THE LAW ON BRAIN TECHNOLOGIES IN WARFARE

ELGAR INTERNATIONAL LAW AND PRACTICE

The Elgar International Law and Practice series is a library of works by leading practitioners and scholars covering key areas in the field of International Law. Each title is analytical in approach, highlighting and unpicking the legal issues that are most critical and relevant to practice. Designed to be detailed, focused reference works, the books in this series aim to offer an authoritative statement on the law and practice in key topics within the field.

For a full list of Edward Elgar published titles, including the titles in this series, visit our website at www.e-elgar.com.

THE LAW ON BRAIN TECHNOLOGIES IN WARFARE

WILLIAM H. BOOTHBY
Visiting Professor, University of Johannesburg, South Africa

ELGAR INTERNATIONAL LAW AND PRACTICE

Edward Elgar
PUBLISHING

Cheltenham, UK · Northampton, MA, USA

Published by

Edward Elgar Publishing Limited
The Lypiatts
15 Lansdown Road
Cheltenham
Glos GL50 2JA
UK

Edward Elgar Publishing, Inc.
William Pratt House
9 Dewey Court
Northampton
Massachusetts 01060
USA

Authorised representative in the EU for GPSR queries only: Easy Access System Europe – Mustamäe tee 50, 10621 Tallinn, Estonia, gpsr.requests@easproject.com

A catalogue record for this book is available from the British Library

Library of Congress Control Number: 2026934084

This book is available electronically in the Elgaronline
Law subject collection
https://doi.org/10.4337/9781035394456

MIX
Paper | Supporting responsible forestry
FSC® C013056
FSC www.fsc.org

ISBN 978 1 0353 9444 9 (cased)
ISBN 978 1 0353 9445 6 (eBook)
ISBN 978 1 0353 9446 3 (ePub)

Printed in Great Britain
by TJ Books, Padstow, Cornwall

CONTENTS

EXTENDED CONTENTS

LIST OF ABBREVIATIONS

AB systems	has the meaning given in sections 1.6 and 2.5.
AI	artificial intelligence.
AMW Manual	Program on Humanitarian Policy and Conflict Research at Harvard University (HPCR), *Manual on the International Law Applicable to Air and Missile Warfare* (March 2010).
API	Protocol Additional to the Geneva Conventions of 12 August 1949, and Relating to the Protection of Victims of International Armed Conflicts, Geneva, 8 June 1977.
API Commentary	International Committee of the Red Cross, *Commentary on the Additional Protocols of 8 June 1977* (Y Sandoz, C Swinarski and B Zimmermann (eds), 1987).
BBI	has the meaning given in section 2.5.3.
BCI	has the meaning given in section 1.6.
Brain technologies	has the meaning given in sections 1.9 and 2.5.
Brussels Declaration	Project of an International Declaration concerning the Laws and Customs of War, Brussels, 27 August 1874.
Customary Law Study	International Committee of the Red Cross, *Customary International Humanitarian Law*, Vol.1 (J-M Henckaerts and L Doswald-Beck (eds), Cambridge University Press, 2005).
Danish MOD Manual	Danish Ministry of Defence, Military Manual on international law relevant to Danish armed forces in international operations, September 2016.
Deep brain stimulation	has the meaning given in section 3.11.
Hague Convention V	Convention respecting the Rights and Duties of Neutral Powers and Persons in Case of War on Land, The Hague, 18 October 1907.
Hague Convention XIII	Convention concerning the Rights and Duties of Neutral Powers in Naval War, The Hague, 18 October 1907.
Hague Cultural Property Regulations	Regulations for the Execution of the Convention for the Protection of Cultural Property in the Event of Armed Conflict, The Hague, 1954.
Hague Draft Rules	Rules concerning the Control of Wireless Telegraphy in Time of War and Air Warfare, Drafted by a Commission of Jurists at The Hague, December 1922.
ICRC	International Committee of the Red Cross.

IHL	international humanitarian law.
Lieber Code	Instructions for the Government of Armies of the United States in the Field, 24 April 1863.
LOAC	law of armed conflict.
Neurotechnology	has the meaning given in section 2.5. The word has also been described as an array of devices and systems that interact with the central nervous system through electrical, magnetic, optogenetic and other means. Some of them primarily serve to understand the brain's functioning while others may consist of methods aimed at directly intervening in mental processes with the purpose of restoring lost functions and enhancing cognitive capabilities.[1]
NIAC Manual	M N Schmitt, C H B Garraway and Y Dinstein, *The Manual on the law of non-international armed conflict with commentary* (International Institute of Humanitarian Law, 2006).
NWP 1-14 M	US Navy, US Marine Corps, US Coast Guard, *The Commander's Handbook on the Law of Naval Operations* (March 2022).
Oslo Manual	Y Dinstein and A-W Dahl (eds), *Oslo Manual on Select Topics of the Law of Armed Conflict* (2020).
Protecting Power	A Protecting Power is a State that is not involved in the conflict and that has been designated by a party to the conflict and has been accepted by the enemy party and has agreed to carry out the functions assigned to a Protecting Power under the law of armed conflict.
Reliably and consistently	refers to the need for systems to perform the specific function to an acceptable standard and with appropriate reliability. The required degree of reliability and consistency will depend on the nature of the obligation and on the severity of the consequences that a failure to maintain the required standard may be expected to cause.
San Remo Manual	International Institute of Humanitarian Law, *San Remo Manual on International Law Applicable to Armed Conflicts at Sea* (L Doswald-Beck (ed), 1995).
Tallinn Manual 2.0	M N Schmitt (ed), *Tallinn Manual 2.0 on the International Law Applicable to Cyber Operations* (Cambridge University Press, 2017).
US DoD Manual	US Department of Defense, *Law of War Manual* (June 2015) as subsequently amended.
UNCLOS	United Nations Convention on the Law of the Sea, Montego Bay, 10 December 1982.
Woomera Manual	J Beard and D Stephens (eds), *The Woomera Manual on the International Law of Military Space Operations* (Oxford University Press, 2024).

1 Impact, opportunities and challenges of neurotechnology with regard to the promotion and protection of all human rights, A/HRC/57/61 dated 8 August 2024 available at https://digitallibrary.un.org/record/4060417?ln=en&v=pdf, para.4.

TABLE OF CASES

INTERNATIONAL COURT OF JUSTICE

INTERNATIONAL CRIMINAL COURT

INTERNATIONAL CRIMINAL TRIBUNAL FOR RWANDA (ICTR)

INTERNATIONAL CRIMINAL TRIBUNAL FOR THE FORMER YUGOSLAVIA (ICTY)

EXTRAORDINARY CHAMBERS IN THE COURTS OF CAMBODIA

EUROPEAN COURT OF HUMAN RIGHTS (ECtHR)

COURT OF JUSTICE OF THE EUROPEAN UNION (CJEU)

ARBITRAL AWARDS

TABLE OF LEGISLATION

INTERNATIONAL LEGISLATION AND INSTRUMENTS

MANUALS AND HANDBOOKS

OTHER DOCUMENTS

1

THE LAW ON BRAIN TECHNOLOGIES IN WARFARE: INTRODUCTION

1.1 INTRODUCTION

The human brain is a mysterious object. Most of us realise that we've got one, **1.001** but none of us fully understands how it works. The majority of us know that the brain is where the development of thoughts and emotions, the acquisition of knowledge, the processing of information, including that received by the senses, and the control of various parts of our bodies, among many other things, are achieved; but ask almost any of us which bit does what, and only the specialist few will offer sensible answers, and not all functions are fully understood. This tale of complacent ignorance, this assumption that the object of unknowable complexity will continue to work perfectly, until it doesn't, this gratitude for all that it gives us without any idea of how, indicates a void in understanding that will, over time, be replaced piece by piece, crumb by crumb, with insights that will come to us through scientific research.

Make no mistake, the author is a fully paid-up member of the ignorant major- **1.002** ity. But the author has, in the last two or three years, become aware that science is opening up new possibilities. In the medical sphere, research is offering possible treatments for conditions such as Parkinson's disease and locked-in syndrome. The possibility of interpreting brain activity is starting to reveal various exciting opportunities and treatments. There is even talk of the creation of artificial brains, whether in the form of numerous intricate computer systems or synthetic biological brain material in association with computer systems. Notions once restricted to science fiction, such as systems enabling a brain to interact directly with another brain without the need for physical activity by those involved, seem poised to make the transition from fantasy to reality.

1.003 These concepts, opportunities and hopes offer what many who suffer will have regarded as an unattainable prospect – the chance to engage with others to a degree that they have hitherto assumed was denied by disease, injury or one of the many other grave challenges that life throws our way. And let us be clear, anything that can alleviate the suffering of these brave souls, anything that can improve their lot, is absolutely to be welcomed and developed as far as humanly possible. But technological advance that has welcome applications in the commercial or medical fields can frequently also have utility in connection with military activities. Brain technology,[1] the collective term which will often be used in this book to refer to a selection of brain-related technologies, is no exception.[2]

1.2 APPLYING LAW IN AN EMERGING FIELD OF SCIENCE

1.004 There are important aspects of brain technology that are discussed in this book which, at the time of writing, are at the experimental stage, but that is not the case with regard to all of the technologies. As will become apparent in the next couple of chapters, one of the important technologies is already being employed for the treatment of patients. Other kinds of brain technology, by contrast, have been the subject of relatively recent scientific discoveries, to which, where relevant, reference is made in the following pages. As is noted in Chapter 6, a large majority of states are obliged to consider the relevant international law that binds them when studying possible new weapons. It is therefore sensible, where science has demonstrated new possibilities in the field of brain technology, to consider what current international law provisions would be applicable to the possible weaponisation of those scientific discoveries. To be clear, there is an important distinction between science fiction and science fact. In this book, care is taken to ensure that the brain technologies that are

1 Neurotechnology is the term more usually employed; the two terms are intended to have the same meaning, and both will appear in the book.

2 Consider Hai Jin, Li-Jun Hou and Zheng-Guo Wang, 'Military Brain Science – How to Influence Future Wars' (2018) 21 *Chinese Journal of Traumatology* 5, cited in N A Farahany, *The Battle for your Brain* (St Martin's Press, 2024), 178.

contemplated are based on scientific developments that have been published in the literature.

The author, therefore, hopes that the observations made in the following pages will prove helpful to those who may find themselves tasked with interpreting sometimes familiar legal rules in this distinctly unfamiliar 'neurocontext'. The citing of relevant scientific papers is intended to show that while the discoveries may have taken place in recent years, the substance of what is being discussed is not fanciful. Inevitably, the discussion and analysis will be based on assumptions and hypotheses, for example as to the general form that the emerging technology and its potential military application will take. Those are, the author hopes, sensible assumptions and hypotheses and are intended to be useful illustrations of how the law may be expected to apply. So the intention is to point out what has been achieved, to look at what may as a result emerge as possible capabilities in the military sphere, and then to work out how the existing body of law would apply. **1.005**

It will be for the reader to assess whether those projections as to possible future systems seem to be realistic or far-fetched. All that the author would suggest is that the legal implications of these developments should now be addressed, and this book aims to help that process. The author cannot, and does not, claim to have got everything right. There will be technical errors; actual applications of the process may differ from what is hypothesised in the following pages, and unforeseeable further scientific advance may also have a role to play. Frankly, none of that matters. What does matter is that we start to think about the direction in which science seems to be going and the legal issues that are thrown up. The author hopes that the following pages are helpful in that sense. **1.006**

The law that is discussed in the following pages is the law that we have, that is *lex lata*. The discussion of how it applies to the potential product of recent scientific discoveries is *lex ferenda*, in the sense that it remains to be seen how states will interpret the application of current law in these novel contexts, what, if any, new customary rules will emerge from a general practice among states, backed by perceived legal obligation, and what, if any, new treaty provision will be agreed by states. It is states that make international law, not the present author. **1.007**

1.3 WHAT IS THINKING?

1.008 As Renée Descartes observed in 1637, 'je pense, donc je suis' which can loosely be translated as 'I think therefore I am' or 'cogito, ergo sum'.[3] This quotation from Descartes' writing leads to the perplexing question in the context of artificial brain technology, namely: 'It thinks, so what does that make it?' I guess the first thing to ponder is whether artificial brain technologies do actually think, which of course requires us to ask, what does 'think' mean? The dictionary definition includes: '1 have a particular opinion, belief, or idea about someone or something; 2 use the mind to form connected ideas about someone or something; 3 (think of/about) take someone or something into account or consideration; 4 (think of/about) consider the possibility or advantages of …'[4] Numerous related notions emerge from this definition and these should also be clarified. An opinion is '1 a personal view not necessarily based on fact or knowledge; 2 the views of people in general [in the sense, for example, of public opinion]; 3 an estimate of quality or worth; 4 a formal statement of advice by an expert or professional'.[5] Belief means '1 a feeling that something exists or is true, especially one without proof; 2 a firmly held opinion; 3 (belief in) trust or confidence in'.[6]

1.009 While addressing these important preliminary definitions, we should also address the distinction between the notions of 'brain' and 'mind'. While the anatomical composition of certain kinds of brain will be considered in Chapter 2, it suffices for the present purposes to note that a brain, for the purposes of this book, is 'an organ of soft nervous tissue inside the skull, functioning as the co-ordinating centre of the nervous system'.[7] Contrast the idea of mind when used as a noun, namely '1 a person's faculty of consciousness and thought; 2 a person's ability to reason or remember things; 3 a person's attention or will; an intelligent person'.[8] Put perhaps rather simplistically, therefore, the mind consists of the functionality that the physical object, the brain, provides. These definitions should be borne in mind when explanations of artificial brain technologies are discussed in Chapter 2.

---

3 W E Burns, *The Scientific Revolution: An Encyclopedia* (ABC-CLIO, 2001), 84.
4 *Compact Oxford English Dictionary*, 3rd edn (Oxford University Press, 2005), 1077.
5 *Compact Oxford English Dictionary*, 3rd edn (Oxford University Press, 2005), 710.
6 *Compact Oxford English Dictionary*, 3rd edn (Oxford University Press, 2005), 81.
7 *Compact Oxford English Dictionary*, 3rd edn (Oxford University Press, 2005), 112.
8 *Compact Oxford English Dictionary*, 3rd edn (Oxford University Press, 2005), 646.

1.4 THE PURPOSE OF THE BOOK

The intended purpose of this book is to answer a number of perplexing questions that arise from work that is currently underway to develop technologies that are associated with the human brain and to replicate activities associated with brain functioning. The questions are as follows: 1.010

1. Isn't brain technology really the same thing as artificial intelligence (AI)?
2. What are the brain technologies that seem likely to be of most relevance to military operations?
3. Which of these brain technologies have been demonstrated in some form and which are entirely theoretical?
4. What are brain-computer interfaces, artificial brain technologies and brain-to-brain interfaces?
5. How do the principles and rules of the *jus in bello*, as they apply to targeting, special protection, weapons, methods of warfare and neutrality, and the law on the resort to the use of force, apply to the use of the three technologies referred to in serial 4?
6. What are the legal rules dealing with the enhancement of the human brain?
7. What are the legal rules dealing with degradation of the human brain?
8. Are there other issues that are relevant?

The author is an international lawyer. He has no training in anatomy, computer science, or indeed in any of the technologies discussed in the following pages. In describing the functioning of the brain and the nature and projected capabilities of brain technologies in Chapters 2 and 3, he therefore relies heavily on the writings of those who have the appropriate specialisms and acknowledges this reliance appropriately below. The technologies to which reference will be made, and the relevant science, are evolving rapidly. Consequently, the assessments of them that are offered and the linked legal implications are, to a degree, provisional in nature. Legal assessments will need to be revisited as technology, and understanding of its capabilities and implications, evolve. Moreover, legal assessments will have to be made with regard to particular systems, although doing so may require consideration of issues associated with the technologies in general. 1.011

As was indicated in section 1.1, the author rather suspects that it will be potential medical and commercial applications of brain technologies that will incentivise their development. Accordingly, it is imaginable that legal regulation of them in those contexts will emerge first. That evolving body of law may be expected to influence, to a degree, how law of armed conflict rules are understood and applied in the new, cognitive environment and the evolution of legal 1.012

rules as to their application in warfare. It must, however, be remembered that it is the current principles and rules of the law of armed conflict that apply when the legal acceptability of new weapons, weapon systems and methods of warfare is being considered.[9]

1.013 The focus of the book is on the law as it currently exists, *lex lata*, and on how that law may be expected to apply in connection with these new technologies. If, at any point in the discussion, reference is made to the law as the author considers it ought to be, *lex ferenda*, this will be made clear in the relevant part of the discussion. The discussions as to law will by and large be concerned with the law as it applies to states in general. While Additional Protocol I (API)[10] is referred to frequently in the text, it is appreciated that not all states are party to that Treaty. The extensive participation by states in API is, however, considered to justify reference to it in the manner adopted in the book. Inevitably, on occasion the law relating to a particular state or legal tradition will sometimes be the focus of a specific legal issue, in which case this will again be made clear. Where the law as it applies to one state is cited, this is generally done for illustrative purposes, for example to illustrate the kinds of legal consideration that the state in question considers to be applicable to the specific use of the technology.

1.014 The author has striven to produce a treatment of this topic which is as comprehensive and intelligible as possible. The topics that are addressed are complex, and the author has endeavoured to ensure that intelligibility is not achieved at the expense of factual or legal accuracy.

1.5 THE BACKGROUND

1.015 Readers of this book may well approach the topic of artificial brain technology with their own perspectives, influenced heavily, no doubt, by each reader's background and, perhaps, professional experience. The author's background is in the military sphere, and it may help some readers if the author explains how he interprets the developments over recent decades that seem likely to culminate in the emergence of the technologies that are the subject of this book.

9 Consider for example the obligation to conduct weapon reviews, discussed in Chapter 6.

10 Protocol Additional to the Geneva Conventions of 12 August 1949, and Relating to the Protection of Victims of International Armed Conflicts, Geneva, 8 June 1977, 1125 UNTS 3 (Additional Protocol I or API).

In the commercial sector, automation in manufacturing has been traced back by Nathan Bong to the 1st century BC and the use by the Greeks and Romans of water wheels to grind grain into flour. Bong notes the use of wind and water mills by the Persians in the 7th to 9th centuries to grind grain and for other mechanical purposes; the development in 1785 by Oliver Evans of a completely automated industrial process (for flour milling); the Industrial Revolution and the age of steam; accelerated introduction of industrial automation between 1900 and the 1950s associated with electrification; and the introduction of computers and robotics into manufacturing processes from 1971 until the present day.[11] **1.016**

In the military context, and specifically in connection with air operations, the first pilotless air vehicles, Aerial Target and Kettering Bug, were respectively developed by the UK and the US during the First World War but were not used operationally. In 1935 the British produced radio-controlled aerial targets, including the DH 82B Queen Bee which may have given rise to the generic term, drone. On 6 August 1946 a remote-controlled prototype based on the B17 Flying Fortress aircraft flew the 2,600 miles from Hawaii to California while remotely controlled by US Army Air Forces (USAAF) personnel. In the 1960s, the UK Royal Artillery acquired surveillance drones and, more recently, in 2012 the UK Royal Artillery operated Watchkeeper unmanned aircraft for intelligence, surveillance, target acquisition and reconnaissance purposes in Helmand Province, Afghanistan during Operation Herrick. MQ-9 Reaper remotely piloted aircraft are in current service with the UK Royal Air Force in reconnaissance, surveillance and air strike roles.[12] **1.017**

In the commercial context, automated processes are now a key element of very many manufacturing processes from automobile construction to the processing of foodstuffs. In commercial logistics and retail, automation has revolutionised the way in which many classes of goods and services are marketed and purchased. In the military sphere, automated systems are used in the control of platforms and weapon systems in all environments: land, sea, air, outer space, and cyberspace. The Oslo Manual defines a highly automated weapon system as: 'a system that, once activated, is capable of identifying and engaging a target without further human input, while being constrained by algorithms that **1.018**

---

11 N Bong, 'The Evolution of Automation', *Progressive Automations*, 26 April 2022, available at https://www.progressiveautomations.com/blogs/news/the-evolution-of-automation.

12 This paragraph is based in large measure on the Imperial War Museum, 'A Brief History of Drones', available at https://www.iwm.org.uk/history/a-brief-history-of-drones#:~:text=The%20Aerial%20Target%2C%20a%20British,was%20tested%20in%20March%201917.

determine its responses by imposing rules of engagement and setting mission parameters which limit its ability to act independently.'[13] The Manual recognised that systems may be automated to varying degrees, and this is also likely to be the case in the commercial context, in the sense that some parts of the manufacturing process may be automated while others may require human, manual activity.

1.019 The distinct and significantly more advanced notion of autonomy is the subject of ongoing research in both the commercial and military contexts, and autonomous systems are increasingly being employed in a wide variety of industries and applications. The commercial use of autonomous vehicles in Los Angeles,[14] the use of a fully autonomous heavy-haul freight rail network in Australia,[15] the use of AI to enable autonomous bricklaying,[16] and the integration of robotic systems with varying degrees of autonomy for the execution of surgical procedures[17] are simply illustrative of the disparate kinds of commercial activity in which autonomous systems are being applied.

1.020 In the military context, an autonomous weapon system can be understood as: 'a weapon system that is programmed to apply human-like reasoning to determine whether an object or person is a target, whether it should be attacked, and if so, how and when.'[18] While the author would dispute the necessity for the reasoning to be 'human-like', the experts who prepared the Oslo Manual explained that they were using that term to 'express the process of human judgment in which disparate facts are assessed and sometimes compared in order to reach an evaluative decision which will require the application of judgment'.[19] Much more could be said about the use of AI in warfare[20] but these brief remarks suffice for the current purposes.

13 Y Dinstein and A W Dahl (eds), *Oslo Manual on Select Topics of the Law of Armed Conflict* (2020) (Oslo Manual), Rule 37, 33.

14 See https://waymo.com/waymo-one-los-angeles/.

15 See https://www.hitachirail.com/case-studies/australia-world-first-fully-autonomous-heavy-haul-rail-network/.

16 See https://www.newcivilengineer.com/latest/dutch-firm-raises-20m-to-upscale-its-ai-driven-autonomous-bricklaying-robots-across-europe-15-02-2024/.

17 A Muacevic and J R Adler (eds), *Autonomous Robotic Surgery: Has the Future Arrived?* (Cureus, 14 January 2024), available at https://pmc.ncbi.nlm.nih.gov/articles/PMC10862530/.

18 Oslo Manual, n.13, Rule 38, 34.

19 Oslo Manual, n.13, para.3 of the Commentary to Rule 38.

20 W H Boothby, 'AI, Warfare and the Law' (2025) 104 *International Law Studies*, available at https://digital-commons.usnwc.edu/ils/vol104/iss1/1/. For reference to some of the issues that may arise from the use of AI and BCIs in conjunction with one another, see N Lubell and K Al-Khateeb, 'Cyborg Soldiers: Military use of Brain-Computer Interfaces and the Law of Armed Conflict' (11 April 2022), later published in L A Dickinson and E Berg (eds), *Big Data and Armed Conflict: Legal Issues Above and Below the Armed Conflict Threshold* (Oxford University Press, 2024), 11–12.

Put somewhat simplistically, autonomous systems can be regarded as an application of AI. They are computer-based systems that enable complex processes to be undertaken without human involvement at that time. Brain technologies constitute the next step change in the evolutionary process that we have been discussing in this section.[21] What exactly those technologies comprise and, to a degree, how they will work will be the subjects of Chapters 2 and 3. 1.021

1.6 HOW THE BOOK CAME TO BE WRITTEN

The author first wrote on the subject of autonomy in warfare approximately 18 years ago when preparing a paper in connection with the project that produced the HPCR Air and Missile Warfare Law Manual.[22] The author maintained an interest in the application of these technologies in the commercial and military environments, noting how the law sought to address autonomous systems in both of those contexts.[23] More recently, the author has looked at the application of AI in general in the conduct of military operations in warfare.[24] Whereas in 2007–08 the use of autonomy seemed to be at the horizon of technical development in this field, now the author would suggest that it is the development of various brain technologies that can properly be described in those terms. Readers will interpret the evolution of the science associated with systems in their own way. Remembering well the days when the card index was the basis for most organisational and administrative processes in commerce and the public service,[25] the author views the subsequent revolution in system methods as a continuum which started with computerisation, progressed with computer-based automation and which now seems likely to develop further with the advent of AI and, in due course, brain technology. Accordingly, now seems to be the right time to discuss the law that will apply to the development and application of brain technologies in the military sphere. It is at this stage, as research is underway to develop these technologies 1.022

21 As to the fundamental difference between AI and the way in which the human brain operates, see Oxford University News and Events, 'Study shows that the way the brain learns is different from the way that artificial intelligence systems learn', 2024, available at https://www.ox.ac.uk/news/2024-01-03-study-shows-way-brain-learns-different-way-artificial-intelligence-systems-learn.

22 *HPCR Manual on the International Law Applicable to Air and Missile Warfare* (Bern, 15 May 2009), available at https://cdn.ca9.uscourts.gov/datastore/library/2013/09/06/Flores_Manual.pdf.

23 W H Boothby, *New Technologies and the Law in War and Peace* (Cambridge University Press, 2019), 137–81.

24 Boothby, n.20.

25 In 1974 the author obtained his first employment in a law office where his task was to file fine cards in alphabetical order; the office was that of the Clerk to the Justices at Harrow Magistrates' Court in Middlesex, England.

and potentially apply them, that relevant law should be considered, for example to avoid the expenditure of costly research resources on ventures that the law would prohibit.

1.7 OUTLINE OF THE TEXT

1.023 This book will aim to present a logical and clear appreciation of what are, in truth, complex technologies the development and implementation of which seem likely to pose some difficult legal issues. Common sense suggests that an appropriate starting point is to explain in non-technical and brief terms the anatomy of the human brain. Reference will also be made to the size and certain characteristics of certain animal brains so that the generic idea of a brain can be understood. A non-exhaustive selection of the facilities and capabilities generated by a human brain will be considered. Elements of the science associated with certain brain technologies, as currently understood and to the extent that these are available on an open-source basis, will then be explained in summary, non-technical terms. The consideration of those matters in Chapter 2 will be developed and, to a degree, applied in Chapter 3.

1.024 It is in Chapter 4 that the focus will shift to the law by dealing with the implications of targeting law for brain-computer interfaces, for artificial brain technologies and for brain-to-brain interfaces. Each of the principles and key rules of targeting law will be addressed in turn in order to determine how each of them will apply to the three technologies. In Chapter 5 the focus will be on the more specific rules dealing with the protection of specific types of object and of person, looking in suitable detail at each category of object and person individually in order to assess the nature of the protection that the law affords and to work out the specific implications for brain technology of those rules.

1.025 In Chapters 6 and 7, an essentially similar analytical process is applied to the principles and rules of weapons law and, respectively, to the specific provisions dealing with a variety of methods of warfare. Chapter 8 then assesses the implications of relevant rules of the law of neutrality for the use of brain technologies and Chapter 9 performs a similar task in respect of the rules of the *jus ad bellum*. In Chapter 10 the enhancement of brain performance, both by the use of drugs and alcohol and by means of brain technologies, is reviewed, and in Chapter 11 a similar analysis is conducted, this time in relation to technologies intended to degrade brain performance. The next chapter (Chapter 12) reports on some of the views expressed by some states and organisations on these matters, and in the final substantive chapter (Chapter 13) the application of international criminal law to these technologies is addressed. In Chapter 14 some brief concluding remarks will be offered.

With a view to keeping the analysis throughout as clear as possible, the brain technologies will usually be considered in the same sequence by reference to each legal rule or type of activity. That sequence will start by considering the implications for what are termed 'brain-computer interfaces', abbreviated throughout the text to BCIs. The nature and meaning of BCIs will be explained in Chapters 2 and 3. The next brain technology to be considered in this sequence will be artificial brain technologies. As will be explained in Chapter 2, for the purposes of this book there are really two kinds of artificial brain technology, namely those consisting exclusively of computer-based systems and those which include biological brain matter, which may have been synthetically produced. For the purposes of the discussion in Chapter 3 and thereafter, those two kinds of artificial brain will be combined in a single category of brain technology, namely artificial brains and will be referred to as AB, or AB systems as the context may require. The third type of technology is brain-to-brain interfaces, a concept that will also be explained in Chapters 2 and 3. This technology will be referred to throughout the book as BBI. **1.026**

1.8 INTENDED READERSHIP

This book will be of interest to anyone who is involved with or interested in brain technologies. In particular, the book is designed to be of use to: **1.027**

- those whose role is to design and/or develop any kind of brain technology for use in any role in the military sphere;
- those who manufacture and market brain technology systems for use by armed forces, ministries of defence, governments, and others in the military context;
- those who want to know how current international law applies to military brain technology systems and the capabilities that they enable;
- those who wish to assess the adequacy of current law and to consider the generation of new law to deal with the challenges posed by these technologies;
- those who are involved in developing policy in this field for potential users of these technologies, including governments, governmental agencies, companies and others;
- Ministries of Defence, armed forces personnel, procurement agencies, military lawyers and others considering the application of law to emerging brain technologies to be applied for military purposes;
- members of think tanks, non-governmental organisations and others with a policy interest in this topic;

- lawyers with an interest in all aspects of the law applying to military brain technologies; and
- those with an academic interest in these matters.

1.9 IS IT THE SCIENCE, THE TECHNOLOGY OR THE FUNCTION, AND WHAT ARE BRAIN TECHNOLOGIES?

1.028 While it is important to have some kind of background understanding of the science that underpins brain technologies, and while therefore some appreciation of the workings of the particular technology will also be important, the author would suggest that it is the function that the technology is being employed to discharge that will perhaps be of greatest importance. Of similar importance will be the extent to which the particular brain technology performs in a reliable and consistent way. So, while the technical discussion in Chapter 2 is an essential foundation on which the book's analysis should be built, our focus must ultimately be on what the technologies are, or must be, designed to do if their employment in particular ways is to be lawful. This will tell us what the legal implications of the diverse circumstances of use of brain technologies might be. So the answer to the first question in the title to this section is that it is the science, the technologies and the functions that we must address, and an attempt has been made to do this in a manner that is as clear and logical as possible.

1.029 In answer to the second question in the title to this section, brain technologies for the purposes of this book consist of BCIs (referred to in section 1.6 above and discussed in Chapters 2 and 3), the two kinds of artificial brain technology mentioned in section 1.6, brain enhancement technologies (discussed in Chapter 10) and brain degradation technologies (discussed in Chapter 11) and BBIs (discussed in Chapters 2 and 3). BCIs, AB systems and BBIs will be discussed individually by reference to each of the principles, rules or topics discussed in Chapters 4 to 9. The various forms of brain enhancement and brain degradation technology will then be reviewed, to the extent that the current state of technical development permits, by reference to applicable law.

1.10 IS ANTHROPOMORPHISING JUSTIFIED?

To anthropomorphize is to 'show or treat an animal, god or object as if it is human in appearance, character or behaviour'.[26] In the context of a book dealing with the application of law to novel technologies, care is usually required in the use of language to describe the processes that those technologies employ, particularly when they replace activities that have usually been undertaken by humans. When preparing a relatively recently published book on AI,[27] the author was careful to avoid anthropomorphising that discussion. Accordingly, when AI processes that replicated human decision-making were being discussed there, the word 'determine' was used, and a particular non-anthropomorphising meaning was given to that word. **1.030**

There are ongoing discussions at the United Nations (UN) in Geneva among states that are party to the Conventional Weapons Convention,[28] focusing on possible legal or other arrangements addressing lethal autonomous weapon systems. In the course of those discussions a number of Guiding Principles were agreed in 2018. One of these Principles stated that '[h]uman responsibility for decisions on the use of weapon systems must be retained since accountability cannot be transferred to machines'.[29] This is probably right where systems based on AI are concerned. AI implies the mechanisation of key processes. However, those AI-mechanised elements in a weapon system or in a method of warfare consist of a computer program applying lessons learned from the data that is fed into it, or that it has acquired, relating to past events, in order to inform how it should act when confronted with particular circumstances.[30] While this may have some similarity to human learning, to suggest that the AI system is making a decision, based on that perceived similarity or analogy seemed to involve an unacceptable intellectual leap, that is, anthropomorphising the machine. **1.031**

---

26 Cambridge online dictionary, 'Anthropomorphise', available at https://dictionary.cambridge.org/dictionary/english/anthropomorphize.

27 Boothby, n.20.

28 Convention on Prohibitions or Restrictions on the Use of Certain Conventional Weapons Which May be Deemed to be Excessively Injurious or to Have Indiscriminate Effects, Geneva, 10 October 1980, 1342 UNTS 137.

29 *Report of the 2018 Session of the Group of Governmental Experts on Emerging Technologies in the Area of Lethal Autonomous Weapons Systems*, CCW/GGE.1/2018/3, dated 23 October 2018, (2018 Report), para.21, Guiding Principle (b).

30 A R Greipl, 'Artificial Intelligence Systems and Humans in Military Decision-Making: Not Better or Worse, but Better Together', Lieber Institute, 14 June 2024, available at https://lieber.westpoint.edu/artificial-intelligence-systems-humans-military-decision-making-better-worse/.

1.032 Accordingly, while in the AI book the author was right to avoid anthropomorphising AI, this approach only remained appropriate on the basis that the AI remained a tool for the human user. As the author pointed out, '[t]hat approach will start to break down when future technologies do indeed enable machines to make decisions in the conventional sense of the word'.[31] The discussion of AI continued:

> when the machine starts to determine from which datasets it will learn, what it will learn, when it will commence its mission, where it will go and what it will do when it gets there, and so on, the "determination/decision" distinction may be challenged, but even then, so long as there are human beings that are commanding and/or that are closely involved in the operation of the system, those human beings, and those behind them in the supply chain, will be responsible for the performance of the capabilities that they release.[32]

1.033 It follows from this that the question summarised in the heading to this section, namely whether anthropomorphising the discussion of brain technologies can be justified, will depend critically on the capability of the particular system. Where operations using BCI systems are concerned, the decisions will be made by the planners and commanders of such operations and, notably, by the operator whose thought, wish or intent is conveyed to the relevant weapon by the BCI. The BCI does not make the decision; it communicates it, so anthropomorphising the role of the BCI would make no sense. With BBI systems, the BBI is again a communication system for the transmission of thoughts, ideas, information and, no doubt, commands and intent between brains without the necessity for physical measures such as writing, speech, hand signals and so on. It is therefore those persons who are involved in the BBI activity who are making the decision, and the question of anthropomorphising the BBI communication process that they are using again does not arise. As to AB technologies, the purpose of the technology will be to replicate in whole or in part the processes employed by the human brain, and the functions to which AB technologies will be applied are likely, in the military context, critically to involve the making of decisions. It is on this basis that the author thinks it right to refer in this book to activities normally associated with human capabilities in the belief that any anthropomorphising effect is justified where AB systems are concerned.

---

31 Boothby, n.20, 11.
32 Boothby, n.20.

2

PRELIMINARY CONCEPTS

2.1 INTRODUCTION

Any discussion of artificial brain (AB) technologies must, in the author's view, start with an explanation of the constituent elements of a brain and must say something about the contributions that some of those elements make to the functioning of the body as a whole. By starting with brain functions in nature, and the anatomy of brains in nature, we can begin to develop an understanding of what a piece of technology needs to be capable of producing in order to be regarded as an AB. There is, however, an immediate problem here. Not all brains are equal and, to further adapt the famous quote from *Animal Farm*, some brains are more equal than others.[1] **2.001**

In this chapter, the human brain is taken to be the most highly developed natural brain and in section 2.2 some basic observations about its anatomy and the functions its elements perform will be offered. In section 2.3 it is noted how the size of brains of certain other animals compare with one another and how they differ from human brain size. In section 2.4 some of the capabilities that derive from the human brain will be considered. Whether all of these capabilities are necessarily unique to humans is a debatable question which is not particularly relevant to the topic of this book. The purpose of discussing **2.002**

1 G Orwell, *Animal Farm: A Fairy Story* (Secker & Warburg, 1945: 'All animals are equal but some animals are more equal than others.'

the chosen examples of human cognitive capabilities is to help us to think about some of the skillsets that an AB may need to have in order to be acceptable for employment in particular military tasks. It is not at this stage being asserted that, to be acceptable for military use, AB technology will have to have all of the listed capabilities or indeed any particular capability. Rather, it is believed that the list, although probably incomplete at present, will, when improved over time, help to provide a checklist of the capabilities that military systems in the field of AB technologies will in practice need to have in order to be capable of lawful employment in warfare. The author appreciates that there is extensive ongoing research in this field. Understanding of the functioning of the human brain, of AB technologies and of related fields can be expected to develop rapidly. The author therefore approaches the discussion in section 2.4, and indeed in the whole chapter, with significant hesitancy. Section 2.5 will then describe the three brain technologies that are the focus of the next several chapters, namely brain-computer interfaces (BCIs), artificial brains (ABs) and brain-to-brain interfaces (BBIs).

2.003 On a related point, it is worth noting that the term 'artificial brain technology' does not specify whether it is the functioning of a human or animal brain that is being synthesised. The author suggests that the sensible way of looking at this is to ask which brain functions are being synthesised by the applied technology and for what purposes. This will start to form a realistic basis for comparison of performance and will then enable an assessment to be made as to the acceptability or otherwise of a particular AB capability.

2.2 THE HUMAN BRAIN, ITS PARTS AND THEIR FUNCTIONS

2.004 Any discussion of AB technologies should start with an explanation of the human brain, its anatomy and the functions that its elements fulfil, and that is the focus of this section. The present author is by training a lawyer, not a brain surgeon. The explanations in the following pages will therefore of necessity be based on materials published by experts in brain anatomy and will be expressed as far as possible in language intended to be readily intelligible to the non-specialist reader.

2.005 The US National Institute of Neurological Disorders and Stroke[2] (NINDS) explains that, weighing three pounds, the human brain is the most complex

2 Part of the US National Institutes of Health.

part of the human body.[3] The NINDS notes that intelligence, interpreting the senses, initiating body movement and controlling behaviour are all functions of the brain. While all of the parts of the human brain work together, each part has its own functions. Johns Hopkins Medicine points out that functions of the brain also include control of thought, memory, emotion, touch, motor skills, vision, breathing, temperature, hunger, and every process that regulates the body.[4]

Broadly, the human brain can be divided into three elements: the forebrain, the midbrain and the hindbrain. Taking these in reverse order, the hindbrain 'includes the upper part of the spinal cord, the brain stem and a wrinkled ball of tissue called the cerebellum'.[5] It is the hindbrain that controls key functions like respiration and heart rate. The cerebellum is located at the back of the head and 'co-ordinates movement and is involved in learned movements'.[6] It has two hemispheres and its function is to 'co-ordinate voluntary muscle movements and to maintain posture, balance and equilibrium'.[7] **2.006**

The midbrain is the upper part of the brain stem. It controls some reflex actions and 'is part of the circuit involved in the control of eye movements and other voluntary movements'. The Johns Hopkins Medicine text explains that the complex structures in the midbrain facilitate hearing, movement, calculation of responses and environmental changes and contain, inter alia, part of the basal ganglia that enables movement and co-ordination.[8] Linking the midbrain with the medulla, the pons enables 'a range of activities such as tear production, chewing, blinking, focusing vision, balance, hearing and facial expression'.[9] The medulla is where the brain meets the spinal cord. It regulates 'heart rhythm, breathing, blood flow, oxygen and carbon dioxide levels'.[10] It also produces reflexive actions such as sneezing, vomiting, coughing and swallowing.[11] **2.007**

---

3 National Institute of Neurological Disorders and Stroke, 'Brain Basics: Know Your Brain', 17 July 2024, available at https://www.ninds.nih.gov/health-information/public-education/brain-basics/brain-basics-know-your-brain#:~:text=The%20brain%20can%20be%20divided,as%20respiration%20and%20heart%20rate (hereinafter NINDS text). This text forms the basis of the discussion in this section. Where other material is used in this section, its provenance is cited appropriately.

4 Johns Hopkins Medicine, 'Brain Anatomy and How the Brain Works', available at https://www.hopkinsmedicine.org/health/conditions-and-diseases/anatomy-of-the-brain (hereinafter Johns Hopkins text).

5 NINDS text, n.3.

6 NINDS text, n.3.

7 Johns Hopkins text, n.4.

8 Johns Hopkins text, n.4.

9 Johns Hopkins text, n.4.

10 Johns Hopkins text, n.4.

11 Johns Hopkins text, n.4.

2.008 The forebrain 'consists primarily of the cerebrum and the structures hidden beneath it'.[12] The cerebrum, located at the topmost part of the brain, is the 'source of conscious thoughts and actions'.[13] It holds memories and permits planning, imagination and thought. It permits recognition of friends, reading and game playing.[14] The Johns Hopkins Medicine text identifies functions of the cerebrum as including initiation and co-ordination of movement, regulating temperature, enabling speech, judgement, thinking and reasoning, problem solving, emotions and learning, as well as functions relating 'to vision, hearing touch and other senses'.[15] 'The cerebrum is split into two halves (hemispheres) … [which] … communicate with each other through a thick tract of nerve fibers that lie at the basis of' a fissure between them 'called the corpus callosum'. The ability to form words 'seems to lie primarily in the left hemisphere, while the right hemisphere seems to control many abstract reasoning skills'.[16] The 'right cerebral hemisphere primarily controls the left side of the body, and the left hemisphere primarily controls the right side'.[17]

2.009 The surface of the cerebrum and of the cerebellum is coated with a layer of grey tissue called the cortex and '[m]ost of the actual information processing in the brain takes place in the cerebral cortex'.[18] As Johns Hopkins Medicine explains:

> [i]n the brain, gray matter refers to the darker, outer portion, while white matter describes the lighter, inner section underneath … Gray matter is primarily composed of neuron somas (the round central cell bodies), and white matter is mostly made of axons (the long stems that connects [sic] neurons together wrapped in myelin (a protective coating) … Each region serves a different role. Gray matter is primarily responsible for processing and interpreting information, while white matter transmits that information to other parts of the nervous system.[19]

2.010 Each of the cerebral hemispheres can be divided into sections, or lobes, each of which has particular functions. The two frontal lobes, behind the forehead, are employed for schedule planning, imagining the future, and using reasoned arguments. Behind each frontal lobe is a motor cortex 'which helps plan, control and execute voluntary movement'.[20] The parietal lobes support reading,

12 NINDS text, n.3.
13 NINDS text, n.3.
14 NINDS text, n.3.
15 Johns Hopkins text, n.4.
16 NINDS text, n.3.
17 NINDS text, n.3.
18 NINDS text, n.3.
19 Johns Hopkins text, n.4.
20 NINDS text, n.3.

arithmetic, taste and smell, and between the parietal lobes and the motor area is the somatosensory cortex, where information about temperature, taste, touch and movement is received from the rest of the body. The occipital lobes at the back of the brain 'process images from the eyes and link that information with images stored in memory'.[21] Beneath the parietal and frontal lobes are the temporal lobes, at the top of which is an area that receives information from the ears. The undersides of the temporal lobes have an important 'role in forming and retrieving memories including those associated with music'. Other parts of the temporal lobes 'integrate memories and sensations of taste, sound, sight and touch'.[22]

In the inner brain, there are structures which 'not only determine our emotional state, but they also modify our perceptions and responses and allow us to initiate movements … without thinking about them'.[23] These structures are duplicated for each half of the brain. The hypothalamus is associated with awakening and adrenaline flow and controls chemicals associated with exhilaration, anger and unhappiness.[24] Also deep within the brain, the pituitary gland 'governs the function of other glands in the body, regulating the flow of hormones from the thyroid, adrenals, ovaries and testicles. It receives chemical signals from the hypothalamus through its stalk and blood supply.'[25] The amygdalae are located under each hemisphere of the brain and 'regulate emotion and memory and are associated with the brain's reward system, stress and the "fight or flight" response when someone perceives a threat'.[26] Nearby, the thalamus is involved with the passage of information to and from the spinal cord and cerebrum.[27] 'An arching tract of nerve cells leads from the hypothalamus and the thalamus to the hippocampus. This tiny nub acts as a memory indexer – sending memories out to the appropriate part of the cerebral hemisphere for long term storage and retrieving them when necessary.' Clusters of nerve cells surrounding the thalamus initiate and integrate movements (and are affected by Parkinson's disease).[28] **2.011**

21 NINDS text, n.3.
22 NINDS text, n.3.
23 NINDS text, n.3.
24 NINDS text, n.3.
25 Johns Hopkins text, n.4.
26 Johns Hopkins text, n.4.
27 NINDS text, n.3.
28 NINDS text, n.3.

2.012 The key functional unit within the brain is the neuron,[29] a kind of cell through which signals pass leading to sensations, movements, thoughts, memories and feelings. Branches extend from the body of these cells, called dendrites. The dendrites receive messages from other nerve cells and '[s]ignals then pass from the dendrites through the cell body and travel away from the cell body down an axon to another neuron, a muscle cell, or cells in some other organ'.[30] These axons 'may be very short, such as those that carry signals from one cell in the cortex to another cell less than a hair's width away', whereas other 'axons may be very long, such as those that carry messages from the brain all the way down the spinal cord'.[31]

2.013 When the signal reaches the end of the axon it stimulates the release of tiny sacs called vesicles. These vesicles release chemicals known as neurotransmitters into the synaptic cleft. The neurotransmitters cross the synapse and attach to receptors on the neighbouring cell. These receptors can change the properties of the receiving cell. If the receiving cell is also a neuron, the signal can continue the transmission to the next cell.[32] Neurotransmitters are chemicals that the brain cells use to communicate with one another, some of which cause the cells to become more active while others dampen activity.[33] Efforts continue to create wiring diagrams of the brain showing the synaptic connections between neurons, but this is only one method for the transmission of signals through the nervous system. 'Another key neural communication pathway is via signalling molecules – in particular via neuropeptides – that modulate synaptic communication and allow communication between neurons that are not linked by synapses.'[34]

2.014 Finally, mention should be made of the 12 cranial nerves that are located within the cranium.

---

29 The human brain comprises two kinds of cells: neurons and glial cells. The latter are approximately 50 times more numerous than the former. Neurons send and receive nerve signals, whereas glial cells 'provide support and nutrition, maintain homeostasis, form myelin and facilitate signal transmission in the nervous system': American Association of Neurological Surgeons, 'Anatomy of the Brain', 14 June 2024, available at https://www.aans.org/patients/conditions-treatments/anatomy-of-the-brain/.

30 NINDS text, n.3.

31 NINDS text, n.3.

32 NINDS text, n.3.

33 NINDS text, n.3. The Johns Hopkins text, n.4, also refers to the brain sending and receiving electrical signals throughout the body.

34 University of Cambridge Neuroscience, 'First Map of Wireless Communication in the Nervous System', 15 November 2023, news report, available at https://neuroscience.cam.ac.uk/first-map-of-wireless-communication-in-the-nervous-system/. The entire neuropeptide signalling network of a whole animal, the Nematode worm C. Elegans, has been mapped for the first time; University of Cambridge, ibid.

It will be appreciated that this has been a somewhat basic discussion of the anatomy of the human brain and of the functions of its constituent elements. As indicated in section 2.1, the discussion in the next section will now shift to considering how human brain size compares with the physical brain capacities of insects and mice. The purpose of this is to put the brain capacities of each into some kind of perspective as a prelude to discussing, in section 2.4, some of the brain-related capabilities that, in the author's view, seem to characterise human beings. **2.015**

2.3 ANIMAL BRAIN SIZES

Brain volume varies enormously between animals and humans. To give some idea of the degree of this variance, note that the brain of the roundworm, *Caenorhabditis elegans*, has a volume of 5x10 to the fourth cubic microns, which can, for comparison purposes, be represented as 50cms or the width of an economy airline seat. The brain volume of a fruit fly, *Drosophila melanogaster*, is 5x10 to the seventh microns, which, on the same scale, would equate to 500m or the length of a Boeing 747 airliner. The brain volume of a mouse, *Mus musculus*, is 5x10 to the eleventh cubic microns, or equivalent, again on the same scale, to the distance from Boston (MA) to Lisbon, that is 5,000km. Finally, the brain volume of *Homo sapiens* is 1.26x10 to the fifteenth cubic microns, equating, on the same scale, to 12.6 million km or nearly 40 times greater than the distance from the Earth to the Moon.[35] **2.016**

Research has shown that the smallest insects, despite their body sizes, do have complex brains and behaviours.[36] However, for the purposes of the main topic of this book, namely brain technologies and the lawfulness of their employment in particular contexts, it suffices to note that it is the more sophisticated capabilities that the human brain achieves that are going to be of greatest **2.017**

35 L F Abbott and others, 'The Mind of a Mouse' (2020) 182(6) *Cell* 1372–6. Pointing out that there is no exact correspondence between brain size and intelligence, the Canine Brains Project notes that dog brains weigh anywhere between 50 and 150g, with smaller dog brains about the size of a lemon and larger dog brains similar to a small pear. In comparison, the human brain weighs between 2.5 and 3lb; Harvard University, 'The Canine Brains Project' (2025), available at https://sites.harvard.edu/caninebrainsproject/brain-size/#:~:text=Dog%20brains%20weigh%20anywhere%20between,tend%20to%20have%20larger%20brains. At birth, the average brain weighs about one pound and grows to about two pounds during childhood; the average weight of an adult female brain is 2.7lb and of a male brain is 3lb: American Association of Neurological Surgeons, n.29. As to the relationship between brain size and body weight in a selection of 20 mammals, see P A M van Dongen, 'Brain Size in Vertebrates', in R Nieuwenhuys and others, *The Central Nervous System of Vertebrates* (Springer, 1998), 2099, at 2100.

36 See for example A Makarova, A Polilov and D M Chklovskii, 'Small Brains for Big Science' (2021) 71 *Current Opinion in Neurobiology* 77–83.

relevance. With that in mind, the discussion will now shift to considering some of the key features of human brain activity. It is thought that identifying some of these key general features will help us when it comes to considering whether specific capabilities associated with brain technologies are going to be legally and ethically acceptable for employment in specific contexts.

2.4 FEATURES THAT TYPIFY HUMAN BRAIN CAPABILITIES

2.018 The purpose in this section is to consider, in no particular order, some of the facilities that the human brain has and that essentially define what it is to be human. The author makes no claim to having identified all such features. Rather, the purpose is to use what follows as a stepping stone to clarifying what must be achieved for an AB to be acceptable for employment in the military sphere. Having made that point, it must be recognised that a piece of new technology may, in practice, be described as an AB even if some of the features of a human brain are not present. From a legal perspective, the key issue will be not so much whether what is developed complies with any particular definition of an AB; the issue will really be whether what the specific technology does is such that it can be lawfully used.

2.019 Before going through the sample features, it is important to note that the issue of which features are unique to humans and which are shared to a greater or lesser extent with animals is imperfectly understood. It is noteworthy that, until the 1960s, it was believed that the ability to use tools was a uniquely human characteristic until, that is, Jane Goodall observed chimpanzees using tools.[37] This is by no means unique. Capuchin monkeys use rocks to smash open hard fruit and nuts, selecting the more durable materials for the purpose. Use of rocks for similar purposes has also been observed in certain fish species, including the California Sheephead Wrasse. New Caledonian crows bend twigs, and so on to use as hooked tools to extract larvae from bark, indicating advanced motor skills, planning and insight. Kea birds in captivity can use stick tools to extract food from puzzle boxes. Also indicative of planning, certain octopuses have been observed carrying coconut shells around for future use. African elephants, confronted with a floating object task, have learned to add more water to the tube, thereby raising the water level and thus rendering

37 See J Goodall, 'Tool-Using and Aimed Throwing in a Community of Free-Living Chimpanzees' (1964) 201 *Nature* 1264–6, available at https://www.nature.com/articles/2011264a0.

the reward accessible.[38] The purpose of the summary in this paragraph is to show that some at least of the skills that we may traditionally have thought unique to humans are, to an extent, shared by certain animals. The relevant point is therefore that, whether animals also have a particular skill, in basic form or not, is not the key issue. What matters from the perspective of this book is that human beings do indeed have the relevant skillset, and it is this aspect that must be considered when assessing whether AB technologies are being considered for employment in particular tasks.

Human beings have, for thousands of years, demonstrated the ability to engage in *philosophical thought*.[39] The ability to develop hypotheses, to consider abstract phenomena, to engage in theoretical debate, to express theorems in algebraic terms and to analogise are all activities which, the author suggests, are typically available to humans. The same can be said of the possibility of developing fictional and illustrative examples to clarify explanations. Whether these are all features of the workings of the human brain that mark us out from animals can be debated. Indeed, that is a question that ongoing research may be expected to clarify. The important observation is that these are features that human beings possess. This philosophical capacity is, the author suggests, clearly linked to the capacity of human beings to observe the world around them, to observe the cosmos and to interpret what they see, thereby developing their understanding of the world and their role within it, their perception of the planet on which we all live and their perception of the status of the Earth within the solar system and beyond. These observations featured significantly in the writings of the early philosophers[40] and continue, for example, in the **2.020**

38 The discussion so far in this paragraph is based on L Williams, '11 animals that use tools in surprising and clever ways – including a few you may not expect', *BBC Discover Wildlife*, 26 March 2025 available at https://www.discoverwildlife.com/animal-facts/animals-that-use-tools.

39 Consider for example Hesiod (7th century BC); Thales (early 6th century BC); Anaximander (6th century BC); Anaximenes (6th century BC); Xenophanes (6th–5th century BC); Pythagoras (6th–5th century BC); Heraclitus (6th–5th century BC); Parmenides (born approx. 510 BC); Zeno of Elea (born approx. 490 BC); Melissus of Samos (flourished approx. 440 BC); Anaxagoras (flourished mid-5th century BC); Leucippus (mid-5th century BC); Empedocles (late 5th century BC); Democritus (born approx. 460 BC); Philolaus of Croton (late 5th century BC); Diogenes of Apollonia (late 5th century BC); Archytas (5th–4th century BC); Socrates (469–399 BC); Hippocrates (died approx. 380 BC); Plato (429–347 BC); Diogenes of Sinope (approx. 404–323 BC); Aristotle (384–322 BC); and Xenocrates (395–313 BC); King's College London, 'History of Philosophy Without Any Gaps', available at https://www.historyofphilosophy.net/timelines/classical-greece.

40 Note for example that in the 5th century BC Empedocles and Anaxagoras argued for the spherical nature of the Earth. Note also the distinction the Greeks drew between what they saw as fixed and wandering stars, the latter comprising the sun, moon, Jupiter, Mars, Saturn, Mercury and Venus; Library of Congress, 'Ancient Greek Astronomy and Cosmology', factsheet, available at https://www.loc.gov/collections/finding-our-place-in-the-cosmos-with-carl-sagan/articles-and-essays/modeling-the-cosmos/ancient-greek-astronomy-and-cosmology.

form of ever more sophisticated observations of deep outer space, to the present day.[41]

2.021 The philosophical capacity of the human brain is also, the author suggests, linked to notions of *religious belief*, belief in an afterlife, in a hereafter of some kind. For example, the Celts of Gaul believed in an afterlife and hence buried their dead with food, weapons and ornaments.[42] Ancient Greek mythology is, for these purposes, a linked notion referring as it does to oral and literary traditions developed by the ancient Greeks with regard to their gods, their heroes and to the nature of the cosmos.[43]

2.022 Sophisticated technological and mathematical concepts also seem to mark out the workings of the human mind. So, for example, concepts like the notion of infinity would seem to be a product of the operation of the human brain. The concept of infinity as such will not necessarily need to be addressed by an AB in a particular application. The point here is that, if that kind of level of sophistication in thought process can be achieved by AB technology, should human characteristics be attributed to such a system? This goes to the very root of the anthropomorphising discussion in Chapter 1.

2.023 A somewhat linked feature of human brain capability is the formulation, and subsequent application, of theoretical analysis. Under this heading, we can perhaps include intellectual thought, ethical thought and ideas of morality with their links to cultural tradition. Indeed, cultural tradition itself is a key aspect of human thinking that ought to be included in this discussion.

2.024 Human beings communicate using numerous diverse media, including speech, other sounds, facial expressions, 'body language', film, audio recordings, handwriting, typescript, photographic images, cartoons, diagrammatic representations, diverse languages, broadcasts and social media and so on. Creativity, including artistic creativity in all of its many forms, also seems to belong in this category of activity. While animals communicate in various ways, it is arguably the number and diversity of ways in which humans communicate and

41 Consider for example the Hubble Space Telescope, launched on 24 April 1990 and orbiting the Earth in low Earth orbit: NASA, 'Hubble Space Telescope' factsheet, available at https://science.nasa.gov/mission/hubble/.

42 P M Cana and M Dillon, 'Beliefs, practices and institutions in Celtic religion', *Encyclopaedia Britannica*, 18 November 2024 available at https://www.britannica.com/topic/Celtic-religion/Beliefs-practices-and-institutions. Consider also the notion of the Elysian Fields in ancient Greek mythology.

43 Consider 'Greek mythology', *Encyclopaedia Britannica*, available at https://www.britannica.com/topic/Greek-mythology.

represent their culture, knowledge, art and beliefs that seem to be of a different order to the behaviour of most members of the animal kingdom.

The capacity for introspection, the achievement of insight, both into the causes of one's own problems and into the failings, vulnerabilities, intentions and options available to oneself and to others ought to get a mention here. Both admirable and less desirable products of the working of the human brain can include compassion, empathy, research in diverse fields, the ability to organise collective activity towards the achievement of a common goal, knowledge that death comes at the end of life and, indeed, that there is an end of life, notions of time and deadlines, the knowledge that there are things that one does not know, masochism, sadism, hatred and suspicion. Another peculiarly human characteristic that has been observed[44] is second order desire, that is we can 'want to have (or not to have) certain desires and motives'. **2.025**

There are, of course, numerous other features of human thinking that are not mentioned here. For example, a suggested unique capability of human beings is to create fire.[45] As noted above, not all of these abilities need to feature for a novel piece of technology properly to be described as an AB; these are nevertheless among the tools in the toolbox that a human being can call upon when undertaking the kinds of tasks that AB technology may be employed to undertake in the future. To the extent that each such feature is relevant to the proper performance of the relevant task, the presence or absence of that feature in the particular AB system will be one of the factors that will influence the acceptability of that artificial system for the performance of that task. **2.026**

2.5 WHAT ARE BRAIN TECHNOLOGIES?

The title of this book refers to brain technologies. That is a significantly wider notion than ABs. It encompasses any technology that is designed to influence or to replicate elements of the performance of the human brain. The remaining pages of this chapter will therefore start by giving a brief and simplified explanation of two kinds of AB technology. The discussion will then turn to technologies that can be used to monitor and influence the human brain by means of BCIs. Then, the idea of direct BBIs using a linking computer will **2.027**

44 H G Frankfurt, 'Freedom of Will and Concept of a Person' (1971) 68 *Journal of Philosophy* 1, 5, 7, cited in N A Farahany, *The Battle for Your Brain* (St Martin's Press, 2024), 161.

45 See Z Cormier, 'Did Neanderthals learn to make fire before us?', *BBC Earth*, available at https://www.bbcearth.com/news/did-neanderthals-learn-to-make-fire-before-us, where the debate as to whether the ability to make fire is unique to Homo sapiens or was understood previously by Neanderthals is discussed.

be outlined. In Chapters 10 and 11, similar technologies that may be used respectively to enhance and degrade the performance of the human brain will also be assessed.

2.028 For the purposes of this book, an AB technology, referred to hereafter as an AB, will refer to any kind of system that is designed to synthesise functioning that is normally associated with a natural brain, whether human or animal. It is therefore an overarching concept that encompasses distinct methods of achieving that functioning. It is a broad notion that ranges from synthesising the performance of multiple brain functions to systems that replicate the functioning of a human brain as a whole.

2.029 In the literature, reference is made to a distinct notion of neurotechnology which:

> encompasses a wide variety of approaches but can be broadly defined as "devices and procedures that are used to access, investigate, assess, manipulate, and emulate the structure and function of neural systems". This includes: medical devices from prosthetics and diagnostic devices, such as cochlear implants and MRIs; cutting-edge implants and wearable devices that may be used in medical settings such as treating neurodegenerative conditions; and increasingly for commercial uses, such as workplace monitoring.[46]

2.030 This is the meaning that will be given to the word neurotechnology when used in this book.

2.5.1 Artificial brains (ABs)

2.031 One method of seeking to synthesise brain performance as a whole is called Artificial General Intelligence (AGI), which has been described as: 'the hypothetical intelligence of a machine that possesses the ability to understand or learn any intellectual task that a human can. It is a type of artificial intelligence that aims to mimic the cognitive abilities of the human brain.'[47] While it is not currently believed to exist, it is the focus of ongoing research. Its suggested applications include: the solution of complex problems beyond human capabilities; optimisation of industrial productivity and efficiency; improved medical diagnoses, treatment planning and medical outcomes; self-driving vehicles; AGI-powered chatbots and virtual assistants.[48]

---

46 'Neurotechnologies', in UK Information Commissioner's Office, *Tech Horizons Report 2024*, available at https://ico.org.uk/about-the-ico/research-reports-impact-and-evaluation/research-and-reports/technology-and-innovation/tech-horizons-report-2024/neurotechnologies/.

47 Google Cloud, 'What is Artificial General Intelligence (AGI)?', available at https://cloud.google.com/discover/what-is-artificial-general-intelligence.

48 Google Cloud, ibid.

Research that aims to *reverse-engineer the human brain* bases itself on the belief that working out how living brains work will offer the best guide to engineering the artificial variety.[49] So, the Wu Tsai Neurosciences Institute at Stanford University has pioneered the growing of simplified human brain circuits from human stem cells, thereby enabling the study of 'the assembly and wiring of the human brain – and the molecular rules that orchestrate it – in real time'.[50] Using this technology, 'the team can now "re-boot" skin cells from a healthy research subject or a patient with a neuropsychiatric disorder, then guide the resulting stem cells to develop into various types of brain cells'.[51] More than a dozen kinds of brain and nervous system tissue can now be grown in laboratory dishes 'as floating spheres of cells called "organoids". Organoids recapitulating different brain regions can then be combined to grow simplified human brain circuits, dubbed assembloids.'[52] These techniques are being used to directly observe the rules regarding the self-assembly of neural circuitry and to pinpoint how the process can go wrong, resulting in brain disorders.[53] Difficult ethical issues are raised by this line of research. It is unclear at what point the development of assembloids will produce a form of consciousness and associated sensations such as suffering. If the object of research is to generate an approximation to a human brain unattached to a body, the moral, ethical and perhaps legal implications of such research are, at the very least, challenging.[54] **2.032**

Another field of research also pursues the possibility of *reverse-engineering* the brain, but aims to do so *by means of computer technologies*. The reverse engineering might be achieved 'through architecting a prototype of a *brain-derived* **2.033**

49 National Academy of Engineering Grand Challenges, 'Reverse-Engineer the Brain', 19 September 2025 available at https://www.nae.edu/20782/grand-challenges-project.

50 N Weiler, 'Q and A: Reverse Engineering the Human Brain by Growing Neural Circuits in the Lab', Wu Tsai Neurosciences Institute, 21 January 2022, available at https://neuroscience.stanford.edu/news/qa-reverse-engineering-human-brain-growing-neural-circuits-lab.

51 Weiler, ibid.

52 Welier, ibid. Pasca recalls his concern that it would be difficult to get the organoids to fuse with each other. However, in the event, not only did the cells recognise one another, they also started to self-organise in a manner resembling human brain development. 'In our very first assembloid we fused ventral forebrain and dorsal forebrain (cortex) organoids and right away saw new-born GABA-ergic interneurons start to migrate towards the cerebral cortex, which is an unique and important aspect of human brain development.': Weiler, ibid.

53 Weiler, ibid. See also K W Kelley and N Paşca, 'Human Brain Organogenesis: Toward a Cellular Understanding of Development and Disease' (2022) 185(1) *Cell* 42–61; and B Goldman, 'Human Brain Cells Transplanted into Rat Brains Hold Promise for Neuropsychiatric Research', Wu Tsai Neurosciences Institute, 12 October 2022, available at https://neuroscience.stanford.edu/news/human-brain-cells-transplanted-rat-brains-hold-promise-neuropsychiatric-research.

54 Consider C Cottier, 'Artificial Brains May Pose a Startling Ethical Dilemma', *Discover*, 28 February 2023, available at https://www.discovermagazine.com/mind/artificial-brains-may-pose-a-startling-ethical-dilemma.

neuromorphic[55] computing system consisting of artificial electronic, ionic,[56] photonic[57] materials, devices and circuits with dynamicity[58] resembling the bio-plausible molecular, neuro-synaptic, neuro-circuit, and multi-structural hierarchical macro-circuits of the brain based on well-tested computational models'.[59] The researchers recognise that, if successful, it can lead to profound changes in the way we lead our lives as well as improved understanding of brain functioning. New nanoscale materials, the researchers suggest, may be able to resemble mechanisms in biological neural systems, thus enabling further research.[60]

2.034 A further line of research recognises the fundamental difference between the brain's computing principles, based as they are on neurons, synapses and information carriers, and the operating systems of conventional computers. This line of research presents: 'an acqueous memristor that emulates the brain's short-term synaptic plasticity features through ion transport in water, mirroring the natural processes of the brain. This device, which is inspired by and understood through a theoretical model, is applied as a synaptic element for reservoir computing, a brain-inspired machine learning framework.'[61]

2.035 In an apparent application of this kind of technology, scientists in China have reportedly developed a 'brain-on-chip' system which combines human brain matter grown in a laboratory with a neural interface chip to produce what the report describes as an organoid robot. The report indicates that 'the artificial brain has been grown in vitro using stem cell technology, allowing scientists

55 'The word neuromorphic comes from two Greek words, neuro meaning nerves and morphic meaning shape. A system is neuromorphic if it is modelled on a biological nervous system such as the human brain': 'What is Neuromorphic Computing?', *Conscium*, 7 June 2024, available at https://conscium.com/explainers/what-is-neuromorphic-computing/.

56 Meaning '1 relating to ions; 2 (of a chemical bond) formed by the attraction of ions with opposite charges': *Compact Oxford English Dictionary*, 3rd edn (Oxford University Press, 2005), 536.

57 A photon is a particle representing a quantum of light or other electromagnetic radiation: *Compact Oxford English Dictionary*, 3rd edn (Oxford University Press, 2005), 766.

58 Dynamic, in the context of physics, means 'relating to forces producing motion': *Compact Oxford English Dictionary*, 3rd edn (Oxford University Press, 2005) 310.

59 S J Ben Yoo and others, 'Towards Reverse-engineering the Brain: Brain-derived Neuromorphic Computing Approach with Photonic, Electronic and Ionic Dynamicity in 3D Integrated Circuits', *Cornell University arxiv*, 28 March 2024, available at https://arxiv.org/abs/2403.19724.

60 Yoo and others, ibid. Consider in this regard the reported design of a 'brain on a chip' made from tens of thousands of artificial brain synapses, known as memristors, that mimic the information transmitting synapses in the human brain; J Chu, 'Engineers put tens of thousands of artificial brain synapses on a single chip', *MIT News*, 8 June 2020, available at https://news.mit.edu/2020/thousands-artificial-brain-synapses-single-chip-0608.

61 T M Kamsma and others, 'Brain-inspired Computing with Fluidic Iontronic Nanochannels' (2024) 121(18) *Proceedings of the US National Academy of Sciences*, available at https://www.pnas.org/doi/10.1073/pnas.2320242121.

to create a brain-like organ out of simplified versions of brain tissue that have a similar function and structure to the brain'. While certain issues remain, 'the technology is a form of brain-computer interface, which provides a direct communication link between electrical activity in the brain and an external device, such as a computer or robotic limb'.[62]

2.5.2 Brain-computer interfaces (BCIs)

A BCI is a system that determines, directly from brain activity, a functional intent such as a wish to change, move, control or interact with an object and that translates that intent or wish into action.[63] The intended effect is that a device can be controlled directly by using the mind. The system bypasses the need to have muscular control, for example, muscles causing the arm to reach out to take hold of an object and causing the hand to grip the object in question. The computer translates the desired action into direct control of the object by the mind.[64] The neurons of the brain communicate using electrochemical signals, and the neurons operate in large networks. It is the electrical activity that is produced by the operations of these neural networks that can be detected from outside the brain using electroencephalography (EEG) by means of a headset or, from the surface of the brain, by means of inserted electrodes called invasive BCIs. Invasive BCIs receive stronger signals and this may be advantageous for the development of more complex BCI systems. So, a BCI consists of three key elements, namely: the headset or inserted electrode to detect and measure brain activity; a computer to process and analyse that activity employing specialised processes and algorithms to interpret from the incoming brain activity the action that the user wishes; and an application or device – once the computer has determined what the user wants the device to do, the computer sends a signal to the device or application to perform the required action.[65] A feedback process in which the decision or intended action that the computer was able to interpret is made known to the user is **2.036**

62 C Trueman, 'Chinese Scientists Develop Artificial Brain to Control "brain-on-chip organoid" Robot', *Data Center Dynamics*, 3 July 2024, available at https://www.datacenterdynamics.com/en/news/chinese-scientists-develop-artificial-brain-to-control-brain-on-chip-organoid-robot/.

63 See S H Scott, 'Converting Thoughts into Action' (2006) 442(7099) *Nature* 141–2 and J P Donoghue, 'Bridging the Brain to the World: A Perspective on Neural Interface Systems' (2008) 60(3) *Neuron* 511–21.

64 See University of Calgary, Cumming School of Medicine, 'What is a Brain Computer Interface', 2025, available at https://cumming.ucalgary.ca/research/pediatric-bci/bci-program/what-bci#:~:text=A%20brain%20computer%20interface%20(BCI,device%20using%20only%20your%20mind.

65 For a discussion of these three elements, the acquisition system, the signal processing system and the effector, see T Bonaci and others, 'App Stores for the Brain: Privacy and Security in Brain-computer Interfaces' (2015) 34(2) *IEEE Technology and Society Magazine* 32–9, available at https://ieeexplore.ieee.org/document/7128844.

an important learning element of a BCI system.[66] Moreover, BCIs can: 'work from the computer to the brain, delivering targeted electrical stimulation to the brain without concurrent signal detection. Bidirectional BCIs combine these functions, as they are simultaneously capable of recording neural activity and delivering targeted stimulation. This two-way communication enables a real-time and interactive exchange between the user and the computer.'[67]

2.037 It is also now possible to use BCIs to translate the image of brain activity that functional magnetic resonance imaging can produce into a description of what a person sees.[68] It remains to be seen whether a person's thoughts can similarly be identified.

2.038 So, in summary, a BCI as discussed above can be described as: 'encompass[ing] an array of neuro-technologies which enable direct communication between the brain and an external device. BCIs detect and interpret the brain's electrical signals and convert these neural impulses into computer-executable commands, enabling users to interact with computers or control devices purely through mental processes while bypassing the need for physical movement.'[69]

2.039 There are obvious applications, potential or actual, of this technology in the treatment of patients with various forms of brain damage or deficit. These include restoring upper limb function to patients with paralysis (for example using BCI to orient a robotic arm and pick up and move objects);[70] generating sensations that feel as if they are coming from, for example, the patient's hand; stimulating lateral parts of the spinal cord to restore sensation from missing limbs; and decoding and producing speech[71] without the patient opening

---

66 The explanation in this paragraph is based heavily on the University of Calgary, Cumming School of Medicine website, ibid.

67 Council of the European Union, Analysis and Research Team Research Paper, 'From Vision to Reality: Promises and risks of brain-computer interfaces', September 2024, available at https://www.consilium.europa.eu/media/fh4fw3fn/art_braincomputerinterfaces_2024_web.pdf?utm_source=linkedin.com&utm_medium=social&utm_campaign=20241002-art-research-paper&utm_content=visual (CEU Research Paper), 4. For a useful description of BCIs, and of potential applications of AI in conjunction with BCIs, see N Lubell and K Al-Khateeb, 'Cyborg Soldiers: Military use of Brain-Computer Interfaces and the Law of Armed Conflict' (11 April 2022), later published in L A Dickinson and E Berg (eds), *Big Data and Armed Conflict: Legal Issues Above and Below the Armed Conflict Threshold* (Oxford University Press, 2024), 3–6.

68 K Nahas, 'AI Re-creates What People See by Reading their Brain Scans', *Science News*, 7 March 2023, available at https://www.science.org/content/article/ai-re-creates-what-people-see-reading-their-brain-scans.

69 CEU Research Paper, n.67, 4.

70 L R Hochberg and others, 'Reach and Grasp by People With Tetraplegia Using a Neurally Controlled Robotic Arm' (2012) 485(7398) *Nature* 372–5.

71 D A Moses and others, 'Real Time Decoding of Question-and-Answer Speech Dialog Using Human Cortical Activity' (2019) 10 Nat Commun 1, 1–14.

their mouth.[72] Further potential applications that have been suggested include lie and deception detection and perhaps the revealing of subconscious brain information.[73]

If the preceding form of BCI can be understood in terms of passively observing the brain's wishes and intent and using computer means to translate those wants and intentions into action, another form of BCI involves manipulating the activity of the brain with the purpose of either stimulating or impeding particular responses from the brain.[74] The method chosen may be electrical or optical stimulation. An example of this form of BCI is the therapeutic use of deep brain stimulation in which electrodes are implanted under the cortex in order to stimulate particular brain locations with the stimulation being controlled externally.[75] **2.040**

The UN Human Rights Committee Advisory Council Report[76] describes the two kinds of neurotechnology as consisting first of: **2.041**

> "neuroimaging", employed for the diagnosis of mental states, includes devices and techniques used to observe the structure or functioning of the brain and map or measure its activity. Such procedures are capable of detecting neural signals and allow the interpretation of mental states and behaviours – reading – but cannot generally modify such processes. Second, altering and modulating the functioning of the brain – writing into – is what "neuromodulation" techniques and devices normally do through the inhibition or stimulation of targeted parts of the brain.[77]

M Ienca and others suggest that the current state of the technology does not permit mind-steering or mind-reading.[78] **2.042**

---

72 See S K Mudgal and others, 'Brain-computer Interface Advancement in Neurosciences: Applications and Issues' (2020) 20 Interdiscip Neurosurg 1–8; Z Abrams, 'The Future of Brain-computer Interfaces', *IEEE Pulse*, 25 January 2023 available at https://www.embs.org/pulse/articles/the-future-of-brain-computer-interfaces/; G K Anumanchipalli and others, 'Speech Synthesis from Neural Decoding of Spoken Sentences (2019) 568(7753) *Nature* 493–8.

73 P R Roelfsema and others, 'Mind Reading and Writing: The Future of Neurotechnology' (2018) 22(7) Trends Cogn Sci 598–610.

74 Consider J Rafferty, 'Brain Computer Interfaces: A New Existential Risk Factor' (2021) 26(2) *Futures Studies* 51–65.

75 M L Kringelbach and others, 'Translational Principles of Deep Brain Stimulation' (2007) 8(8) Nat Rev Neurosci 623–35.

76 UN Human Rights Council, Impact, opportunities and challenges of neurotechnology with regard to the promotion and protection of all human rights, A/HRC/57/61, 8 August 2024, available at https://digitallibrary.un.org/record/4060417?ln=en&v=pdf (HRC Report).

77 HRC Report, ibid, para.6.

78 M Ienca and others, 'Towards a Governance Framework for Brain Data' (2022) 15 *Neuroethics* 2.

2.5.3 Brain-to-brain interfaces (BBIs)

2.043 In August 2014, Charles Grau and others observed that the then recent development of BCIs constituted an important development in the creation of brain-to-brain communication systems and that 'precise brain stimulation techniques are now available for the realization of non-invasive computer-brain interfaces'.[79] As those experts explained, by combining BCI with computer-brain interfaces the vision of non-invasive, computer-mediated brain-to-brain communication between subjects could be realised. 'Our results provide a critical proof-of-principle demonstration for the development of conscious B2B communication technologies.'[80]

2.044 The research was taken significantly further by Jiang and others. In their report, they explain: 'Direct brain to brain interfaces (BBIs) in humans are interfaces which combine neuroimaging and neurostimulation methods to extract and deliver information between brains, allowing direct brain-to-brain communication. A BBI extracts specific content from the neural signals from a "sender" brain, digitizes it, and delivers it to a "receiver" brain.'[81] Non-invasive technologies, such as EEG, are used to record the neural activity and transcranial magnetic stimulation then delivers information to the brain. Jiang and colleagues then refer to the results of their research, stating that '[t]he interface allows three human subjects to collaborate and solve a task using direct brain-to-brain communication'.[82] In the experiment, the sender's decisions are delivered to the receiver's brain via magnetic stimulation of the occipital cortex and the receiver integrates the information from two senders and uses an EEG interface to make a decision.[83]

2.045 Vakilipour and Fekrvand describe BBIs as being 'made up of two parts known as the brain-computer interface part which reads a sender's brain activity and

---

79 C Grau and others, 'Conscious Brain-to-Brain Communication in Humans Using Non-invasive Technologies', *PLOS One*, 19 August 2014 available at https://journals.plos.org/plosone/article?id=10.1371/journal.pone.0105225.

80 Grau and others, ibid. See also W Lee and others, 'Non-invasive Transmission of Sensorimotor Information in Humans Using an EEG/Focused Ultrasound Brain-to-Brain Interface', *PLOS One*, 9 June 2017, available at https://journals.plos.org/plosone/article?id=10.1371/journal.pone.0178476.

81 L Jiang and others, 'BrainNet: A Multi-person Brain-to-Brain Interface for Direct Collaboration Between Brains', *Nature Scientific Reports*, 16 April 2019, available at https://www.nature.com/articles/s41598-019-41895-7.

82 Jiang and others, ibid.

83 Jiang and others, ibid.

digitalizes it, and the computer-brain interface part, which writes the delivered brain activity to a receiving brain'.[84]

It is clear that this technology is in its very early stages of research, but there is evident potential for its use in numerous contexts, including military activities. In this regard, it should be borne in mind that the 175 states that are party to API are required by Article 36 of that Treaty to conduct a weapon review when a means or method of warfare is being studied. While each state will have its own view as to the stage at which the study of a weapon has commenced, now is thought to be the right time to start to develop views as to the application of international law to the potential employment of the technologies discussed in this chapter in the armed conflict context. **2.046**

2.5.4 Brain enhancement and brain degradation

Various technologies have been used for a number of years either to enhance or, indeed, to degrade the performance of the human brain. These technologies and their legal implications are discussed respectively in Chapters 10 and 11 below. **2.047**

84 P Vakilipour and S Fekrvand, 'Brain-to-Brain Interface technology: A Brief History, Current State and Future Goals' (2024) 84(5) Int J Dev Neurosci 351–67.

3
OPPORTUNITIES, RISKS AND ISSUES

3.1 INTRODUCTION

3.001 In July 2006, scientists announced that a paralysed man had been able to use a new brain sensor to move a computer cursor, to open an email and to control a robotic device simply by thinking about it. The BrainGate sensor, which involved planting electrodes in the brain, was recognised then as offering new hope to patients suffering from paralysis. A small silicon chip with 100 electrodes was implanted into the motor cortex, cell activity was recorded and sent to a computer, the commands were translated by the computer and the patient was able to move and control the external device.[1] Research in this field is starting to accelerate, for example in the US and China,[2] enabled in

1 'Paralysed Man Masters Thought Control', *NBC News*, 12 July 2006, available at https://www.nbcnews.com/id/wbna13830825.

2 See US Department of Defense, *Military and Security Developments involving the People's Republic of China, Annual Report to Congress* (2024) available at https://media.defense.gov/2024/Dec/18/2003615520/-1/-1/0/MILITARY-AND-SECURITY-DEVELOPMENTS-INVOLVING-THE-PEOPLES-REPUBLIC-OF-CHINA-2024.PDF; B Maiseli and others, 'Brain-Computer Interface: Trend, Challenges and Threats' (2023) 10(1) *Brain Informatics* 20; and S Saha and others, 'Progress in

part by developments in relevant technologies, including nanotechnology and artificial intelligence. It is becoming increasingly clear that brain-computer interface (BCI) technologies may be expected radically to change our way of life, and it is the purpose of this chapter to consider some of the opportunities, risks and issues that brain technologies, including BCIs, may offer and present.

The key applications of BCI technologies to date have been in medicine, specifically in the treatment of patients suffering from paralysis,[3] patents suffering from 'locked in' syndrome,[4] patients who have lost limbs whether through illness or injury,[5] or those whose illness has resulted in loss of mobility, speech or other facility. There are, however, recognised challenges confronting the further development of these technologies. The first is the sheer complexity of the human brain with its estimated 86 billion neurons, each of which potentially has thousands of synaptic connections with nearby cells.[6] The second category of challenges includes numerous psychophysiological, neurological and technological issues.[7] Some of the challenges and risks are discussed later in this chapter. **3.002**

3.2 POTENTIAL BCI APPLICATIONS AND SOME CHALLENGES

BCIs that are currently available enable patients with paralysed limbs to regain control of those limbs.[8] Moreover, BCIs 'that measure movement-related neural activity with implanted electrodes can restore some … lost arm and hand function as the cortex remains capable of generating neural activity **3.003**

Brain-computer Interface: Challenges and Opportunities' (2021) 15 *Frontiers* available at https://www.frontiersin.org/journals/systems-neuroscience/articles/10.3389/fnsys.2021.578875/full.

3 J F M Brannigan and others, 'Endovascular Brain-computer Interfaces in Post-stroke Paralysis' (2023) 55(2) Stroke 474–83.

4 Locked in syndrome refers to paraplegic patients who are unable to move any part of their body, even their eyes, but who still have active minds.

5 T Yanagisawa and others, 'BCI Training to Move a Virtual Hand Reduces Phantom Limb Pain', *National Library of Medicine*, 28 July 2020, available at https://pubmed.ncbi.nlm.nih.gov/32675074/.

6 C Caruso, 'A New Field of Neuroscience Aims to Map Connections in the Brain', *Harvard Medical School*, 19 January 2023.

7 Saha and others, n.2, Section 2.

8 Consider, for example, T Freeman, 'Brain-spine Interface Enables Natural Walking After Spinal Cord Injury', *Physics World*, 1 June 2023. For an assessment of the potential use of BCIs in conjunction with traditional, complementary and integrative medicine, see J Y Ng, 'Exploring the Intersection of Brain-computer Interfaces and Traditional, Complementary, and Integrative Medicine' (2025) 14(2) *Integrative Medicine Research* 101142, available at https://www.sciencedirect.com/science/article/pii/S2213422025000228.

that controls arm and hand motion'.[9] Another use of BCIs that has been suggested is to monitor employee brain activity,[10] the suggested purpose being to enhance performance and productivity and, say, to ensure the safe undertaking by personnel of hazardous tasks. The author would suggest that while the medical use of such systems, for example to ensure the correct operation of devices to control prostheses or to address paralysis, is likely to be unobjectionable, they would raise profound legal and perhaps ethical issues if applied to the employment setting. Consider, for example, the potential for a BCI that is not primarily intended for a thought monitoring purpose to collect data indicating the thought processes of an identifiable individual employee. Problems under data protection and human rights law rules relating to privacy, for example, are likely to arise.

3.004 Numerous other applications for BCI technologies have been either demonstrated or suggested, including mind control of a computer cursor,[11] precision control of machines,[12] the sending of emails, online shopping, communicating[13] and controlling the settings for lighting, heating and other systems, thought-driven typing and data tasks, accelerated digital workflows, say in the office context, and the development of new collaborative tools thereby facilitating more immersive and more natural remote working.[14] Other possibilities include the creation of new art or music simply by thinking about it and the generation of direct learning interfaces in which complex concepts are rapidly

---

9 S N Flescher and others, 'A Brain-computer Interface That Evokes Tactile Sensations Improves Robotic Arm Control' (2021) 372(6544) *Science* 831–6, available at https://pmc.ncbi.nlm.nih.gov/articles/PMC8715714/#:~:text=Brain%2Dcomputer%20interfaces%20(BCIs),controls%20arm%20and%20hand%20motion.

10 Note, A Kies and others, 'Wired for Work: Brain-computer Interfaces' Impact on Front Line Employees' Well-being' (2024) 36(1) *Journal of Service Management* 1–26, available at https://www.researchgate.net/publication/386172938_Wired_for_work_brain-computer_interfaces'_impact_on_frontline_employees'_well-being.

11 'Neuralink's First Human Patient Able to Control Mouse Through Thinking, Musk says', *Reuters*, 20 February 2024, available at https://www.reuters.com/business/healthcare-pharmaceuticals/neuralinks-first-human-patient-able-control-mouse-through-thinking-musk-says-2024-02-20/#:~:text=The%20study%20uses%20a%20robot,or%20keyboard%20using%20their%20thoughts.

12 Consider, for example, a brain implant permitting biological connection to the internet, enabling wireless connection with any person with a similar implant and computer setup; see R Mack, 'Neuralink Implanted a Device in a Patient's Brain, Elon Musk says', *New York Times*, 29 January 2024.

13 Consider, for example, the use of a BCI to enable a stroke patient to speak again; J Osborne and S Zakaria, 'Silent Speech, Loud Questions: The Dawn of Brain-computer Communication', *Rand*, 15 May 2025, available at https://www.rand.org/pubs/commentary/2025/05/silent-speech-loud-questions-the-dawn-of-brain-computer.html.

14 Council of the European Union, Analysis and Research Team Research Paper, 'From Vision to Reality: Promises and Risks of Brain-computer Interfaces', September 2024, available at https://www.consilium.europa.eu/media/fh4fw3fn/art_braincomputerinterfaces_2024_web.pdf?utm_source=linkedin.com&utm_medium=social&utm_campaign=20241002-art-research-paper&utm_content=visual (CEU Research Paper), 9.

assimilated and in which educational experiences are adjusted to suit the learning styles of individuals.[15] The prospect is even being discussed of humans engaging with animal cognitive processes leading, potentially, to inter-species communication.[16] If BCIs were to be used in the marketing sphere, they might provide 'real-time insights into emotional and cognitive responses which could lead to a deeper understanding of consumer behaviour'.[17] Much of the discussion in the present paragraph is likely to provoke alarm. That alarm may be magnified by the realisation that, while research in this field is advancing rapidly, regulation of it in the commercial setting is not developing at the same pace.[18] The present author believes that legislation will be required in which human and other rights, such as privacy rights, and the data rights of citizens are carefully safeguarded,[19] in which punitive provisions are set forth and in which appropriate transparency of BCI processes is assured.[20]

Non-invasive BCI technologies have been employed for various medical **3.005**
purposes including the treatment of brain and spinal cord deficits[21] and the monitoring of brain activity. They are also capable of commercial application in enhancing feelings of well-being, in the workplace and in education; the purpose may be to improve cognitive and sporting performance, or to assist with concentration, relaxation or sleep.[22] The effectiveness of these devices is

15 CEU Research Paper, ibid. See also F Caiado and A Ukolov, 'The History, Current State and Future Possibilities of the Non-invasive Computer-brain Interfaces' (2025) 25 *Medicine in Modern Technology and Devices* 100353, available at https://www.sciencedirect.com/science/article/pii/S2590093525000049.

16 M Adnan, 'Communicating with Cats: The Future of Human-feline Interaction Using Brain-computer Interfaces (BCIs)', *LinkedIn*, 28 October 2024, available at https://www.linkedin.com/pulse/communicating-cats-future-human-feline-interaction-using-adnan-qic4c.

17 CEU Research Paper, n.14, 10.

18 AJOB Neuroscience UN Human Rights Council, Impact, opportunities and challenges of neurotechnology with regard to the promotion and protection of all human rights, A/HRC/57/61 dated 8 August 2024, available at https://digitallibrary.un.org/record/4060417?ln=en&v=pdf (HRC Report), paras 12 and 13. For suggestions as to an international declaration on the topic, see, for example, J C Bublitz, 'What an International Declaration on Neurotechnologies and Human Rights Could Look Like: Ideas, Suggestions, Desiderata' (2023) 15(2) AJOB Neuroscience *AJOB Neuroscience* 96–112 available at https://www.tandfonline.com/doi/full/10.1080/21507740.2023.2270512#abstract.

19 Consider M Ienca and others, 'Brain Leaks and Consumer Neurotechnology' (2018) 36 *Nature Biotechnology* 805–10.

20 Note, for example, D Berrick, 'BCI Technical and Policy Recommendations to Mitigate Privacy Risks', *Future of Privacy Forum*, 15 February 2022, available at https://fpf.org/blog/bci-technical-and-policy-recommendations-to-mitigate-privacy-risks/.

21 Consider, for example, DARPA, 'BG+: Bridging the Gap Plus', available at https://www.darpa.mil/research/programs/bridging-the-gap-plus, which 'aims to develop new approaches for treating spinal cord injury by integrating injury stabilization, regenerative therapy, and functional restoration' involving the employment of two systems of implantable and adaptive devices.

22 HRC Report, para.10.

not generally proven and there is a relative lack of research on the effects of long-term use.[23]

3.006 A study of the use of BCI applications for training and rehabilitation of students with neurodevelopmental disorders has suggested, among other things: the potential use of BCI-related systems in connection with dyslexia; that BCI spatial abilities training can improve cognitive skills such as speed, memory, attention, flexibility and problem solving; that students' immersion, creativity, emotional skills and ADHD symptoms can be improved by BCI training; and that there have been positive findings in relation to attention, memory, language and visuospatial abilities.[24] Other indicated applications of BCI technology include attention-span training and memory power. Many challenges, however, remain.[25]

3.3 POTENTIAL BRAIN-TO-BRAIN INTERFACE (BBI) APPLICATIONS AND CHALLENGES

3.007 In 2014, Rajesh Rao and others described the first BBI in humans.[26] Linxing Jiang and his colleagues[27] explain that their BBI system, BrainNet, expands the scale of BBIs to multiple human subjects working collaboratively to solve a task; is the first BBI to combine brain recording (EEG) and brain stimulation (TMS) in a single human subject, thus eliminating the need for physical movements to convey information; and enables the recipients of information, by means only of information received through BrainNet, to learn the reliability of information conveyed to their brains by other participants and choose the most reliable sender. The researchers explain that with sufficient hardware their system can be scaled to the case where every participant can both send and receive information using the BBI, and hold out the prospect of what they describe as a social network of brains.[28] Potential applications of BBIs that

23 A Wexler and P Reiner, 'Oversight of Direct-to-Consumer Neurotechnologies (2019) 363 *Science* 6424.

24 G Papanastasiou and others, 'Brain Computer Interface Based Applications for Training and Rehabilitation of Students with Neurodevelopmental Disorders: A Literature Review' (2020) 6(9) *Heliyon* e04250 available at https://pmc.ncbi.nlm.nih.gov/articles/PMC7482019/#bib81.

25 Papanastasiou and others, ibid.

26 R P N Rao and others, 'A Direct Brain-to-Brain Interface in Humans' (2014) 9(11) *PLoS One* e111332, available at https://pmc.ncbi.nlm.nih.gov/articles/PMC4221017/.

27 L Jiang and others, 'BrainNet: A Multi-person Brain-to-brain Interface for Direct Collaboration Between Brains', *Nature Scientific Reports*, 16 April 2019, available at https://www.nature.com/articles/s41598-019-41895-7.

28 Jiang and others, ibid. Note also S McQuate, 'How You and Your Friends Can Play a Video Game Together Using Only Your Minds', *UW News*, 1 July 2019, available at https://www.washington.edu/news/2019/07/01/play-a-video-game-using-only-your-mind/.

have been suggested include the establishment of social networks similar to current social media networks, monitoring, encryption, and silent commands, including in the military context.[29]

It is clear that a great deal of further research work will be required before it will be feasible to apply technology based on this science to the solution of the kinds of complex problems that are encountered in the military sphere. However, it is evident that that level of sophistication is the goal of the researchers. While the use of BBIs to solve complex issues, including military ones, probably therefore lies in the medium- to long-term future, it is nevertheless sensible to consider now the kinds of issues that such processes might be expected to raise in the context of warfare-related decision-making.[30] Accordingly, the discussion in the following pages will include, where relevant, consideration of the implications of the various principles and rules of international law for the use of BBIs. **3.008**

3.4 POTENTIAL ARTIFICIAL BRAIN (AB) APPLICATIONS AND CHALLENGES

Before getting into the possible militarisation of AB concepts, a topic that will be addressed briefly later in this chapter, we should reflect on which general classes of activity are likely to be controlled or undertaken by AB technologies. The answer, the author suggests, is that any function that a human being can perform should, subject to certain limitations, be capable of performance using an AB-enabled system. The limitations will include: **3.009**

1. whether it is technically feasible to design an AB system to undertake the range of tasks associated with the particular function;
2. whether it is ethically acceptable for an AB system to fulfil the relevant function;

29 E Hildt, 'Multi-person Brain-to-Brain Interfaces: Ethical Issues' (2019) 13 Front. Neurosci., available at https://www.frontiersin.org/journals/neuroscience/articles/10.3389/fnins.2019.01177/full#B2. Consider also telepathic communication to relay important battlefield information, as contemplated by Margaret Kosal and Joy Putney; M Kosal and J Putney, 'Neurotechnology and International Security: Predicting Commercial and Military Adoption of Brain-computer Interfaces in the United States and China' (2023) 42(1) *Politics and the Life Sciences* 81, 87, Scenario 1.

30 It should be borne in mind that in Article 36 of the Protocol Additional to the Geneva Conventions of 12 August 1949, and Relating to the Protection of Victims of International Armed Conflicts, Geneva, 8 June 1977, 1125 UNTS 3 (Additional Protocol I or API), States Parties are required 'in the study … of a new weapon, means or method of warfare … to determine whether its employment would, in some or all circumstances, be prohibited by th[e] Protocol or by any other rule of international law applicable to the' state. The study of such a method of warfare might arise somewhat sooner than the perfected technology.

3. specifically, whether there is a legal or practical requirement that the function be performed by a human being; and
4. whether the function in question is linked to some other activity for which human involvement is required so that human performance of the function is also necessary.

3.010 In the author's view, determining whether performance of a task or function by an AB system will be legally and practically acceptable will require first that the task or function be broken down into its required elements so that the feasibility of the AB system satisfying each of those elements to an appropriate standard can then be considered. That is the approach that is adopted in this book in relation to each of the three technologies, namely BCIs, ABs and BBIs.

3.011 The term 'artificial brain' does not presuppose that it is a human brain with all of its complexities and sophisticated capabilities that is being replicated. In principle, therefore, an artificial brain that does not reflect all of the characteristics of a human brain, what might be described as a 'human brain minus', or maybe an AB that only includes a few of the features of a human brain, might also be classed as an AB. For the purposes of the discussion in this book, the assumption must be that when an AB is being referred to in this book, it is an AB that has all of the socialisation, learning, evaluation, comparison and judgement skills of a human brain, to the extent that those skills are required for the proper performance of the designated role or function. This may have implications for how AB systems are developed and tested; for example, a human being learns from their mistakes and, as a child, a human is allowed to make mistakes as part of learning. Allowing a child to fall and hurt itself in order to learn to take more care in future is a case in point. If a child is never permitted to fall it may never understand the consequences of falling and this may adversely affect its action choices later. It remains to be seen to what extent learning from error will be built into AB system training.

3.012 One imagines that the objective in scientific research will be to get ABs as close as possible to the healthy human brain, but not all human brains are necessarily equal. The author assumes that replication of capabilities at the level of an average human brain will be the research goal, at least initially.

3.5 DISTINGUISHING AB FROM ARTIFICIAL INTELLIGENCE (AI) TECHNOLOGIES

In a previous book, the author understood AI to be 'the application of computer-based technology to simulate the human ability to gain knowledge and skills by means of experience, training and/or education'.[31] AI technology therefore focuses on using computers to mimic what a human does to gain knowledge and new skills by employing the various learning tools. AB, by contrast, is simulating the brain itself in whole or in part, that thoroughly complex collection of structures that provides the myriad skills, features and facilities that lie at the core of our very humanity. It is the scope and complexity of the facilities that the natural brain provides, the intricacy of its mechanisms, and the way in which such diverse aspects ranging, for example, from emotion through objective calculation to analysis, judgement and intent, that, taken together, mark out the development of an AB as an endeavour to be distinguished from AI. Accordingly, artificial general intelligence will only truly represent an AB if the scope and complexity aspects briefly summarised in the previous sentence are achieved.[32] **3.013**

Moreover, it is the intensely personal nature of many aspects of natural brain function, including thought, reflection and emotion, that causes AB technologies to raise such profound issues. As noted in section 3.4, the analysis in this book assumes that AB is synthesising the human brain with all its capabilities and facilities, or at least with the capabilities and facilities that are required for the proper, lawful performance of the role in which the AB is to be employed. The 'AB minus' concept then becomes a synthetic human brain in which key features or facilities of a natural brain are missing. If the absence of those missing features or facilities does not affect the correctness, reliability and consistency of performance of the designated task(s) by the AB, then their absence is irrelevant when assessing the acceptability of using the AB for the task. Addressing this aspect can only really be done by reference to a particular technology and its undertaking of a given task. **3.014**

---

31 W H Boothby, *AI Warfare and the Law* (2025), 5. US Naval War College International Law Studies.

32 Note, however, endeavours to bridge the gap between AI and AB technologies, such as H Xiong and others, 'The Digital Twin Brain: A Bridge Between Biological and Artificial Intelligence' (2023) 2 *Intelligent Computing* 0055, available at https://spj.science.org/doi/10.34133/icomputing.0055. See also D Orf, 'AI is Breaking into a Higher Dimension – Literally – to Mimic the Human Brain and Achieve True Intelligence', *Popular Mechanics*, 15 July 2025, available at https://www.popularmechanics.com/science/a65397906/human-brain-ai/; K Dickman, 'Neuromorphic Computing: the Future of AI', 31 March 2025, Los Alamos National Laboratory, available at https://www.lanl.gov/media/publications/1663/1269-neuromorphic-computing.

3.6 POTENTIAL MILITARY USES OF BCI TECHNOLOGY

3.015 BCI technology can enable a human being to control a virtual drone using just their mind.[33] The sensor that detects human brain activity may take the form of a skull cap.[34] There is the risk that the signals received by the skull cap from the brain will be imprecise.[35] If improved signals representing the brain activity are required for the particular BCI system to operate correctly, invasive surgery may be needed.[36] That surgery may involve the implanting of a very small electronic device 'beneath the skull, directly into the brain, to target specific sets of neurons. BCI implants currently under development are tiny and can engage up to a million neurons at once.'[37] Any invasive surgery is likely to involve health risks which, in the case of invasive brain surgery, may be significant. Many legal issues, including the obtaining of freely given and appropriately informed consent, are likely to arise. An alternative to the skull cap discussed earlier in this section has been developed relatively recently. This involves the fitting of a microstructure brain sensor that is inserted into the minute spaces between hair follicles slightly beneath the skin. Reportedly, the device produces high-fidelity signals and means that the BCI can be used continuously.[38] In order to avoid or minimise some of the risks identified earlier in this paragraph, it would clearly be desirable to avoid the need for a craniotomy to deliver penetrating or surface electrodes to the brain. This issue was the subject of a 2023 study with the catchy title 'Stentrode With Thought-Controlled Digital Switch Study'. The participating scientists reported, inter alia, as follows: 'Endovascular access to the sensorimotor cortex is an alternative to

---

33 V Sankaran, 'Paralysed Man Learns to Fly Virtual Drone With Mind Using Breakthrough Brain Implant', *The Independent*, 21 January 2025 available at https://www.independent.co.uk/tech/brain-implant-paralysed-man-drone-b2683334.html; see also Rand article, 'Brain-computer Interfaces are Coming – Will We Be ready?', *Rand*, 27 August 2020, available at https://www.rand.org/pubs/articles/2020/brain-computer-interfaces-are-coming-will-we-be-ready.html.

34 M Jochumsen and others, 'Evaluation of EEG Headset Mounting for Brain-computer Interface Stroke Rehabilitation by Patients, Therapists, and Relatives' (2020) 14 Front. Hum. Neurosci. available at https://www.frontiersin.org/journals/human-neuroscience/articles/10.3389/fnhum.2020.00013/full.

35 J J Shih and others, 'Brain-computer Interfaces in Medicine', *Mayo Clinic Proceedings*, March 2012, available at https://pmc.ncbi.nlm.nih.gov/articles/PMC3497935/pdf/main.pdf.

36 Z-P Zhao, 'Modulating Brain Activity With Invasive Brain-computer Interface: A Narrative Review' (2023) 13(1) *Brain Science* 134, available at https://pmc.ncbi.nlm.nih.gov/articles/PMC9856340/#:~:text=Invasive%20BCI%2C%20in%20comparison%20to,higher%20signal%2Dto%2Dnoise%20ratio.

37 Rand, n.33. The sensors are reportedly roughly the size of a grain of sand.

38 Georgia Tech Research, 'New Wearable Brain-Computer Interface', 7 April 2025 available at https://research.gatech.edu/new-wearable-brain-computer-interface#:~:text=Georgia%20Tech%20researchers%20have%20developed,BCI)%20in%20everyday%20life%20possible.

placing BCI electrodes in or on the dura by open brain surgery…. it is possible to record neural signals from a blood vessel.'[39]

In the military context, freely given and appropriately informed consent from the relevant soldier, discussed later in this chapter, would be required before any electrode, invasive or otherwise, is fitted to that individual. **3.016**

In addition to mind control of drones and other systems,[40] other applications of BCI technology in the military sphere that have been discussed include: more rapid sharing of information; improving situational awareness; making more accurate decisions more speedily; improving human memory, attention span and cognitive performance; the monitoring of people for excessive stress or cognitive workload; improving understanding of how physiological states affect cognitive and motor performance; improving the ability to succeed in challenging circumstances, such as search and rescue operations in remote or inaccessible environments; and silent communication without risk of radio interference.[41] The Defense Advanced Research Projects Agency (DARPA) Next-generation Non-surgical Nanotechnology programme aimed to develop high performance, bi-directional brain-machine interfaces for able-bodied service members. These systems are envisaged for use in connection with the control of unmanned aerial systems, active cyber defence systems, and 'teaming with computer systems to successfully multitask during complex military missions'. The aim of the DARPA project was to produce a device that does not require surgical implantation but which 'is capable of specifically interacting **3.017**

39 P Mitchell and others, 'Assessment of Safety of a Fully Implanted Endovascular Brain-computer Interface for Severe Paralysis In Four Patients: The Stentrode With Thought-Controlled Digital Switch (SWITCH) Study', (2023) 80(3) JAMA Neurol 270–8, available at https://pubmed.ncbi.nlm.nih.gov/36622685/.

40 Consider, for example, the combination of BCI and exoskeleton technologies as discussed by Dov Greenbaum, who argues that the combined technology represents a discrete category of augmentation which blurs the traditional distinction between operator and tool; it is further argued that governance arrangements are required that reflect both the requirements of operational effectiveness and ethical considerations, a framework for which is proposed; D Greenbaum, 'Enhancing the Warfighter: Ethical, Legal, and Strategic Implications of Brain Machine Interface-enabled Military Exoskeletons' (2025) 16(4) AJOB Neuroscience 222–47, available at https://www.tandfonline.com/doi/full/10.1080/21507740.2025.2530952?scroll=top&needAccess=true.

41 Rand, ibid. See N Lubell and K Al-Khateeb, 'Cyborg Soldiers: Military Use of Brain-Computer Interfaces and the Law of Armed Conflict' (11 April 2022), later published in L A Dickinson and E Berg (eds), *Big Data and Armed Conflict: Legal Issues Above and Below the Armed Conflict Threshold* (Oxford University Press, 2024), 7–9 where military uses of BCIs are discussed under the headings of monitoring, control, communications, and enhanced functions. See also S Reis, 'Expert paper: Strategic considerations for brain-computer interface military R&D', *Oxford Expert Emerging Threats Group*, 6 July 2025, available at https://emergingthreats.co.uk/paper-strategic-considerations-for-brain-computer-interface-military-rd/.

with sub-millimetre[42] regions of the brain with a spatial and temporal specificity that rivals existing invasive approaches'. Research in this field continues.

3.018 Another approach proposes the employment of BCI technology in conjunction with the use of a joystick. This hybrid interface reportedly shows high accuracy and robustness when used as a brain-robot interface. The performance of the system has been demonstrated in real-time control of a swarm of quadrotors.[43]

3.019 It will be apparent during the discussion in the following chapters that the author refers to the advisability of the BCI associated with a weapon system being switched off until it has been determined that the contemplated attack or other military operation can lawfully proceed. This is because if a mere thought of the operator of the BCI can result in the attack or other operation being initiated, it will be important to ensure that the legally required precautions have in fact been taken. It is recognised that in some systems, what this would require is the switching off of the system while in others selecting a deactivation or similar mode may be sufficient to achieve a like effect. In that regard, references to either switching off or deactivating the BCI should be interpreted accordingly.

3.020 The potential employment of BCIs during combat to reduce pain and to regulate emotions raises numerous concerns. The experience of fear is clearly linked to the fearful individual taking precautions in order to keep that individual safe. The author suggests that it will be important to ensure that any use of BCI is accompanied by measures to give the BCI user at least the same level of personal protective awareness that conventional fear would arouse. Of course, the potential for BCIs to augment human capabilities, say by enhancing human cognitive functions, by accelerating human decision-making and by increasing situational awareness might also achieve the purpose referred to in the preceding sentence. The possibility that BCIs will facilitate the provision of immersive, realistic, engaging and more individually tailored training should also be borne in mind.[44]

---

42 DARPA, 'NC3: Next Generation Non-Surgical Neuro-Technology', available at https://www.darpa.mil/research/programs/next-generation-nonsurgical-neurotechnology#:~:text=The%20envisioned%20N3%20technology,of%20neural%20tissue%20within%2050ms.

43 G K Karavas and others, 'A Hybrid BMI for Control of Robotic Swarms: Preliminary Results, 2017 IEEE/RSJ International Conference on Intelligent Robots and Systems, available at https://bpb-us-w2.wpmucdn.com/sites.udel.edu/dist/b/9405/files/2019/08/IROS17_Karavas.pdf.

44 Rand, n.33.

3.7 IN THE MORE DISTANT FUTURE

Scientific development seems likely to permit thoughts in the human brain to be decoded by accessing the patterns of neural activity;[45] if scientific discoveries in that field can be made and then converted into technology that can be refined, this will facilitate a number of possible new processes, some welcome and some not. The possibility for individuals to communicate through thought alone without the necessity for speech or writing[46] could, for example, enable communication with patients whose communicative powers have been adversely affected by trauma or illness. 'Brain-computer interfaces have been developed that can translate brain signals into words. Such devices have the potential to aid communication for people who are unable to speak.'[47] On the more troubling side, the technical possibility of decoding a person's thoughts, not necessarily with their consent, raises the most profound issues involving personal privacy rights.[48] While legal rules would be required limiting the circumstances in which such technology might lawfully be used, the very existence of such a capability raises the prospect of its potential employment, perhaps by the unscrupulous, outside of those desirable, therapeutic contexts and suggests that measures will be needed to protect individuals from unwanted, unwarranted and potentially most invasive activity. **3.021**

Other future possibilities may include the development of imagery from the subconscious and the uploading of the contents of the human mind onto a computer.[49] Brain-to-brain connections indicate the possibility of controlling or influencing another person's movements or decisions through direct neural **3.022**

45 A Krausová, 'Legal Aspects of Brain Computer Interfaces' (2014) 8(2) Masaryk University Journal of Law and Technology 199–208.

46 S Duraivel and others, 'High-resolution Neural Recordings Improve the Accuracy of Speech Decoding (2023) 14 *Nature Communications* 6938, available at https://www.nature.com/articles/s41467-023-42555-1.

47 National Institutes of Health Research Matters, 'Brain Decoder Turns a Person's Brain Activity into Words', 16 May 2023 available at https://www.nih.gov/news-events/nih-research-matters/brain-decoder-turns-person-s-brain-activity-into-words#:~:text=Brain%2Dcomputer%20interfaces%20have%20been,to%20have%20invasive%20brain%20surgery; and D Thompson, 'Mind-reading Technology Can Turn Brain Scans Into Language', Columbia University Department of Neurology, 1 May 2023, available at https://www.neurology.columbia.edu/news/mind-reading-technology-can-turn-brain-scans-language. See also G Conroy, A mind-reading brain implant that comes with password protection, Nature News, 2025 Aug available at https://pubmed.ncbi.nlm.nih.gov/40813479/.

48 C M L Brown, 'Neurorights, Mental Privacy and Mind Reading (2024) 17 *Springer Nature Link* 34, available at https://link.springer.com/article/10.1007/s12152-024-09568-z.

49 N Collins, 'Hawking: "In the future, brains could be separated from the body"', *The Telegraph*, 20 September 2013.

connection,[50] and an animal's activity through cross-species connections.[51] Work is also underway to devise brain-machine-brain systems that, in the future, would enable people to communicate globally through simple thought control and without typing or speaking.[52]

3.023 These areas of technological research cause one to wonder at what point machines take on the characteristics of humans or, for that matter, at what point does the human being become a component in a machine system. While this may seem to be an entirely theoretical question, it may become increasingly realistic as technology advances, and the ethical, legal and social issues that it raises are likely to prove numerous and complex. It is therefore, the author believes, appropriate and indeed necessary for us to consider these issues now so that the beneficial consequences of BBIs can be experienced while the potential risks and dangers are either excluded or at least minimised.

3.8 RISKS AND CHALLENGES

3.8.1 Implanting electrodes

3.024 There are numerous concerns associated with the implantation of electrodes on or in the human brain for the purposes of invasive BCI. While the implantation can be achieved surgically, there are associated risks, for example, of haemorrhage, infection and, depending on the precise technique that is employed, tissue damage.[53] The alternative method of insertion is, reportedly, by transmission through the blood stream.[54] Reliability concerns and ignorance as to the effects of long-term use of such implanted devices are further important

50 M L Latash and X Huang, 'Neural Control of Movement Stability: Lessons From Studies of Neurological Patients (2015) 301 *Neuroscience* 39–48, available at https://pmc.ncbi.nlm.nih.gov/articles/PMC4504804/.

51 'Our results demonstrate the feasibility of computer-mediated interfacing of the neural signals between human and animal to generate simple motor responses': S-S Yoo and others, 'Non-invasive Brain-to-brain Interface (BBI): Establishing Functional Links Between Two Brains', *PLOS One*, 3 April 2013, available at https://journals.plos.org/plosone/article?id=10.1371/journal.pone.0060410.

52 As reported by E J P Fisher in 'Direct Brain to Brain Communication Without Interface Applications – Fact or Fiction?' (2022) 5(1) Neurol Res Surg 1–10, 3.

53 Note, J Volkmann, 'Deep Brain Stimulation for the Treatment of Parkinson's Disease' (2004) 21(1) J Clin Neurophysiol 6–17; B Maiseli and others, n.2; A N Dalrymple and others, 'Overcoming Failure: Improving Acceptance and Success of Implanted Neural Interfaces' (2025) 11 *Bioelectronic Medicine* 6, available at https://bioelecmed.biomedcentral.com/articles/10.1186/s42234-025-00168-7.

54 E Waltz, 'The Brain Implant Company Going for Neuralink's Jugular', *IEEE Spectrum*, 20 December 2023; X Wang and others, 'Intravascular Delivery of an Ultraflexible Neural Electrode Array for Recordings of Cortical Spiking Activity' (2024) 15(9442) Nat Commun, available at https://pmc.ncbi.nlm.nih.gov/articles/PMC11530632/. The purpose is to create a secure interface for communication with the thought process.

issues that will need to be addressed.[55] There are also risks associated with the selection of frequencies and power settings[56] and there are problems arising from the limited current understanding of the exact functioning of these BCIs. Moreover, predicting which brain tissue will be affected by the stimulation and the exact damage that may be caused is problematic[57] and there are issues associated with the precise locating of the electrodes.

3.8.2 Device failure and risks for particular individuals

The possibility that an implanted device may fail raises concerns as to whether implants can be removed safely, and whether a failed device will cause the brain harm during the period before and/or during removal.[58] If the implanted electrode requires upgrading or renewal, the likely and possible medical consequences of such procedures will need to be known, fully disclosed and taken into account when the decision to proceed with the implant is made. **3.025**

Indeed, in a more general context, it will also be necessary to establish before the implant of electrodes, or before the commencement of non-intrusive BCI processes, what the effect of such procedures on the physical, psychological and psychiatric health of the particular individual will be. The literature suggests that: '[i]ndividuals may experience cognitive fatigue, skin irritation, headaches or eyestrain from extended use. There is also a psychological dimension to consider as BCIs have the potential to influence emotions, personality and memory. For example, the brain's natural mechanism to suppress traumatic memories could be compromised. Currently, knowledge in this domain is very limited…'[59] The author would comment that legal issues will, of course, arise if relevant BCI procedures are undertaken before the physical, psychological, **3.026**

55 T Buller, 'Brain Computer Interfaces and the Translation of Thought into Action' (2021) 14(2) *Neuroethics* 155–65; S J Bensmaia and L E Miller, 'Restoring Sensorimotor Function Through Intracortical Interfaces: Progress and Looming Challenges' (2014) 15(5) Nat Rev Neurosci 313–25.

56 S Kim and others, 'Behavioural Assessment of Sensitivity to Intracortical Microstimulation of Primate Somatosensory Cortex' (2015) 112(49) Proc Nat Acad Sci (USA) 15202–07; D A Bjånes and C T Moritz, 'A Robust Encoding Scheme For Delivering Artificial Sensory Information Via Direct Brain Stimulation' (2019) 27(10) IEEE Trans Neural Syst Rehabil Eng 1994–2004. Moreover, prolonged stimulation can apparently increase safety risks to nerves within the brain; C L Hughes and others, 'Neural Stimulation and Recording Performance in Human Sensorimotor Cortex Over 1500 Days' (2021) 18(4) J Neural Eng. 1–13.

57 A L Benabid, 'Spotlight on Deep Brain Stimulation' (2015) 519(7543) *Nature* 299–300.

58 E C Leuthardt, D W Moran and T R Mullen, 'Defining Surgical Terminology and Risk for Brain Computer Interface' (2021) 15 Neurosci, available at https://www.frontiersin.org/journals/neuroscience/articles/10.3389/fnins.2021.599549/full. Consider a possible solution at K Mabry, 'Brain Implants That Don't Leave Scars', *The Harvard Gazette*, 14 August 2025 available at https://news.harvard.edu/gazette/story/2025/08/brain-implants-that-dont-leave-scars/.

59 CEU Research Paper, n.14, 14.

psychiatric, emotional, personality, memory and other relevant implications for the specific individual are known. The author points out that consent is only real consent if it is appropriately informed. It follows that if those applying the procedure do not know its potential consequences, the consent of the user cannot possibly be informed. Informed consent may not necessarily require those conducting the BCI process to know what the consequences for the particular individual will actually be. What it will require, at a minimum, is that those applying the BCI procedure know the risks for the particular individual, and make those risks known to and understood by that individual.

3.8.3 Informed consent

3.027 So, those undertaking the relevant BCI programme will need to be as sure as they can be that the effects of the particular BCI technique on persons having the same characteristics as the particular prospective user are known and the informed consent of the prospective user will be required before the BCI process can proceed.[60] That informed consent must be freely given. This will raise particular issues in connection with certain types of individuals such as military personnel, the young (minimum age limits will be required), the vulnerable (the capacity to consent will be critical here), those who may not understand for language reasons, those who may not understand for mental impairment reasons, those who are not capable of communicating unambiguously that they do or do not understand and/or consent and so on. Protocols that already exist to deal with patients giving advance consent to medical procedures should be capable of adaptation to deal with BCI activities in the military sphere. Where BCI consent in general is concerned, however, the complex nature of BCI treatments and the complex and multifaceted nature of potential risks may make it hard to be sure the consent is both appropriately informed and freely given. Regulations will need to specify what is acceptable in this respect.

3.8.4 Using BCIs to detect signals

3.028 The discussion so far in this section has been largely concerned with the risks and dangers arising from the use of BCIs to influence brain activity, and in particular the use of implanted electrodes in that endeavour. In this and subsequent subsections, we look at the somewhat different issues that arise from the

60 Ng, n.8, Section 5.1 (citing S Goering and others, 'Recommendations for Responsible Development and Application of Neurotechnologies' (2021) 14(3) *Neuroethics* 365–86) where the point is made that as 'BCIs collect sensitive neural data, patients should be fully informed about potential risks and benefits'.

use of BCIs to detect and record signals generated by the brain and then to use specialised algorithms to interpret those signals so that they can be translated into the action desired by the subject's brain. While the sensors can be placed on the scalp, thus avoiding the concerns associated with implantation, signal interference may adversely affect the process of converting the brain signals into the desired action and there is the risk of error in decoding the activity in the brain.[61]

If the use of invasive electrodes is being considered, it must be borne in mind that the implantation of invasive BCI in brain tissue can damage nerve cells and blood vessels, thereby risking infection. There are also risks that the recipient's body may reject the implant and that scar tissue formed following surgery may adversely affect BCI performance. Maiseli also notes that daily decoder training can be burdensome for the user and may need to be automated to make BCI use more user friendly.[62] **3.029**

3.8.5 Privacy

Maiseli and colleagues explain that what is wanted is BCI that enhances our lives while considering human factors. The latter are stated to be 'convenience, ease of use, privacy, security and safety'. Under the privacy heading is the risk that a BCI application may extract sensitive information from a user without the latter's knowledge. So, in addition to the brain data required for the BCI to perform its function, the BCI may, for example, also extract information about the individual's physical state or behaviours. That sensitive information may, the Council of the European Union paper recognises, include information ranging from thoughts and emotions to preferences and intentions; the paper notes that the intimate nature of the information that BCIs can gather from the brain will require stringent privacy protections and will involve ethical considerations.[63] Maiseli advocates the adoption of standards to define, inter alia, acquisition methods, access controls and encryption techniques. The point remains, however, that legal and other provisions will be required to address these and related privacy concerns. Those provisions will likely include rights to access and delete personal data, obligations to obtain individuals' consent before certain, or perhaps all, uses of such data, restrictions on the **3.030**

---

61 J Xu and others, 'A Bi-directional Neuromodulation Technology for Nerve Recording and Stimulation' (2018) 9(11) *Micromachines* 1–14. Consider also the risk that hackers exploit vulnerabilities and thereby prejudice the confidentiality of relevant data, ibid.

62 Maiseli and others, n.2, 9 and 10.

63 CEU Research Paper, n.14, 15.

collection of such data, and restrictions on the lawful uses to which such data may be applied.[64] In addition, appropriately stringent security measures to protect such information will be required, and regulatory provisions may need to specify such measures, it being recognised that data relating to brain functioning that identifies individuals will be classed as personal data having the highest level of sensitivity.[65]

3.031 Similarly profound privacy concerns arise from the news that researchers have developed the first non-invasive[66] method of determining the gist of imagined speech.[67] The idea is that the output from brain scans can be used in association with AI to decode imagined speech. The opportunities arising from this technology relate, of course, to the potential for expression by those suffering from relevant disabilities. The concern relates to the dangers of unwanted intrusion into the brain functioning of individuals, both disabled and otherwise. Misuse of the material by those who extracted it and hacking of the associated data by unauthorised and potentially unscrupulous third parties are just two of the risks that arise here. One can imagine the use of such data in commercial, marketing and armed conflict settings, and, even more troublingly, its use in ways that diminish the security of the affected individuals.

3.8.6 Security and other issues

3.032 Under the security heading is the risk of cyber intrusion enabling the hacker to interfere with the proper performance of the BCI application; for example: 'attackers may alter commands derived from the feature translation component

64 The CEU Research Paper mentions targeted advertising, which is one field in which such use might be restricted. Moreover, the potential for the processes used to capture, collect, and transmit information acquired using BCIs to be hacked or for the resulting information to be inappropriately shared implies an obligation on those engaged in such capturing, collection, and transmission processes to employ suitable methods to ensure the security of that information. 'This underscores the importance of clarifying who owns this data, how consent is obtained and managed, the purposes for which the data can be collected and used, the conditions under which it can be shared, and the security measures in place to prevent unauthorised use and protect privacy rights'; consider CEU Research Paper, n.14, 16.

65 Consider O Landau and others, 'Mind Your Privacy: Privacy Leakage Through BCI Applications Using Machine Learning Methods' (2020) 198 *Knowledge-Based Systems* 105932, available at https://www.sciencedirect.com/science/article/abs/pii/S0950705120302641?via%3Dihub, noting that personality traits can be deduced from electroencephalogram (EEG data).

66 Non-invasive neurotechnological techniques will not penetrate the skin, skull or brain tissue and may employ helmets, glasses, wristbands, electrode patches, tattoos or earphones; HRC Report, n.18, para.9.

67 M Zhang, 'GPT AI Enables Scientists to Passively Decode Thoughts in Ground-breaking Study', *Artisana*, 1 May 2023, available at https://www.artisana.ai/articles/gpt-ai-enables-scientists-to-passively-decode-thoughts-in-groundbreaking; S Reardon, 'Mind-reading Machines Are Here: Is It Time to Worry?', *Nature News Explainer*, 2 May 2023, available at https://www.nature.com/articles/d41586-023-01486-z. Reportedly, a GPT AI model was used to reconstruct human thoughts with up to 82% accuracy based on recordings of non-invasive signals obtained using MRI technology; Zhang, ibid.

and cause adverse effects to the target subject. Therefore researchers should investigate security threats and vulnerable BCI components that can be easily attacked, then find robust solutions.'[68]

Another aspect of security is the need to ensure that BCI-derived medical data is obtained, stored and processed securely. Imagine, for example, a situation in which hackers gain access to the personal details of individuals who, through the use of BCI technologies, have been diagnosed as suffering from epilepsy. The possible use of that information by unscrupulous hackers to target the relevant individuals with material that includes strobing images, thereby triggering epileptic episodes, illustrates the importance of carefully maintaining the security of such data.[69] **3.033**

Other issues identified by Maiseli and colleagues include the sheer amount of data associated with research and activity in this field, the availability of participants for clinical trials, the need for a multidisciplinary approach to BCI issues, the cost, complexity and bulkiness of BCI systems, and issues surrounding the battery lifetime of implantable BCIs. Perhaps the key issue that Maiseli raises, and that is central to the topic of this book, is the need for standardisation and approval of BCI applications by regulatory authorities. Moreover, the Council of the European Union paper points out that the cost and technical sophistication associated with BCI technology may cause existing socioeconomic inequalities to be exacerbated.[70] **3.034**

Certain matters will require careful thought and, perhaps, regulatory action or judicial decision-making in the foreseeable future. For example, does a BCI operator become legally responsible for having had a particular thought if, say, that thought caused the BCI to initiate unlawful action? It is uncontroversial that performing an act, such as pulling the trigger of a firearm resulting in the death of a civilian, renders the relevant individual legally responsible for the unlawful attack; the question therefore becomes whether it makes a difference **3.035**

---

68 Maiseli and others, n.2. See also proposals to help protect BCI users from undue risks, including relating to personal health and genetic information: 'Regulators should mandate non-surgical device update methods, strong authentication and authorization schemes for BCI software modifications, encryption of data moving to and from the brain, and minimize network connectivity where possible.' The authors also designed a hypothetical, average case threat model; T Schroder and others, 'Cyber Risks to Next-gen Brain Computer Interfaces: Analysis and Recommendations' (2025) 18(2) *Neuroethics*, available at https://papers.ssrn.com/sol3/papers.cfm?abstract_id=5138265.

69 E Wolfe and S Ahmed, 'A Twitter Cyberattack on the Epilepsy Foundation Posted Strobing Images that Could Trigger Seizures', CNN, 17 December 2019, available at https://edition.cnn.com/2019/12/17/tech/epilepsy-strobe-twitter-attack-trnd/index.html.

70 CEU Research Paper, n.14, 15; the paper emphasises the need to ensure that vulnerable populations, including individuals with chronic illnesses and disabilities, are prioritised.

that the initiating event consists of a thought as opposed to an overt act. The Oslo Manual deals with the responsibilities of those involved in the conduct of cyber operations, including attacks, and in the conduct of operations, including attacks, using remotely piloted aircraft, highly automated weapon systems and autonomous weapons. The Manual asserts that such persons 'are responsible for their respective roles and, commensurate with their involvement, have obligations to ensure that such operations are conducted in accordance with the applicable principles and rules of LOAC'.[71] This may suggest that the triggering of an unlawful event by the formation of a thought will involve potential responsibility under the law of armed conflict (LOAC). That does, however, imply that the law would restrict what the operator is allowed to think, a proposition that may be problematic, given the tendency of the brain to drift from thought to thought not necessarily predictably. This in turn leads one to wonder whether thought control through training would become a requirement to seek to prevent unlawful outcomes. There are very many difficult controversies here which states will need to consider sooner rather than later.

3.9 AUTONOMY AND FREEDOM

3.036 Technologies such as BCIs that have the capacity to enhance an individual's cognitive ability and potential for informed decision-making can also be misused to exert an inappropriate influence on the decision-making, or even thought processes, of that individual, thus eroding their freedom of thought and action. Political processes that rely on the formation of opinions by individuals, such as elections in a democratic society, may be distorted due to the exercise of undue influence over the thought and opinion-forming processes, perceptions[72] and autonomy of those individuals. Similarly, BCI activity that is designed to enhance the autonomy of, say, a paraplegic individual, may also have a contrary effect if it stimulates the individual to perform acts that do not accord with the individual's wishes. Totalitarian regimes and others could use such technologies to identify dissenters before overt action has been taken by them.[73]

71 Y Dinstein and A W Dahl (eds), *Oslo Manual on Select Topics of the Law of Armed Conflict* (2020) (Oslo Manual), Rules 22 and 44.

72 BCI use can affect the user's conceptions of themselves and how others perceive them; E Versalovic and others, '"Re-identifying Yourself": A Qualitative Study of Veteran Views on Implantable BCI For Mobility in ALS' (2022) 17(7) *Disability and Rehabilitation: Assistive Technology* 807–14.

73 Consider J Rafferty, 'Brain-Computer Interfaces: A New Existential Risk Factor' (2021) 26(2) *Journal of Futures Studies* 51–65.

3.10 WHO IS ACCOUNTABLE?

If the use of BCI technology has the effect of changing an individual's personality, thought processes, risk appreciation, recklessness level, impulsivity and/or behaviours, important questions arise as to where responsibility lies for the subsequent actions of that individual. The complex question that arises is at what point and in what circumstances do individuals cease to be responsible for their own actions? These are of course issues that are now being, and have in the past been, tackled with reference to mental illness,[74] intoxication,[75] extreme events diminishing perceived responsibility,[76] mistakes of fact and of law[77] and so on. Some of the legal approaches that have been adopted to deal with those circumstances may, of course, be found suitable to deal with this aspect of BCI use. The issue for consideration is, therefore, whether attributing the relevant behaviours to BCI activity makes a material difference such that a new approach to responsibility and accountability is required.[78] When considering the allocation of responsibility in circumstances in which BCI technology is used to influence brain activity, difficult questions arise if the person whose brain has been affected goes on to perform some unacceptable and/or unlawful act. Consideration of that issue may be assisted by contemplating the following questions: **3.037**

1. Can a causal link between the use of the BCI and the subsequent unacceptable act be established?
2. Did the user give fully informed consent to the BCI use?
3. Was the BCI user made aware in advance of the risk that the unacceptable act may result?
4. Was the BCI user aware of the degree and nature of risk, and if not, should they have been, or been made, aware of it?
5. Were all relevant and applicable rules and guidance complied with?
6. Can the BCI user, or some other person such as a commander linked to the decision to use the BCI properly, be regarded as responsible for the unacceptable act?

---

74 See, for example, UK Crown Prosecution Service (CPS), *Mental health conditions and disorders: Draft prosecution guidance* (12 March 2019), available at https://www.cps.gov.uk/publication/mental-health-conditions-and-disorders-draft-prosecution-guidance.

75 UK CPS, ibid.

76 See UK Sentencing Council, *Manslaughter by reason of diminished responsibility,* Guideline (1 November 2018), available at https://sentencingcouncil.org.uk/guidelines/manslaughter-by-reason-of-diminished-responsibility.

77 See K W Simons, 'Mistake of Fact or Mistake of Criminal Law? Explaining and Defending the Distinction', Boston University School of Law Working Paper 08-32, 17 November 2008, available at https://core.ac.uk/reader/270213540.

78 Consider Maiseli and others, n.2, p 9.

3.038 While academic discussion may include consideration of potential responsibility for unethical actions by the BCI operator following the BCI use, the focus of this book will be on legal responsibility. Assessing legal, and particularly criminal, responsibility may involve answering the following questions:

1. Has it been established that the unacceptable event was caused by the wrongful act of the BCI operator?
2. Is that wrongful act attributable to their use of the BCI to perform an act?
3. Can it be shown that if the operator had not been using BCI to perform the act but had done so using some other technology or system, the unacceptable or criminal act would, or would not, have occurred?
4. Did the BCI activity affect the operator in a way or to a degree that was not sufficient to excuse the operator from criminal responsibility for the unacceptable act?
5. Are the circumstances such that the BCI operator shares responsibility for the wrongful act with some other person, such as the person who gave instructions for the BCI system to be used?

or

6. Are the roles of the BCI and of the BCI operator such that the operator cannot properly be deemed to have any responsibility for the unacceptable act?

3.039 Much will depend on the availability of relevant evidence, and gaps in that evidence may render it impossible to answer these questions with the level of assurance that the commencement or continuance of proceedings requires.

3.11 DEEP BRAIN STIMULATION

3.040 The discussion of different types of BCI has, to this point, focused on the distinction between the use of an 'external to the brain' headset to detect the electrical signals, as against the alternative, somewhat intrusive, use of implanted electrodes within the cranium and, even, inside the structure of the brain. The term deep brain stimulation is used to refer to the use of electrodes implanted under the deep cortex to stimulate particular target sites. The stimulation is controlled externally to treat conditions such as Parkinson's disease, tremor and certain other disorders.[79] This kind of BCI has been developed specifically to

---

79 K E Lyons and R Pahwa, 'Deep Brain Stimulation and Tremor' (2008) 5(2) *Neurotherapeutics* 331–8. For an assessment of how deep brain stimulation has progressed to 2025, see A Fasano and A Horn, 'Deep Brain Stimulation for Movement Disorders: 2025 and Beyond' (2025) 18(1) *Brain Stimulation* 274, available at https://www.brainstimjrnl.com/article/S1935-861X(24)00375-9/fulltext and A E Martinez-Nunez and others, 'Editorial: Deep Brain Stimulation Think Tank: Updates in Neurotechnology and

stimulate or inhibit particular kinds of brain activity.[80] Deep brain stimulation can also, for example, be achieved by means of a cochlear prosthesis, that is an artificial implant, to stimulate auditory nerves thereby enabling persons with hearing disabilities to hear.[81] The technique is also used in the treatment of Alzheimer's disease, depression and obsessive compulsive disorder.[82]

3.12 IDENTITY

As Emily Postan explains, there are numerous regulatory regimes that may apply to the information that can be derived from the processes discussed in this chapter. If the information can be classed as personal data, data protection law is likely to apply. If it is classed as patient records, the particular rules dealing with medical records will be relevant. If the information constitutes research findings or is commercially sensitive, different rules will apply. Ms Postan points out that there is an additional area of concern, namely the potential for a person's encounter with information generated by neurotechnologies to impact on their own sense of identity.[83] **3.041**

The concept of identity, as used in this discussion, has to do with the perception that an individual has of him/herself. It refers to the kind of person the individual regards him/herself as being and involves numerous elements. The literature suggests that certain important factors will tend to impact on whether a person's identity will be affected, for example by a BCI activity. The author suggests that these factors include cultural traditions and religious beliefs; patterns of thought, approaches to thinking and individual thoughts; perceptions, whether they are factually accurate or not; patterns of behaviour, habits and routines; emotional attachments and usual emotional responses; and perhaps a general understanding of oneself, what one stands for, what is important to one, and, in very general terms, one's priorities in one's family life, social life, professional life and so on.[84] Xiao-yu Sun and Bin Ye observe **3.042**

Neuromodulation' (2025) 19 Hum Neurosci, available at https://www.frontiersin.org/journals/human-neuroscience/articles/10.3389/fnhum.2025.1609727/full.

80 J Rafferty, 'Brain Computer Interfaces: A New Existential Risk Factor' (2021) 26(2) *Journal of Futures Studies* 51–65.

81 R Andersen and M Ross, 'The Intention Machine' (2019) 320(4) *Scientific American* 24–31.

82 See for example, V Visser-Vandervalle and others, 'Deep Brain Stimulation For Obsessive-compulsive Disorder: A Crisis of Access' (2022) 28(8) Nat Med 1529–32.

83 E Postan, 'Narrative Devices: Neurotechnologies, Information and Self-constitution' (2021) 14 *Neuroethics* 231–51.

84 Consider Postan, ibid, 231–51; J Pugh, 'Clarifying the Normative Significance of "Personality Changes" During Deep Brain Stimulation' (2020) 26 Sci Eng Ethics 1655–80; N V Colman and P Williams,

that the use of certain BCIs: 'may change users' cognition, behaviours, and self-perception, thereby affecting their identity. Researchers have delved into the connection between BCIs and identity, investigating the potential for BCIs to modify a user's identity and induce psychological changes, among various other factors.'[85]

3.13 HUMAN RIGHTS

3.043 Human rights law is concerned with the relationship between a state's citizens and the government or other state authorities. During periods when armed conflict is not taking place, the activities of state security forces and other agencies of the government are regulated by the domestic laws of the country and by the human rights law rules that apply to that country. The discussion in this section will be by reference to the International Covenant on Civil and Political Rights (International Covenant)[86] and the European Convention on Human Rights (ECHR).[87] The International Covenant requires a State Party to 'respect and to ensure to all individuals within its territory and subject to its jurisdiction the rights recognized in the present Covenant, without distinction …'[88] The ECHR requires participating states to 'secure to everyone within their jurisdiction' ECHR rights and freedoms.[89] It follows, therefore, that if a state is engaged in activity involving the use of brain technology within its own territory, that would mean that jurisdiction, and thus the rights prescribed by the human rights instrument of which the state is a party, will therefore apply to that activity.

3.044 If an armed conflict is taking place, it is well established that the law of human rights continues to apply. In its *Palestinian Wall* judgment,[90] the International Court of Justice confirmed this, subject to any permissible derogation that a state may have made. When addressing the relationship between human

'Feeling Like My Self: Emotion Profiles and Social Identity' (2013) 40(2) J Consum Res 203–22.

85 Xiao-yu Sun and Bin Ye, 'The Functional Differentiation of Brain-computer Interfaces and its Ethical Implications' (2023) 10 Humanit and Soc Sci Commun 878, available at https://www.nature.com/articles/s41599-023-02419-x citing, inter alia, S Aggarwal and N Chugh, 'Ethical Implications of Closed Loop Brain Device: 10 Year Review' (2020) 30(1) Minds Mach 145–70.

86 International Covenant on Civil and Political Rights, adopted on 16 December 1966 by UN General Assembly Resolution 2200A (XXI) (International Covenant).

87 European Convention for the Protection of Human Rights and Fundamental Freedoms, Rome, 4 November 1950, 213 UNTS 221 (ECHR).

88 International Covenant, n.86, Art.2(1).

89 ECHR, n.87, Art.1.

90 Advisory Opinion on the Legal Consequences of the Construction of a Wall in the Occupied Palestinian Territory, 9 July 2004 [2004] ICJ Reports 136 (Wall Case).

rights law and the LOAC, the Court described three possible situations. Some may be exclusively matters for international humanitarian law, others may be exclusively matters for human rights law and yet others may have to be considered by reference to both bodies of law.[91]

The ECHR permits a state to derogate from its obligations in times of war or other public emergency threatening the life of the nation to the extent strictly required by the exigencies of the situation and provided the measures taken are not inconsistent with other provisions of international law.[92] However, a State party to the ECHR cannot derogate from Article 2 (right to life) other than for lawful acts of war, nor from Articles 3 (torture), 4(1) (slavery and servitude) and 7 (no punishment without law). Similar but not identical circumstances would allow a state to derogate from its obligations under the International Covenant;[93] a state cannot derogate from Articles 6 (right to life), 7 (torture, cruel, inhuman or degrading treatment or punishment), 8(1) and (2) (slavery and servitude), and 18 (freedom of thought, conscience and religion). **3.045**

A key issue will be whether the relevant persons are within the jurisdiction of the relevant state for human rights purposes. The European Court of Human Rights (ECtHR) stated, in the case of *Loizidou v Turkey (Preliminary Objections)*,[94] that jurisdiction can apply if, through military action, a state exercises effective control of an area outside its national territory. Jurisprudence of the ECtHR[95] since *Loizidou* seems to show that if a state exercises authority and control over a person outside its national territory, that will cause the individual to be within its jurisdiction for human rights law purposes. The case of *Jaloud v The Netherlands*[96] reinforced the criterion of authority and control as establishing human rights jurisdiction over individuals. In the case of *Georgia v Russia II*,[97] having noted the absence of effective control in an area where competing state forces are fighting to try to establish control, the Court then, consistent with its earlier cases, applied the authority and control test to determine whether individuals came within human rights law jurisdiction. **3.046**

91 Wall Case, ibid, para.106.
92 ECHR, n.87, Art. 15(1).
93 International Covenant, n.86, Art.4.
94 *Loizidou v Turkey*, Appn No.15318/89, Judgment on Preliminary Objections dated 23 March 1995, para.62.
95 Note *Ocalan v Turkey*, App No.46221/99, 12 May 2005, para.91; ECtHR, *Issa and Others v Turkey*, App No.31821/96, 16 November 2004, paras 71 and 72; ECtHR, *Al-Skeini and Others v United Kingdom*, App No.55721/07, 7 July 2011, generally and at para.149.
96 ECtHR, *Jaloud v The Netherlands*, App No.47708/08, 20 November 2014, para.152 and the concurring judgments of Judges Spielmann and Raimondi.
97 ECtHR, *Georgia v Russia II*, App No.38263/08, 21 January 2012, paras 126 and 127.

3.047 This raises the obvious issue of which brain technology-related activities would have the effect of bringing a person located extraterritorially within the jurisdiction of a state employing that technology. The author suggests that the use of BCI technology by State A to control a weapon system that is then used to attack State B personnel on State B territory will not have the effect of bringing the State B personnel within the jurisdiction of State A. This is because the use of the BCI technology in that way does not, alone, constitute the required exercise of authority and control. Equally, the use of autonomous weapons that employ AB technology will not, alone, amount to the required exercise of authority and control. The human rights law implications of using BCI technology to degrade the cognitive performance of an adversary are discussed in Chapter 11. If State A were to use a BCI-enabled system to control the actions of a soldier from enemy State B on State B territory, although one cannot be certain until the Court has taken a definitive position on the matter, there is every prospect that the Court would find the State B soldier to be subject to State A authority and control with the effect that State A would be required to respect the soldier's human rights.

3.048 If a BCI-controlled system or an AB-enabled system were to be used to interfere with the cognition of an enemy individual, it would be for a Court to decide whether the interference had the effect of placing the individual within the acting state's authority and control, and thus its jurisdiction. The author suspects that, in appropriate cases, the Court might so decide. It would then be for the Court to determine whether the BCI- or AB-enabled interference amounts, for example, to 'arbitrary or unlawful interference with his privacy, family, home or correspondence'.[98] It should also be noted that '[e]veryone shall have the right to freedom of thought, conscience and religion'[99] and 'to hold opinions without interference'.[100] These would seem to be the human rights of particular significance where cognitive interference is concerned.[101] If the cognitive interference has the effect of placing the individual temporarily within the acting state's authority and control and it is taking place in

98 International Covenant, n.86, Art.17(1).

99 International Covenant, n.86, Art.18(1).

100 International Covenant, n.86, Art.19(1).

101 Note, however, discussion of a right to mental integrity; S Ligthart, 'The Right to Mental Integrity in the Age of Neurotechnology: Constructing Scope and Exploring Permissible Limitations' (2025) 12(1) *Journal of Law and the Biosciences*, available at https://academic.oup.com/jlb/article/12/1/lsaf010/8156051. Marcello Ienca and Roberto Andorno propose the establishment of four new human rights to address the issues arising from neurotechnological developments: M Ienca and R Andorno, 'Towards New Human Rights in the Age of Neuroscience and Neurotechnology', *Springer Nature Link*, 26 April 2017, available at https://link.springer.com/article/10.1186/s40504-017-0050-1.

the course of, and as part of, armed conflict hostilities, the LOAC, with its principles and rules regarding targeting and weaponry, discussed respectively in Chapters 4, 5 and 6 below, will apply. To provide an example, if, while the affected individual is within the authority and control of the adverse party, they are caused to take less care, to behave in a negligent manner and to issue statements or orders that expose them to ridicule, this would not arguably satisfy the act of violence requirement for classification as an attack. Equally, those effects may, in the factual circumstances, be insufficiently serious for the superfluous injury/unnecessary suffering principle to be breached. If the conclusion is reached that no LOAC rules apply, there is the risk that human rights law would be seen as the body of law against which the acceptability of the BCI use must be judged. Indeed, to make a more general point, it seems to the author that as the LOAC is not being updated to address new and emerging technologies, individuals and perhaps states may be expected to increasingly look to human rights law to address the perceived gaps.

Moreover, if, during an armed conflict, the act of cognitive interference is taking place other than in connection with the hostilities, and if the jurisdiction aspect of human rights law is satisfied, the rights mentioned earlier in the present paragraph will likely apply. **3.049**

Much of what has been discussed earlier in this chapter feeds into concerns that certain uses of brain technologies may conflict with human rights norms. The UN Special Rapporteur on the right to privacy has, for example, submitted a report to the Human Rights Council on 12 March 2025 in which she noted that neurotechnologies 'that record or alter brain activity and generate neurodata … not only allow us to identify a person, but also provide an unprecedented depth of understanding of their individuality'. The report recommends: the development of a regulatory framework for neurotechnologies and processing of neurodata to ensure responsible use; that existing right to privacy principles be incorporated into national legal frameworks; that ethical practices be promoted in this field; and that education on neurotechnologies and neurodata be promoted to support informed consent.[102] On 2 April 2025 the Human Rights Council adopted a resolution requesting its Advisory Committee to draft recommended guidelines 'for applying the existing human rights framework to the conception, design, development, testing, use **3.050**

102 UN General Assembly, Human Rights Council, A/HRC/58/58, 16 January 2025.

and deployment of neurotechnologies and to present [the guidelines] to the Council …'[103]

3.051 The use of brain technologies to monitor and interfere with thought processes of individuals raises the most profound ethical concern.[104] Because of the jurisdictional issues discussed briefly earlier in this section, human rights law is unlikely to apply in many cases where such activity is undertaken against persons who are not in the territory of the user state and where the affected individuals are not subject to the user state's authority and control. This may suggest that new law will be required. It will be for states to decide whether that new law should apply both in situations of armed conflict and peace. The issues are complex, the drafting of such legal provisions will not be easy and securing sufficient international consensus in favour of such legal provisions will probably be even more challenging. In the interim, the ECtHR and other human rights bodies may have to address the challenging issue of what degree of cognitive interference has the effect of placing an individual under the authority and control of the user state.

3.14 DATA PROTECTION

3.052 The first question that might occur to the reader is why there is even a section in this book dealing with data protection. The author's position is that data protection law issues are unlikely to arise where personal data is obtained in order, for example, to support lawful targeting as part of ongoing hostilities during an armed conflict. Consider, however, the use of BCI technology to monitor the brain functioning and thought processes of a state's own personnel. Consider also the information and insight as to private thoughts that a state may access as a result of the introduction of BBI technology into the decision-making procedures employed by its own military and civilian personnel. Consider lastly the possibility, perhaps likelihood, that the use of BCIs, ABs or BBIs may give the user state access to personal information due to the way in which these technologies interact with other systems. While there can be no certainty that a particular operation using any of these technologies will necessarily produce personal information to which the data protection rules apply, it is unnecessary for completeness to include the present section. Moreover,

103 UN General Assembly, Human Rights Council, A/HRC/RES/58/6, 3 April 2025.

104 X-Y Sun and B Ye, 'The Functional Differentiation of Brain-computer Interfaces (BCIs) and its Ethical Implications' (2023) 10 *Humanities and Social Sciences Communications* 878, available at https://www.nature.com/articles/s41599-023-02419-x.

even in situations to which the rules do not explicitly apply, the application of corresponding safeguards may be seen as a matter of best practice.

European Union regulation of these matters is to be found in the General Data Protection Regulation (GDPR).[105] Of central importance are the data protection principles which, briefly summarised, involve requirements that personal data processing be lawful, transparent and fair; that it be collected for an explicit and lawful purpose and that it should not be further processed for an inconsistent purpose; that it be adequate, relevant and limited to what is necessary; that it be accurate, kept up to date and that reasonable steps are taken to ensure that inaccurate personal data is rectified without delay; that it is kept in a form that enables the identification of data subjects for no longer than the purpose for which they were processed requires; and that it is processed in a manner that ensures appropriate security of the personal data.[106] **3.053**

Personal data is any data relating to an identified or identifiable natural person. Processing of such data includes any operation or set of operations performed on personal data, by automated means or otherwise, including collecting it, organising it, recording it, structuring it, storing it, adapting it, altering it, ordering it, retrieving it, consulting it, using it, disclosing it, disseminating it, making it available, combining it, erasing it or destroying it.[107] This has the effect that virtually any kind of handling of personal data constitutes processing. Consent, for the purposes of the Regulation, must be a 'freely given, specific, informed and unambiguous … agreement to the processing of personal data relating to' the relevant person.[108] Biometric data is then specifically defined as 'personal data resulting from specific technical processing relating to the physical, physiological or behavioural characteristics of a natural person, **3.054**

105 Regulation (EU) 2016/679 of the European Parliament and of the Council of 27 April 2016 on the protection of natural persons with regard to the processing of personal data and on the free movement of such data, and repealing Directive 95/46/EC (General Data Protection Regulation) (GDPR), available at http://eur-lex.europa.eu/legal-content/EN/TXT/PDF/?uri=CELEX:32016R0679&from=EN. For recognition that the GDPR was not designed to address neurodata as such, and an assessment of how neurodata fits within the GDPR's existing framework, see L Pudliak, 'GDPR and Neurotechnology: Protecting Brain Data in Emerging BCI Applications' (2025) 11(2) *European Data Protection Law Review* 177–85.

106 GDPR, ibid, art.5. The European Court of Justice has found that, confronted with data on the internet that appears unfair, one-sided or wrong, an individual has the so-called 'right to be forgotten', that is the right, for example, for Google to delete information that is inadequate, irrelevant or no longer relevant; A Travis and C Arthur, 'EU Court Backs Right to be Forgotten: Google Must Amend Results on Request', *The Guardian*, 13 May 2014, available at https://www.theguardian.com/technology/2014/may/13/right-to-be-forgotten-eu-court-google-search-results and see GDPR EU, 'Everything You Need to Know About the "Right to be Forgotten"', available at https://gdpr.eu/right-to-be-forgotten/.

107 GDPR, ibid, art.4(1) and (2).

108 GDPR, ibid, art.4(11).

which allow or confirm the unique identification of that natural person, such as facial images or dactyloscopic data'.[109] It is foreseeable that thought processes will be found to be unique to an individual and will also be treated as biometric data.

3.055 An 'identifiable natural person' is then stated to be 'one who can be identified, directly or indirectly, in particular by reference to an identifier such as a name, an identification number, location data, an online identifier, or to one or more factors specific to the physical, physiological, genetic, mental, economic, cultural, or social identity of that natural person'.[110] The reference to 'mental identity' is of obvious importance to the present discussion in the sense that it will be the identifiability of an individual by reference to their thought processes that brings the identification of the individual by that means within Article 4(1). Perhaps this presupposes the existence of a database of such records in relation to specified individuals.

3.056 For the processing of personal data to take place, one of six criteria must be satisfied. These, in summarised form, are: that the data subject consents to the processing; that the processing is necessary for the performance of a contract to which the data subject is a party; that processing is necessary to comply with a legal obligation binding the controller; that processing is necessary to protect the vital interests of the data subject or someone else; that processing is necessary for the performance of a task carried out in the public interest or in the exercise of authority vested in the controller; or where there are third-party interests, unless these are overridden by the interests, rights or freedoms of the data subject.

3.057 Perhaps the most important ground for lawful processing of personal data is that the data subject, that is the person referred to in the data, consents to the particular processing.[111] This, as was explained in section 3.8.3, can be expected to raise complex issues where the brain technologies discussed in this book are being used to obtain the information. The author suspects that, to comply with the GDPR, it would be necessary for the relevant individual specifically to consent in advance to the collection of whatever personal data is acquired as a result of the use of the technology during the period when it is being employed. There would thereafter, the author believes, need to be

109 GDPR, ibid, art.4(14).

110 GDPR, ibid, art.4(1).

111 See GDPR, ibid, art.7, Recital 32 and GDPR-info.eu, 'Consent', available at https://gdpr-info.eu/issues/consent/.

specific further consent by the individual to any use of the collected personal data. That may presuppose disclosing to the individual what items of personal data have been collected and then obtaining their consent to specific uses of each. It will be for the relevant national authorities to work up rules and guidance on these matters. The author suggests, however, that the intensely personal nature of private thoughts will prompt those authorities to introduce restrictive and protective arrangements.

Special rules apply to the processing of personal data that reveals racial or ethnic origins, political opinions, religious or philosophical beliefs, trade union membership, genetic data, biometric data, and data relating to health or sex life or sexual orientation. It is at least foreseeable that some of the data that may be obtained using the technologies discussed in this book fall into some of these categories, for example the health category. Processing of such data is prohibited by Article 9, but there are exceptions, including explicit consent of the data subject (if the state's law allows such consent), necessary processing for the data controller's employment law obligations and rights, protection of the vital interests of the data subject or another person where the data subject is incapable of giving their consent, very limited processing by certain non-profit organisations for limited purposes and with specified safeguards, or the processing relates to data manifestly made public by the data subject or is necessary to establish, exercise or defend legal claims. The Article provides for limited medical and public interest-related exemptions. To the extent that Article 9 data is the subject of greater protection, classification under that Article of personal data obtained through the use of brain technologies would be appropriate. **3.058**

The Regulation clarifies the obligations arising from the requirement for transparency and makes detailed provision as to, for example, the information that must be provided when data is being collected from a data subject, the information to be given when personal data is not obtained from a data subject, the right of the data subject to confirmation of whether personal data relating to them is being processed and, if so, their right to have access thereto and the right of rectification, erasure and to restrict the processing of personal data. A complex issue here is that the data may be obtained directly from the data subject's brain without the data subject being aware that they have provided it. Maybe that should and will be interpreted in such a way as to give the personal data the highest level of protection. **3.059**

There are important exclusions from the application of GDPR. Article 2(2) stipulates that the Regulation does not apply to the processing of personal **3.060** data 'in the course of an activity which falls outside the scope of Union law'. Recital 16 to the Regulation repeats this exclusion and cites, as an example of excluded matters, 'activities concerning national security'.[112] Under Recital 19, processing of personal data by competent authorities 'for the purposes of the prevention, investigation, detection or prosecution of criminal offences, including the safeguarding against and the prevention of threats to public security …' lies outside the scope of the GDPR and is regulated by Directive 2016/680.[113] Exactly which matters fall within the scope of national security but outside the scope of 'threats to public security' is not clear to the author and will, the author believes, be a matter for national interpretation. Under Directive 2016/680, Member States are required to protect rights and freedoms, including the right to the protection of personal data. Importantly, the Directive applies to the processing of personal data wholly or partially by automated means. The Directive applies similar principles to those discussed earlier in connection with the GDPR and requires Member States, for example, to make provision as to time limits for storage of personal data and as to the limitation of processing to that which is necessary.

3.061 The UK arrangements for data protection are based on the UK's version of the GDPR and on the Data Protection Act 2018.[114] In 2023, the UK Information Commissioner's Office produced a report on neurotechnologies and neurodata in which concerns related to discrimination, accuracy and fairness were identified. Engagement was promised with a view to producing specific guidance in the longer term.[115]

3.062 While the focus in this section has been on the highly developed EU regulations, non-EU states will have their own applicable legislation which must, so far as applicable, be complied with.[116]

---

112 Similarly excluded by the same Recital are activities concerning the Common Defence and Security Policy of the European Union.

113 Directive (EU) 2016/680 of the European Parliament and of the Council of 27 April 2016 on the protection of natural persons with regard to the processing of personal data by competent authorities for the purposes of the prevention, investigation, detection or prosecution of criminal offences or the execution of criminal penalties, and on the free movement of such data, and repealing Council Framework Decision 2008/977/JHA (the Directive).

114 2018 c.12.

115 UK Information Commissioner's Office, *ICO Tech Futures: Neurotechnologies* (1 June 2023), available at https://ico.org.uk/media2/about-the-ico/research-and-reports/ico-tech-futures-neurotechnology-0-1.pdf.

116 It should also be noted that the Council of Europe's Consultative Committee of the Convention for the Protection of Individuals with regard to Automatic Processing of Personal Data, issued, on 5 March 2025, *Draft Guidelines on Data Protection in the context of Neurosciences*, T-PD(2025)1. This extensive document is available at https://rm.coe.int/t-pd-2025-1-draft-guidelines-neuroscience-without-tc-comments/1680b4a10b.

4

TARGETING USING BRAIN TECHNOLOGY

4.1 INTRODUCTION

Having discussed the nature of brain technologies and some of the roles which the associated technologies may be expected to fulfil, in this chapter attention shifts to the law of armed conflict (LOAC). The chapter discusses the principles and rules of the LOAC that determine whether an attack or other military operation should proceed against a specific target. Those who are involved in making targeting decisions will tend to focus on numerous issues, including: the object(s) or person(s) that are the object(s) of the planned operation or attack and their military value; the kind of military action that is to be taken; the intended effect of that military action; what is going on in the vicinity of the target; the preferred timing and nature of the operation; and the weapon or method that is to be used. **4.001**

4.002 While weapons law[1] and targeting law are distinct topics, they are linked. A member of the armed forces who has been issued by their state with, or assigned to use, a weapon should be entitled to assume that that weapon complies with the law that binds their state, both in terms of the weapon and the circumstances in which it is being made available for use.[2] Accordingly, any restrictions on lawful use identified when the weapon is subjected to legal review should be reflected in the concepts of use documents supplied to the military units that receive the weapon and in instructions to relevant personnel.

4.003 This chapter will deal, respectively, with the principles and rules governing the targeting of persons and objects. The principles and rules that are customary in nature will be distinguished from those that only bind states party to a specific treaty. How treaty law rules apply to a specific state may, however, depend on whether that state made reservations or interpretive statements when becoming party to the treaty.

4.004 Fundamental customary principles of the LOAC underpin targeting law. The most obviously relevant among these are humanity,[3] military necessity[4] and distinction.[5] There are, in addition, customary targeting law rules[6] as well as treaty law provisions. Additional Protocol I (API) codified the law of targeting and, while those treaty law rules bind the 175 states that are party to that

---

1 Weapons law is discussed in Chapter 6.

2 Not least because all states are subject to an implied obligation legally to review the weapons that they acquire and states that are party to the Protocol Additional to the Geneva Conventions of 12 August 1949, and Relating to the Protection of Victims of International Armed Conflicts, Geneva, 8 June 1977, 1125 UNTS 3 (Additional Protocol I or API) are bound by Article 36 of that Treaty; see section 6.10 below.

3 The principle of humanity 'forbids the infliction of suffering, injury or destruction not actually necessary for the accomplishment of legitimate military purposes'; UK Manual, para.5.2.3; see also US DoD *Law of War Manual* (June 2015) as subsequently amended (US DoD Manual), para.2.3 and UK Ministry of Defence, *The Manual of the Law of Armed Conflict*, UOP (2004) (UK Manual).

4 'Military necessity is now defined as "the principle whereby a belligerent has the right to apply any measures which are required to bring about the successful conclusion of a military operation and which are not forbidden by the laws of war". Put another way, a state engaged in an armed conflict may use that degree and kind of force, not otherwise prohibited by the law of armed conflict, that is required in order to achieve the legitimate purpose of the conflict, namely the complete or partial submission of the enemy at the earliest possible moment with the minimum expenditure of life and resources.': UK Manual, ibid, para.2.2, as amended. For a broadly similar notion differently expressed, see US DoD Manual, ibid, para.2.2.

5 See section 4.3 below.

6 See International Committee of the Red Cross, *Customary International Humanitarian Law*, Vol.1 (J-M Henckaerts and L Doswald-Beck (eds), Cambridge University Press, 2005) (Customary Law Study), particularly Parts I–III. However, consider also Memorandum for Assistant General Counsel (International), Office of the Secretary of Defense, 1977 Protocols Additional to the Geneva Conventions: Customary International Law Implications, 8 May 1986 and M J Matheson, 'The United Kingdom Position on the Relation of Customary International Law to the 1977 Protocols Additional to the 1949 Geneva Conventions' (1987) 2 AU JILP 419.

treaty, many of those rules also reflect customary law which binds all states. Where this is the case, it will be pointed out.

Each section of the chapter will start by setting forth a particular principle or rule, noting its legal basis and status in the law and explaining its meaning. The principle or rule will then be applied to brain technology capabilities, and the issues raised by those capabilities will be identified. The capabilities that will be considered are: the use of brain-computer interface (BCI) technology to control a military operation, including an attack; the use of an artificial brain (AB) technology to decide upon and initiate the execution of an operation, including an attack; and the use of a brain-to-brain interface (BBI) for a similar purpose. Computer-based ABs and ABs that include biological brain material (whether synthetic or not) will be considered as a single category of technology for these purposes. **4.005**

The final preliminary point to note is the scope of application of the codified targeting law rules in Articles 48–67 of API. They apply as treaty law to 'any land, air or sea warfare which may affect the civilian population, individual civilians or civilian objects on land'. The Articles also apply 'to all attacks from the sea or from the air against objectives on land, but do not otherwise affect the rules of international law applicable in armed conflict at sea or in the air'. [7] This means that the mere possibility of civilians or civilian objects on land being affected will cause these treaty law provisions to apply to military activities undertaken on land, in the air or at sea. The treaty does not mention operations conducted from outer space or from cyberspace. That is largely a rather moot point, as most, if not all, of the Article 48–67 rules reflect customary international law, so outer space[8] and cyber operations will, in practice, be subject to the same rules. Maritime engagements and air-to-air combat in which there is no possibility of civilians or civilian objects on land being affected are not, however, regulated by Articles 48–67.[9] **4.006**

---

7 AP1, n.2, Art.49(3).

8 Consider Article III of the Treaty on Principles Governing the Activities of States in the Exploration and Use of Outer Space, including the Moon and other Celestial Bodies, UN General Assembly Resolution 2222 (XXI), January 1967.

9 For an authoritative assessment of the rules applicable to warfare at sea, see the International Institute of Humanitarian Law, *San Remo Manual on International Law Applicable to Armed Conflicts at Sea* (L Doswald-Beck (ed), 1995). (San Remo Manual) and for a similarly authoritative assessment of the rules relating to air and missile warfare, see Program on Humanitarian Policy and Conflict Research at Harvard University (HPCR), *Manual on the International Law Applicable to Air and Missile Warfare* (March 2010) (AMW Manual), available at https://cdn.ca9.uscourts.gov/datastore/library/2013/09/06/Flores_Manual .pdf.

4.2 THE LAW IMPOSES LIMITS

4.007 The first basic principle of the law of targeting dates back to 1899 and 1907.[10] Its most recent articulation is as follows: 'In any armed conflict, the right of the Parties to the conflict to choose methods or means of warfare is not unlimited.'[11] The principle is customary, binds all states and makes it clear that the law insists on there being limits to what is legally acceptable in the conduct of hostilities and that the law determines what those limits consist of by prescribing the relevant rules. So states do not have an unfettered right to choose how to employ brain technologies in warfare. Moreover, to the extent that those brain technologies are, themselves, deciding on the taking of hostile action, their decisions must also be constrained so as to comply with the principle. In short, this is the principle that makes it clear that brain technologies may only be used in a lawful manner and that those systems must be employed and, to the extent that this applies, must conduct themselves in accordance with the law. It is therefore critically important that the decisions and actions taken by such systems must be capable of being limited in accordance with the law.

4.008 This immediately raises a potential issue in respect of BCIs. Will the BCI reliably and consistently translate the wish or intent that the operator formulated in their mind into action that accurately reflects that wish or intent? If not, the particular BCI system would likely fail this first fundamental principle. Careful testing of the BCI and of the systems to which it is linked will be required to check this point. The observation is not, it should be stressed, being put forward in relation to BCIs in general. The legal issue is whether the specific BCI system translates the operator's thought or intent reliably and consistently into the desired action. By way of example, State A acquires an unmanned surface vessel that employs BCI technology. The vessel is armed with a naval gun that can be used for littoral attacks of coastal targets on land. In testing it is found that the BCI has a tendency to misinterpret the operator's instructions relating to the required elevation of the barrel. The use of the weapon would therefore be prohibited by this first principle.

4.009 Where AB systems are concerned, similar questions arise, such as will the AB system perform as designed or intended or will it for some reason act in a manner that was not contemplated when it was brought into service? To be more

10 Regulations annexed to Hague Convention (IV), 18 October 1907, Respecting the Laws and Customs of War on Land, The Hague, 18 October 1907 (Hague Regulations 1907), Art.22.

11 API, n.2, Art.35(1).

specific, can those planning to use the AB system be sufficiently confident that the system will not act outside pre-set parameters by:

1. forgetting or misinterpreting the instructions fed into it at the pre-mission stage;
2. choosing to ignore mission constraints;
3. choosing to deceive its own operator;
4. its decision-making systems being corrupted, for example, because of inadequate protection against adversary or third-party hacking (suitable cyber security arrangements will be an important safeguard here); or
5. other reason?

With BBIs one rather suspects that the connectivity into and from the computer that sits in the middle of the process and indeed that computer itself might potentially be vulnerable to external interference if insufficient steps are taken to become aware of vulnerabilities and take suitable protective action. There will also be a concern as to whether the central computer's output is being conveyed accurately to the recipient brain. If important decisions are to be the subject of BBI discussion or decision/order-communication processes, it is correspondingly important that those three sources of potential vulnerability or error be regularly and carefully checked. The observations made in this and the previous two paragraphs apply not just in relation to Article 35(1) but also in connection with the other targeting law rules. This should be borne in mind throughout the discussion regarding each of the following rules/principles, even where not specifically noted in the text. **4.010**

A discrete potential issue concerning BBIs is whether, after the exchange of thoughts or the sending of instructions has been completed, it can be shown what the respective participants contributed to the process. This aspect is likely to be of critical importance if responsibility is to be allocated. It is unlikely to be a significant issue if the resulting decision is both militarily satisfactory and legally compliant. In the discussion of the various principles and rules in the rest of the book, it will be assumed that the BBI is working as it should, with the contributions of those participating in the BBI activity being accurately transmitted to and understood by the other participants. **4.011**

4.3 THE PRINCIPLE OF DISTINCTION

The principle of distinction is the second basic principle of targeting law. It applies to attacks and to military operations that fall below the threshold of attacks. The origins of the principle go back at least to the St Petersburg **4.012**

Declaration,[12] the Preamble of which states that 'the only legitimate object which States should endeavour to accomplish during war is to weaken the military forces of the enemy'.[13] The API formulation of the principle is authoritative, reflects customary law,[14] binds all states and is as follows:

> In order to ensure respect for and protection of the civilian population and civilian objects, the Parties to the conflict shall at all times distinguish between the civilian population and combatants and between civilian objects and military objectives and accordingly shall direct their operations only against military objectives.[15]

4.013 The principle appears in API under the heading 'Basic Rule' and is considered by the International Court of Justice in its Nuclear Weapons Advisory Opinion as 'cardinal' and 'intransgressible'.[16] It is indeed the very foundation of the law of targeting. Article 48 refers to 'operations', as distinct from the reference in many of the other rules of targeting law to 'attacks'. The author's position is that if the drafters of API had intended the principle of distinction to apply only to attacks, it could have made this clear in Article 48. It did not do so. Attacks are defined in Article 49(1) of API as 'acts of violence against the adversary, whether in offence or defence'. The author's position is that 'military operations' is wider than attacks, and that it includes any activity undertaken in connection with hostilities and that adversely affects the enemy.

4.014 If BCIs are to be used in connection with attacks, it will be planners, commanders and operators who will be responsible for ensuring that the principle is complied with. This may best be achieved by keeping the BCI switched off while the status of the object of the attack as a military objective is confirmed and while the lawfulness of the planned attack under targeting law is assessed. Only when the distinction principle has been carefully considered, when it has been determined that the attack will not be indiscriminate, when it has been

---

12 Declaration Renouncing the Use, in Time of War, of Explosive Projectiles under 400 Grammes Weight, St Petersburg, 11 December 1868 (St Petersburg Declaration).

13 Ibid, preambular para.2.

14 See Customary Law Study, n.6, Rules 1 and 7.

15 API, n.2, Art.48 and Customary Law Study, n.6, Rules 1 and 7. Frits Kalshoven observed that while early 19th-century treaties included an 'implicit recognition that the civilian population itself does not represent a legitimate target of war', since those days military operations have been 'deliberately planned and carried out against the civilian population', with the result that war became a 'struggle of nation against nation, not army against army'. He noted, however, that the reaffirmation of the principle of distinction by the international community of states is authoritative; F Kalshoven, 'Arms, Armaments and International Law' (1985-II) 191 *Recueil des Cours* 207.

16 See International Criminal Court (ICJ) Advisory Opinion on the Legality of the Threat or Use of Nuclear Weapons (1996) ICJ Reports 226, 35 ILM 809, paras 78–9.

found not to breach proportionality and when precautions have been addressed should the attack take place.

For example, State A is involved in an armed conflict against State B. State A's Alpha unit will be using, inter alia, a BCI-enabled mobile artillery system. The Alpha unit commander receives information that a civilian library is being used by enemy units for the storage of ammunition. The BCI operator, in consultation with the commander, has decided to switch off the BCI while steps are taken by planners and intelligence staffs to verify the information, and thus the status of the library as a military objective. **4.015**

If AB systems are to be used to decide who or what is to be made the object of attack, will the AB system consistently and reliably: **4.016**

1. distinguish between combatants and civilians?
2. distinguish between objects which are military objectives and those which are civilian objects?
3. only direct military operations, including attacks, against combatants and military objectives?

Where BBIs are used to decide on military operations, the requirements will be similar to those applying where no brain technology is involved, that is that the persons making the decisions take into account all available and relevant information, that they apply the principle and that they distinguish throughout between combatants and military objectives on the one hand and civilians and civilian objects on the other. It will therefore be important to ensure that the information that is relevant to compliance with the principle is available to those involved in the BBI decision-making process. **4.017**

The armed forces may be undertaking certain activities that are not linked to hostilities and that do not adversely affect the enemy. Activities of that kind may lawfully be directed at civilians or civilian objects. This would apply, for example, to propaganda, psychological operations, some kinds of cyber operation and some kinds of information operation. The principle of distinction will apply, however, to military action that does not cause death, injury, damage or destruction but that does have an adverse effect on the enemy. **4.018**

The distinction principle applies in both international and non-international armed conflicts. The difference, where the latter are concerned, is that the **4.019** decision to be made is between (1) the fighters,[17] that is members of the armed forces, members of dissident armed forces, members of organised armed groups and civilians who are directly participating in hostilities and (2) peaceable civilians.

4.020 It follows from this that if BCI, AB or BBI systems are to be used in connection with military operations, an assessment as to whether the operation is expected to have an adverse effect on the enemy must be made, in the case of BCI and BBI by planners, commanders and operators using such systems, and in the case of AB either by the system itself or by responsible planners, commanders and/or operators.

4.4 APPLYING DISTINCTION TO PERSONS

4.021 The principle of distinction obliges parties to an armed conflict to always distinguish between civilians and military objectives when conducting military operations. If this is to make sense, we need to understand who, respectively, are military objectives and civilians. The persons classed as military objectives by API consist of combatants and civilians who are taking a direct part in hostilities. The first of these, combatants, comprise members of the armed forces of a party to a conflict, but do not include medical personnel and chaplains who are collectively referred to as non-combatants.[18] Article 43 of API explains that the 'armed forces of a Party to a conflict consist of all organized armed forces, groups and units which are under a command responsible to that Party for the conduct of its subordinates, even if that Party is represented by a government or an authority not recognized by an adverse Party'.[19]

4.022 API stipulates that combatants have the right to take a direct part in hostilities,[20] with the result that they cannot be prosecuted for their acts of war that comply with the LOAC. Combatants may be lawfully targeted throughout the period of the international armed conflict unless they have been rendered *hors*

17 Consider M N Schmitt, C H B Garraway and T Dinstein, *The Manual on the Law of Non-International Armed Conflict, With Commentary* (San Remo, International Institute of Humanitarian Law, 2006), paras 1.1.2 and 2.1.1.

18 API, n.2, Art.43(2); Customary Law Study, n.6, Rule 3. US DoD Manual, n.3, para.4.3 refers to lawful combatants, unlawful combatants, privileged and unprivileged belligerents. In this book, the word combatant will describe the status of the relevant individual in accordance with Art.43.

19 API, n.2, Art.43(1), which also requires that the armed forces be subject to an internal disciplinary system which, among other things, must enforce compliance with international humanitarian law (IHL). As to the meaning of armed forces, see also Customary Law Study, n.6, Rule 4.

20 API, n.2, Art.43(2). See also Customary Law Study, n.6, Rule 3 as to meaning of combatants.

de combat.[21] If combatants are captured by an adverse Party, they have the right to prisoner of war status.[22]

The law on these matters that binds states that are not party to API is to be found in the 1907 Hague Regulations. Article 1 provides: 'The laws, rights, and duties of war apply not only to armies, but also to militia and volunteer corps fulfilling the following conditions: 1. To be commanded by a person responsible for his or her subordinates; 2. To have a fixed distinctive emblem recognizable at a distance; 3. To carry arms openly; and 4. To conduct their operations in accordance with the laws and customs of war.' If an irregular force meets these four conditions, its members will be entitled to combatant status, to participate in the hostilities, to combatant immunity and to prisoner of war status if captured.[23] The four criteria listed above reflect the attributes common to armed forces of a state.[24] **4.023**

It follows from this that combatants can lawfully be made the object of attack during operations involving the use of BCI, AB or BBI systems unless the combatants have been rendered *hors de combat*. The factors that the AB system uses to classify a person as a combatant will depend on whether the relevant state is party to API. If it is, it will apply the Article 43 criteria. If it is not, it will apply Article 1 of the Hague Regulations. **4.024**

Civilians who are taking a direct part in hostilities may also lawfully be made the object of attack. This is because under API civilians 'shall enjoy the protection afforded by [Section 51], unless and for such time as they take a direct part in hostilities'.[25] This provision is generally accepted as amounting to a customary rule that binds all states.[26] However, while the binding nature of the rule is accepted, there is disagreement as to aspects of the meaning of the term 'direct part in hostilities'.[27] While firing a weapon in the course of armed conflict hostilities is widely seen as taking a direct part in hostilities, certain **4.025**

21 As to the definition of persons who are *hors de combat*, see section 5.14 below.

22 Geneva Convention (III) relative to the Treatment of Prisoners of War, Geneva, 12 August 1949, 75 UNTS 135 (GCIII), Art.4A(1) and API, n.2, Art.44(1).

23 GCIII, ibid, Art.4A(2).

24 US DoD Manual, n.3, para.4.6.1.

25 API, n.2, Art.51(3) and see Customary Law Study, n.6, Rule 6.

26 Note, the US position, as expressed in the US DoD Manual, n.3, that while the Manual 'uses the phrase "direct part in hostilities" to indicate what activities cause a civilian to forfeit his or her protection from being made the object of attack' that does not mean that the US has adopted the direct participation in hostilities rule that is expressed in API, n.2, Art.51: US DoD Manual, n.3, para.5.8.1.

27 See articles by W Hays Parks, M N Schmitt, K Watkin, W H Boothby and N Melzer in (2010) 42 *New York Journal of International Law and Politics*.

other activities associated with hostilities may be less clear-cut. It will be for each state to form its own reasonable interpretation of the provision's meaning.

4.026 A civilian is defined in API as 'any person who does not belong to one of the categories of persons referred to in article 4A(1), (2), (3), and (6) of the Third [Geneva] Convention and in article 43 of' AP1.[28] 'In case of doubt whether a person is a civilian, that person shall be considered to be a civilian.'[29] The UK has expressed the view that this doubt rule only arises where the person making the assessment considers that there is substantial doubt after having considered the information from all sources that is reasonably available at the relevant time. The UK has also stated that this doubt rule does not override the commander's duty to protect the safety of troops under his command or to preserve his military situation in conformity with other rules in AP1.[30] As a corollary of the principle of distinction, '[t]he civilian population as such, as well as individual civilians, shall not be made the object of attack'. The civilian population comprises all persons who are civilians.[31] These two customary law rules bind all states in relation to both international and non-international armed conflicts.[32] The presence within the civilian population of persons who are not civilians does not deprive the population of its civilian character.[33]

4.027 Accordingly, where BCI systems are employed in relation to military operations, the direct participation in hostilities rule, the requirement to protect non-combatants, the rule as to classification of civilians and the doubt rule must be applied by planners, commanders and by the operators whose thoughts or intent are being translated by the BCI system into action by the linked weapon or other military capability to which the BCI is connected.

4.028 Where AB systems are being used to undertake autonomous attacks, the AB system must reliably and consistently:

---

28 API, n.2, Art.50(1) and Customary Law Study, n.6, Rule 5.

29 AP1, n.2, Art.50(1). See also changes made to the US DoD Manual, n.3, on 31 July 2023: List of Changes promulgated on 31 July 2023 annexed to the DoD Manual (as amended), para.5.4.3.2.

30 Statement (h) made by the UK on ratification of AP1, n.2, on 28 January 1998.

31 API, n.2, Art.50(2).

32 API, n.2, Art.51(2) and Protocol Additional to the Geneva Conventions of 12 August 1949, and relating to the Protection of Victims of Non-International Armed Conflicts (Protocol II), 8 June 1977, 1125 UNTS 609 (APII), Art.13(2). Note also US DoD Manual, n.3, paras 5.3, 17.7; AMW Manual, n.9, Rule 11; NIAC Manual, para.2.1.1.1; Customary Law Study, n.6, Rule 1; Rome Statute of the International Criminal Court, 17 July 1998, Art.8(2)(b)(i) and (ii), (e)(i) and (ii); Israel, *Rules of Warfare on the Battlefield,* 2nd edn (Military Advocate-General's Corps Command, IDF School of Military Law, 2006), 8 and 29.

33 API, n.2, Art.50(2) and (3).

1. distinguish between combatants, non-combatants and civilians and only direct operations against the first of these;
2. distinguish between peaceable civilians and civilians who take a direct part in the hostilities and only direct military operations against the latter (it will be necessary for the AB system to be able to identify the activities that, according to the position taken by the relevant state, constitute direct participation);
3. if the available information does not clearly show that the civilian is directly participating, treat the individual as a peaceable civilian;
4. classify as civilians all persons who are not combatants/non-combatants;
5. detect, having taken all relevant information into account, that there is doubt as to the status of a person as a combatant; and
6. where doubt exists, assume civilian status pending resolution of the matter and/or refer the decision about the military operation to a human operator.

If BBI systems are being used either to link personnel who are deciding upon attacks or to communicate decisions as to attack to operators whose task is to carry those thought-instructions out, it will be important for the system: **4.029**

1. to be operating correctly and, specifically, to be robust against interference by an adversary or third party;
2. to reliably and consistently detect the thoughts/intents of all participants in the BBI system;
3. to reliably and consistently transmit the thoughts and intentions of the participants to each other as each participant intends;
4. to reliably and consistently represent the conclusions of the BBI-enabled process to the participants; and
5. to reliably and consistently communicate any instruction or order arising from the BBI process to those to be tasked with carrying it out.

The complexities involved in the use of BCI, AB and BBI systems are likely to be such that planners, commanders and operators will need the assistance of technical experts who are likely to be civilians. At least some of the activities of those experts are likely to be classed by the adverse party as 'direct participation'. This raises the following potential issues: **4.030**

1. Such employees should be informed of their position under the LOAC.
2. There is the risk that they will cease to perform their duties as hostilities approach.
3. It may be possible to recruit such pivotal personnel to the armed forces, thereby granting them combatant immunity.[34]

34 For a discussion of some of the issues, see P W Singer, *Corporate Warriors: The Rise of the Privatised Military Industry* (Cornell University Press, 2004), 151–68.

4. Taking action under point 3 is likely to secure their continued performance of their duties during periods of armed conflict hostilities.
5. The state employing such experts should ensure that the terms on which they are recruited and employed preclude their classification as mercenaries.[35]

4.031 A person is the object of an attack if the person is intended to be injured or killed by the attack. If death or injury to particular civilians occurs but was not the intended outcome of the attack, those civilians will not have been the object of the attack. It would only be lawful to make a civilian the object of attack if, and for such time as, they take a direct part in the hostilities.[36]

4.032 If a BCI system is being used in connection with attacks, it will be the planner, commander and/or operator who will decide on which person(s) and/or which object(s) constitute the object of the planned attack, that is against whom or what the attack is to be directed. It will be the BCI operator who executes the attack by forming the required thought or intent that will, via the BCI, initiate the firing of the linked weapon system.

4.033 If an AB system is being used to undertake an attack, much will depend on the degree of discretion that is granted to the AB system. It may be programmed so that it has a very restricted choice of target, or it may be given a greater degree of latitude over targets. Determining who or what was the object of attack may therefore involve considering the input of planners, commanders and operators as well as examining the decision-making of the AB system.

4.034 'Acts or threats of violence the primary purpose of which is to spread terror among the civilian population are prohibited.'[37] If violence is not being employed or threatened, the rule will not apply.[38] To be 'among' the civilian population, the terror must, the author suggests, affect a significant portion

35 In API, n.2, Art.47 the term mercenary is defined for purposes of LOAC. The person must have been specially recruited to fight in an armed conflict. This would, arguably, not be the case if it is a company with which the state has contracted, as there is no contractual arrangement between the relevant individuals and the state that is involved in the armed conflict. Article 47 requires that the person be motivated by a desire for private gain 'and, in fact, is promised, by or on behalf of a Party to the conflict' compensation that exceeds what is paid to combatants of similar ranks and functions in the recruiting state's own armed forces. If it is the employing company that is paying the employee and if the required skills are not available in the recruiting state's armed forces, as may well be the case with experts in the use of brain technologies in warfare, this may have the effect that the definition of mercenary would not apply to such experts, but much will depend on the facts of a specific case.

36 API, n.2, Art.51(3).

37 API, n.2, Art.51(2), second sentence; APII, n.32, Art.13(2), second sentence. The rule applies in international and non-international armed conflicts. See Customary Law Study, n.6, Rule 2.

38 Copying false news reports that cause panic among the population, and attacks that are primarily intended to damage a military objective will not generally breach this rule.

of the population, even if the violence or threatened violence is more localised. The BCI and AB implications of this rule are discussed in Chapter 7, section 7.9.

4.5 APPLYING DISTINCTION TO OBJECTS

4.5.1 Military objectives

The distinction principle requires the parties to an armed conflict at all times to distinguish between civilian objects and military objectives, and only to direct their military operations against the latter. Understanding the implications of the principle where objects are concerned therefore requires a clear appreciation of what exactly military objectives and civilian objects respectively consist of. If a BCI-enabled operation is to take place, it will be for the planner, commander and/or operator to consider the points made in the rest of this section and then decide whether the proposed target constitutes a military objective and is, thus, a lawful target. **4.035**

Where objects are concerned: 'military objectives are limited to those objects which by their nature, location, purpose or use make an effective contribution to military action and whose total or partial destruction, capture or neutralization, in the circumstances ruling at the time, offers a definite military advantage.'[39] This wording has been widely used by states in military manuals[40] and reflects customary law applicable to international and non-international armed conflicts.[41] The International Committee of the Red Cross (ICRC) Commentary to API explains that an object is something that is 'visible and tangible'.[42] It follows that the definition does not include national morale, the **4.036**

---

39 API, n.2, Art.52(2) and Customary Law Study, n.6, Rule 8. Professor Dinstein argues that the definition ought to have been composite in nature, amalgamating an abstract statement with a non-exhaustive catalogue of specific examples; Y Dinstein, *The Conduct of Hostilities under the Law of International Armed Conflict*, 4th edn (Cambridge University Press, 2022), 119–20. For an early formulation of the notion, see Rules concerning the Control of Wireless Telegraphy in Time of War and Air Warfare, Drafted by a Commission of Jurists at The Hague, December 1922, Art.24(1).

40 US DoD Manual, n.3, para.5.6.3; see also AMW Manual, n.9, Rule 1(y); NIAC Manual, n.32, para.1.1.4; Customary Law Study, n.6, Rule 8; San Remo Manual, n.9, Rule 40. See also Protocol on Prohibitions or Restrictions on the Use of Mines, Booby-Traps and Other Devices as amended on 3 May 1996 (Protocol II to the 1980 Convention on Certain Conventional Weapons as amended on 3 May 1996) (Amended Mines Protocol), Art.2(4); Protocol on Prohibitions or Restrictions on the Use of Incendiary Weapons (Protocol III to the 1980 Convention on Certain Conventional Weapons), Geneva, 10 October 1980, Art.1(3).

41 Customary Law Study, n.6, Commentary to Rule 8.

42 International Committee of the Red Cross, *Commentary on the Additional Protocols of 8 June 1977* (Y Sandoz, C Swinarski and B Zimmermann (eds), 1987) (API Commentary), paras 2007, 2008.

political views of the population or economic well-being. Important elements in the definition should be clarified as follows.

4.037 The word 'nature' refers to the inherent character of an object. Accordingly, weapon launch platforms such as combat aircraft, warships and submarines, as well as missiles, small arms, ammunition, armoured personnel carriers and artillery weapons are all clear examples of objects that are military objectives by nature. Similarly, military command, control and communications equipment, depots, barracks and military air and naval bases will also be military objectives by nature. BCI, AB and BBI systems that are designed to be used exclusively in connection with attacks or with the performance of other military operations will also be military objectives by nature. The fact that civilians may be involved in the operation of such facilities will not affect this classification.[43]

4.038 If a BCI-enabled weapon system is to be used in connection with attacks:

1. Has the system been adequately tested to ensure that the thoughts or intent of the operator will be reliably and consistently translated into action by the weapon system that corresponds with the relevant thought or intent?
2. Is the BCI system free from faults and sufficiently robust against enemy or third-party interference?
3. Are the human and other arrangements associated with the use of the BCI-enabled weapon system organised so as to promote compliance with the LOAC?

4.039 If an AB system is to be used in connection with attacks:

1. Has it been tested sufficiently in a manner that replicates as closely as possible the intended circumstances of use?
2. Do the results of those tests give confidence that it will reliably and consistently distinguish between objects which are and are not military objectives by nature?
3. Will the AB reliably and consistently decline to make objects which are not classed as military objectives by nature the object of attack on that basis (it being recognised that an object may be a military objective on the grounds of location, purpose or use)?
4. Does what is known about the decision-making process employed by the AB also give the confidence referred to in point 2 above?
5. Is the AB system free from known faults of any kind and free from any disturbance, including interference by adverse or third parties?

---

43 M N Schmitt (ed), *Tallinn Manual 2.0 on the International Law Applicable to Cyber Operations* (Cambridge University Press, 2017) (Tallinn Manual 2.0), Commentary to Rule 100, para.8 and see API Commentary, ibid, para.2020.

If a BBI system is to be used as part of the targeting procedure, a key question will be whether the BBI is operating correctly in the sense that all contributions made by all participants in the discussion conducted through BBI are accurately received and shared in a form that can readily be understood by other participants. Another key question will be whether the BBI will accurately deliver the instruction formulated during the BBI-enabled consultations to those tasked with the execution of that instruction. **4.040**

These considerations will apply similarly when location, purpose and use are being considered. **4.041**

An object becomes a military objective on the basis of location if its location or geographical situation renders it[44] of military importance.[45] Geographical features such as an elevated area of ground with commanding views of a plain, a mountain pass or a narrow gorge may all, depending on the operational context, be examples of locations that make an effective contribution to military action in the circumstances applying at the relevant time.[46] **4.042**

To be used to decide that an object is a military objective by virtue of location, an AB system must reliably and consistently: **4.043**

1. assess the military usefulness of the object in its location in light of the operational context; and
2. identify that the object, by virtue of its location, is making an effective contribution to military action.

It may not be necessary to rely on the decision of the AB system if a person is in a position to make that determination before or during the mission. Prior programming of factors that alone or in association with each other will cause an object to be a military objective by location into an AB system may, but will not necessarily, enable point 1, above, to be satisfied. Careful testing will be necessary to determine whether the use of the factors by the system leads to **4.044**

44 Note, the Danish MOD Manual (Danish Ministry of Defence, Military Manual on International Law relevant to Danish armed forces in international operations, September 2016), which states that location means '[o]bjects that must be assumed to have a direct military function or use due to their location even though the adversary does not (yet) have an intention in that respect' and objects that due to their location make an effective contribution to the adversary's military action: 304.

45 API Commentary, n.42, para.2021.

46 Yoram Dinstein points out that an area of land 'must obviously have exceptional traits' to be a military objective by virtue of purpose and that the incidence of location as a determinant factor cannot be too sweeping. 'Commonly accepted illustrations are an important mountain pass or defile; a trail in the jungle or in a swamp area; a river crossing; or a spit of land controlling the entrance of a harbour': Dinstein, n.39, 134.

sufficiently reliable and accurate determinations. If an AB system cannot make the assessment in point 1 above to an acceptable level of reliability, the matter will need to be referred to a human operator.

4.045 The word 'purpose'[47] in the definition of military objective refers to the intended future use of the object.[48] If, therefore, good quality intelligence were to show that, in the event of the runway at its military airbase being rendered unusable by bombing, the enemy would use the runway at a local civilian airfield for its combat aircraft squadrons, that civilian runway becomes a military objective now because of the enemy's intended future military use of it.

4.046 It will be for the operator of a BCI-enabled weapon system, in consultation, no doubt, with the commander, planners and others, to decide whether the available information supports the conclusion that the enemy intends to use the object in the future for military purposes.

4.047 For an AB system to decide that an object has become a military objective by virtue of purpose, the system must reliably and consistently:

1. access and assess information as to the enemy's intended future use of the object;
2. analyse whether that future use is such as will make an effective contribution to military action; and
3. assess whether the available information is sufficient to render the analysis in point 2 above reliable. This will include deciding whether any of the available information calls into question the suggested intention to use the object for military purposes in the future.

4.048 The author believes that, if there is conflicting information, the AB system should be programmed not to classify the object as a military objective on the basis of purpose. It should be programmed either to assess whether any of the other three criteria apply or simply to refer the issue for a decision by a human operator.

---

47 The US DoD Manual, n.3 characterises 'purpose' in this context as meaning 'the intended or possible use in the future'; para.5.6.6.1. Examples of possible future use in this context are said to include civilian runways that could be used in the event that the military runways become unserviceable and bridges or tunnels that would possibly be used to assist future adversary military operations. This, in the author's view, is an over-inclusive approach. The preferred interpretation is that it must be intended to use the object for military purposes in the future. That future intended use of the object may of course have to be inferred from the circumstances applying at the time. See Dinstein, n.39, 133.

48 Danish MOD Manual, n.44, 302, UK Manual, n.3, para.5.4.4; *Australian Law of Armed Conflict Manual*, ADDP 06.4 (11 May 2006), para.5.29.

The use criterion means that an object that is used for military purposes is a military objective. The tower of a church is, prima facie, a civilian object. However, if that church tower is currently used by the enemy, for example as an observation post from which to direct force movements or to call in artillery fire, that military use will convert what otherwise would be a civilian object into a military objective. Accordingly, civilian communications networks such as roads, bridges, railway lines, television and radio stations, ports, airports and harbours will frequently be military objectives either because of their current use for military purposes or due to the enemy's intended future use of them. The same can be said of factories, warehouses, other buildings and many other objects, but there must be clear information on which it can correctly be concluded that the object has become a military objective.[49] **4.049**

The operator of a BCI-enabled weapon system should consult, to the degree necessary, with the commander, planners and others to decide whether the available information supports the conclusion that the object of potential attack has become a military objective by virtue of use. **4.050**

To apply the use criterion, an AB system must reliably and consistently: **4.051**

1. detect the uses to which an object is being put by the enemy and
2. assess whether any of those uses makes an effective contribution to enemy military action. The AB system should be programmed to recognise that objects which meet only one of the uses of which satisfies point 2 are still a military objective.[50]

The customary military objective definition in Article 52(2) requires that twin tests be applied when determining whether an object is in fact a military objective. The object must make an effective contribution to military action by virtue of its nature, location, purpose or use (the first test) and its destruction, capture or neutralisation, in the prevailing circumstances, must offer a definite military advantage (the second test).[51] While the two tests are clearly linked, both must be applied when an AB system, or indeed a human operator, considers any of the four criteria. **4.052**

49 Note, AMW Manual, n.9, commentary accompanying Rule 22(c), paras 2 and 3.

50 US DoD Manual, n.3, para.5.7.1.2; AMW Manual, n.9, commentary accompanying Rule 22(d); Customary Law Study, n.6, commentary accompanying Rule 8.

51 J Dill, *Legitimate Targets? Social Construction, International Law and US Bombing* (Cambridge University Press, 2015), 71.

4.053 For example, State A is using BCI technology to control the missile firing mechanisms aboard its fleet of remotely piloted aircraft. Planned targets are assessed in the usual way by the targeting board. However, the BCI-controlled system has been found useful for attacking targets of opportunity. A surveillance drone detects that enemy commanders are meeting in a civilian factory building. Video footage of the commanders entering the building enables its military use to be verified, and the object is classed as a military objective. Deciding whether to attack the building will involve consideration of other targeting law rules.

4.054 'In case of doubt whether an object which is normally dedicated to civilian purposes … is being used to make an effective contribution to military action, it shall be presumed[52] not to be so used.'[53] It should be emphasised that the doubt rule in respect of objects only arises if the doubt relates to the current use of the object. Additionally, the doubt rule only applies in the case of objects that are normally dedicated to civilian purposes – it does not therefore apply in the case of dual-use objects.

4.055 For example, the operator of State A's BCI-enabled mobile artillery piece consults with the commander, planners and others about the status of a proposed target. The object is a house that, it is believed, is being used for the storage of enemy weapon systems, including BCI-controlled weapons. That belief is based on information from a single informant who has not previously supplied information to State A. The operator and commander agree that the doubt rule applies and that the house cannot yet be classed as a military objective. A surveillance drone is used to monitor movements in the vicinity of the house and confirms the accuracy of the intelligence from the informant. The doubt rule therefore no longer applies as the status of the house as a military objective on the basis of that use has been confirmed.

4.056 Operators, commanders and planners must consider all available information in order to decide whether the doubt rule applies. If it does, they must decide not to attack the relevant object. While there may be doubt as to the current use of an object, available information may support the conclusion that the object is a military objective on some other basis, such as purpose.

---

52 Customary Law Study, n.6, commentary to Rule 10. Yoram Dinstein states that this is a rebuttable presumption that only arises if there is reasonable doubt: Dinstein, n.39, 131.

53 API, n.2, Art.52(3). This Rule applies in both international and non-international armed conflicts.

An AB system that is used in connection with deciding upon attacks must reliably and consistently detect when circumstances render the doubt rule applicable and if it is, the AB system must reliably and consistently: **4.057**

1. assess whether the relevant object is normally dedicated to civilian purposes, noting that dual-use objects are not normally dedicated to civilian purposes;
2. only apply the doubt rule where the doubt relates to current use, noting that the rule does not apply where there is doubt as to nature, location or purpose; and
3. decline to attack the object if there is doubt as to whether its current use makes an effective contribution to military action.[54]

If an object was a military objective due to its use but that military use has ended, it will become a civilian object if none of the other three criteria, nature, location or purpose apply to it. Allowing an AB system that has determined that an object is not a military objective on the basis of use to consider the other three criteria would only be appropriate if there is a suitable degree of confidence that the AB can consider the alternative criteria independently and to an acceptable level of consistency and reliability. **4.058**

It perhaps goes without saying that a BBI system that is facilitating considerations of this kind must be performing in such a way that the information is being accurately presented to those tasked with making the decision, and that the views of those considering the matter are being accurately transmitted to each other. **4.059**

4.5.2 Civilian objects

'Civilian objects are all objects which are not military objectives' and 'shall not be the object of attack'.[55] So attacks must not be aimed at objects that are not military objectives. The focus here is on the target of the attack, not on incidental damage arising from an attack that is aimed at a military objective. This rule is also not dealing with the situation where an attack the object of which is a military objective fails for whatever reason, including error or technical fault, to hit the chosen target. **4.060**

---

54 Note, the amended US DoD view in the US DoD Manual, n.3, para.5.4.3.2, as amended 31 July 2023: 'Under the principle of distinction, commanders and other decision-makers must presume that persons or objects are protected from being made the object of attack unless the information available at the time indicates that the persons or objects are military objectives.'

55 API, n.2, Art.52(1); Customary Law Study, n.6, Rule 7; US DoD Manual, n.3, para.5.6.2; UK Manual, n.3, para.5.24; AMW Manual, n.9, Rule 11 and see the accompanying commentary; Rome Statute, n.32, Art.8(2)(b)(ii).

4.061 The way in which the definition of civilian objects is drafted has the effect that all objects are either military objectives (and thus are liable to be attacked) or civilian objects (and thus are protected from being made the object of attack). So civilian objects lose their protection if, for example, they are used for military purposes.[56]

4.062 The implications of this rule for the use of BCI, AB and BBI systems are clear. If an object is not a military objective, planners, commanders, operators and systems employing brain technologies must not make it the object of attack. Where BCI-enabled weapon systems are being used, operators, commanders and planners will be responsible for ensuring that civilian objects are not targeted.

4.063 AB-enabled weapon systems used for autonomous attack missions must be programmed so that they will reliably and consistently refrain from making civilian objects the object of attack. This presupposes that the system reliably and consistently detects when an object is a civilian object and, as a distinct requirement, that it also reliably and consistently refrains from attacking objects that it has identified as being civilian objects.

4.064 With BBI systems, the obligation will be to ensure that the decision-making process that the BBI enables and the instruction transmission process that it provides operate accurately and reliably.

4.6 INDISCRIMINATE ATTACKS

4.065 'Indiscriminate attacks are prohibited. Indiscriminate attacks are: (a) those which are not directed at a specific military objective; (b) those which employ a method or means of combat which cannot be directed at a specific military objective; or (c) those which employ a method or means of combat the effects of which cannot be limited as required by th[e] Protocol; and consequently, in each such case, are of a nature to strike military objectives and civilians or civilian objects without distinction.'[57]

4.066 This is a customary law rule that binds all States and applies in both international and non-international armed conflicts.[58] Subparagraphs (b)

---

56 Customary Law Study, n.6, 34 and Rule 10.

57 API, n.2, Art.51(4) and AMW Manual, n.9, Rule 13(b).

58 Customary Law Study, n.6, Rules 11 and 12 and see AMW Manual, n.9, Rule 13(a) and associated commentary.

and (c) are concerned with weapons law and are therefore discussed in Chapter 6. Subparagraph (a) deals with the situation in which the attack itself is indiscriminate, irrespective of the discriminating or non-discriminating nature of the weapon that is used.

Planners, commanders and operators involved in attacks using BCI, AB and BBI systems must therefore ensure that the system will direct the attack at a lawful target, whether it is a military objective, combatants or directly participating civilians.[59] Where a BCI-enabled weapon system is being used, care must be taken to ensure that the BCI operator only forms the thought or intent that will initiate the attack when it has been determined, probably with the assistance of planners, commanders and others, that the attack will engage a military objective, that is a lawful target. **4.067**

Where the use of an AB weapon system to undertake autonomous attacks is concerned, it will be necessary for commanders and others involved in initiating the mission to be satisfied, on the basis of system design, system testing and other information about the AB mechanisms, that the AB will, in the prevailing circumstances, reliably, consistently and exclusively target persons or objects that are military objectives, that is lawful targets. With BBI systems, the obligation will be to ensure that the decision-making process that the BBI enables and the instruction transmission process that it provides operate accurately and reliably. **4.068**

Consider the example of a remotely piloted aircraft system that carries a BCI-enabled air-to-ground missile system. The sensors aboard the aircraft detect and photograph what might be an enemy tank. However, the image is unclear due to cloud and air pollution in the area, and the photo interpreters are not able to confirm the nature of the observed object. The operator of the BCI-enabled weapon consults with the commander and it is decided not to proceed with an attack. As a further example, consider an AB-enabled weapon system that is being employed in autonomous mode. The weapon system detects a group of large vehicles, one of which is in fact a tank, while the remainder are civilian heavy goods vehicles located in a vehicle park. It is known from tests that, in particular light conditions, the AB system lacks the ability to distinguish between tanks and large civilian vehicles. The AB system is programmed to detect when the relevant light conditions apply and to refrain from undertaking an attack in such circumstances. On the occasion mentioned **4.069**

---

59 That is objects that come within the API, n.2, Art.52(2) definition, combatants who are not *hors de combat* or directly participating civilians who are not *hors de combat*.

in the scenario, the AB system decides not to attack, thus ensuring that the indiscriminate attack prohibition is complied with.

4.7 EXAMPLES OF INDISCRIMINATE ATTACKS

4.070 API specifies carpet bombing as an example of an indiscriminate attack. The provision gives as an example of an indiscriminate, and thus unlawful, attack 'an attack by bombardment by any methods or means which treats as a single military objective a number of clearly separated and distinct military objectives located in a city, town, village or other area containing a similar concentration of civilians or civilian objects;'.[60] The treaty does not specify the degree of separation that is required for the military objectives to be regarded as clearly separated and distinct. Neither is it made clear how a similarity between a concentration of civilians or civilian objects and a number of military objectives is to be judged. So this is a legal rule that is not easy to apply. In the author's view, the decision-maker should assess whether it is reasonable, given what is then known, to treat the military objectives as a single target.

4.071 If a BCI system is being employed in connection with attacks, the planner, commander and operator will be responsible for making that judgment.

4.072 If it is an AB system that is making the decision, it must reliably and consistently:

1. detect that the military objectives it is observing are clearly separate and distinct;
2. detect that those military objectives are located in an area containing a concentration of civilians or civilian objects;
3. assess whether the concentration of civilians or civilian objects is similar to the clearly separated and distinct military objectives; and
4. if that is the case, refrain from treating those military objectives as a single military objective for the purposes of attack.

4.073 If the planner, commander or operator of such an operation is able to monitor the AB system's processes and has the capability to intervene and stop an attack that would be unlawful or that would breach the commander's intent,

60 Note, UK Manual, n.3, para.5.23.2; AMW Manual, n.9, Rule 13(c); NIAC Manual, n.32, commentary accompanying Rule 2.1.1.3; and Customary Law Study, n.6, Rule 13. AMW Manual, n.9, Rule 13(c), commentary, para.2 points out that the Rule 'does not deny the possibility that a number of lawful targets, which are not clearly separated and distinct, may be treated as a single lawful target'. Amended Protocol II provides '[s]everal clearly separated and distinct military objectives located in a city, town, village or other area containing a similar concentration of civilians or civilian objects are not to be treated as a single military objective'; Amended Mines Protocol, n.40, Art.3(9).

this may be sufficient to ensure compliance with the rule. If that is not possible, such an operation can only proceed if the AB system will reliably and consistently apply the judgements required by this rule.[61]

If a BBI is facilitating the discussion by those individuals of these issues, the BBI must be operating correctly so that proper inputs are received and fully considered in a structured way. **4.074**

Imagine that the commander has instructed the operator of a BCI-enabled missile system to attack four buildings located in an industrial park where the numerous remaining buildings are civilian retail outlets or civilian manufacturing facilities. The BCI operator is supplied with a plan showing the location of the four targets. He notices that two of them are next door to one another and uses his thought or intent to initiate the firing of a single missile with two warheads with the desired effect of destroying both of the adjoining structures at the same time and as part of a single attack. No carpet-bombing objection arises. If, by contrast, multiple missiles were to be used to attack all four targets and everything in between them, Article 51(5)(a) and, by extension, the prohibition of indiscriminate attacks in Article 51(4) and in customary law would be breached. Instead, and having targeted the two adjoining structures, by targeting the two remaining targets individually using single missiles, the BCI operator complies with the rule. **4.075**

Article 51(5)(b) sets forth the proportionality rule by prohibiting 'an attack which may be expected to cause incidental loss of civilian life, injury to civilians, damage to civilian objects, or a combination thereof, which would be excessive in relation to the concrete and direct military advantage anticipated'.[62] It is a forward-looking rule because, as the words 'expected' and 'anticipated' make clear, it is concerned with decision-making in advance of an attack. It prohibits a decision to undertake an attack where excessive civilian injury and/or damage should be expected or where the attacker intends to cause excessive civilian injury and/or damage. Considerable incidental civilian injury and/or damage is not enough, per se, to render a planned attack unlawful. It is only if that expected incidental civilian injury/damage is excessive when compared with the military advantage that is anticipated as accruing from a successful **4.076**

---

61 It will be noted that the emphasis here and elsewhere in the book is on what the AB system will actually do, not on what it might theoretically be capable of doing.

62 API, n.2, Art.51(5)(b) and see also Amended Mines Protocol, n.40, Art.3(8)(c). In the application of the proportionality rule to precautions, see the discussion in sections 4.9–4.11 below. In its application to cultural property, see Second Protocol to the Hague Convention of 1954 for the Protection of Cultural Property in the Event of Armed Conflict, The Hague, 26 March 1999, Art.2.

prosecution of the attack that the rule is broken if the attack proceeds. This is a customary rule that therefore binds all states, including states that are not party to API, and that applies in both international and non-international armed conflicts.[63]

4.077 If a BCI system is being used in connection with attacks, the planner, commander and operator will be responsible, in accordance with their respective roles, for ensuring compliance with this rule. Achieving that requirement with suitable reliability may require that the BCI is switched off until proper collateral damage and proportionality evaluations have been completed and properly considered. As with the application of other rules of targeting law, the operator whose thoughts or intent are designed to initiate an attack using the BCI-enabled weapon will no doubt be relying on the proper performance by planners, commanders and others of their roles in relation to the attack.

4.078 If an AB system is being used to decide upon attacks, it must consistently and reliably:

1. assess the civilian injury and/or civilian damage that should be expected to result from the attack;
2. assess the military advantage that can be anticipated from the successful prosecution of the attack;
3. compare the assessments in points 1 and 2; and
4. assess whether the result of the point 1 assessment would be excessive in relation to the result of the point 2 assessment.

4.079 There are no generally accepted scales of measurement of civilian injury/damage and of military advantage, and even if there were, those units of measurement would differ. This is not, therefore, an easy test to apply, either by a person or an AB system. The AB system should be programmed to consider and apply the same decision that a reasonable military commander in possession of the same information would make.[64]

---

63 Customary Law Study, n.6, Rule 14; UK Manual, n.3, paras 5.23.2 and 15.15.1; US DoD Manual, n.3, paras 5.12 and 16.5.1.1; AMW Manual, n.9, Rule 14 and the commentary thereto; NIAC Manual, n.32, para.2.1.1.4. Shereshevsky deploys the interesting arguments for and against the equal application of the proportionality rule as between enhanced and unenhanced soldiers; Y Shereshevsky, 'Are all Soldiers Created Equal? – On the Equal Application of the Law to Enhanced Soldiers, SSRN, 3 September 2020, available at https://papers.ssrn.com/sol3/papers.cfm?abstract_id=3684645, later published in the (2021) 61(2) *Virginia Journal of International Law* 271–323.

64 See *Final Report to the Prosecutor by the Committee Established to review the NATO Bombing Campaign against the Federal Republic of Yugoslavia,* available at https://www.icty.org/en/press/final-report-prosecutor-committee-established-review-nato-bombing-campaign-against-federal, para.50. See also M Bothe,

If an operator is able to observe the AB's processes and intervene if they suggest that an unlawful or undesired attack is going to be undertaken, this may be an appropriate safeguard. **4.080**

If a BBI is being used, for example, to facilitate the assessment of these matters by a group of the responsible staff, it must be established in advance that the BBI system is operating correctly in such a way that information and views can be shared accurately, effectively and efficiently among all of the members of the group. **4.081**

There is a difference of view as to the position of medical personnel and medical objects under the proportionality rule. The ICRC view is that they should respectively be classed as civilians and civilian objects.[65] The US Department of Defense (DoD) disagrees.[66] The author considers that, while the proportionality rule does not refer to medical personnel and objects specifically, such personnel are, prima facie, not combatants under API, Article 43, and medical objects, including medical units, hospitals and medical transports including medical aircraft, are, prima facie, not military objectives. This means that medical personnel and medical objects are, respectively, civilians and civilian objects and are thus protected, inter alia, by the proportionality rule. Such protection would of course cease if they were to take a direct part in the hostilities or in some other way become military objectives. Accordingly, the position taken in this book is that medical personnel and objects count on the collateral damage side of the proportionality rule and that they must be considered when the attacker's precautions are being complied with.[67] It is therefore suggested that planners, commanders and operators should also apply this interpretation when undertaking attacks using BCI systems and when using BBI systems to plan or consider attacks. It is also suggested that AB systems should be programmed to apply this interpretation when applying the proportionality rule to future attacks. **4.082**

K J Partsch and W A Solf, *New Rules for Victims of Armed Conflicts: Commentary on the Two 1977 Protocols Additional to the Geneva Conventions of 1949* (Martinus Nijhoff Publishers, 1982), 363.

65 ICRC Report for the 32nd International Conference, *International Humanitarian Law and the Challenges of Contemporary Armed Conflicts*, Geneva, 8–10 December 2015, 31–2.

66 See the discussion in M W Meier, 'The Principle of Proportionality in the DoD Law of War Manual', *Just Security*, 18 January 2024 available at https://www.justsecurity.org/91319/the-principle-of-proportionality-in-the-dod-law-of-war-manual/.

67 See, however, Yoram Dinstein's analysis: Dinstein, n.39, 178–9.

4.8 HUMAN SHIELDING

4.083 Article 51(7) of API provides: 'The presence or movements of the civilian population or individual civilians shall not be used to render certain points or areas immune from military operations, in particular in attempts to shield military objectives from attacks or to shield, favour or impede military operations.[68] The Parties to the conflict shall not direct the movement of the civilian population or individual civilians in order to attempt to shield military objectives from attacks or to shield military operations.'[69]

4.084 Accordingly, attempts to shield military objectives from attack by placing civilians in the vicinity of lawful targets thereby altering the proportionality calculus associated with potential attack are prohibited. The rule is really directed at unscrupulous action by the human shielder that seeks to exploit the adversary's adherence to the principle of distinction, and in particular the proportionality rule.[70] Human shields may be present voluntarily or under compulsion; both forms of human shielding are prohibited under Article 51(7). Moreover, the obligation to take precautions against the effects of attacks, set forth in Article 58 of API, requires the parties to the conflict to 'endeavour to remove the civilian population, individual civilians and civilian objects under their control from the vicinity of military objectives' to the maximum extent feasible.[71]

4.085 Article 51(8) makes it clear that '[a]ny violation of these prohibitions shall not release the Parties to the conflict from their legal obligations with respect to the civilian population and civilians, including the obligation to take the precautionary measures provided for in Article 57 [of API]'.[72] So, while Article 57 precautions must be applied by the attacker, the treaty gives no guidance as to the values that should be given to the human shields when

---

68 Intentionally using human shields in order to persuade an adversary not to undertake an otherwise lawful attack is explicitly prohibited and breaches the API, n.2, Art.58 requirement that all parties to the conflict remove civilians from the vicinity of military objectives and take other necessary precautions to protect civilians under their control.

69 API, n.2, Art.51(7). The US DoD Manual asserts: 'Parties to a conflict may not use the presence or movement of protected persons or objects 1 to attempt to make certain points or areas immune from seizure or attack; 2 to shield military objectives from attack; or 3 otherwise to shield or favour one's own military operations or to impede the adversary's military operations': para.5.16.

70 Dinstein, n.39, 208, para.612. Human shielding is a war crime; Rome Statute, n.32, Art.8(2)(b)(xxiii). Yoram Dinstein points out the complexity of the issue in the context of urban warfare, where it may be hard to establish whether 'stay-behind civilians' are in fact human shields and, if they are, whether they are there voluntarily or not; ibid, 209.

71 API, n.2, Art.58(a). This obligation is without prejudice to Geneva Convention (IV) relative to the Protection of Civilian Persons in Time of War, Geneva, 12 August 1949, 75 UNTS 287 (GCIV), Art.49.

72 Consider the criticism of this rule in N A Canestaro, 'Legal and Policy Constraints on the Conduct of Aerial Precision Warfare' (2004) 37 Van JTL 431, 461.

the proportionality rule is being applied. The AMW Manual distinguishes between voluntary and involuntary human shields[73] and notes that among the participating experts there were three divergent views about the status of voluntary human shields. 'One view was that voluntary human shields are not counted in the calculation of collateral damage because they are directly participating in hostilities. A second view held that voluntary human shields do not qualify as civilians directly participating in hostilities. Hence, they remain protected civilians who count fully under the proportionality analysis. Finally, the third view agreed with the second view as to the status of voluntary human shields, but asserted that the principle of proportionality will apply to them in a modified (more relaxed) way, since they have deliberately put themselves in harm's way in order to affect military operations.'[74]

The experts took the view that involuntary human shields included 'both those who have been compelled to stay at or in the vicinity of a lawful target, and those who do not know or lack the capacity to understand their situation, such as school children'.[75] There was agreement among the experts that involuntary human shields count as civilians in the proportionality evaluation. 'There was, however, disagreement as to whether the principle of proportionality will be applied to such a situation in the usual form, or whether it can be applied in the circumstances in a modified (more relaxed) way because the enemy has caused the situation by bringing the civilians in harm's way.'[76] If there is doubt as to the voluntary/involuntary status of the human shields, that doubt should be resolved in favour of increased protection for the shields, that is they should be assumed to be present involuntarily.[77] **4.086**

If the attacking party is using BCI or AB technology in connection with attacks and if the planner, commander or operator associated with the mission becomes aware of the presence of human shields in the vicinity of the target, that planner, commander or operator will have responsibilities in accordance with their respective role. Those responsibilities will be to ensure that the legally required precautions are taken in accordance with the level of protection of the shields that the state understands the law to prescribe. If an AB system is deciding on and undertaking attacks, it will be the AB system that must reliably and consistently discharge the same responsibility. If a person is **4.087**

73 AMW Manual, n.9, Rule 45, para.5.
74 AMW Manual, n.9, Rule 45, para.6.
75 AMW Manual, n.9, Rule 45, para.7.
76 AMW Manual, n.9, Rule 45, para.7.
77 AMW Manual, n.9, Rule 45, para.8.

monitoring the performance of the AB system, that person must be enabled to intervene and must actually do so if intervention becomes necessary to prevent an unlawful attack or one with an undesired outcome. Assuming that the state using an AB system to decide upon attacks interprets the law as explained in this section, compliance with this rule requires that the AB system must reliably and consistently:

1. detect that persons are in the vicinity of the military objective;
2. detect whether some or all of those persons are civilians;
3. distinguish between civilians who are human shields and those who are in the vicinity of the military objective for non-shielding reasons (civilians who are present for non-shielding reasons that do not amount to direct participation must count fully in the proportionality assessment);
4. distinguish between human shields that are present voluntarily and involuntarily;
5. if it cannot distinguish as required in point 4 above, treat any persons it identifies as human shields as being involuntarily present;
6. if both voluntary and involuntary human shields are present and it cannot distinguish between them, treat all human shields as involuntary; and
7. apply the proportionality and precaution rules in accordance with Articles 51(5)(b) and (8) and 57.

4.088 As an example, State A is involved in an armed conflict against State B. State A wishes to use a BCI-controlled missile system to attack a building that is used for military command, control and communications functions. A reconnaissance drone sends images showing the presence of civilians on the roof of the building. The imagery does not make it clear whether the civilians are present voluntarily or have been compelled to stand there. The commander of the unit that operates the missile system therefore assumes that the civilians are present involuntarily. State A adopts the view that the civilians count in the proportionality assessment but with a reduced value. The BCI facility is switched off while the expected civilian casualties are assessed and compared with the anticipated military advantage in destroying the building. That advantage is anticipated to be very high and the commander assesses that the expected collateral damage will not be excessive. Precautions are taken, to the extent feasible, to minimise civilian casualties. The commander authorises the attack, the BCI system is switched on, and the operator forms the thought or intent that will cause the missile to be fired.

4.9 CONSTANT CARE PRINCIPLE

The LOAC requires that precautions be taken by attackers and against the effects of attacks. The purpose of these essentially complementary precautions is to seek to ensure the protection of civilians and civilian objects. The attacking party[78] and the party in control of territory where attacks are liable to occur[79] each have their own precautionary obligations. If the party in control of the territory fails to take its precautions, that does not excuse the attacking party from complying with its required precautions.[80] If an attack results in excessive damage or injury to protected objects or persons, it is the circumstances that applied when the decision was made to proceed with the attack that are important. The action and inaction of both attackers and of parties in control of territory must be carefully considered before responsibility is allocated. **4.089**

The general rule under Article 57(1) of API states: 'In the conduct of military operations, constant care shall be taken to spare the civilian population, civilians and civilian objects.'[81] **4.090**

In the author's view, this reflects a customary principle which binds all states in connection with international and non-international armed conflicts. The principle means that all persons who are involved in the conduct of military operations, including but not limited to attacks, must take care, and that there is no time during the preparation and undertaking of such operations and attacks when the requirement to take care can be dispensed with.[82] **4.091**

Article 57(1) refers specifically to 'military operations'. The majority of other targeting law provisions in API refer equally specifically to attacks. If the negotiators of the treaty had intended Article 57(1) to apply only to attacks, they could easily have done so by using that word. They did not do so, and a military operation is clearly a different concept from an attack, although the former will of course include the latter. The API Commentary describes military operations as 'all movements and acts related to hostilities that are undertaken by armed forces'[83] which the author considers to be over-inclusive. For the purposes of this book, a military activity that is intended, or may be **4.092**

78 API, n.2, Art.57.
79 API, n.2, Art.58.
80 API, n.2, Art.51(8).
81 Customary Law Study, n.6, Rule 15; AMW Manual, n.9, Rule 30, the commentary to which notes that the same norms apply equally in all domains of warfare: land, sea, and air; commentary to Rule 30, para.2.
82 There are no exceptions to the duty to seek to spare the civilian population, civilians and civilian objects; AMW Manual, n.9, commentary to Rule 30, para.3.
83 API, n.2, commentary, para.1875.

expected, to have an adverse effect on the enemy not necessarily amounting to death, injury, damage or destruction, will constitute a military operation. That activity will therefore come within the Article 57(1) principle meaning that all persons who are involved in the preparation or conduct of such an activity must take care at all times to spare civilians and civilian objects.

4.093 The implications of this for planners of military BCI, AB and BBI operations are that they must exercise care in the preparation and subsequent refinement and confirmation of the plans, that is they must consider the extent to which civilians may be injured or killed and/or civilian objects may be damaged or destroyed, and they must, consistent with the accomplishment of the military purpose, plan the operation and adjust those plans in a way that is consistent with sparing civilians and civilian objects.

4.094 Commanders of military BCI, AB and BBI operations must satisfy themselves that care is taken at all times with the preparation and execution of each operation for which they are individually or jointly responsible with a view to sparing the civilian population.

4.095 Operators must, commensurate with their roles and responsibilities and so far as is practical, seek to ensure that BCI, AB or BBI systems that they are using will operate as intended, that is that the system is correctly set up, that it appears to be operating correctly, that any faults in its operation are promptly put right and so on. If the operator becomes aware that, for whatever reason, civilians will be exposed to greater risk than was notified to planners and commanders, this should, where possible, be notified to commanders.[84]

4.096 Planners, commanders and operators will need to assess whether the way in which the BCI, AB system or BBI has been set up, its interface with the weapon and the way in which data input is handled promote reliable, accurate and legally compliant operation of the weapon system, and thus the reliability, accuracy and lawfulness of the operation as a whole. If an alternative way of achieving the military purpose would give greater assurance that targeting law rules will be complied with, that alternative should generally be chosen.

4.097 The constant element in the care obligation means that the assessments discussed in this section must be repeated up to the point when no further revision or cancellation of the operation or attack is possible.

---

84 Consider Y Dinstein and A-W Dahl (eds), *Oslo Manual on Select Topics of the Law of Armed Conflict* (2020) (Oslo Manual), Rule 44, para.3.

The persons who are involved in the conduct of a BCI, AB or BBI military operation may not be limited to planners, commanders and operators. There are numerous individuals who have roles in the manufacture, design, supply, procurement, legal review and introduction into service of military capabilities. The issue to consider is which of these roles can properly be described as involvement in the conduct of the ensuing operations. Much will depend on how the system operates, on the role it fulfils, and in particular on the directness of the link between the individual's function and the subsequent military operation. Clearly, the manufacturer of a more traditional weapon system, such as a rifle or a general purpose bomb, cannot usually be described as involved in the subsequent decision to use it in connection with a particular attack. However, if, for example, the actions of a software designer determine not only what effect the weapon has on a target but also which specific targets the weapon engages, that might, depending perhaps on other factors, be seen as involvement by the designer in the subsequent operation. **4.098**

BBI technology will foreseeably be used in the military context to facilitate rapid decision-making and decision implementation where two or more individuals, who may include, inter alia, commanders, planners, subject matter specialists, advisers and operators are involved. In the targeting context, BBI may have positive legal implications by enabling rapid interaction where otherwise time pressures might preclude this. It will be important to ensure that the BBI is operating correctly throughout its periods of use, that all actors that should be contributing to a decision or interaction are, so far as is practical, connected, that all connected actors remain fully connected throughout, that all can transmit and receive and that the quest for speed of decision or action does not erode the quality of the process leading thereto. These are, the author suggests, the key factors relating to the use of BBIs in the taking of precautions, and these points will not therefore be repeated in the discussion of detailed precautions in section 4.11. **4.099**

4.10 APPLYING THE CONSTANT CARE PRINCIPLE

Where the military use of a BCI system is concerned, the position taken in this book is that those who design BCI systems to translate the thoughts of an operator into the actual operation of the weapon system are not involved in the conduct of the actual operation because it is the relevant operator who decides on the conduct of the operation. The system designers will have other responsibilities, for example under the weapon procurement contract, but their activities will not usually come within the Article 57(1) precautionary obligations. **4.100**

4.101 The same considerations apply to those who manufacture and supply the BCI systems, to those who procure such systems for use in the relevant kinds of operation or attack, and to those who specify the generic circumstances in which it is intended to use them. All such persons are similarly not involved in the conduct of the actual operation and are therefore also not included within the Article 57(1) obligations.

4.102 Persons who, before the state acquires the relevant weapon system, test the performance of the BCI systems to assess their suitability for employment in operations and attacks of the kind that are being contemplated, those who review the lawfulness of the employment of such systems in the intended circumstances of use, and those who decide on the procurement of the system are, in the author's view, also sufficiently removed from the decision to conduct an actual operation to be excluded from the Article 57(1) obligations.

4.103 Arguably, persons who transmit the limitations on the permitted manner and circumstances of use of the BCI weapon system to the units that will receive and use it, and those who train relevant personnel in the correct operation of such systems, are responsible for performing their duties properly, but will not, without more, have Article 57(1) responsibilities. The author would stress, however, that much will depend on the particularities of the specific BCI system and on how broadly states choose to interpret the notion of involvement in the decision to conduct military operations.

4.104 The author believes that, if AB technology is developed, involving the use of an AB to control a weapon system and to make decisions as to whether, where and when military operations, including attacks, should take place and as to the targets to be engaged, a broader selection of individuals is likely to be regarded as involved in the decision to undertake the ensuing military operations. These individuals will all have key roles in ensuring that the AB, as applied to the relevant weapon system, is appropriate for the task and is likely to operate in accordance with targeting law.[85]

4.105 The distinction here between BCIs and AB systems is crucial. The BCI is interpreting the action that the operator is wanting to take and is the instrumentality through which that wished-for action is translated into an actual act.

85 Consider the Oslo Manual observation that '[a]ll those involved in the conduct of operations, including attacks, using … highly automated weapon systems or autonomous weapons, are responsible for their respective roles and, commensurate with their involvement, have obligations to ensure that such operations are conducted in accordance with the applicable principles and rules of LOAC': Oslo Manual, ibid, Rule 44.

The operator, as formulator of their wish or intent, is, in principle, in control of the system.[86] Where AB systems are concerned, it is the AB that is controlling the system. It is the AB that is forming the wish or intent and which is then translating that wish or intent into subsequent action. Accordingly, the Article 57(1) duty to take constant care applies as follows.

The designers of such AB systems must exercise constant care to ensure that the system can only form a wish or intent that complies with targeting law constraints, meaning all of the limitations and constraints that are discussed in this chapter and in Chapter 5. This will be the duty of the designer if the designer is made aware of the intended application of the AB system to undertake military operations. It may be, however, that the AB system that is being designed is of a more generic character, that is that it is capable of application in a variety of uses, some of them, say, for commercial, consumer purposes and only one or a few linked to the conduct of hostilities. In the author's view, the designer's activity will only potentially come within Article 57(1) if it is made known to them at design stage that the system that is being developed is to be used for the directing of operations or the targeting of attacks in armed conflicts. **4.106**

The position of manufacturers and suppliers is rather different. A manufacturer or other person who supplies an AB weapon system to a state will clearly be aware of the purposes for which the system will foreseeably be employed. Indeed, it is likely that those intended or designed purposes will have been set forth in the marketing materials associated with the particular weapon system. Logically, by producing and selling a system that is designed to formulate a wish or intent to undertake an attack and that is also designed to translate that wish or intent into associated hostile action, the manufacturer and/or supplier are clearly persons who are involved in the subsequent decision to undertake a military operation or attack. There will, however, be those who object that the manufacturers and suppliers are too remote from such subsequent decisions and sometimes that will indeed be the case. **4.107**

The author wonders whether, with time, the creation and supply of such systems will be interpreted as necessarily involving a duty to do everything practically possible to ensure that the wishes or intents that the system generates **4.108**

86 If the operator is no longer in control of the system, complex issues may arise depending upon whether the operator was, at the material time, aware of the loss of control, whether the operator was under pressure, say from a commander, to proceed notwithstanding the loss of control, whether available information suggested the operation would be satisfactory despite the loss of control, the degree to which, or time period during which, control is lost and so on.

can only ever be translated into lawful action. This will require the careful preparation of a 'legal governor' (to borrow the language applied by Ron Arkin).[87] For these purposes, the legal governor must take the form of an absolute constrainer, perhaps in the form of an immutable filter, that considers the wishes and intents, that assesses the circumstances that are applying at the relevant time, that reflects all of the principles and rules of targeting law (and indeed of other applicable law such as the law of neutrality) and that will only permit lawful action pursuant to those wishes or intents. This 'legal governor' will need to be robust against enemy and third-party interference or manipulation, will need to be extensively tested to prove its correct performance in a full selection of the intended circumstances of system use and will have to be demonstrably free from manufacture-level faults and design failings.

4.109 Those who procure AB weapon systems for use by a state, who specify the generic circumstances and manner of use of the weapon system by that state, who test the AB weapon system for that state, who conduct the weapon review of such a system and who transmit the resulting guidance on use to the ultimate military users of the system all have key responsibilities. The Oslo Manual explains that '[a]ll those involved in the conduct of operations, including attacks ... are responsible for their respective roles and, commensurate with their involvement, have obligations to ensure that such operations are conducted in accordance with the applicable principles and rules of LOAC'.[88] The Commentary to that Rule recognises that 'numerous individuals may have various roles that may be relevant to the conduct of an ... operation' and, in the ensuing list, mention is made of 'those who prepared the software'.[89] In the author's view, those relevant roles, and thus the responsibility reflected in the Rule, will extend certainly to system designers, manufacturers and suppliers subject to the caveat mentioned earlier, but also to those whose roles are listed earlier in the present paragraph. Indeed, the various individuals mentioned in this paragraph will tend to be mutually dependent on each other in the sense that the performance of each role will depend on proper performance of their roles by the other actors. Thus, only if the testing of the system is properly undertaken can the legal reviewer correctly identify the limitations on lawful use, but only if the intended circumstances of use are correctly transmitted to the testers can suitable tests be organised, and only if the results of those tests are accurately reflected in the legal review can the correct limitations on use be

---

87 R C Arkin and others, *An Ethical Governor for Constraining Legal Action in an Autonomous System*, CSE Technical Reports (2009), 163.

88 Oslo Manual, n.84, Rule 44.

89 Oslo Manual, n.84, para.2 of the commentary to Rule 44.

made available by the responsible military authorities to the military units that will ultimately be tasked with employing the AB weapon system. The mutual dependencies are numerous. For the present purposes, it suffices to note that the constant care obligation, when applied to AB weapon systems, extends beyond commanders and operators to certain individuals who can, perhaps, be summarised as the members of the 'supply chain'.

4.11 DETAILED PRECAUTIONS IN ATTACK

Paragraph (2) of Article 57 requires that '[w]ith respect to attacks, the following precautions shall be taken:' This wording is important. It shows that the following rules apply specifically to attacks,[90] and that paragraph (2)'s precautions are obligatory, but it leaves open the question of who must take those precautions, or indeed whether the precautions must be taken by a human operator as opposed to by some other phenomenon or machine. What is clear is that the law requires that the precautions be taken.[91] **4.110**

The author believes that the six precautionary rules that are referred to in this section reflect customary law. While it is appreciated that the US has concerns with regard to the sixth rule[92] to the extent that each rule is essential to compliance with the precautionary principle in Article 57(1), it derives its customary status from that principle. **4.111**

The six precautionary rules will be discussed in turn, in each case dealing first with BCI operations and thereafter with the use of an AB technology. It is hoped that this approach will make the relevant points clear. **4.112**

'[T]hose who plan or decide upon an attack' are the persons who are obliged to take the first three precautions in Article 57(2). 'Those' has traditionally been interpreted as applying to human beings.[93] If a BCI system is being used to translate the wish or intent of the operator into the act that amounts to an attack, it will be the operator who is deciding upon the attack and who is therefore tasked by Article 57(2) with taking the three precautions. As to planning, if a person is planning operations in which attacks employing BCI **4.113**

90 Which are defined in API, n.2, Art.49(1) as 'acts of violence against the adversary, whether in offence or defence'.

91 As to the relationship between the precautionary rules, distinction and discrimination, consider Dill, n.51, 73–6.

92 Note, however, US DoD Manual, n.3, paras 5.11.7 and 5.11.7.1.

93 Consider API Commentary, n.42, para.2197.

technologies are going to form an integral part, or in which such operations may reasonably be expected to form such a part, that planner and the BCI operator must both undertake the first three precautions.

4.114 Where AB technologies are concerned, it is the AB that will be deciding what or who is to be attacked, which weapon is to be used (if there is a choice), how the attack is to be undertaken, when the attack is to take place and so on. The legal requirement is that the AB system, and the way in which the AB mission is configured, shall be such that the first three precautions can in fact be applied. This might, for example, involve decisions by the AB system or by commanders and/or operators in advance of the commencement of the mission. Much will depend on the proven capabilities of the AB system. If it is shown that the AB system will reliably apply precautions 1, 2 and 3 to an acceptable standard, this may be sufficient to permit reliance on the AB system where precautions 1, 2 and 3 are concerned. If reliable performance of those requirements in the relevant circumstances of use cannot be shown, human performance of the specified precautions in advance of the mission is likely to be necessary. If human action in advance of the mission would also not result in the reliable performance of the precautionary task, some other operational method should be chosen.

4.11.1 The first detailed precaution

4.115 The first precautionary rule requires those who plan or decide upon attacks to:

> do everything feasible to verify that the objectives to be attacked are neither civilians nor civilian objects and are not subject to special protection but are military objectives within the meaning of paragraph 2 of Article 52 and that it is not prohibited by the provisions of this Protocol to attack them;[94]

4.116 Objects and persons that are 'subject to special protection' are discussed in Chapter 5. The word 'feasible' has been interpreted as meaning what is practicable or practically possible, taking into account of all circumstances ruling at the time, including humanitarian and military considerations.[95]

---

94 API, n.2, Art.57(2)(a)(i) and see Customary Law Study, n.6, Rule 16. In a statement that it made when becoming party to API, the UK interpreted 'feasible' 'to mean that which is practicable or practically possible, taking into account all circumstances ruling at the time, including humanitarian and military considerations'; statement (b) made on ratification of API on 28 January 1998. Similar statements were made by France, Germany and Canada.

95 Statement (b) made by the UK on ratification of API. Note, W Heintschel von Heinegg and P Dreist, 'The 2009 Kunduz Air Attack: The Decision of the Federal Prosecutor-General on the Dismissal of Criminal Proceedings Against Members of the German Armed Forces' (2009) 53(1) *German Yearbook of International Law* 38–9.

The obligation is to do everything that is practicable or practically possible to verify. This does not imply a duty to achieve certainty. It simply means doing what one can to be as sure as possible.[96] Enemy deception operations, the speed of modern hostilities and other factors may affect what precautions it is possible to take to verify the status of the target as a military objective. The dynamic nature of the battlespace may also affect the currency, and thus the reliability of the data on which military objective assessments are based, and the decision-maker may be unaware that the data on which decisions are being based have become unreliable.[97] Dinstein describes the overall precautions requirement as 'due diligence and acting in good faith', which, in the author's view, is an admirably succinct and accurate clarification of what is required, a clarification that also applies to the requirements of modern high-speed warfare. **4.117**

As this precautionary rule is addressed to those who plan or decide upon the attack, where attacks are pre-planned, both the planners and those executing the attack must take precautions to verify that it is a lawful target. The operational planning team will verify that the object(s) or person(s) to be targeted are military objectives at the time when the plans are drawn up. If the attack is to be undertaken using a BCI-enabled weapon system, the operator whose thought process or intent will initiate the attack must, prior to initiation, verify or receive information that verifies the status of the target(s) as military objective(s). If AB technology is to be employed to decide upon the attack, and if a human operator cannot fulfil these requirements in advance of the mission, the AB system will need to fulfil the following requirements: **4.118**

1. Its decision-making system must be programmed to appreciate the distinction between military objectives and persons/objects that are protected by the law.
2. The decision-making system must actually make that distinction reliably and consistently in respect of both persons and objects.
3. It must reliably and consistently refrain from making protected persons/objects the object of attack. This must have been demonstrated in tests that accurately replicate the intended circumstances of use.
4. It must receive and consider all available information, including information from sources other than its own sensors, before making that judgment.

96 Tallinn Manual 2.0, n.43, Rule 115, para.4.

97 Bothe, Partsch and Solf, n.64, 279 and F Green, Remarks in ASIL Proceedings, 'Implementing Limitations on the Use of Force: The Doctrine of Proportionality and Necessity' (1992) 62, 66, quoting General Schwarzkopf.

4.119 The information that will need to be made available to the operator of the BCI system, or that will need to be fed into the AB technology that controls the mission, will include the target co-ordinates, the image of the target (particularly in the case of an attack using AB technology incorporating the use of televisual sensors), the timing of the attack, the weapon to be used (there may be no choice), the collateral damage estimate and the image of the area surrounding the target as reviewed by the planners. Complying with the first precautionary rule will also require that the operator of the BCI-enabled weapon system is instructed not to develop the thought process that will initiate the attack if any change is detected to the target or to the area surrounding the target indicating: that the target is no longer a military objective; that the target is subject to special protection (as to which see Chapter 5); or that the attack will be indiscriminate (see sections 4.6 and 4.7).

4.120 There is no requirement for an attacker to expose their own forces to enhanced risk in order to reduce the risk to civilians below a level that complies with the discrimination rule.[98] Moreover, there is no obligation to pre-plan attacks. In the author's view, the military context will be among the factors that determine whether particular precautions are practically possible, and thus feasible.

4.11.2 The second detailed precaution

4.121 The second precautionary rule requires that those who plan or decide upon attacks:

> take all feasible precautions in the choice of means and methods of attack with a view to avoiding, and in any event to minimizing, incidental loss of civilian life, injury to civilians and damage to civilian objects;[99]

4.122 It should be made clear as a matter of law that the expectation that collateral damage (death or injury to civilians and/or damage to civilian objects) will occur does not necessarily render an attack unlawful. This rule merely requires that everything possible be done to either avoid collateral damage or, at least, keep it to a minimum. This implies that the operator of a BCI-enabled weapon

---

98 See H E Shamash, 'How Much is Too Much? An Examination of the Principle of *Jus in Bello* Proportionality' (2005–6) 2 IDFLR 103, 125; M Roscini, 'Targeting and Contemporary Aerial Bombardment' (2005) 54 ICLQ 411, 416; and E Cannizzaro, 'Contextualising Proportionality: *Jus ad Bellum* and *Jus in Bello* in the Lebanese War' (2000) 864 IRRC 779, 789. Note, however, the Australian statement on ratification of API on 21 June 1991, referring to Arts 51(5)(b) and 57(2)(a)(iii), that 'the term "military advantage" involves a variety of considerations including the security of attacking forces'. See also the US DoD Manual, n.3, para.5.2.3.2.

99 API, n.2, Art.57(2)(a)(ii) and see Customary Law Study, n.6, Rule 17.

system must adopt the method of attack which is most likely to achieve that outcome. That in turn suggests that such an operator must receive the information that will enable them to achieve that outcome. This will include details of the weapon systems that are available to achieve the desired military purpose and the implications of the employment of each of them for the expected incidental death/injuries to civilians and damage to civilian objects. The BCI operator must then be empowered to choose the option that minimises collateral damage.

If an AB system is to be employed for the attack, and if a human operator cannot fulfil these requirements in advance of the mission, the AB must reliably and consistently: 4.123

1. Be aware of the alternative weapon systems that are available for the attack. These will not necessarily be limited to the weapon systems controlled by the AB system.
2. Evaluate the target, its location, the persons and objects in the vicinity, and the characteristics of each of the weapons available to the commander.
3. Assess the collateral damage that is to be expected from the use of each of the alternative weapon systems against the chosen target to achieve the desired military purpose.
4. Assess the angle of attack, fuse setting, altitude of weapon release, timing of attack (if this can be varied),[100] and guidance and weapon control arrangements that will achieve the desired military purpose while keeping collateral damage to a minimum. This will also involve deciding which specific object or part of an object should be made the focus of the attack (if that will affect the danger posed to civilians and/or civilian objects), whether the attack should use a ground- or air-mounted platform, the explosive fill of the munitions to be used, and other relevant factors.
5. Choose the weapon system that avoids or minimises collateral damage.
6. Consider whether there is an alternative method of attack that would achieve the same military purpose while avoiding or minimising collateral damage. This may involve choosing between, for example, air attack using a manned or unmanned aircraft, a special forces ground attack operation, or artillery fire.
7. If there is an appropriate alternative method, choose that alternative method.

It must be emphasised that the rule only requires precautions that are feasible, that is that are practicable or practically possible taking military and humanitarian interests into consideration. The API Commentary notes that 'circumstances of combat and the control of airspace may render it more difficult to 4.124

---

100 Depending on the circumstances, there may be other aspects of the attack that the AB system will need to address.

observe this rule'.[101] While the use of precision weapon systems is sometimes necessary if collateral damage is to be minimised, there is no targeting law rule that specifically mandates their employment. Locating a tank or artillery piece near a civilian object does not immunise that military objective from being attacked. Indeed, it may be lawful to use a non-precision weapon against such an objective if a limited stock of precision weapons is required for use against more challenging targets.

4.11.3 The third detailed precaution

4.125 The third precautionary rule requires that those who plan or decide upon attacks:

> refrain from deciding to launch any attack which may be expected to cause incidental loss of civilian life, injury to civilians, damage to civilian objects, or a combination thereof, which would be excessive in relation to the concrete and direct military advantage anticipated;[102]

4.126 The feasibility aspect that we have noted in relation to sections 4.11.1 and 4.11.2 does not apply to this rule. It is an absolute rule and practicability issues do not arise. Operators that will employ BCI-enabled weapons must therefore be appropriately briefed, and AB weapon systems must be so set up that the rule will always be applied.

4.127 The timing of the application of the rule is important. It applies when the decision to undertake the attack is being made. The planning process may not necessarily involve a decision actually to undertake the attack. Rather, planning may simply involve the development of options. Whenever an actual decision is to be made that an attack will take place, the rule will apply. Accordingly, if an AB system is used to develop attack options, that will not be regarded as making a decision to launch an attack. If, by contrast, an AB system is developed which is designed to develop those attack options, to select which among them is the preferred option and then to select that option for implementation, this rule will apply to such a process. Accordingly, such an AB system will need consistently and reliably to do the following:

1. Distinguish between civilians and combatants.
2. Distinguish between civilians who are, and who are not, taking a direct part in the hostilities. (The AB system may have been programmed or developed to

101 API Commentary, n.42, para.2200.

102 API, n.2, Art.57(2)(a)(iii) and consider Customary Law Study, n.6, Rule 18.

identify certain acts as constituting DPH thus rendering the actor liable to be attacked. If so, does it perform that function reliably and consistently? If the AB system is unable to recognise activities as constituting direct participation, it should be programmed or developed to regard the relevant actor as a peaceable civilian. Alternatively, it should be so configured that, in doubtful cases, the issue will be referred to human decision-making.)

3. Distinguish between objects that are military objectives and those which are not. (If the AB system is able, reliably and consistently, to identify certain activities as having the effect of rendering an otherwise civilian object a military objective, it would be appropriate for it to treat that object as a military objective in applying the proportionality rule. If, however, some uses of an object cannot be reliably categorised by the AB system in a correct manner, it should be programmed or developed to grant civilian object protection as the default setting.)
4. Assess (probably by quantification) the death and injury that the chosen method of attack may be expected to cause to peaceable civilians and the damage that is to be expected to civilian objects.
5. Assess the military advantage that the successful attack of the intended target is anticipated to produce in the relevant circumstances. (This will probably involve assessing the degree and nature of the anticipated military advantage. Military advantage is concrete and direct if it is 'substantial and relatively close'.[103] It will not be concrete and direct if it is speculative, theoretical or if it only accrues as an indirect consequence of the attack. The AB system will need to reflect this.)
6. Compare the values under points 4 and 5 above.
7. Refrain from deciding to undertake the attack if point 4 would be excessive in relation to point 5.

The reference to the AB system performing these tasks consistently and reliably reflects the need that the performance of that system must have been the subject of extensive (perhaps exhaustive would be a better word), realistic testing in order to verify not just that the AB system is capable of undertaking each of these discrete tasks, but that it will actually do so in all of the intended circumstances and with reference to all of the kinds of attack in which it is intended to be employed. **4.128**

The rule, and the proportionality assessment that it requires, does not set forth an arithmetical formula for assessing whether the death and/or injury to civilians and/or damage to civilian objects (that is collateral damage) is going to be excessive in relation to anticipated military advantage. There are no established units for the measurement of collateral damage and military advantage, and **4.129**

103 API Commentary, n.42, para.2209. Bothe interprets 'concrete' as specific and perceptible to the senses while 'direct' is taken to mean without necessitating any intervening agency: Bothe, Partsch and Solf, n.64, 365.

those two phenomena are fundamentally different in nature anyway.[104] There is also the point that the cultural background of a commander is bound to affect, to a degree, that commander's evaluation of a specific scenario.

4.130 The generally accepted understanding is that judgement is required and that the required standard of judgement is that of the reasonable military commander.[105] This, therefore, is the method of assessment that the AB system must reliably and consistently apply when undertaking the task identified under points 6 and 7 above. The task of software developers, system designers and manufacturers is to produce such a decision-making capability and the task for system testers is to ensure that the AB fulfils the task to an acceptable standard of accuracy, reliability and consistency. The reasonableness standard suggests that the system will not need to achieve perfection in its decision-making – rather, the requirement is that the decisions that the system makes should be within the scope of decisions that a reasonable commander might be expected to make in the given circumstances.

4.131 This rule is concerned with the collateral damage that is the incidental consequence of an attack that is directed at a lawful target, that is an object that is a military objective, combatants or civilians taking a direct part in the hostilities. The obligation to verify that the object of the attack is a lawful target is reflected in the first detailed rule (discussed in section 4.11.1).

4.11.4 The fourth detailed precaution

4.132 The fourth precautionary rule requires:

> an attack shall be cancelled or suspended if it becomes apparent that the objective is not a military one or is subject to special protection or that the attack may be expected to cause incidental loss of civilian life, injury to civilians, damage to civilian objects, or a combination thereof, which would be excessive in relation to the concrete and direct military advantage anticipated;[106]

4.133 This rule is not limited to those who plan or decide upon attacks. It therefore applies to all those who have a role in the planning, decision-making or conduct of attacks. The rule also does not include the feasibility caveat. It is therefore an absolute rule. This rule is dealing with the situation in which an

---

104 Consider Cannizzaro, n.98, 789.

105 Final Report, n.64, para.50 states: 'Although there will be room for argument, there will be many cases where reasonable military commanders will agree that the injury to non-combatants or the damage to civilian objects was clearly disproportionate to the military advantage gained.'

106 API, n.2 Art.57(2)(b) and note Customary Law Study, n.6, Rule 19.

attack has previously been planned or in which the attack process may already have begun.[107] The requirement is quite straightforward. It will be necessary for the AB system and/or other systems or persons to continue to monitor the planned target and the area surrounding it within which damage or injury can be expected given the nature of the weapon it is intended to use and the planned method of using that weapon. If it becomes clear that any of the circumstances set forth in the rule apply, the attack must be cancelled or suspended. The three circumstances are: that the object of the attack ceases to be a lawful target, that the target has special protection, or that the proportionality rule would be breached.

If an AB system is to be used to decide upon attacks, it will be necessary for that system and/or for other systems or persons: **4.134**

1. to continue to monitor the target to ensure that the target has not ceased to be a lawful target;
2. to continue to monitor the target to ensure that it has not become specially protected (the point here is that it might become clear, for example, that the target building where some weapons are being stored is being used as a medical facility such that the special warning and other special precautions referred to in Chapter 5 are required before an attack can be considered);
3. to continue to monitor the target to ensure that the planned attack will not breach the proportionality rule; and
4. to cancel or at least to suspend the attack if information received by the sensors aboard the weapon platform, or information from other sources, indicates that any of the circumstances referred to in points 1, 2 or 3 will apply.

Persons and objects may cease to be lawful targets for a variety of reasons. Civilians who were directly participating in the hostilities may no longer be doing so; targeted persons or objects may now be entitled to special protection;[108] an object may no longer be used for military purposes; an object that the enemy intended to use for military purposes may no longer be intended for such use; a location may no longer have military value; combatants or directly participating civilians that it was intended to attack may have been rendered *hors de combat*. An AB system that is making attack decisions **4.135**

107 For cases when disproportionate attacks have been cancelled consider: C Greenwood, 'Customary International Law and the First Geneva Protocol of 1977 in the Gulf Conflict', in P Rowe (ed), *The Gulf War 1990–91 in International and English Law* (Routledge, 1993), 83; 'Israel Releases Goldstone Response', *HonestReporting*, 1 February 2010, available at http://honestreporting.com/israel-releases-goldstone-response-2/, 97.

108 For example, if an object that was previously being used to accommodate able-bodied troops is now being used as a field hospital.

must reliably and consistently cancel or suspend the attack decision if any of these circumstances arise.

4.136 If a BCI is being used in connection with attacks, it will be necessary for the operator, and for the commander of such a mission, to be aware of any relevant changes in the circumstances of the target and to be in a position to cancel or suspend any attack decision. This implies the need for a constant updating of relevant information from all sources to the BCI operator and commander. It also implies that the operator, and perhaps the commander, should have the ability to call off the attack at any time when it is practical to do so after the operator has transmitted the intent to attack to the weapon system and before the attack takes place. What is practical in this respect will depend on the nature of the weapon, on how the control mechanisms are structured, and on the circumstances of the operation among other things.

4.137 The important question, which arises in connection with both AB-enabled attacks and attacks involving BCI weapons, is at what point does the obligation to cancel or suspend cease to apply? As noted in the previous paragraph, the nature of the control mechanisms may be a significant factor here. Imagine, for example, that an AB system decides to fire an intercontinental ballistic missile at a target with a transit time from the launch pad to the target of approximately 30 minutes. During that time a large column of civilian refugees approaches the target area. Space-based sensors operated by the attacking state detect these refugees for the first time while the missile is transiting to target. If the missile is not equipped with an abort or divert facility, the lawfulness of the attack will be judged by reference to the information available to the decision-maker, that is the AB system, at the time when the decision was made to launch the missile. However, if, for example, the operator has ongoing connectivity with the missile during transit to target and if the missile is equipped with such an abort or divert capability, the obligation to activate that facility would arise when the operator receives the relevant information. This raises the following questions in relation to an AB-enabled system:

1. Will there be a significant time gap between launch and detonation?
2. Will the AB system continue to observe the target area throughout the period of transit to target?
3. If not, will other sensors do so?
4. Will the AB system have ongoing control of the weapon system during transit to target, and will the weapon system be equipped with an abort/divert/disarm facility?
5. Will the AB system reliably and consistently activate the abort/divert/disarm facility when circumstances require this?

There may be no abort/divert/disarm facility and/or no sensor to detect changes in the target area during a substantial transit period from launch to target. Equally, the AB system may not be programmed to respond to such changes or may not be programmed to abort/divert/disarm having so responded. If this is the case, it will be for the weapon reviewer to consider whether the AB weapon system is consistent with the application of this detailed precautionary rule and, indeed, with the obligation to take constant care to spare civilians and civilian objects. **4.138**

If a BCI weapon is being employed, the human operator of the weapon system, along with the commander, will be the agencies with responsibility for ensuring that the obligation set forth in this rule is complied with. The BCI operator will therefore have the responsibility for intervening, to the extent that it is practically possible in the circumstances to do so, in order to abort/divert/disarm the weapon if the circumstances in the target area or in relation to the target change in any of the ways discussed earlier in this section. It seems to the author that, if technically highly sophisticated systems of the AB and BCI variety are to be developed and employed in the use of weapons, it is only reasonable to expect that equally sophisticated technology be employed to cancel or suspend attacks when it is appropriate to do so, and to detect when such situations are arising. **4.139**

4.11.5 The fifth detailed precaution

The fifth precautionary rule requires: **4.140**

> effective advance warning shall be given of attacks which may affect the civilian population, unless circumstances do not permit.[109]

The word 'affect' is not defined but is widely recognised as referring to death or injury among the civilians as opposed to mere annoyance, inconvenience, fear or stress.[110] A warning may be somewhat general in nature and does not have to specify the time and place of a planned attack.[111] **4.141**

The effectiveness requirement implies that the warning must be given in a language or manner that is understood by the persons to whom it is being directed. It may be difficult to achieve translation into local language(s), in which case the appropriate action might be communicated effectively by means **4.142**

---

109 API, n.2, Art.57(2)(c); Customary Law Study, n.6, Rule 20 and US DoD Manual, n.3, para.5.11.5.

110 Consider Tallinn Manual 2.0, n.43, para.4

111 US DoD Manual, n.3, para.5.11.5.2.

of drawings. The warning must be designed to reach those who are likely to be endangered by the planned attack.[112] The media to be selected should, again, be designed to achieve effective communication to the persons liable to be affected by the planned attack. Relevant media may include radio and/or television transmissions, posts on social media, the dropping of leaflets from the air, communications through a humanitarian organisation that is active in the area, or even communication through the Protecting Powers.[113] The measures that are appropriate will depend on the circumstances.[114]

4.143 The rule only requires the giving of a warning if the civilian population may be affected.[115]

4.144 In the case of a BCI-enabled attack, the human operator of the BCI weapon system must consider all available information before making a determination as to whether a warning is required. That determination, and the warning action that is decided upon, must take place before the operator's thought is translated by the BCI into the commencement of the attack. Irrespective of whether a warning is given, all other required precautions in attack must be taken.[116]

4.145 An AB system that is being used to decide upon and then execute attacks must exercise judgement to determine whether civilians may be killed or injured as a result of the planned attack. If it determines that that is possible, it must formulate a warning in appropriate terms, must communicate the warning to the potentially affected persons using appropriate media, and must give sufficient time for the appropriate action to be taken by the warned civilians. An operator of a BCI-enabled weapon system and the commander of such an operation will be responsible for making the same assessments and decisions. In practical terms, it is likely that the BCI will need to be switched off while this is taking

---

112 Note, AMW Manual, n.9, Rule 37 and commentary; UK Manual, n.3, para.5.32.8. For a comprehensive discussion of the topic, see P S Baruch and N Nauman, 'Warning Civilians Prior to Attack under International Law – Theory and Practice' (2011) 87 *International Law Studies* 359.

113 A Protecting Power is a State that is not involved in the conflict and that has been designated by a party to the conflict and has been accepted by the enemy party and has agreed to carry out the functions assigned to a Protecting Power under the law of armed conflict; see ICRC How does law protect in war, Chapter 13, IV.1 available at https://casebook.icrc.org/law/implementation-mechanisms#iv_1.

114 'The purpose of a warning is to facilitate the protection of the civilian population so that civilians and the authorities in control of the civilian population can take measures to reduce the risk that civilians will be harmed by military operations … a warning should be designed to accomplish this purpose to the extent feasible': US DoD Manual, n.3, para.5.11.5.2.

115 See for example Heintschel von Heinegg and Dreist, n.95, 21.

116 AMW Manual, n.9 Rule 37, para.16.

place and should only be activated after the appropriate period following the warning has expired.

The location of an attack may be such that the civilian population will not be affected by it. Attacks in remote, unpopulated or depopulated locations are examples of this. However, populations move during armed conflicts, and areas may become populated if groups of people are, for example, fleeing from the hostilities in a nearby place.[117] **4.146**

A warning is only required if the circumstances, including the military circumstances, permit. This means that if an AB system is deciding upon attacks, that AB system must assess whether the circumstances, including the military and humanitarian circumstances, permit the giving of a warning. If, for example, the AB system has decided that a surprise attack against the enemy from a direction that the enemy is unlikely to expect is what is required, a warning will frustrate the military purpose of the attack in which case the warning is not required. The issue is whether the AB system will be able to detect 1. what the purpose of the attack is, 2. that that purpose would be frustrated by the giving of a warning, and 3. that because of this a warning does not have to be given even though civilians are liable to be killed or injured as a result of the attack. It may be that, in advance of the initiation of the mission, whether it involves an AB system or a BCI-enabled capability, warning arrangements that will satisfy the rule can be made by or on behalf of the mission commander.[118] **4.147**

4.11.6 The sixth detailed precaution

The sixth precautionary rule requires: **4.148**

> When a choice is possible between several military objectives for obtaining a similar military advantage, the objective to be selected shall be that the attack on which may be expected to cause the least danger to civilian lives and to civilian objects.[119]

This rule becomes relevant if more than one military objective can be attacked in order to achieve a specific military purpose. However, the rule only applies if the military benefit to be derived from attacking the alternative military objectives is similar. In those circumstances, the obligation is to choose the **4.149**

---

117 Note, R Geiss and M Siegrist, 'Has the Armed Conflict in Afghanistan Affected the Rules on the Conduct of Hostilities?' (2011) 881 IRRC 11, 39, where it is suggested that it is only if the possibility can be ruled out that the obligation, subject to the circumstances, does not arise.

118 As to the customary status of the rule as to warnings, see AMW Manual, n.9, Rule 37, para.2 basing that view on the Hague Regulations, 1907, n.10.

119 API, n.2, Art.57(2)(c) and Customary Law Study, n.6, Rule 21 and associated commentary.

objective the attack of which poses the least danger to civilians. This rule seems to be a logical development of the constant care principle in Article 57(1) of API in the sense that breaching the rule would be inconsistent with compliance with that principle. The US objects to the API wording. In the US view, the attacker must not be prevented from pursuing every military advantage they believe warrants pursuit, and must be permitted to attack an objective involving higher civilian risk if the objective affords a greater likelihood of achieving the military advantage.[120] The issue raised by the US DoD *Law of War Manual* is all about whether enhanced risk to own or allied forces is a factor to be taken into account when determining the degree of military advantage to be anticipated from an attack. The key point in the Article 57(3) wording, however, is that the military advantage arising from the alternative targets must be similar for the rule to apply. Yoram Dinstein acknowledges that 'the [US] proposition is often contested (at least in part)',[121] but concludes that 'force protection is a valid concern in determining the military advantage of an attack'. He suggests that '[w]hat is called for is a reasonable "allocation of risk" between the attacker's military personnel and the collateral damage to civilians/civilian objects'.[122] The position taken in this book is that, in principle, the risk to own or allied forces is indeed a valid consideration in determining, in the context of the present rule, whether the military advantage to be achieved from attacking the alternative military objectives is indeed similar. However, reasonableness must be applied. This means that if there is a trifling difference in the degree of risk to attacking forces but a significant difference in the danger to civilians/civilian objects, the rule should be applied so as to favour the attack of the military objective that poses the least danger to civilians/civilian objects.

4.150 If a BCI system is being used so that the thought or intent of the BCI operator activates an associated weapon to undertake an attack, it will be necessary for the thoughts or intent of the operator to be incapable of activating the weapon while this, and the other detailed precautions, are being applied. This is likely to be achieved simply by switching off the system. It will be for the operator, linked supporting staff and/or the commander to consider the rule, and the five issues listed below, and when the responsible individuals are satisfied

---

120 At para.5.11.7, the US DoD Manual, n.3, cites similar wording to API, n.2, Art.57(3) but uses the wording 'provided all other factors are equal'.

121 R Geiss, 'The Principle of Proportionality: Force Protection as a Military Advantage' (2012) 45 IsLR 71–89.

122 Dinstein, n.39, 193 citing B L Bengs, 'Legal Constraints Upon the Use of a Tactical Nuclear Weapon Against the Natanz Nuclear Facility in Iran' (2008) 40 GWILR 323, 369.

that the constant care principle and the detailed precautionary rules have been complied with, the BCI-enabled attack can proceed.

If an AB weapon system is deciding between alternative targets of attack: **4.151**

1. Will it detect that there are, in fact, alternative targets that will yield the intended military advantage?
2. Will it evaluate the military advantage that attacking each of the alternative targets will yield?
3. Will it detect, reliably and consistently, that each target is a military objective, that is a lawful target?
4. Will it, reliably and consistently, assess the risk to civilians and civilian objects posed by each of the alternative attacks and, to the extent discussed above, the risk to own or allied forces associated with the attack of each alternative target?
5. Will it compare the advantages and risks and reliably and consistently apply the 'reasonable allocation of risk' discussed earlier in this section?

4.12 PRECAUTIONS AGAINST THE EFFECTS OF ATTACKS

Article 58 of API prescribes precautions that must be taken by those who control territory where attacks are likely to occur. The author takes the view that these are customary law obligations[123] which bind all states in international armed conflicts. Applying the precautions discussed in this section will involve human decision-making by military commanders, officials and others who are responsible for the government and administration of the relevant territory. **4.152**

Article 58 states the following: **4.153**

> The parties to the conflict shall, to the maximum extent feasible:
>
> (a) without prejudice to article 49 of the Fourth Convention, endeavour to remove the civilian population, individual civilians and civilian objects under their control from the vicinity of military objectives;
> (b) avoid locating military objectives within or near densely populated areas;
> (c) take the other necessary precautions to protect the civilian population, individual civilians and civilian objects under their control against the dangers resulting from military operations.[124]

123 Dinstein, n.39, 199.

124 See Customary Law Study, n.6, Rules 22 to 24; US DoD Manual, n.3, para.5.14 and as to particular measures, see paras 5.14.1, 5.14.2 and 5.14.3. More detailed precautionary measures are discussed in the ensuing subparas.

4.154 It is clear that all of the parties to an international armed conflict must take the three listed precautions. The words 'to the maximum extent feasible' indicate that the three listed obligations must be complied with to the extent that it is practicable to do so, taking into account humanitarian and military considerations.[125]

4.155 Taking the required precautions in order, precaution (a) is stated to be 'without prejudice to Article 49 of the Fourth Convention'. Article 49 prohibits '[i]ndividual or mass forcible transfers, as well as deportations of protected persons from occupied territory to the territory of the Occupying Power or to that of any other country' irrespective of the motive.[126] Evacuations are permitted if the security of the population or imperative military reasons so require.[127] If it can be avoided, such evacuation must not, however, take the protected persons outside the occupied territory and the persons concerned must be returned home as soon as the relevant hostilities end.[128] There are additional safeguarding provisions that apply to such transfers. In addition, the occupying power 'shall not deport or transfer parts of its own civilian population into the territory it occupies'.[129]

4.156 Subject to these Convention rules, the parties to the conflict must try to move the civilians and civilian objects that they control away from military objectives.

4.157 There is an evident link between precaution (a) and precaution (b) which addresses both permanent and movable military objectives. Accordingly, military barracks, military stores and ammunition, tanks and artillery pieces, concentrations of armed forces personnel, military helicopters and vehicles, military communications equipment, military radar systems (mobile or

125 Consider statement (b), UK statement on ratification of API on 28 January 1998; Statement 3 made by Belgium on ratification of API on 12 December 1977; Statement E by Canada on ratification of API on 12 December 1977; Statement B by Italy on ratification of API on 12 December 1977; Statement 2 by Germany on ratification of API on 23 December 1977; and Statement 6 by Ireland on ratification of API on 12 December 1977. The API Commentary notes that the use of 'feasible' illustrates the fact that no one can be required to do the impossible. As Yoram Dinstein notes, some intermingling of civilians and civilian objects with military objectives is going to be almost inevitable; Dinstein, n.39, 199; and the author would add that the practical ability of the party in control of territory to achieve separation such as to provide effective protection to civilians and civilian objects may well be limited.

126 GCIV, n.71, Art.49(1).

127 GCIV, n.71, Art.49(2), first sentence. Consider, for example, extensive evacuations undertaken in the UK and on continental Europe of children and other civilians from areas that were likely to be the focus of attacks during the Second World War.

128 GCIV, n.71, Art.49(2), sentences 2 and 3.

129 GCIV, n.71, Art.49(5) and (6).

otherwise), military weapon systems of all kinds, and all other persons and objects classed as military objectives must, as far as possible, be kept away from densely populated areas.[130] While from a practical point of view, such precautions should be considered during the transition to armed conflict, the legal obligation only applies once an armed conflict is underway.

Precaution (c) is, in a sense, the catch-all provision which obliges parties to an armed conflict, to the maximum extent feasible, to take the precautions that are necessary for the protection of the civilian population, individual civilians and civilian objects that are under the control of that party. This necessarily requires each party to the armed conflict to think about the kinds and methods of attack that its enemy can be expected to employ. **4.158**

The actions required by these rules that are of specific relevance to the kinds of technology discussed in this book will, the author suggests, so far as is feasible, include the following: **4.159**

1. To avoid locating civilians and the civilian population in the vicinity of facilities that are linked to AB- and BCI-enabled military operations, BBI-enabled military activities and brain enhancement and brain degradation activities associated with the armed conflict.
2. Likewise, to avoid positioning the facilities mentioned in point 1 above within or near densely populated areas.
3. To avoid locating civilians and the civilian population in the vicinity of facilities involved in the development, manufacture, storage, and so on of equipment associated with the activities mentioned in point 1 above.
4. Similarly, to avoid locating such facilities in or near densely populated areas.
5. If it is known that brain technology will be used by the enemy in association with specific munition types, to take necessary precautions to protect civilians and civilian objects from the dangers linked to the use of those kinds of weapon systems using such technology. What exactly those dangers are will become clearer as the nature of the relevant weapons becomes known and as brain technology evolves. It will be for states involved in an armed conflict against an opposing party that is using such capabilities to determine what precautions are feasible, and to take them.

So far as the author is aware, there are no relevant actions that AB or BCI technology can be used to undertake but, again, as understanding of these **4.160**

130 Consider API Commentary, n.42, para.2251; and AMW Manual, n.9, Rule 42, which provides that belligerent parties 'must, to the maximum extent feasible, avoid locating military objectives within or near densely populated areas, hospitals, cultural property, places of worship, prisoner of war camps and other facilities which are entitled to specific protection'.

technologies evolves, that aspect will also likely become clearer. In the realm of conventional hostilities, feasible precautions tend to include:

1. clear marking, with the protective emblems, of medical facilities, transports and personnel in ways that are visible to anticipated methods of attack;
2. clear marking of cultural objects, again in ways that will be detectable during anticipated attacks;
3. appropriate marking of works and installations containing dangerous forces (as to which see Chapter 5);
4. providing the enemy with information as to non-defended localities (discussed in Chapter 5);
5. making agreements between the parties that systems that are not military objectives and that are indispensable to the survival of the civilian population will not be attacked;
6. provision of facilities to protect civilians from the effects of air raids;
7. removal of children to places of safety; and
8. removal of cultural objects to places of safety.

4.161 The exact nature of the precautions that should be taken will depend on the circumstances that apply to the particular armed conflict. The object of the precautions that are taken should be the reduction, as far as possible, of the dangers that civilians will face as a result of the use of any weapon, including AB- and BCI-enabled weapon systems, as well as limiting the damage and destruction that is inflicted on civilian and cultural objects.

4.13 A CONCLUDING OBSERVATION

4.162 In the opening lines of section 4.7, the author pointed out the complementary nature of the rule as to the precautions to be taken by attackers and, respectively, against the effects of attacks. As to this complementary relationship, the ICRC Commentary to API sensibly points out: 'Belligerents may expect their adversaries to conduct themselves fully in accordance with their treaty obligations and to respect the civilian population, but they themselves must also co-operate by taking all possible precautions for the benefit of their own population as is in any case in their own interest.'[131] It follows from this that the attacker has the right to assume that those in control of the territory where the attack is to take place will discharge their obligations, and that those in control of territory have the right to expect that attackers will apply their required precautions. The important legal point is that the fact that one party is not taking

131 API Commentary, n.42, para.2240.

its precautions, or is not doing so fully, does not excuse the other party from its own precautionary obligations.[132]

Nevertheless, if an attack leads to an unsatisfactory outcome, the subsequent determination of responsibility for that outcome ought to reflect the compliance, or otherwise, of each party with its precautionary obligations, to the extent that such failures led to the civilian casualties and damage. If, therefore, an AB-enabled attack is found to have caused excessive casualties among civilians or damage to civilian objects, and if the party in control of the relevant territory placed the relevant military objective in a densely populated area, this is a factor that should be properly considered when responsibility for a resulting disproportionate attack, for example one undertaken using an AB-enabled system, is assessed. An AB system that is carefully programmed accurately to apply the proportionality rule may be impeded in doing so if the military objective has been located in a congested and densely populated location. That said, the proper decision for the attacker, and thus for the AB, may well be to cancel the attack. **4.163**

One can imagine that technologies may emerge that will enable the decision-making processes central to AB and BCI systems to be interfered with. Imagine a situation in which a party to an armed conflict that is in control of territory is able to deceive an AB system into believing that a civilian object is a military objective. If that deception were to cause an AB weapon system to target a civilian object, such as a primary school, causing distressing civilian casualties, actual responsibility for the civilian casualties would lie with the party perpetrating the deception. However, it may be difficult to detect the deception either before the attack, long after it, or indeed at all. And yet, such a scenario may have profound and unsatisfactory strategic consequences. **4.164**

---

132 Note, the observation in Customary Law Study, n.6: 'State practice indicates that an attacker is not prevented from attacking military objectives if the defender fails to take appropriate precautions or deliberately uses civilians to shield military operations. The attacker remains bound in all circumstances, however, to take appropriate precautions in attack … and must respect the principle of proportionality … even though the defender violates international humanitarian law': Customary Law Study, ibid, commentary accompanying Rule 22, 71.

5

PERSONS AND OBJECTS ENTITLED TO SPECIAL PROTECTION

5.1 INTRODUCTION

5.001 In Chapter 4, the basic principles of the law of targeting and the rules that implement the principle of distinction were applied to hostilities involving brain-computer interface (BCI) and artificial brain (AB) technologies. In this chapter, the focus shifts to objects and persons that the law of armed conflict (LOAC) specifically protects. Again, the aim of the discussion is to examine the implications of these specific protection provisions for the employment of BCI, AB and brain-to-brain interface (BBI) systems in military operations including attacks. As will be explained below, some objects and persons receive what are described as specific protection, meaning that the particular class of person or object is specifically mentioned in the law, but the level of protection that is given equates to that given to civilians or civilian objects. Journalists and their equipment are a case in point. Other persons and objects receive special protection, in the sense that the LOAC contains rules that have a greater protective effect than the rules addressing civilians and civilian objects in general. Where this is the case, the nature of the enhanced protection will be pointed out along with its implications for the employment of AB, BCI and, to the extent that is relevant, BBI systems in the associated hostilities.

5.002 One general point should be made at this early stage. If BCI or AB systems are to be used in connection with attacks, it will be necessary for such systems to be tested thoroughly. Such testing must, inter alia, establish whether the AB system will, reliably and consistently, fulfil the identified requirements arising from each of the rules and whether the use of the BCI system will facilitate the provision of the required protection.

5.2 PROTECTION OF MEDICAL PERSONNEL, UNITS AND TRANSPORTS, THE WOUNDED, SICK AND SHIPWRECKED

5.003 Geneva Convention I states: 'The fixed establishments and mobile medical units of the Medical Service may in no circumstances be attacked, but shall at all times be respected and protected by the Parties to the conflict.'[1] The 'respect' obligation means that no action can be taken to prevent or impede them from performing their medical or religious function. It would therefore be forbidden to make objects or persons benefitting from this 'respect' protection the object of an attack, and it would similarly be prohibited to interfere with their medical work.[2] This element of the rule does not, however, prohibit incidental damage when a military objective is targeted. The 'protect' obligation is distinct and involves taking suitable precautions to ensure that others respect the objects or persons that are thereby protected.[3] In addition, 'medical personnel exclusively engaged in the search for, or the collection, transport, or treatment of the wounded or sick', chaplains and certain other staff including those who administer medical units must be respected and protected.[4]

1 Geneva Convention I for the Amelioration of the Condition of the Wounded and Sick in Armed Forces in the Field, Geneva, 12 August 1949, 75 UNTS 31 (GCI), Art.19(1). See also International Committee of the Red Cross, *Customary International Humanitarian Law*, Vol.1 (J-M Henckaerts and L Doswald-Beck (eds), Cambridge University Press, 2005) (Customary Law Study), Rule 28 and US DoD *Law of War Manual* (June 2015, as subsequently amended) (US DoD Manual), para.7.10.

2 J S Pictet, 'Commentary to Geneva Convention I (1952)', Commentary to Article 19(1), Section B.

3 Pictet, ibid.

4 GCI, n.1, Art. 24. Auxiliary medical personnel must also be respected and protected while carrying out those duties when they come into contact with the enemy; GCI, ibid, Art.25. See Customary Law Study, n.1, Rule 25.

Additional Protocol I to the Geneva Conventions (API) applies this special level of protection to civilian medical and religious personnel.[5] Similarly protected are the wounded, sick and the shipwrecked, all of whom must be respected and protected.[6]

5.004 If a BCI system is being used in connection with attacks, planners, commanders and operators must:

1. identify fixed medical establishments, mobile medical units, the medical personnel, chaplains and other staff referred to in the previous paragraph, civilian medical personnel, the wounded, sick and the shipwrecked; and
2. apply the respect and protect obligations as described in the previous paragraph.

5.005 Accordingly, if a BCI system is employed to translate the thoughts or intent of the operator into attacks, that operator will be responsible for ensuring that no such thought or intent is communicated to the weapon system if the object of the thought or intent is medical personnel, religious personnel or medical objects. This will either involve the operator ensuring that no such thought or intent is formed in the first place or, more likely, that the BCI mechanism is switched off until such time as the operator can be sure that this rule will be complied with. The latter approach would seem to be the preferred one.

5.006 *Scenario 1.* State A is involved in an international armed conflict with State B. State A is using BCI-controlled land-based fighting vehicles to attack buildings that are used by the enemy for military command and communications functions. The operator of one of the BCI-controlled vehicles is observing a building using a televisual sensor. The BCI system is switched off while they are doing this. The BCI vehicle operator can see that injured persons are being wheeled into the building, that persons wearing white coats occasionally appear in front of the building and that vehicles outside the building carry the red crescent emblem. They refrain from attacking the building, do not activate the BCI and inform their commander accordingly.

5.007 If an AB system is to be used to undertake attacks, either the personnel initiating the mission or the AB system itself must, consistently and reliably:

---

5 Protocol Additional to the Geneva Conventions of 12 August 1949, and Relating to the Protection of Victims of International Armed Conflicts, Geneva, 8 June 1977, 1125 UNTS 3 (Additional Protocol I or API), Art.15(1) and (5); Customary Law Study, n.1, Rule 27.

6 GCI, n.1, Art.12(1) and Convention (II) for the Amelioration of the Condition of Wounded, Sick and Shipwrecked Members of Armed Forces at Sea, Geneva, 12 August 1949, 75 UNTS 85 (GCII), Art.12(1).

1. detect that persons it observes are medical personnel, religious personnel, wounded, sick or shipwrecked personnel as referred to in this section;
2. detect that objects it observes are medical objects of a kind listed in this section;
3. refrain from making any person or object referred to under points 1 or 2 the object of attack;
4. refrain from otherwise interfering with the work of the medical and religious persons and the objects referred to in points 1 and 2 above;[7]
5. to the extent relevant, must take suitable action to ensure others respect the protected persons and objects.[8]

Scenario 2. Some of State A's land-based fighting vehicles are equipped with AB technology to enable autonomous use. One of the vehicles is also observing the building referred to in Scenario 1. The AB detects that the building is being used for medical purposes and fulfils the obligation in point 5 above by informing the unit commanders who, in turn, inform allied states of the status of the building as a protected medical establishment. **5.008**

If reliance is being placed on the AB system to satisfy these requirements, this will involve designing or programming and perhaps training of the AB system to detect the protected persons and objects and to act accordingly. It will also involve proper testing of the AB system to ensure that it actually performs in accordance with the five stated criteria. At the practical level, it will be important for the AB system reliably and consistently to detect the emblem that the adverse party uses to identify medical and religious personnel, units and transports. It will also be important for the AB system, in the absence of such an emblem, reliably and consistently to detect that the personnel, units and transports it is observing are entitled to the special protection discussed in this section. Specifically identifying wounded, sick and shipwrecked personnel using an AB system may be challenging. The testing of the system should be designed to reveal whether this will be achieved sufficiently consistently and reliably. **5.009**

The special protection of 'fixed establishments and mobile medical units of the Medical Service … shall not cease unless they are used to commit, outside their humanitarian duties, acts harmful to the enemy'.[9] Even then, protection only ceases 'after a due warning has been given, naming, in all appropriate cases, **5.010**

7 Consider API, n.5, Art.16(1) and (2) and International Committee of the Red Cross, *Commentary on the Additional Protocols of 8 June 1977* (Y Sandoz, C Swinarski and B Zimmermann (eds), 1987) (API Commentary), para.663 et seq.

8 This may involve those initiating the mission or the AB system itself, having detected that an object or person has medical status, passing that information to others with a view to ensuring protection.

9 GCI, n.1, Art.21, first sentence.

a reasonable time-limit, and after such warning has remained unheeded'.[10] Certain conditions must not be considered as depriving the medical facility of its protection, namely:

1. That the personnel of the unit or establishment are armed, and that they use the arms in their own defence, or in that of the wounded and sick in their charge.
2. That in the absence of armed orderlies, the unit or establishment is protected by a picket or by sentries or by an escort.
3. That small arms and ammunition taken from the wounded and sick and not yet handed to the proper service, are found in the unit or establishment.
4. That personnel and material of the veterinary service are found in the unit or establishment, without forming an integral part thereof.
5. That the humanitarian activities of medical units and establishments or of their personnel extend to the care of civilian wounded or sick.[11]

5.011 It should be noted that those in control of the relevant facilities 'shall ensure that the said medical establishments and units are, as far as possible, situated in such a manner that attacks against military objectives cannot imperil their safety'.[12]

5.012 Planners, commanders and operators involved in operations entailing the use of BCI systems must determine if the unit or establishment is being used in the manner referred to in the first sentence of Article 21. If so, a warning must be given. They must determine whether the circumstances are appropriate for the giving of a reasonable time limit associated with the warning. The warning must specify the activity that must cease and the reasonable time within which it must cease. The commanders, planners and operators must then decide whether the warning has been heeded within that time. If it has, the special protection of the medical unit or establishment continues. If the warning has not been heeded, planners, commanders and operators must apply the principles and rules set forth in Chapter 4, that is the rules of targeting law, before undertaking any attack against the unit or establishment.

5.013 If a BCI is being used to translate the operator's thought or intent into attack action, the BCI-enabled operator or those who are supporting that individual will be responsible for applying these requirements. Steps should be taken to ensure that no thought or intent to attack is communicated to the BCI system until it has been established that the exceptions in Article 22 do not apply. This will likely require that the BCI system be switched off until those actions and

10 GCI, n.1, Art.21, second sentence.
11 GCI, n.1, Art.22 and Customary Law Study, n.1, commentaries to Rules 25 and 28.
12 GCI, n.1, Art.19(2).

assessments have been completed and it has been determined that it is lawful for the unit or establishment to be attacked.

If an AB system is being used to undertake autonomous attacks, Articles 21 and 22 of the Geneva Convention I (GCI) raise a number of important issues to be addressed either by an operator in advance of the mission, or by the AB system itself. If an operator is addressing these issues in advance of the mission, it will be important for the AB system reliably and consistently to comply with the restrictions imposed by the operator that are designed to ensure compliance with these rules. If no such operator is in a position to implement these steps in advance of the mission, the AB system itself will need reliably and consistently to fulfil the following requirements. **5.014**

1. The AB system will need to detect whether the medical unit, establishment, transport or personnel is being used to, outside its humanitarian duties, commit acts that are harmful to the enemy. If the AB system cannot do this and if no operator can do it in advance of the mission, the AB system should be programmed simply not to target any facility that exhibits the protective emblem or that it detects is performing medical tasks.
2. If the AB system detects that the medical unit, establishment, transport or personnel is being used in the manner referred to in point 1 above, the AB system, or an operator who is in a position to do so, will need to issue the warning discussed earlier in this section. This will require the operator or the AB system to formulate the warning, to determine whether a reasonable time limit is appropriate, to determine what that reasonable time limit is, to include that time limit in the warning and then to communicate the warning to the enemy in a suitable way.
3. The commander or operator, or the AB system, must reliably and consistently assess whether the warning has been heeded within such time limit as is stipulated under point 2 above.
4. If the commander or operator, or the AB system, determines that the warning has not been heeded during the time limit, the operator or the AB system must then apply the principles and rules explained in Chapter 4 before undertaking any attack.

It must be remembered that the warnings to which these special protection provisions refer should point out the misuse by the enemy of the specially protected object and should warn as to the consequences that will ensue if the misuse does not cease within a specified and reasonable time period. The issue here is whether the AB system, or arrangements associated with its use, is capable of formulating and issuing such a warning. If not, an operator must be in a position, in advance of the mission, to give such a warning to the unit, establishment or transport that is the prospective target. **5.015**

5.016 It should be noted that the warning required by Article 57 of API, as to which see Chapter 4, section 4.11.5 above, is different in nature from the warning discussed in the present section and must, subject to the exception stated in that Article, be given where an attack may affect the civilian population.

5.017 If an AB system is being used to undertake attacks, the chances are that, in its general programming, the AB system will identify armed military personnel, sentries and accumulations of weapons and/or ammunition as constituting military objectives. The following additional issues therefore arise:

1. Will the AB system apply the provisions of Article 22 of GCI reliably and consistently?
2. Alternatively, will an operator, in advance of the AB mission, take the action that is necessary to ensure compliance with Article 22? This will likely require careful programming and training of the AB system, extensive subsequent testing to verify the reliability of the AB's performance in this respect and careful training of the operator(s).

5.018 *Scenario 3.* Continuing with the situation described in *Scenario 1*, the BCI operator's televisual sensor shows that on the roof of State B's identified medical unit an anti-aircraft missile position has been set up and its operator is about to start firing at State A helicopters. A warning is therefore sent to State B's military authorities which includes the following text: 'You are setting up an anti-aircraft missile firing position on the roof of the medical building (insert co-ordinates). This is a misuse of the medical unit. Immediate action will be taken to neutralise that firing position.' It is determined that the nature of the threat to allied aircraft is so great that a reasonable time for compliance with the warning is not appropriate. The missile firing position is therefore attacked in a manner that limits the damage as far as possible to the firing position and that causes as little damage/injury as possible to the medical facility and its personnel.

5.019 *Scenario 4.* Continuing with *Scenario 2*, the AB system and linked sensors also detect the setting up of the anti-aircraft missile firing position on the roof of the medical establishment. The AB system has been programmed to issue warnings and issues a text in identical terms which is forwarded by State A's Command HQ to State B. The AB seeks permission from the unit commander to attack the firing position. Knowing that the warning has been issued and that the circumstances do not require the giving of a reasonable time limit for compliance, the unit commander authorises the AB to initiate the necessary attack. The AB system has been programmed to apply the precautions required by targeting law.

GCI makes it clear that '[t]ransports of wounded and sick or of medical equipment shall be respected and protected in the same way as mobile medical units'.[13] So, the same special level of protection applies to all vehicles employed on medical transport work, whether on a permanent or temporary basis, which is why the same issues identified earlier in this section apply also in the case of medical transports. **5.020**

The protective emblem, namely the red cross, red crescent or red crystal, indicates the protected status of medical personnel, units, establishments or transports, but it is the medical function that the facility or transport is fulfilling that entitles it to special protection.[14] A vehicle may be used to transport ammunition to the place where hostilities are taking place and, on the return journey, the same transport may be used to carry wounded and sick persons. Using the transport in that way does not deprive it of its special protection as a medical transport during the times when it is being exclusively used to transport the wounded, the sick or medical supplies.[15] **5.021**

Where BCI systems are being used, the implications are clear. The responsibility of operators, and anyone assisting the operators, will be to pay careful attention and, when the emblem is observed, to recognise that the associated facility or transport has specially protected status. **5.022**

Where AB systems are being used to undertake autonomous attacks, the following issues arise: **5.023**

1. The AB system must reliably and consistently detect the presence of the protective emblems or of indicators provided for in the Annex to API.[16]
2. The AB system must refrain from making personnel, facilities or transports displaying the protective emblem the object of an attack.
3. Irrespective of whether the personnel, unit or transport is displaying the emblem, the AB, or an operator in advance of the mission, must reliably and consistently detect when persons, a unit or transport are exclusively engaged in a medical function.
4. The AB system must reliably and consistently detect when a transport that may, on a previous journey, have been transporting military materials is now being exclusively used for medical purposes.
5. The AB system must reliably and consistently refrain from undertaking an attack if point 1, 2, 3 or 4 applies.

---

13 GCI, n.1, Art.35(1); as to the meaning of 'respect' and 'protect', see earlier in this section.
14 Customary Law Study, n.1, Rule 30, Interpretation, para.1.
15 Pictet, n.2, 281–2.
16 See API, n.5, Annex I: Regulations Concerning Identification.

5.024 *Scenario 5.* State A's autonomous unmanned aircraft are equipped with AB-controlled air-to-ground missile systems and with televisual sensors. The imagery that the sensors have supplied shows, inter alia, an enemy land vehicle transporting ammunition to a forward position. The aircraft was, at the time the sensors observed this, engaged in another priority task. That task has now been completed, and the same vehicle is now observed by the sensor travelling in the opposite direction. Sensor imagery shows the enemy truck displaying a red crescent on its sides and on the roof. The AB has been programmed to recognise that the vehicle has protected status, and the AB system refrains from attacking the vehicle.

5.025 API defines medical aircraft as 'any medical transports by air'[17] and medical transports comprise 'any means of transportation, whether military or civilian, permanent or temporary, assigned exclusively to medical transportation and under the control of a competent authority of a Party to the conflict'.[18] As with medical transports generally, the aircraft may be assigned exclusively to medical duties on a permanent or temporary basis.[19] Medical aircraft must be respected and protected.[20] API deals with the operation of medical aircraft by reference to three classifications of airspace. These are: (1) in and over land areas 'controlled by friendly forces, or in and over sea areas not physically controlled by an adverse Party' (where respect and protection of medical aircraft is stated not to be dependent on agreement with the adverse party, but where notification to that party may afford 'greater safety');[21] (2) in and over parts of the contact zone areas either controlled by friendly forces or where physical control is not clearly established (where protection is only fully effective by prior agreement between the parties and absent such agreement medical aircraft operate at their own risk but must be respected after they are recognised as such);[22] and (3) over land or sea areas physically controlled by an adverse party (where medical aircraft must be protected provided prior agreement to such flights has been obtained from the adverse party).[23]

---

17 API, n.5, Art.8(j).

18 API, n.5, Art.8(g).

19 GCI, n.1, Art.36 and Pictet, n.2, 288–9.

20 API, n.5, Art.24.

21 API, n.5, Art.25.

22 API, n.5, Art.26(1). 'Contact zone' means an area on land where the forward elements of opposing forces are in contact with each other, especially where they are exposed to direct fire from the ground.

23 API, n.5, Art.27(1). Article 27(2) provides the steps to be taken if, through error or emergency, a medical aircraft flies over an area physically controlled by an adverse party without or in deviation from an agreement.

The US Department of Defense (DoD) *Law of War Manual* describes medical aircraft as aircraft exclusively employed for the removal of the wounded, sick and shipwrecked and for the transport of medical personnel and equipment. It stipulates that such aircraft shall not be attacked but shall be respected by the belligerents while flying at heights and at times and on routes specifically agreed upon by the belligerents concerned.[24] The US DoD Manual goes on to explain that while the use of medical aircraft generally depends on agreement between the belligerents, known medical aircraft when performing their humanitarian functions must be respected and protected.[25] GCI Article 36, after specifying arrangements over the marking and means of identification of medical aircraft,[26] stipulates that '[u]nless agreed otherwise, flights over enemy or enemy-occupied territory are prohibited'.[27] **5.026**

The fluid nature of hostilities in some modern conflicts may, but will not necessarily, render the distinctions in airspace reflected in API unhelpful. While movements of medical aircraft in airspace securely controlled by friendly forces are unlikely to present problems, such movements in all other airspace will require an agreement between the parties, that: when identified as a medical aircraft, the respect and protect obligations apply; that aircraft that are lost or in distress should identify themselves and their status and, having so identified themselves, should not be attacked; and that, absent an agreement, medical aircraft outside securely controlled airspace operate at their own risk. **5.027**

If a BCI system is being used to translate the thoughts or intent of an operator into an attack, it will be necessary for the operator: **5.028**

1. to decide whether the aircraft that is being observed is a medical aircraft;
2. if it is, not to make it the object of attack and more generally to respect and protect it;
3. to determine whether the medical aircraft is being flown in accordance with a prior agreement between the parties to the conflict;
4. if such a prior agreement has been made and the medical aircraft is not complying with it, to assess whether any deviation from the terms of the agreement is material;
5. if it is not or it becomes clear that the deviation from the agreed route is due to distress, error or aircraft malfunction, to continue to respect and protect the medical aircraft.

24 US DoD Manual, n.1, para.7.14, reflecting GCI, n.1, Art.36(1).
25 IUS DoD Manual, n.1, para.7.14.1.
26 GCI, n.1, Art.36(2).
27 GCI, n.1, Art.36(3).

5.029 If, after considering these matters, the operator considers that the aircraft has lost its protected status, the principles and rules in Chapter 4 must be applied before any attack is decided upon and the BCI system should probably be switched off until it has finally been decided that an attack would be lawful.

5.030 *Scenario 6.* State A has agreed with adversary State B for the movement of its medical aircraft in airspace that is controlled by neither state. The agreement specifies dates, departure and arrival locations and times, altitudes, speeds, the types of aircraft, the markings of aircraft and the call signs and other identification and communication requirements associated with the medical flights. State B's ground-based air defence systems are operator-controlled using BCI technology. State B sensors detect an aircraft that is marked as a medical aircraft and that is complying with all of the requirements in the agreement except that it is deviating from its prescribed route. The BCI operator reports this to their commander and at the same time mayday transmissions from the aircraft are received requesting permission to land as a technical emergency has arisen. State B's BCI operator respects the medical status of the aircraft, does not activate the BCI system and permission to land at a nearby airfield is granted.

5.031 The issues for AB systems will be:

1. Will the details of agreements as to enemy medical aircraft movements be fed into the AB system?
2. Will the AB system detect, or receive external information (such as a distress call from those in control of the aircraft) that shows that a medical aircraft is deviating from its flight plan due to distress or navigational error?
3. Will the AB system reliably and consistently recognise flights undertaken in accordance with agreements between the parties and refrain from attacking them?
4. (And, perhaps) Will the AB system refer to a human operator the decision whether to attack a medical aircraft that has deviated from the agreed flight plan?

5.032 *Scenario 7.* The facts are as explained in *Scenario 6* but the ground-based air defence facility employs AB technology autonomously to attack intruding military aircraft and missiles. The AB technology has fed into it the details of the agreements between States A and B as to the movement of State A medical aircraft. The AB system recognises that the medical aircraft is deviating from the course specified in the agreement. By automated processes, the moment that the aircraft broadcasts its mayday signal, this is forwarded to the air defence system which recognises the continued protected status of the aircraft and therefore does not make it the object of attack.

5.3 CIVILIAN MEDICAL FACILITIES

Civilian medical units that belong to a party to the conflict, or that are recognised and authorised as provided for in GCI and API, 'shall be respected and protected at all times and shall not be the object of attack'.[28] 'The protection to which civilian medical units are entitled shall not cease unless they are used to commit, outside their humanitarian function, acts harmful to the enemy.' That protection only ends 'after a warning has been given setting, whenever appropriate, a reasonable time-limit, and after such warning has remained unheeded'.[29] The rule then lists the following as acts that shall not be regarded as harmful to the enemy for these purposes, namely: **5.033**

a) that the personnel of the unit are equipped with light individual weapons for their own defence or that of the wounded and sick in their charge;
b) that the unit is guarded by a picket or by sentries or by an escort;
c) that small arms and ammunition taken from the wounded and sick, and not yet handed to the proper Service, are found in the units;
d) that members of the armed forces or other combatants are in the unit for medical reasons.[30]

Civilian medical facilities can only, therefore, become military objectives as a result of their current use, not due to their nature, location or purpose. **5.034**

Where BCI systems are being used to translate the thoughts or intent of an operator into attacks, planners, operators and commanders must: **5.035**

1. recognise the status of an object as a civilian medical unit;
2. decide whether any of the limited circumstances that would cause the civilian medical unit to lose its protected status apply;
3. if that is the case, give a warning;
4. if appropriate, give a reasonable time limit for compliance;
5. determine if the warning has been complied with;
6. if not, apply the principles and rules in Chapter 4 before any attack takes place.

While these decisions are being made, it would be prudent to switch off the BCI system. **5.036**

---

28 API, n.5, Art.12(1).
29 API, n.5, Art.13(1) and (2).
30 API, n.5, Art.13(2).

5.037 Where the use of AB systems in connection with attacks is concerned:

1. the AB system must reliably and consistently recognise the target as a civilian medical facility; and
2. the AB system must reliably and consistently refrain from attacking the object if there is no information to show that the object is currently being used for military purposes.

5.038 The other element in Article 13(2) which constitutes special protection for civilian medical facilities is the obligation to give a special warning before attack. That obligation is expressed in similar terms to the warning that is discussed in section 5.2. The issues that are discussed in that section, and associated explanations, will therefore apply in respect of the warning required by Article 13(2) and, even if those requirements are met, the targeting law rules discussed in Chapter 4 must be complied with.

5.4 HOSPITAL SHIPS, SICK-BAYS, OTHER MEDICAL SHIPS AND CRAFT

5.039 Hospital ships must 'in no circumstances be attacked or captured'. They are defined as 'ships built or equipped by the Powers specially and solely with a view to assisting the wounded, sick and shipwrecked, to treating them and to transporting them'.[31] They must 'at all times be respected and protected, on condition that their names and descriptions have been notified to the Parties to the conflict ...'.[32]

5.040 Where BCI systems are being used to translate the thoughts or intent of an operator into attacks, planners, operators and commanders must ensure that any ship coming within the definition of a hospital ship is not attacked but is respected and protected. Those individuals will need to be aware of the descriptions and locations of hospital ships and must, it is suggested, apply this rule with suitable care.

---

31 GCII, n.6, Art.22, and see Arts 24 and 25; note also International Institute of Humanitarian Law, *San Remo Manual on International Law Applicable to Armed Conflicts at Sea* (L Doswald-Beck (ed), 1995) (San Remo Manual), para.47 and UK Ministry of Defence, *The Manual of the Law of Armed Conflict*, OUP (2004), para.13.33.

32 GCII, n.6, Art.22(1). The Convention requires that the names and descriptions (registered gross tonnage, length, number of masts and funnels) of the hospital ships shall have been notified to the parties to the conflict ten days before their employment. Note that GCII, n.6, Art.27 gives similar protection to coastal rescue craft ('small craft employed by the State or by the officially recognized lifeboat institutions for coastal rescue operations'), 'so far as operational requirements permit'.

Where AB systems are to be used for the conduct of attacks where hospital ships are operating, the issues to be considered include the following: 5.041

1. Will the AB system reliably and consistently identify that a vessel is a hospital ship? If not, the AB system must not be permitted to operate in any location where hospital ships are or may be.
2. If the AB system does reliably and consistently identify hospital ships, will it reliably and consistently refrain from attacking such vessels?

GCII Article 43 specifies the external marks to be applied to hospital ships[33] and API specifies light signals, radio signals, electronic identification, radio communications, international codes, and other means of communication for exclusive use by medical units and transports.[34] 5.042

The key issue for the use of AB systems in connection with attacks is whether the AB system will recognise the stipulated means of identification and, having done so, whether it will act accordingly, that is refrain from attacking the unit or transport. 5.043

If hostilities take place on board a warship, the sick-bays 'shall be respected and spared as far as possible'.[35] Personnel undertaking hostilities using BCI systems will need to apply this requirement to the extent that this is possible. 5.044

An AB system will need to be so constructed that whatever action is possible in the circumstances to protect and spare the sick-bay is in fact done. Doing what is possible may involve using a system other than the AB system (or, as the case may be, a BCI-enabled system) to undertake the operation if such an alternative system is available and if its use would indeed enhance the protection of the sick-bay. 5.045

'The protection to which hospital ships and sick-bays are entitled shall not cease unless they are used to commit, outside their humanitarian duties, acts harmful to the enemy. Protection may, however, cease only after due warning has been given, naming in all appropriate cases a reasonable time limit, and after such warning has remained unheeded.'[36] It will be noted that these provisions are similar in nature to the protective arrangements discussed earlier 5.046

33 All exterior surfaces of the ship must be white and one or more large red crosses must be painted and displayed on each side of the hull and on the horizontal surfaces so as to achieve maximum visibility from the sea and from the air.
34 API, n.5, Annex I, Chapter III, Arts 5–11.
35 GCII, n.6, Art.28.
36 GCII, n.6, Art.34(1).

in relation to medical units and transports. The explanations given in section A.2 will therefore apply, *mutatis mutandis*, to the platforms and other objects discussed in the present section, and the implications for BCI operations will therefore be similar.

5.047 If AB systems are to be used:

1. AB systems that are to operate in a maritime environment where hospital ships are also believed to be located must be fed with data including the list of enemy hospital ships, their notified details, distinctive signals and communication arrangements that they will be using, and their markings so that they can be recognised as protected hospital ships;
2. AB systems must reliably and consistently refrain from attacking vessels recognised as hospital ships or coastal rescue craft.
3. A limited list of acts that are harmful to the enemy, that are outside the humanitarian function of the hospital ship or coastal rescue craft and that unambiguously render the ship liable to be attacked should be fed into the AB system.
4. The AB system should only be permitted to schedule a vessel for attack if a circumstance on the list mentioned in point 3 above arises, and even then only after the warning has been issued, after it has gone unheeded for a suitable time period and after other targeting law requirements that are applicable in naval warfare have been satisfied.

> The following conditions shall not be considered as depriving hospital ships or sick-bays of vessels of the protection due to them:
>
> 1) The fact that the crews of ships or sick bays are armed for the maintenance of order, for their own defence or that of the sick and wounded.
> 2) The presence on-board of an apparatus exclusively intended to facilitate navigation or communication.
> 3) The discovery on board hospital ships or in sick-bays of portable arms and ammunition taken from the wounded, sick and shipwrecked and not yet handed to the proper service.
> 4) The fact that the humanitarian activities of hospital ships and sick-bays of vessels or of the crews extend to the care of wounded, sick or shipwrecked civilians.
> 5) The transport of equipment and of personnel intended exclusively for medical duties, over and above the normal requirements.[37]

5.048 Where BCI systems are being used to translate the thoughts or intent of an operator into attacks, planners, operators and commanders must ensure that none of the circumstances listed in points 1) to 5) is misinterpreted as depriving the hospital ship or sick-bay of its protection.

---

37 GCII, n.6, Art.35.

If AB systems are to be used in connection with relevant attack operations, the issues will be: **5.049**

1. Will the AB system conclude that the target is a protected hospital ship or coastal rescue craft and thus protected from attack despite the fact that it observes any of the activities referred to in points 1) to 5) above taking place there?
2. Will the AB system therefore reliably and consistently refrain from attacking the target?

API grants special protection on a similar basis to other medical ships and craft.[38] Article 22(2) of API also extends specially protected status to: 'hospital ships made available for humanitarian purposes to a party to the conflict: (a) by a neutral or other State which is not a party to that conflict; or (b) by an impartial humanitarian organization, provided that, in either case, the requirements set out in [Article 25 of Geneva Convention II] are complied with.'[39] This means that the requirements relating to the use of BCI and AB systems identified earlier in this section in relation to hospital ships will also need to be applied in relation to other medical ships and craft and to the hospital ships referred to in Article 22(2) of API. **5.050**

5.5 CIVILIAN AIRLINERS

A civilian airliner in flight is at the same time both vulnerable to attack[40] and capable of posing a serious threat to persons and objects on the ground.[41] **5.051**

38 API, n.5, Art.23(1) and (3). The term 'medical ships and craft' means any medical transports by water, and medical transports are means of transportation, whether military or civilian, permanent or temporary, assigned exclusively to medical transportation and under the control of a competent authority of a party to the conflict; API, n.5, Art.8(g) and (i).

39 These objects acquire special protected status by virtue of the statement in Art.22(2) that it is the (special) protection provided by the Conventions to Article 25 Vessels that is being extended to these additional classes of vessel.

40 Consider, for example, the downing of Iran Air flight 655 by the USS Vincennes on 3 July 1988: US Naval History and Heritage Command, 'H-020-1: The Fog of War – USS Vincennes Tragedy – 3 July 1988', available at https://www.history.navy.mil/content/history/nhhc/about-us/leadership/director/directors-corner/h-grams/h-gram-020/h-020-1-uss-vincennes-tragedy--.html; the shooting down of Korean Air Lines flight 007 by a Soviet air-to-air missile on 1 September 1983 near Sakhalin Island, Russia: 'Korean Air Lines flight 007', *Encyclopaedia Britannica*, 27 February 2025, available at https://www.britannica.com/event/Korean-Air-Lines-flight-007; and the shooting down of Malaysian Airlines flight 17 on 17 July 2014 in Eastern Ukraine by means of a Russian-made surface-to-air missile: 'Malaysia Airlines flight 17', *Encyclopaedia Britannica*, 25 February 2025, available at https://www.britannica.com/event/Malaysia-Airlines-flight-17.

41 Note, for example, the terrorist bombing of Pan American flight 103 over Lockerbie, Scotland on 21 December 1988: 'Pan Am Flight 103', *Encyclopaedia Britannica*, available at https://www.britannica.com/event/Pan-Am-flight-103; consider also terrorists taking control of civilian airliners, flying two of them into the twin towers of the World Trade Centre in New York causing those towers to collapse and flying

It may be carrying large numbers of passengers[42] who may well be civilians whom both parties to an armed conflict are legally obliged to protect.[43] If a party to an armed conflict intends to use a civilian airliner to undertake an attack, or for any other military purpose, the aircraft will become a military objective by virtue of that intended future use; actual use for such purposes will have the same effect.[44] The difficult issue that will confront commanders or other decision-makers is whether an airliner that may be carrying large numbers of passengers has become a threat requiring the use of force. The associated challenge is to gain sufficient information as to who (if anyone) is in control of the aircraft, what their intentions are, and thus what the appropriate response will be. This challenge may arise during periods of armed conflict or in the peacetime context. In armed conflict, the issue is whether the airliner has become a military objective; in peacetime, the issue is likely to be whether the use of force against the airliner is a lawful exercise of the inherent right of self-defence.

5.052 Effective protection of civilian airliners requires that they be recognised as such.[45] Under the Chicago Convention, 'every aircraft engaged in international air navigation shall bear its appropriate nationality and registration marks'.[46] Recognition can also be achieved by civilian airliners employing secondary surveillance radar modes and codes.[47]

---

another airliner into the Pentagon building in Washington DC all on 11 September 2001: Imperial War Museum, 'What Were the 9/11 Terrorist Attacks?', available at https://www.iwm.org.uk/history/what-were-the-911-terrorist-attacks.

42 The maximum certified passenger capacity of an Airbus A380 passenger airliner is 853; R Beresnevičlus and A Mitchell, 'How Many Passengers Can You Fit on an Airbus A380?', *Simple Flying*, available at https://simpleflying.com/how-many-passengers-can-you-fit-on-an-airbus-a380/.

43 A civilian airliner must not be attacked unless it qualifies as a military objective; see Y Dinstein and A W Dahl (eds), *Oslo Manual on Select Topics of the Law of Armed Conflict* (2020) (Oslo Manual), Rule 90b. As civilian objects they are entitled to particular care in terms of precautions; ibid, Rule 91b.

44 Consider also API, n.5, Art.37(1) and Regulations concerning the Laws and Customs of War on Land annexed to Hague Convention IV respecting the Laws and Customs of War on Land, The Hague, 18 October 1907, Art.23(b).

45 As to the shooting down by the USS Vincennes of an Iranian airliner on 3 July 1988, it appears those on the warship mistook the Iranian airliner for an attacking Iranian F14 fighter aircraft and took what they perceived to be appropriate action in self-defence. This highlights the importance of proper identification steps, and the vital importance that proper care is taken over precautions. The Vincennes example also highlights that the attack decision may be being made under pressing time constraints and with less than perfect information. See George C Wilson, 'Navy Missile Downs Iranian Jetliner', *Washington Post*, 4 July 1988, available at http://www.washingtonpost.com/wp-srv/inatl/longterm/flight801/stories/july88crash.htm.

46 Chicago Convention on International Civil Aviation, 7 December 1944, 15 UNTS 295 (Chicago Convention 1944), Art.20.

47 Chicago Convention 1944, ibid, Annex 10, Foreword, Serial 49.

It follows from this that planners, commanders and operators employing BCI systems to translate thoughts or intent into attacks must apply all precautions with particular care and must access and consider all relevant and available information to ensure that civilian airliners are identified as such, that those which are not military objectives are not attacked and that, if action must be taken against a civilian airliner, that action involves the least force that is consistent with the circumstances. Subject to what is stated later in this section about the likely necessity for any decision to attack an airliner in flight to be made by a human commander, AB systems used in connection with the targeting of objects in flight such as enemy rockets, drones and missiles must also be set up in such a way that civilian airliners are not attacked. **5.053**

The doubt rule will often apply. If the civilian airliner is normally dedicated to civilian purposes, as will usually be the case, and if there is doubt as to whether it is currently being used to make an effective contribution to military action, the assumption must be that it is not being so used and that it therefore retains protected civilian object status. Where relevant operations involve the use of a BCI system, planners, commanders and operators will be responsible for ensuring that the doubt rule is correctly applied and it would seem sensible for the BCI system to be switched off until the doubt rule has been addressed and those operating the BCI system are as certain as the circumstances, including the limited available time and information, permit that the airliner is a military objective and that attacking it using, for example the BCI-linked weapon is lawful and appropriate. **5.054**

An AB system that is used in connection with the targeting of objects in flight must therefore be programmed to apply the presumption of protected civilian status. The air defence system should be structured so that all available information as to a relevant aircraft is available to the AB system and to associated commanders. In practical terms, a situation of the kind referred to in this section should be referred by the AB system to those commanders so that the action that is to be taken can be decided by them. **5.055**

Scenario 8. State A is involved in an armed conflict with State B. State A has manned combat aircraft that would be used if any aircraft enters State A airspace without prior permission. Members of 800 Squadron are on what is described as 'speedy alert' 24 hours a day. The aircraft is equipped with BCI-enabled air-to-air missile systems. An airliner that has failed to identify itself to air traffic control enters State A airspace on a course that would lead it to overfly Alpha City, State A's densely populated capital. The on-duty crew of 800 Squadron is scrambled to intercept the airliner. The BCI system is not in **5.056** active mode at this stage. The only communication from the airliner's crew, when instructed to land for inspection, was to reply 'No way'. All attempts to communicate with the airliner are unsuccessful, the intercept and the various manoeuvres undertaken by the intercepting aircraft produce no response, and the airliner's flight crew appear to be ignoring the intercepting aircraft. When the aircraft is 15 minutes' flying time from the outskirts of the city, Alpha TV News carries reports of a statement by State B's Foreign Minister threatening a 9/11-style attack. It would be for the responsible officer to consider all of the circumstances, including the statement, in determining whether, notwithstanding the presumption, the intercepted airliner has become a military objective. If he so decides and orders the shooting down of the airliner, it will be at that stage that the BCI will be activated.

5.057 The AMW Manual notes that '[w]hile civilian airliners (whether enemy or neutral) ought to avoid entering a no-fly or "exclusion" zone, or the immediate vicinity of hostilities, they do not lose their protection merely because they enter such areas'.[48] Accordingly, operations using BCI or AB systems in connection with the targeting of objects in flight must apply the precautionary measures irrespective of the location of the civilian airliner inside or outside such a zone.

5.058 A civilian airliner may become a military objective by:

> Being on the ground in a military airfield of the enemy in circumstances which make that aircraft a military objective.[49]
>
> Engaging in hostile actions in support of the enemy, e.g. intercepting or attacking other aircraft; attacking persons or objects on land or sea; being used as a means of attack;[50] engaging in electronic warfare; or providing targeting information to enemy forces.[51]
>
> Facilitating the military actions of the enemy's armed forces, e.g. transporting troops, carrying military materials or refueling military aircraft.[52]

---

48 Program on Humanitarian Policy and Conflict Research at Harvard University (HPCR), *Manual on the International Law Applicable to Air and Missile Warfare* (March 2010) (AMW Manual), available at https://cdn.ca9.uscourts.gov/datastore/library/2013/09/06/Flores_Manual.pdf (AMW Manual), Rule 60. The Oslo Manual, n.43, adds that if they are intercepted within such a zone, 'civilian airliners continue to be entitled to particular care in terms of precautions'; Oslo Manual, n.43, Rule 91(d).

49 However, some airfields are split into military and civilian parts, so considerable care would be needed to ensure that the aircraft really is in the military part. See further AMW Manual, n.48, Rule 63(a), p.160.

50 Attacks of the sort perpetrated on the US on 11 September 2001 would be an example of such additional forms of attack.

51 AMW Manual, n.48, Rule 63(b), p.161.

52 AMW Manual, n.48, Rule 63(c), p.161.

Being incorporated into or assisting the enemy's intelligence gathering system, e.g. engaging in reconnaissance, early warning, surveillance or command, control and communications missions.[53]

Refusing to comply with the orders of military authorities, including instructions for landing, inspection or possible capture, or clearly resisting interception.[54]

Otherwise making an effective contribution to military action.[55]

Where a BCI system is being employed, planners, commanders and operators involved with the operation of the system will need to assess whether the relevant civilian airliner has become a military objective in at least one of the ways on this list. If those persons conclude that none of the listed circumstances applies, the airliner must not be attacked. The author suggests that before an AB system employed in an air defence role recommends that a civilian airliner be attacked, it will need reliably and consistently to detect that the civilian airliner is performing in at least one of the six ways listed above. **5.059**

The AMW Manual suggests that any decision to attack a civil airliner should be taken by a 'sufficiently high level of command'.[56] This rather reinforces the impression that such a decision should be taken by an appropriately senior officer as opposed to by an AB system. Whether that will continue to be the case if AB systems were, in time, found to be equally reliable to, or perhaps more reliable than, human decision-making remains to be seen. For the foreseeable future, it can perhaps be assumed that human decision-making at a senior level will be necessary, whether or not supported by AB capabilities. **5.060**

Civilian airliners must not be attacked unless their protection is lost[57] and the AMW Manual explains that they 'are civilian objects which are entitled to particular care in terms of precautions'.[58] The AMW Manual experts agreed that 'the general obligation to take every feasible step – in order to ascertain that the target to be attacked is a lawful target – must be meticulously observed'.[59] This means that particular precautionary care must be taken to prevent an accidental, mistaken or otherwise inappropriate downing of the aircraft.[60] The operators of civilian airliners should, however, 'avoid areas **5.061**

53 AMW Manual, n.48, Rule 63(d), p.161.
54 AMW Manual, n.48, Rule 63(e), p.161.
55 AMW Manual, n.48, Rule 63(f), p.161.
56 AMW Manual, n.48, Rule 69 and commentary para.1, p.168.
57 AMW Manual, n.48, Rule 25, para.2.
58 AMW Manual, n.48, Rule 58, p.155. This rule is stated to be based on San Remo Manual, n.31, para.53 and UK Manual, n.31, para.12.28; ibid, Rule 58, para.2.
59 AMW Manual, n.48, commentary, para.6, p.156.
60 AMW Manual, n.48, Rule 58, para.4.

of potentially hazardous military activity, even if civil aviation has not been restricted or prohibited in the respective airspace'.[61] When they are on the ground, civilian airliners are civilian objects unless, for example by virtue of their intended future use, they have become military objectives.

5.062 The author takes the view that, for a decision to attack a civilian airliner in flight to be justified, there must be near certainty that the relevant criteria apply. Absolute certainty will generally be unachievable and the decision will inevitably be contextual. Time available for the decision may be short and information may be incomplete. AB systems may, however, assist the decision-maker, it being recognised that the final decision will likely need to be made by a commander or other designated person. If an AB system is supporting that human decision, it should reliably and consistently:

1. take into account all available information, including that from all available sensors, that is relevant to the decision to be made and only consider relevant information;
2. detect that required information is lacking and initiate action, where possible, to obtain it;
3. consider and make known to the human decision-maker all alternative ways of dealing with the situation that do not involve the use of force against the airliner;
4. only recommend the use of force against the airliner if all less violent options have been carefully considered and if they have proved inadequate or it is considered that they would be inadequate;
5. determine that all available and relevant information is being made available to the human decision-maker;
6. recommend that force should not be used if insufficient information is available to support the use of force;
7. notify the human decision-maker if any factor is present that is impairing the functioning of the AB system;
8. apply the rules as to precautions with the particular care specified by the AMW Manual experts; and
9. if there is national policy for dealing with such a situation, the AB system should reliably and consistently act in accordance with that policy.

5.063 An alternative situation that may involve airliners may arise if air defence missiles are being used to target other airborne threats, such as missiles, rockets or drones.[62] AB systems that are supporting such air defence missiles will need to distinguish between the targets they are designed to engage, that is missiles

61 Oslo Manual, n.43, Rule 96.

62 Consider for example the Iron Dome and Phalanx weapon systems.

and rockets, and civilian aircraft. While there is a requirement that the parties to an armed conflict exercise particular care in terms of precautions,[63] the Oslo Manual experts drew attention to the right, during an armed conflict, whether international or non-international, 'to restrict or prohibit entry into their national airspace'.[64] The experts noted that the 'responsibility of States that provide air-traffic services for the safety of civil aviation remains intact during an armed conflict' and opined that, during an armed conflict, 'States should – whenever necessary for the safety of civil aviation – restrict access to their national airspace (in whole or in part) by civilian airliners'.[65] The Manual goes on to observe that a 'State must keep under review the level of danger to civil aviation under its air traffic control and inform the relevant foreign actors of any imminent dangers to aviation in the airspace for which it is responsible'.[66] Finally, on this point, the Manual, in best practice language, advises that '[c]ivilian airliners should avoid areas of potentially hazardous military activity, even if civil aviation has not been restricted or prohibited in the respective airspace'.[67]

It follows from what the Oslo Manual experts concluded that there should be **5.064** human monitoring of the relevant airspace and there should be connectivity between the military forces responsible for that airspace and civilian air traffic control. If an intruder into the relevant airspace is detected, every effort must be made to communicate with it and to assist it to leave, recognising that its presence might be innocently caused, for example by an aircraft malfunction.

The network of responsibilities identified by the Oslo Manual experts is **5.065** designed to avoid civilian airliners getting into harm's way by entering locations where hostilities are taking place. It does this by identifying the responsibilities of territorial states, states that provide air traffic services, and the civilian airliners themselves (clearly meaning all those involved in their operation). These precautionary steps will all be taken by human decision-makers. In practice, if a civilian airliner is being tracked by the operators of BCI-enabled weapon systems, the BCI control system should be deactivated while the listed precautions, and associated decision-making, are taking place. It is only when the human decision to target the relevant aircraft has been taken

63 Oslo Manual, n.43, Rule 91(b).
64 Oslo Manual, n.43, Rule 87(a).
65 Oslo Manual, n.43, Rules 94 and 95(a).
66 Oslo Manual, n.43, Rule 95(b).
67 Oslo Manual, n.43, Rule 96.

that the BCI-enabled weapon system that is to be used for the attack should be activated.

5.066 If an air defence system is controlled by AB technology, the AB system must reliably and consistently:

1. examine a prospective target up to the point of actual engagement and determine if any characteristics associated with the weapons or vehicles it is designed to target are absent;
2. if they are, refer the situation for human decision-making or, if that is not feasible, decline to target the object it is observing; and
3. distinguish reliably between, on the one hand, the rockets, missiles and other weapons that it is intended to target and a civilian aircraft of whatever kind. Careful testing must have demonstrated that the AB does this reliably and consistently in the circumstances in which it is intended to use the system.

5.067 In the perhaps less likely event that BCI-related weapon systems are used in such a role, planners, commanders and operators, supported by the information from all available sources, will be responsible for making the assessments referred to in points 1 and 3 above.

5.068 Precautions must therefore be taken to ensure that attacks are limited to objects such as inbound rockets, missiles or other weapons, including drones. The obligation to take particular care in the exercise of these precautions is designed to secure the safety of airliners and the potentially large number of civilian passengers on board. If advances in technology, and in particular in BCI and AB technologies, are able to enhance that protection, perhaps in the case of AB systems by enabling the taking of additional precautions such as the more rapid and accurate recognition of the nature and status of an object in flight, this would of course be a positive development.

5.6 CULTURAL OBJECTS

5.069 The Hague Cultural Property Convention,[68] together with its Protocols, gives special protection to cultural property during armed conflict. The definition of cultural property in the Convention is, the author believes, both comprehensive and customary, binds all states, including those which are not party to the Convention and is as follows:

---

68 1954 Hague Convention for the Protection of Cultural Property in the Event of Armed Conflict, adopted 14 May 1954, 249 UNTS 215 (1954 Convention). At the time of writing there are 138 States Parties to the Convention: source: www.icrc.org.

(a) Moveable or immovable property of great importance to the cultural heritage of every people, such as monuments of architecture, art or history, whether religious or secular; archaeological sites; groups of buildings which, as a whole, are of historical or artistic interest; works of art; manuscripts, books and other objects of artistic, historical or archaeological interest, as well as scientific collections and important collections of books or archives or of reproductions of the property defined above;
(b) Buildings whose main and effective purpose is to preserve or exhibit the moveable cultural property defined in sub-paragraph (a) such as museums, large libraries and depositaries of archives, and refuges intended to shelter, in the event of armed conflict, the moveable cultural property defined in sub-paragraph (a);
(c) Centres containing a large amount of cultural property as defined in sub-paragraphs (a) and (b), to be known as "centres containing monuments".[69]

Planners, commanders and operators of BCI systems that are used to translate the thoughts or intent of the operator into attacks using linked weapons must apply the definition in order to identify the objects that are cultural property and, thus, entitled to protection under the 1954 Convention. If an AB system is to be used in connection with target decision-making, it will need, reliably and consistently, to do the following: **5.070**

1. Recognise any object that satisfies any of the descriptions in this definition. The relative imprecision of two key notions in paragraph (a), namely 'of importance' and 'of interest', may make it difficult to develop an AB system that can make that evaluation.
2. Assess whether the relevant object is of great importance to the cultural heritage of every people.

It may be possible, of course, for operators, or those developing the AB mechanisms, to install, in advance of the mission, data identifying all of the objects that are located in the area where the AB system may operate and that are cultural objects. If that has been done, then it will simply be a question of whether the AB system will recognise particular objects as being on the list. If the area in which the AB system is permitted to operate is not defined, satisfying this requirement may prove problematic.[70] The legal requirement will be that either a human operator can apply the judgement that the definition requires to determine whether an object does or does not come within the definition, or the AB system must do so. **5.071**

69 1954 Convention, ibid, Art.1(a)–(c).

70 One wonders whether a possible future legal development (*de lege ferenda*) would be a requirement for those in control of territory to apply a digital 'cultural property shield' that can be recognised by autonomous and AB attack systems; consider the obligations under API, n.5, Art.58(c).

5.072 Under paragraph (b), the operator, in advance of the mission, or the AB system must determine the main and effective purpose of a building that is being considered for attack. A commander, planner or operator may be able, before the mission starts, to examine the area where the AB weapon system is to operate in order to identify buildings 'whose main and effective purpose is to preserve or exhibit' movable cultural property. Any such buildings could then simply be placed on a 'no strike list'. It remains to be seen whether it will be possible to develop AB systems that can be fed with, or that can themselves obtain, the required information to support a suitably reliable decision of that kind. This rather points to the importance of human planning in advance of missions of this sort. That planning process may need to be extensive and burdensome if the AB system is to be permitted to operate in loosely defined areas, or without geographical constraints. Exchange of information between belligerents may be an option here.

5.073 Paragraph (c) includes another imprecise notion, namely a 'large' amount of cultural property in a centre, but the individual cultural property items will benefit from Convention protections anyway.

5.074 The key protective provision in the Convention is:

> 1. The High Contracting Parties undertake to respect cultural property situated within their own territory as well as within territory of other High Contracting Parties by refraining from any use of the property and its immediate surroundings or of the appliances in use for its protection for purposes which are likely to expose it to destruction or damage in the event of armed conflict; and by refraining from any act of hostility directed against such property.
> 2. The obligations mentioned in paragraph 1 of the present Article may be waived only in cases where military necessity imperatively requires such a waiver.[71]

5.075 Paragraph 1 obliges the parties to the conflict to respect cultural property. The respect obligation comprises, most importantly, the obligations elaborated in that paragraph, namely, in the first case, not to use cultural property, its immediate vicinity or its protective systems, for purposes that would expose it to damage or destruction during armed conflict. Secondly, the parties to the conflict must not undertake hostile acts aimed at the cultural property.

71 1954 Convention, n.64, Art.4(1) and (2). The AMW Manual, n.48, suggests that the decision to use cultural property or its immediate surroundings for military purposes can only be implemented after emblems identifying the object as cultural property have been removed; Rule 93(b), p.217. The opinion is expressed there that, whenever circumstances permit, the enemy should be notified a reasonable time in advance of the decision to use cultural property for military purposes: Second Protocol to the Hague Convention of 1954 for the Protection of Cultural Property in the Event of Armed Conflict The Hague, adopted 26 March 1999 (1999 Protocol), Art. 6(d) and AMW Manual, n.48, para.2, p.215.

Planners, commanders and operators of BCI weapon systems will be responsible for ensuring that the prohibitions in Article 4 are complied with. This will include ensuring that the various steps identified below in relation to the use of AB systems are taken.

Assuming that the AB weapon system correctly identifies items of cultural property reliably and consistently, it must, with similar accuracy and reliability: **5.076**

1. refrain from using cultural property in a manner liable to expose it to destruction or damage during an armed conflict;
2. refrain from using the immediate surroundings of cultural property in a manner liable to expose the cultural property to destruction or damage during an armed conflict;
3. refrain from using appliances for the protection of cultural property in a manner liable to expose the cultural property to destruction or damage during an armed conflict;
4. refrain from making cultural property, its immediate surroundings or appliances for its protection the object of attack unless the waiver can lawfully be applied; and
5. detect that imperative military necessity requires the exercise of the waiver.

If the AB system detects that an object is protected under the Convention and that the circumstances permit the exercise of the waiver, it may only be permitted to decide on the use of, or attack against, the object if Article 4 is complied with. If the AB system does not make those determinations reliably and consistently, it must refrain from using any of the objects protected by the Convention for military purposes and must not attack them. **5.077**

When determining whether the imperative military necessity requirement is satisfied, consideration must be given to whether an alternative target would provide a similar military advantage, whether an alternative object could be used to achieve the relevant military purpose, and whether an attack is needed at all. Sometimes, less violent action can produce the desired military outcome; equally, there will be occasions when the cultural object does not need to be exposed to the risk of attack. Perhaps an alternative weapon could be chosen to reduce the likely impact on the cultural object. **5.078**

If a BCI-enabled weapon is being employed, it will be necessary for these assessments to be made before the BCI is activated and, thus, before there is any possibility of the weapon being fired. The operator of the BCI-enabled weapon may be the person who makes those assessments. Equally, the commander, planners or other personnel may do so. What matters is that the assessments are performed before the BCI becomes capable of using a thought **5.079** or intent of the operator as the 'trigger' to fire the weapon. It is assumed to be unlikely that a BCI system would decide on the placement of military objectives, whether in the vicinity of cultural objects or elsewhere. However, an AB system may decide where to locate itself. Clearly, the mere presence of a BCI-enabled weapon system may incentivise acts of violence aimed at neutralising that system, so it follows from the terms of Article 4 that AB-enabled weapon systems should only locate themselves in the vicinity of a cultural object if imperative military necessity so demands. A key question will therefore be whether the AB system will, in practice, reliably and consistently determine that imperative military necessity so requires.

5.080 If an AB weapon system is being used to decide upon attacks, it will be necessary for that system:

1. to determine reliably and consistently whether an attack is necessary to achieve the desired military purpose;
2. if so, to determine reliably and consistently whether that attack needs to be directed at cultural property; and
3. if so, to be programmed to choose the weapon and method of attack that poses the least risk to the cultural property.

5.081 Reach-back to a human operator may be necessary.

5.082 Article 6 of the Convention prescribes the emblem which may be applied to cultural property. It is in the form of a shield consisting of a royal-blue square, one of the angles of which forms the point of the shield and of a royal-blue triangle above the square, the space on either side being taken up by a white triangle.[72] In BCI-enabled operations, it will be for planners, commanders and operators, through personal observation and/or with the assistance of sensors to detect the presence of such a shield and then to act accordingly. If an AB system is being used, the AB system will need, reliably and consistently, to detect the presence of such a shield and, having done so, act in accordance with Article 4 of the Convention.

5.083 A limited number of refuges intended to shelter movable cultural property in the event of armed conflict and centres containing monuments and other immovable cultural property of very great importance may receive special protection provided that they are located far enough from any large industrial

72 1954 Convention, n.64, Art.16(1). The AMW Manual concludes that belligerent parties ought to mark cultural property with the internationally recognised emblem and should provide the enemy with timely and adequate information about its location: AMW Manual, n.48, Rule 94.

centre or important military objective and are not used for military purposes.[73] Information about the location of such refuges and centres will have to be briefed to planners, commanders and operators employing BCI-enabled weapons before the activation of such systems. It will be the responsibility of those individuals to ensure that the required special protection is afforded to such refuges and centres. In advance of a mission employing an AB system, the AB mission control mechanism must have the details of such refuges and centres loaded into it and the AB system must be programmed to provide to such refuges and centres the required special protection. In conducting military operations using either BCI or AB systems, care must also be taken to ensure special protection is provided to cultural property that the adverse party has entered into the International Register of Cultural Property under Special Protection.[74] Planners, commanders and operators will need to ensure that this aspect has been reflected in the planning of a mission using a BCI system; if an AB weapon system is being used, such information will need to be loaded into the AB system's targeting control systems before the mission starts.[75]

The 1999 Protocol to the Convention[76] clarifies the operation of the Article 4(2) waiver by specifying that it 'may only be invoked to direct an act of hostility against cultural property when and for as long as: (1) That cultural property has, by its function, been made into a military objective; and (2) There is no feasible alternative available to obtain a similar military advantage to that offered by directing an act of hostility against that objective'.[77] **5.084**

For states that are party to this Protocol, planners, commanders and operators deciding whether to use a BCI-enabled weapon system to attack cultural property must apply the considerations in items (1) and (2) of Article 6(a) of the Protocol in deciding whether it would be lawful to undertake the attack. If a state party to the Protocol is intending to use an AB-enabled weapon system that may be expected to undertake such an attack, the issue will be whether **5.085**

73 For the notion of 'improvised refuges' see Regulations for the Execution of the Convention for the Protection of Cultural Property in the Event of Armed Conflict, The Hague, 1954 (Hague Cultural Property Regulations), Art.11.

74 As to registration arrangements and the procedures associated with cancellation of registration, see Hague Cultural Property Regulations, n.69, Arts 12–16.

75 A state entering an item of cultural property on this register undertakes to refrain from 'any act of hostility directed against such property and ... any use of such property or of its surroundings for military purposes': 1954 Convention, n.64, Art.9. A violation of this provision releases the opposing party from its obligation to ensure the immunity of the relevant cultural property.

76 Second Protocol to the Hague Convention of 1954 for the Protection of Cultural Property in the Event of Armed Conflict, adopted 26 March 1999.

77 1999 Protocol, n.71, Art.6(a).

that AB system will reliably and consistently apply the same considerations when it, the AB system, decides on the attack. This will, the author believes, need to be programmed into the decision-making processes within the AB system. Accordingly, the AB system must reliably and consistently:

1. determine what function the cultural property in question is fulfilling;
2. determine that it is the function that the cultural property is fulfilling that renders it a military objective; and
3. determine that there is no feasible[78] alternative to directing the attack against the cultural property.

5.086 The 1999 Protocol also obliges states party to it to take precautions that are similar to those provided for in Article 57 of API, that were discussed in Chapter 4.

5.087 The API provision dealing with cultural property is as follows:

> Without prejudice to the provisions of the Hague Convention for the Protection of Cultural Property in the Event of Armed Conflict of 14 May 1954, and of other relevant international Instruments, it is prohibited:
>
> a) to commit any acts of hostility directed against the historic monuments, works of art or places of worship which constitute the cultural or spiritual heritage of peoples;
> b) to use such objects in support of the military effort;
> c) to make such objects the object of reprisals.[79]

5.088 It will be evident to the reader that the more detailed requirements are set forth in the 1954 Convention and in its 1999 Protocol. A state that implements the measures discussed earlier in this section will also comply with the API requirements.

78 It is likely that states will interpret 'feasible' as meaning that which is practicable or practically possible, taking military and humanitarian considerations into account.

79 API, n.5, Art.53.

5.7 STARVATION AND OBJECTS INDISPENSABLE TO THE SURVIVAL OF THE CIVILIAN POPULATION

'Starvation of civilians as a method of warfare is prohibited.'[80] This is a customary law rule that binds all states, the breach of which is a war crime.[81] The implications for BCI and AB operations are simple. Neither of those methods may be used to impose starvation on civilians and both such systems should be used or, as the case may be, programmed accordingly. **5.089**

Article 54(2) of API states that it is: 'prohibited to attack, destroy, remove or render useless objects indispensable to the survival of the civilian population, such as foodstuffs, agricultural areas for the production of foodstuffs, crops, livestock, drinking water installations and supplies and irrigation works, for the specific purpose of denying them for their sustenance value to the civilian population or to the adverse Party, whatever the motive, whether in order to starve out civilians, to cause them to move away, or for any other motive.'[82] **5.090**

In order to comply with this rule, planners, commanders and operators of BCI-enabled weapon systems must: **5.091**

1. assess whether the proposed operation will attack, destroy, remove or render useless the objects that the operation is intended to engage;
2. assess whether the object of the operation is indispensable to the survival of the civilian population (in this regard, it should be noted that the objects specifically referred to in Article 54(2) are merely examples and other kinds of object may, depending on the location, climate and circumstances, also be indispensable to survival); and
3. refrain from deciding upon or cancel the operation if its purpose would be to deny the sustenance value of the relevant object(s) to the civilian population or to the enemy.

---

80 API, n.5, Art.54(1); Customary Law Study, n.1, Rule 53. The Commentary to that Rule notes that the starvation prohibition was generally considered to be a new rule when adopted in 1977 but has since hardened into a rule of customary law. The US DoD Manual explains that starvation is a legitimate method of warfare that must be conducted in accordance with the principles of distinction and proportionality and other law of war rules; para.5.20. The Manual goes on to note that starvation specifically directed against the enemy civilian population is prohibited: para.5.20.1. Starvation would include deprivation of food and deprivation of water.

81 Rome Statute of the International Criminal Court, 17 July 1998, Art.8(2)(b)(xxv), which specifies that the act must be intentional.

82 API, n.5, Art.54(2); note the US position that this rule would not apply to attacks that are carried out for specific purposes other than to deny sustenance, such as destroying a field of crops being used as concealment by the enemy, where the goods are being used solely as sustenance by the enemy armed forces or where they are being used for other military purposes; US DoD Manual, n.1, para.5.20.4.

5.092 It should be noted that the ulterior motive of the act is irrelevant.

5.093 Where AB operations are concerned, can planners, commanders or operators satisfy this requirement in advance of the mission, for example by so programming the AB system that it is incapable of undertaking an activity that would breach Article 54(2)? If not, the following issues arise:

1. Will the AB system reliably and consistently determine that the proposed operation amounts to attack, destruction, removal or a rendering useless of the indispensable object?
2. Will the AB system reliably and consistently determine that the object that it is observing is indispensable to the civilian population's survival?
3. Having made the determination concerning point 2 above, will the AB system reliably and consistently refrain from attacking, destroying, removing or rendering useless the object in question?

5.094 A key question that arises is whether the AB system is capable of forming a purpose. Clearly, a planner, commander or operator of such a system may have a purpose and may so arrange the way in which the AB system is deployed and used with a view to achieving that purpose. Absent such a human purpose, it will be necessary to consider the capability of the particular kind of AB technology with a view to assessing whether the system itself can have a purpose. The author rather doubts that that will be the case, but as the technology develops the possibility cannot be altogether excluded.

5.095 The wording of Article 54(2) indicates that denial of sustenance value to either the civilian population or to the adverse party will cause the rule to be broken. Objects which are used solely as sustenance for members of the armed forces or in direct support of military action are not protected by this rule. However, action cannot be taken against these objects if it may be expected to leave the civilian population with such inadequate food or water as to cause its starvation or to force it to move.[83] It is arguable that the rule will be breached if there was more than one specific purpose for the relevant act, one of which consisted of the prohibited deprivation. Where BCI- or AB-enabled weapons are being employed, the legally safer course would be for planners, commanders and operators to determine which objects are in fact indispensable to the survival of the civilian population in the location where the hostilities are taking place. In the case of BCI-enabled systems, operators must simply avoid forming the intent to fire the weapon against objects coming within Article

83 API, n.5, Art.54(3).

54(2). An AB-enabled weapon should be programmed to identify such objects and, having done so, reliably and consistently decline to make them the object of any of the four activities referred to in Article 54(2).

Scenario 9. State A is contemplating the use of a BCI-enabled missile located on one of its autonomous drones to attack an electricity distribution unit that serves the civilian population of a major town. Its adversary, State B, is located in a region where daytime temperatures regularly reach 50 degrees Celsius or more, and the population relies heavily on air-conditioning for its survival. The assessment is that targeting the electrical unit would cause multiple deaths and would cause large numbers of civilians to move away. State A ultimately decides not to attack the electricity unit and places the unit on the no-strike list that is programmed into the targeting control systems of its AB weapon systems. **5.096**

The objects that are protected by this provision will vary according to the circumstances of the particular population. The rule protects the general population of a locality, not individual civilians. The kinds of objects referred to specifically in Article 54(2) are examples of objects that may be indispensable. The situation of a particular population may render other objects indispensable.[84] **5.097**

Article 54 permits a party to an international armed conflict to derogate from Article 54(2) 'in the defence of its national territory against invasion'. This is termed a scorched earth policy, and the derogating party may pursue such a policy within national territory that is under its control 'where required by imperative military necessity'.[85] It is assumed that any decision to implement a scorched earth policy will be made by suitably senior commanders who will determine whether the 'imperative military necessity' requirement is satisfied. If AB systems are involved in such operations, they will need to be programmed to limit such scorched earth activities to national territory within the control of the party using the AB system. Planners, commanders and operators of BCI-enabled systems employed in such operations will need to ensure that those activities are similarly constrained.[86] **5.098**

84 For a discussion of the kinds of facility covered by these provisions, see Y Dinstein, *The Conduct of Hostilities Under the Law of International Armed Conflict*, 4th edn (Cambridge University Press, 2022), 289.

85 API, n.5, Art.54(5), also noted in US DoD Manual, n.1, para.5.20.4.

86 Consider Dinstein, n.84, p.290.

5.8 AIRCRAFT GRANTED SAFE CONDUCT

5.099 A cartel aircraft 'means an aircraft granted safe conduct by agreement between the Belligerent Parties for the purpose of performing a specific function, such as the transport of prisoners of war or parlementaires'.[87] Any type of aircraft, military or civilian, may be granted safe conduct by agreement between the parties and the purpose does not need to be limited to the carriage of prisoners of war or parlementaires.[88] Such aircraft are specifically protected while they are performing their assigned mission, while travelling to the location where the mission will commence and while returning from the mission.[89] The agreement granting safe conduct should specify the purpose of the flight, details of the flight, arrangements for filing a flight plan and other relevant matters.[90] The protected status is contingent on the aircraft satisfying certain conditions, namely:

1. it must comply with the details of the agreement, including availability for inspection and identification; and
2. it must not 'intentionally hamper the movements of combatants' and must be 'innocently employed in [its] agreed-upon role'.[91]

5.100 However, '[l]oss of specific protection will only take place if the circumstances of non-compliance are sufficiently grave that the aircraft has become or may reasonably be assumed to be a military objective'.[92] In case of doubt as to whether an aircraft granted safe conduct qualifies as a military objective, the assumption must be that it does not.[93]

5.101 It will be the responsibility of planners, commanders and operators of BCI-enabled systems to be aware of agreements between the parties to the conflict under which flights are taking place and to ensure that they take all the measures that are necessary to ensure that aircraft performing such flights are not attacked. Likewise, the details of the relevant flights should be fed into AB systems that are to undertake relevant operations. Before such an AB-enabled

---

87 AMW Manual, n.48, Rule 1(g). A parlementaire is a person who has been authorised by one of the belligerent parties to enter into communication with the enemy; AMW Manual, ibid, Commentary to Rule 1(g), para.2, citing Hague Regulations 1907, n.44, Art.32.

88 AMW Manual, n.48, Commentary to Rule 64, para.2.

89 AMW Manual, n.48, Commentary to Rule 64, para.5.

90 AMW Manual, n.48, Commentary to Rule 64, paras 6 and 7.

91 AMW Manual, n.48, Rule 65(a).

92 AMW Manual, n.48, Rule 65(b).

93 AMW Manual, n.48, Rule 66.

mission involving ground-to-air or air-to-air weapon systems is commenced, the commanders and operators will need to satisfy themselves:

1. that no flights to which this section refers are taking place in or near the location of the AB system; or
2. that the AB system is not technically capable of interfering with the flight; or
3. that the AB system has been so programmed that the planners, commanders and operators can be sure that it will not attack or otherwise adversely affect the flight granted safe conduct.

In this regard, relevant considerations will be whether the AB system will reliably and consistently: **5.102**

1. differentiate between intentional hampering and getting in the way of combatants due, for example, to technical malfunction, negligent navigation or some other innocent cause;
2. detect that an aircraft undertaking a specified flight that it is observing is the subject of an agreement between the parties relating to that flight;[94]
3. detect that the aircraft granted safe conduct is failing to comply with the details of the agreement. The agreement may specify, for example, departure and projected arrival times, the destination, the route taken, the altitude and speed of the flight in the cruise, the particular aircraft used, its markings and call sign, and its availability for inspection. The issues will be: (a) whether the AB system, in conjunction with available sensors, is able to detect that the aircraft has deviated from the terms of the agreement; (b) whether the AB system will assess whether the deviation from the requirements in the agreement justifies action in response and, if so, what kind of action. This may involve considering the possibility of navigational error, disabling of the aircraft or of the crew, on board emergency, weather effects and so on;
4. detect that there is doubt as to whether the aircraft granted safe conduct has become a military objective;[95] and
5. if point 4 above applies, refrain from making the aircraft the object of attack.

Rule 69 of the AMW Manual suggests that any decision to attack an aircraft granted safe conduct 'ought to be taken by an appropriate level of command'.[96] Paragraph 1 of the commentary to that Rule clarifies this as meaning 'a sufficiently high level of command'. It is therefore for suitably senior commanders to make the decision, and it will be important that any relevant BCI and AB systems are suitably programmed or configured to give effect to the decision of the senior individual. **5.103**

94 Such information might of course be fed into the system by a human operator.

95 San Remo Manual, Art.58.

96 AMW Manual, n.48, Rule 69 and Commentary, para.1, p.168.

5.104 *Scenario 10.* State A and State B have agreed to exchange prisoners. They have agreed that the prisoners that State A is releasing will be flown in a chartered airliner belonging to a specified airline. The flight will depart from a stated airfield at 10.00 am local time and will fly an agreed route at agreed speeds and altitudes, arriving at Beta City airport at 11.30 am local time. At 10.35 am local time, when the aircraft has achieved cruise altitude, it starts to deviate from the agreed route, moving towards airspace above a sensitive military facility in State B. State B immediately protests to State A military headquarters which fails to respond to the protest. The cartel aircraft continues on the same course. State B scrambles a combat aircraft equipped with BCI-enabled air-to-air missiles. State B repeats its protest at a more senior level, warning that it will fire on the aircraft if the warning is not heeded. State A acknowledges the protest, apologises, explains the cartel aircraft has suffered a navigation equipment failure and the aircraft soon thereafter resumes the agreed route. The BCI systems are not activated and no air-to-air missiles are fired.

5.105 A warning must be issued whenever circumstances permit before any action is taken.[97] The planners, commander and operator of a relevant BCI-enabled weapon will be responsible for determining: whether the prevailing circumstances permit the giving of a warning; how such a warning should be communicated to the aircraft granted safe conduct; what action the aircraft should be required to take; whether the aircraft appears to be complying with the terms of the warning; if not, whether some other action short of attacking the aircraft is appropriate; if not, when and how the attack should be undertaken.

5.9 WORKS AND INSTALLATIONS CONTAINING DANGEROUS FORCES

5.106 States that are party to API are required by Article 56 to give special protection to dams, dykes and nuclear electrical generating stations, collectively referred to as works and installations containing dangerous forces. The Article does not have customary status and therefore does not bind states that are not party to API. Article 56(1) is as follows:

> 1. Works or installations containing dangerous forces, namely dams, dykes and nuclear electrical generating stations, shall not be made the object of attack, even when these objects are military objectives, if such attack may cause the release of dangerous forces and consequent severe losses among the civilian population. Other military

97 AMW Manual, n.48, Rules 38 and 70. The AMW Manual recognises that a warning may not be feasible if hostile action by the aircraft granted safe conduct is imminent.

> objectives located at or in the vicinity of these works or installations shall not be made the object of attack if such attack may cause the release of dangerous forces from the works or installations and consequent severe losses among the civilian population.[98]

In the conduct of BCI-enabled attacks, planners, commanders and operators must make the assessments referred to in points 1 to 5 below. Before the BCI system is activated, all five points must have been addressed, and the targeting law rules set forth in Chapter 4 must be applied. **5.107**

In the conduct of AB-enabled operations, the following issues arise: **5.108**

1. The AB system must recognise that it is observing a dam, dyke, or nuclear power station.
2. The AB system must recognise when a military objective that it is intending to attack is located at or in the vicinity of a dam, dyke, or nuclear power station. It will be for each state party to API to interpret the meaning of the word 'vicinity', and to program the AB system accordingly.
3. The AB system must assess whether the intended attack on an object referred to in points 1 or 2 above may cause the release of dangerous forces, that is the water held back by the dam or dyke or the dangerous substances contained within the nuclear power station.
4. If the object that the AB system is observing comes within either points 1 or 2 above and if point 3 applies, the AB system must determine whether the dangerous forces, if released, may cause severe losses among the civilian population. It will be for each party to interpret the meaning of the word 'severe' and to program the AB system accordingly.
5. If point 4 above applies, the AB system must reliably and consistently refrain from undertaking the attack.
6. The AB system must then apply the targeting law rules set forth in Chapter 4.

Article 56(2) provides: **5.109**

> 2. The special protection against attack provided by paragraph (1) shall cease:
>   (a) for a dam or a dyke only if it is used for other than its normal function and in regular, significant and direct support of military operations and if such attack is the only feasible way to terminate such support;[99]
>   (b) for a nuclear electrical generating station only if it provides electric power in regular, significant and direct support of military operations and if such attack is the only feasible way to terminate such support;

98 API, n.5, Art.56(1).

99 Consider for example the attack, in May 1953, of the Toksan and Chasan irrigation dams which 'rendered unserviceable the two main railway lines and parallel highways into the military, industrial and political centre of Pyongyang': W Hays Parks, 'Conventional Aerial Bombing and the Law of War', Proceedings, Vol 108/5/951, *Naval Review* (1982), 98 at p.113.

(c) for all other military objectives located at or in the vicinity of these works or installations only if they are used in regular, significant and direct support of military operations and if such attack is the only feasible way to terminate such support.[100]

5.110 When deciding whether Article 56(2) will permit the attack of a dam or dyke, or an attack against an object in the vicinity of a dam or dyke, using a BCI-enabled system, planners, the commander and the operator must consider:

1. Is the object in question a dam or dyke? or
2. Is the object in question at or in the vicinity of a dam or dyke?
3. If point 1 applies, is the function for which the dam or dyke is being used not its normal function (that is holding back the water, one assumes)?
4. If point 1 applies, is the dam or dyke being used to give support to military operations that is regular and significant and direct?
5. If point 2 applies, is the object being used in regular and significant and direct support of military operations?
6. If the answer to point 4 or 5 is yes, what are the feasible (that is practicable or practically possible, taking humanitarian and military considerations into account) ways of bringing to an end the support to military operations given by the object in point 1 or 2?
7. Is such an attack the only feasible way of bringing that support to an end?

5.111 When deciding whether Article 56(2) will permit the attack of a nuclear power station, or against an object in the vicinity of a nuclear power station, using a BCI-enabled system, planners, the commander and the operator must consider:

1. Is the object in question a nuclear power station?
2. Is the object in question at or in the vicinity of a nuclear power station?
3. If point 1 applies, is the function for which the nuclear power station is being used not its normal function (that is generating electric power, one assumes)?
4. If point 1 applies, is the nuclear power station being used to give support to military operations that is regular and significant and direct? That support may consist of military uses of the power station that have nothing to do with the generation of electricity. If the use in support of military operations consists of the supply of electricity that is used, for example by military units or installations, the issue will be whether the associated support is direct. Imagine that the electric power goes from the nuclear power station into an electricity grid from which military and other users take their power. It may be that such an arrangement does not amount to direct support.

100 API, n.5, Art.56(2).

5. If point 2 applies, is the object being used in regular and significant and direct support of military operations?
6. If the answer to point 4 or 5 is yes, what are the feasible (that is practicable or practically possible, taking humanitarian and military considerations into account) ways of bringing to an end the support to military operations given by the object in point 1 or 2?
7. Is such an attack the only feasible way of bringing that support to an end?

Where AB-enabled operations are concerned and taking into account the six points discussed in relation to Article 56(1), the legally safest course may be simply to program the system to identify dams, dykes and nuclear power stations and not undertake any attack directed at any of the three facilities or at any object located near such a facility. Failing that approach, it would be sensible to arrange for the AB system to refer to a human operator or commander situations where it detects that one of these works or installations, or any object in their vicinity, has become a military objective. It is, in this regard, relevant to note the Article 56(3) requirement that: '[i]f the protection ceases and any of the works, installations or military objectives mentioned in paragraph (1) is attacked, all practical precautions shall be taken to avoid the release of the dangerous forces.'[101] It would be for the planner, commander or operator to decide what precautions are practical but it must be borne in mind that any attack must not only comply with the specific requirements of Article 56, but also the general rules of targeting law discussed in Chapter 4, including the detailed customary precautions prescribed by Article 57 of API. **5.112**

Article 56(5) states that: 'installations erected for the sole purpose of defending the protected works or installations from attack are permissible and shall not themselves be made the object of attack, provided that they are not used in hostilities except for defensive actions necessary to respond to attacks against the protected works or installations and that their armament is limited to weapons capable only of repelling hostile action against the protected works or installations.'[102] **5.113**

It will therefore be necessary for an AB system used to undertake attacks to: **5.114**

1. detect that the sole purpose of the installation that it observes is to defend the dam, dyke or nuclear power station from attack; and
2. detect that the installation is only used for defensive actions responding to an attack against the dam, dyke or nuclear power station. This will likely involve

101 API, n.5, Art.56(3), sentence 2.
102 API, n.5, Art.56(5).

feeding into the AB control system lists of weapons that planners, commanders and operators consider would satisfy this inherently imprecise provision.

5.115 Article 56(7) prescribes a special sign to identify objects protected by the Article, namely 'a group of 3 bright orange circles placed on the same axis, as specified in Article 16 of Annex I to th[e] Protocol'. Clearly, when planners, commanders and operators become aware of the presence of this sign, they must apply the Article 56 requirements. An AB system that is used to undertake attacks must recognise this sign and, having done so, must apply the rules as discussed in this section.

5.116 States that are not party to API will not be bound by the rules discussed in this section. They will, however, be bound by the customary targeting law rules. Any decision by such a state to attack a dam, dyke or nuclear power station or a target nearby must comply with targeting law, including the prohibition of indiscriminate attacks, the proportionality rule and the obligation to take precautions in attack.

5.117 *Scenario 11.* State A's AB-enabled air-to-ground missile system detects that a pair of tanks has been parked by State B next to a dam. A reconnaissance mission establishes that the lake formed by the dam is full of water. This information is available to the AB system. The AB system calculates the explosive force that the missile warhead will release and concludes that the possibility of a resulting breach of the dam wall cannot be excluded. The same reconnaissance flight establishes that there are three towns downstream of the dam and that substantial numbers of casualties can be expected if the water in the dam is released. The findings from the reconnaissance flight are communicated digitally to the AB system, which postpones the attack and refers the circumstances to a human operator for a decision as to whether the attack should take place.

5.10 THE NATURAL ENVIRONMENT

5.118 Under the Hague Regulations it is prohibited '[t]o destroy or seize the enemy's property, unless such destruction or seizure be imperatively demanded by the necessities of war'.[103] While this will not necessarily have been the focus of the treaty rule at the time of its adoption, property, for these purposes, will now generally be understood as including the environment.

---

103 Hague Regulations 1907, n.44, Art.23(g).

The general understanding of 'environment' will include man-made objects which contribute to the circumstances in which people live, move and interact. Where the somewhat more specific notion of natural environment is concerned, the Oslo Manual suggests that while there is no mandatory customary law requirement in this respect, '[w]hen planning and conducting operations during an armed conflict, due regard should be had to the natural environment'.[104] **5.119**

The very many states that are party to the Chemical Weapons Convention, 1993, and to the Biological Weapons Convention, 1972 must neither use nor engage in a broad selection of other acts associated with such weapons. This may have an incidental protective effect where the natural environment is concerned. As is noted in Chapter 6, subsections 6.6.7 and 6.6.8, neither BCI nor AB systems may be used in association with such weapons. **5.120**

5.10.1 Environmental Modification Convention

Taking the treaty law rules relating to the environment in the order in which they were adopted, the Environmental Modification Convention (ENMOD)[105] requires that states party to it do not 'engage in military or any other hostile use of environmental modification techniques having widespread, long-lasting or severe effects as the means of destruction, damage or injury to any other State Party'.[106] States Parties also must not assist, encourage or induce prohibited activities.[107] The term 'environmental modification techniques' is defined by the treaty to include any technique for changing, through the deliberate manipulation of natural processes, the dynamics, composition or structure of the Earth, including its biota, lithosphere, hydrosphere and atmosphere, or of outer space.[108] The definition therefore extends to deliberate or intentional action to influence processes, for example modifying the weather, causing floods or drought, and triggering tsunamis or earthquakes.[109] **5.121**

The expression 'wide-spread, long-lasting or severe' has been interpreted as follows: '(a) "widespread": encompassing an area on the scale of several hundred square kilometres; (b) "long-lasting": lasting for a period of months, or **5.122**

104 Oslo Manual, n.43, Rule 138 with Commentary. The experts noted that this best practice provision applies to 'all domains of warfare': ibid, Commentary accompanying Rule 139, para.1.

105 United Nations Convention on the Prohibition of Military or any other Hostile Use of Environmental Modification Techniques, New York, 10 December 1976, 1108 UNTS 151 (ENMOD).

106 ENMOD, ibid, Art.I(1).

107 ENMOD, ibid, Art.I(2).

108 ENMOD, ibid, Art.II.

109 See P J Rowe, *Defence: the Legal Implications* (Brassey's (UK) Ltd, 1987), p.117.

approximately a season; (c) "severe": involving serious or significant disruption or harm to human life, natural and economic resources or other assets.'[110] ENMOD therefore prohibits the use of natural processes to cause this level of destruction and/or loss of life to an adversary State Party during an international armed conflict.

5.123 Both the acting state and the victim state must be parties to the treaty for ENMOD to apply. ENMOD would not apply if the level of harm to human life and/or damage explained earlier is not caused, if only inconvenience is caused, or if the environmental manipulation is undertaken for peaceful purposes. Accordingly, ENMOD is really about using natural processes as a weapon or instrument for causing damage or injury to another state that is party to the treaty.

5.124 If a State Party to ENMOD is using BCI systems in connection with hostilities involving another States Party, the implications of ENMOD are clear. Planners, commanders and operators must not use those systems to trigger an environmental event that would breach the treaty rule. If AB systems are being employed in connection with such hostilities, the AB systems must be prevented from undertaking any operation that would involve the manipulation of natural processes and that would have any of the effects prohibited by the treaty. To be prohibited under the treaty, the manipulation must be deliberate. It will be for the user state to assess the AB system's capabilities and level of sophistication in order to determine whether the AB technology is capable of forming a deliberate intent. It should, however, be borne in mind that if planners, commanders or operators have such an intent, this may suffice to establish a breach of the rule.

5.125 If an environmental modification technique uses either widespread or long-lasting or severe environmental effects to cause damage or injury to another State Party, the treaty prohibits its military or other hostile use. This will need to be reflected in the programming of any relevant AB system.

5.10.2 Articles 35(3) and 55 of AP1

5.126 States that are party to API must comply with the following two rules:[111]

110 Report of the Conference of the Committee on Disarmament, Vol.1, General Assembly Official Records, 31st Session, Supplement No.27 (A/31/27), p.91.

111 These two rules do not have customary law status and do not therefore bind states that are not party to the treaty; Oslo Manual, n.43, Commentary accompanying Rule 140, paras 2 and 4, but note the observations in both paras as to the desirability of ensuring environmental protection as a matter of policy.

> It is prohibited to employ methods or means of warfare which are intended, or may be expected, to cause widespread, long-term and severe damage to the natural environment.[112]

> Care shall be taken in warfare to protect the natural environment against widespread, long-term and severe damage. This protection includes a prohibition of the use of methods or means of warfare which are intended or may be expected to cause such damage to the natural environment and thereby to prejudice the health or survival of the population.[113]

Although 'natural environment' is not defined in API, it seems to refer to the biological environment in which the population is living, encompassing flora, fauna and climatic elements.[114] Article 35(3)'s protective effect is not necessarily limited to the territory of parties to the conflict. The effect of Article 49(3) of API will be to limit the application of Article 55 to situations in which civilians or civilian objects on land may be affected.[115] **5.127**

The API Commentary offers the following understanding of 'widespread, long-term and severe': **5.128**

> The time or duration required (i.e. long-term) was considered by some to be measured in decades. References to twenty or thirty years were made by some representatives as being a minimum. Others referred to battlefield destruction in France in the First World War as being outside the scope of the prohibition ... It appeared to be a widely shared assumption that battlefield damage incidental to conventional warfare would not normally be proscribed by this provision. What the article is primarily directed to is thus such damage as would be likely to prejudice, over a long term, the continued survival of the civilian population or would risk causing it major health problems.[116]

Only very severe environmental damage will, therefore, breach the API rules. **5.129** The survival or health of the population as a whole, as opposed to that of individual civilians, must be prejudiced.[117] The US considers that these API

---

112 API, n.5, Art.35(3).

113 API, n.5, Art.55. See UK statements on ratification of API on 28 January 1998, statement (f), that both provisions (that is both Arts 35(3) and 55) 'cover the employment of methods and means of warfare and that the risk of environmental damage falling within the scope of these provisions arising from such methods and means of warfare is to be assessed objectively on the basis of the information available at the time'.

114 Dinstein, n.84, p.272, referring to the API Commentary, n.84.

115 'A review of the negotiating record suggests that this ambiguous approach was intended to satisfy two competing camps, those who advocated the intrinsic value approach of Article 35(3), and their opponents who advocated framing restrictions in human terms': P J Richards and M N Schmitt, *Mars Meets Mother Nature: Protecting the Environment during Armed Conflict* (1998–99) 28 Stetson LR 1047, p.1063.

116 Rapporteur's Report CDDH/215/Rev.1, para.27, reported in API Commentary, n.7, para.1454. See also L Doswald-Beck, 'The Value of the 1977 Protocols', in M A Meyer, *Armed Conflict and the New Law* (British Institute of International and Comparative Law, 1989), p.162.

117 See also S Witteler, 'Der Krieg im Golf und seine Auswirkungen auf die natürliche Umwelt', Notwendige Überlegungen zu den umweltschützenden Vorschriften des humanitären Völkerrechts (1991) 4 (1–2) *Humanitäres Völkerrecht Informationsschriften* 48; and note P Antoine, *International Humanitarian Law and the Protection of the Environment in Time of Armed Conflict* (IRRC, 1992) p.526.

provisions fail 'to acknowledge that the use of such weapons is prohibited only if their use is clearly excessive in relation to the overall concrete and direct military advantage anticipated'.[118]

5.130 It should, however, be remembered that Article 8(2)(b)(iv) of the Rome Statute sets forth the following war crime:

> Intentionally launching an attack in the knowledge that such attack will cause incidental loss of life or injury to civilians or damage to civilian objects or widespread, long-term and severe damage to the natural environment which would be clearly excessive in relation to the concrete and direct overall military advantage anticipated;[119]

5.131 This drafting of the crime makes it clear that the natural environment is, in principle, a civilian object, although to be considered under Article 8(2)(b)(iv), the damage to the environment must first reach the Article 35(3) level. When the proportionality rule is being applied, it is clear that incidental damage to the natural environment must be treated as damage to a civilian object (unless the relevant part of the natural environment has become a military objective).

5.132 If BCI systems are to be used in the conduct of attacks, it follows that planners, commanders and operators must make themselves aware of the incidental damage that planned operations may be expected to cause to the natural environment and must factor that damage into the proportionality assessments that are made in advance of a BCI-enabled attack. If an AB-enabled autonomous weapon system is to be used in connection with decisions to undertake attacks, the AB system must:

1. detect that there are elements of the natural environment that the attack that is being considered may be expected to affect;
2. assess whether those parts of the natural environment are, or are not, military objectives;
3. assess what damage the attack that is being considered may be expected to cause to those elements of the natural environment that are not military objectives;
4. determine whether the method of attack that is being considered minimises collateral damage as a whole, including the expected damage to the parts of the natural environment that are not military objectives; and
5. add the expected damage to those parts of the natural environment to the other collateral damage that the attack that is being considered may be expected to cause when applying the proportionality rule (discussed in Chapter 4).

---

118 US DOD Manual, n.1, para.6.10.3.1.

119 See also Oslo Manual, n.43, Rule 145 and associated Commentary.

If the state is a party to API, the AB system must also: **5.133**

6. determine whether the attack that is being considered may be expected to cause environmental damage that would breach the Article 35(3) threshold. If this is the case, the attack must not proceed.

Scenario 12. State A and State B are both parties to ENMOD. State A has developed a large explosive device capable of detonation underwater. The war with State B is not going well, and some politicians have suggested that the bomb should be detonated in an area of ocean where a tsunami could be triggered to engulf the coastal areas of State B. The State A authorities have pointed out that the casualties that such an attack may be expected to cause and the loss of life would constitute a breach of the ENMOD Convention, and have accordingly rejected the politicians' suggestion. **5.134**

5.11 CIVIL DEFENCE

'Civil defence means the performance of … [certain] humanitarian tasks intended to protect the civilian population against the dangers, and to help it to recover from the immediate effects, of hostilities or disasters and also to provide the conditions necessary for its survival.'[120] An exhaustive list of civil defence tasks is then provided, including warning, evacuation, managing shelters, rescue, medical services, fire-fighting, protective measures, emergency accommodation provision, emergency repair of utilities, emergency disposal of the dead and certain associated activities.[121] **5.135**

Subject to the provisions of API, '[c]ivilian civil defence organisations and their personnel shall be respected and protected … [and] shall be entitled to perform their civil defence tasks except in case of imperative military necessity'.[122] This special protection also applies to 'civilians who, although not members of civil defence organizations, respond to an appeal from the competent authorities and perform civil defence tasks under their control'.[123] Buildings and matériel[124] used for civil defence purposes and shelters provided **5.136**

120 API, n.5, Art.61(a), first sentence.
121 API, n.5, Art.61(a).
122 API, n.5, Art.62(1).
123 API, n.5, Art.62(2).
124 Civil defence matériel means equipment, supplies and transports used by civil defence organisations for the performance of civil defence tasks: API, n.5, Art.61(d).

for the civilian population are covered by Article 52 (as civilian objects).[125] Civil defence organisations of neutral states or other states not involved in the armed conflict which perform civil defence tasks in the territory of a party to the conflict with that party's consent and under its control are similarly protected but notification of that assistance must be given as soon as possible to other parties to the conflict.[126]

5.137 Article 65 of API states that civil defence protections do not cease unless civilian civil defence organisations, personnel, buildings, shelters and matériel 'commit or are used to commit, outside their proper tasks, acts harmful to the enemy. Protection may, however, cease only after a warning has been given, setting, whenever appropriate, a reasonable time limit, and after such warning has remained unheeded.'[127]

5.138 The following situations are not considered to be harmful to the enemy:

(a) civil defence tasks are carried out under the direction or control of military authorities;
(b) civilian civil defence personnel co-operate with military personnel in the performance of civil defence tasks, or that some military personnel are attached to civilian civil defence organisations;
(c) the performance of civil defence tasks may incidentally benefit military victims, particularly those who are *hors de combat*.[128]

5.139 Under Article 66 of API, '[e]ach Party to the conflict shall endeavour to ensure that its civil defence organizations, their personnel, buildings and matériel [and shelters] are identifiable while they are exclusively devoted to the performance of civil defence tasks'.[129] Provision is made in API for an international distinctive sign for civil defence, namely an equilateral blue triangle on an

---

125 API, n.5, Art.62(3) but they may only be destroyed or diverted from normal use by the party to which they belong.

126 API, n.5, Art.64(1); Office of the Judge Advocate General of Canada, Law of Armed Conflict at the Operational and Tactical Levels, Joint Doctrine Manual dated 13 August 2001, para.440, pp.4-9–4-10. Such activity is not regarded as interference in the conflict, but the activity should be undertaken with due regard to the security interests of the parties to the conflict.

127 API, n.5, Art.65(1).

128 API, n.5, Art.65(2) and see AMW Manual, n.48, Rule 92 and associated Commentary at pp.213–4. Note that the carriage by civil defence personnel of light individual weapons for the maintenance of order does not amount to an act harmful to the enemy, but where fighting on land is occurring or likely, the parties to the conflict will do what is necessary to limit such weapons to handguns: Art.65(3). The AMW Manual notes that civil defence tasks must be humanitarian and must not contribute to the war effort – Rule 1k, para.3 – but notes that fighting a fire at a military objective to protect civilians or civilian objects in the vicinity would be a civil defence activity.

129 API, n.5, Art.66(1).

orange background.[130] In addition, members of the armed forces and military units assigned to civil defence organisations must be respected and protected subject to certain conditions.[131]

If a BCI system is being used in connection with attack operations, it will be necessary for planners, commanders and operators to recognise the buildings, shelters, equipment, supplies and transports used by the civil defence organisation of the adverse party and to ensure that no such personnel or thing is made the object of attack. This will involve ensuring that the operator of the BCI system is not capable of transmitting a thought or intention to attack to the system that would be used to activate the weapon. Perhaps this can best be achieved by ensuring that the BCI is switched off until all required precautions have been completed. **5.140**

If an AB system is being used to decide upon attacks, it will be necessary for that system to: **5.141**

1. recognise the civil defence sign specified in Article 66(4);
2. reliably and consistently not attack any personnel or object displaying that sign;
3. recognise personnel, buildings, shelters, equipment, supplies and transports that are being used for civil defence purposes;
4. reliably and consistently not attack any personnel or object referred to in point 3 above;
5. recognise the civil defence nature of tasks carried out under the control of military authorities;
6. reliably and consistently not attack personnel and matériel involved in such tasks;
7. recognise that military personnel are co-operating with civil defence personnel in the performance of civil defence tasks or are attached to civil defence organisations; and
8. reliably and consistently not attack persons referred to in point 7.

130 API, n.5, Art.66(4) describes the sign as 'an equilateral blue triangle on an orange ground'.

131 API, n.5, Art.67(1). The conditions are that the personnel and the units must be permanently and exclusively assigned or devoted to civil defence tasks, that such armed forces personnel do not perform any other military duties during the conflict, that such personnel are clearly distinguishable from other members of the armed forces by prominently displaying the distinctive civil defence sign (they shall also be issued with an identity card provided for in the Annex to AP1), that such personnel are only issued with light individual weapons to maintain order or for self-defence in accordance with Art.65(3), that such personnel do not directly participate in the hostilities and do not commit acts harmful to the enemy, and that such personnel or units only fulfil civil defence tasks within the national territory of their own party.

5.12 LOCALITIES AND ZONES UNDER SPECIAL PROTECTION

5.12.1 Non-defended localities

5.142 The parties to the conflict must not 'attack, by any means whatsoever, non-defended localities'.[132] Non-defended localities may be unilaterally declared by the appropriate authorities of a party to the conflict if the inhabited place is 'near or in a zone where armed forces are in contact and which is open for occupation by an adverse party'. The following conditions must apply:

a) all combatants, as well as mobile weapons and mobile military equipment must have been evacuated;
b) no hostile use shall be made of fixed military installations or establishments;
c) no acts of hostility shall be committed by the authorities or by the population; and
d) no activities in support of military operations shall be undertaken.[133]

5.143 The presence inside the locality of specially protected persons, such as medical personnel, and of police forces for the sole purpose of maintaining law and order, will not breach the conditions in Article 59(2).[134]

5.144 Article 59 specifies the following procedure:

1. The declaration must be addressed to the adverse party.
2. The declaration must 'define and describe, as precisely as possible, the limits of the non-defended locality'.
3. The party receiving the declaration must acknowledge it and must treat the locality as non-defended unless the Article 59(2) conditions are not fulfilled.
4. If point 3 applies, the party receiving the declaration must inform the declaring party.
5. Even if the conditions set forth here are not met, other targeting law protections apply, including the distinction principle, the prohibition of indiscriminate attacks, the proportionality and precautions rules.[135]

5.145 As a separate matter, the parties to the conflict can agree that a locality will be non-defended.[136]

5.146 If a BCI system is being used in connection with attack operations, it will be necessary for planners, commanders and operators to be aware of any designation by the adverse party to the conflict of a locality or place as a non-defended

132 API, n.5, Art.59(1).
133 API, n.5, Art.59(2).
134 API, n.5, Art.59(3).
135 API, n.5, Art.59(4).
136 As to which see API, n.5, Art.59(5)–(7).

locality. This will involve ensuring that the accurate co-ordinates of the locality have been entered on a no-strike list and that all necessary precautions are taken to ensure that no attack against such a locality takes place while the locality continues to satisfy the conditions set forth in Article 59(2). In particular, the operator of the BCI system must not be capable of transmitting to the BCI system a thought or intention to attack the relevant locality or place. As suggested in the previous section, this can, perhaps, best be achieved by ensuring that the BCI is only activated when any necessary precautions have been completed.

If an AB system is being used to decide upon attacks, it will be necessary for the system: **5.147**

1. to have loaded into it the precise co-ordinates of any non-defended locality, probably as part of a no-strike list;
2. to reliably and consistently not make the non-defended locality the object of attack; and
3. to reliably and consistently recognise the markings of the non-defended locality provided for in Article 59(6) of API and to refrain from making any location within those markings the object of attack.

Any decision to attack a non-defended locality, say because the requirements under Article 59(2) are no longer being complied with, will, it is suggested, need to be made by a human being, probably a commander of appropriate seniority. An AB-enabled autonomous weapon system will therefore need to be programmed not to attack anything within the co-ordinates of such a locality until explicit authority has been received by the AB from a human planner, operator or commander. **5.148**

All weapon-related BCI and AB systems together with their associated weapons that are mobile in nature must be evacuated by the party declaring it from the non-defended locality before it makes the declaration.[137] After the declaration has been made, any BCI- or AB-related weapons or other weapons that remain there must not be used either for hostile purposes or otherwise to support military operations. AB systems must be deactivated and must not be capable of self-reactivation. **5.149**

Scenario 13. State A wants to protect its culturally important town, Albino, from attack. It removes all military equipment from the town, instructs all **5.150**

137 Security considerations will also probably require the removal or destruction of sensitive equipment of this nature.

military units to avoid the town and sends a declaration to State B. The declaration gives the geographical co-ordinates of the area that is to be protected and proposes that the declaration should take effect on a specified date and time. State B initially fails to respond but State B's legal advisers insist that State B's commanders must acknowledge State A's declaration, which they then do. A squadron of State A tanks is located not far from the declared zone but does not enter the zone. State B would be permitted to attack the tanks but must continue to refrain from any attack within the declared zone.

5.12.2 Demilitarized zones

5.151 Article 60 of API recognises that the parties to the conflict may by agreement confer on a zone the status of demilitarised zone. They must not extend their military operations to such zones in breach of the agreement between them.[138] 'The agreement shall be an express agreement, may be concluded verbally or in writing', and can be reached through an intermediary. 'The agreement may be concluded in peacetime, as well as after the outbreak of hostilities, and should define and describe, as precisely as possible, the limits of the demilitarized zone and, if necessary, lay down the methods of supervision.'[139]

5.152 Article 60(3) then sets forth conditions that should normally apply to a demilitarised zone. The listed conditions are similar to those in Article 59(2), although Article 60(3)(d) is expressed a little differently. 'Should normally' indicates that Article 60(3) has the status of guidance, it being appreciated that these zones are set up by agreement between the belligerents. Article 60(4) makes similar provision to Article 59(3). Provision is made for the marking of non-defended localities that have been established by agreement and of demilitarised zones.[140]

5.153 Under Article 60(6): 'if the fighting draws near to a demilitarized zone, and if the Parties to the conflict have so agreed, none of them may use the zone for purposes related to the conduct of military operations or unilaterally revoke its status.' Paragraph (7) refers to a situation in which 'one of the Parties to the conflict commits a material breach of the provisions of paragraphs 3 or 6'. This should, the author suggests, be interpreted as referring, in the case of the paragraph (3) conditions, to the extent that the conditions referred to in paragraph

---

138 API, n.5, Art.60(1).

139 API, n.5, Art.60(1) and (2). For a discussion of the notion of demilitarised zones, see M Roscini and M Longobardo, 'Demilitarized Zones', in E P J Myjer and T Marauhn (eds), *Research Handbook on International Arms Control Law* (Edward Elgar Publishing, 2022), 467–80.

140 API, n.5, Arts 59(6) and 60(5).

(3) are included in the agreement between the parties. This, it seems, is a provision that is reflecting the general obligation for belligerents to comply in good faith with the terms of agreements reached between them. If paragraph (6) applies, 'the other party shall be released from its obligations under the agreement'. In such circumstances, the zone loses its status but the other targeting law protections discussed in this and the previous chapter shall apply.

If a BCI system is being used in connection with attacks, relevant planners, commanders and operators must be fully aware of the terms of any agreement setting up a demilitarised zone in the territory held by the adversary, must know the co-ordinates of the zone and the activities that, respectively, are permitted and prohibited inside the zone. If there is no clear information that the terms of that agreement are being breached, planners, commanders and operators must ensure that military operations involving BCI-enabled weapons are not extended to any location that is within the zone covered by the agreement and that the zone is not used for any purpose relating to military operations. If the party in whose territory the zone is located breaches the terms of the agreement, planners, commanders or operators must assess whether that breach is material (probably meaning whether the breach makes a significant difference in military terms). If it does, they should apply the principles of distinction and discrimination and the proportionality and precautions rules before undertaking any attack. **5.154**

If an AB system is being employed, it must: **5.155**

1. have the co-ordinates of the demilitarised zone, the conditions and other relevant terms of the agreement fed into the mission control system;
2. reliably and consistently recognise the status of the relevant area as a demilitarised zone and refrain from extending its military operations to, or undertaking attacks within, such a zone; and
3 refer to an operator any information suggesting that the zone no longer fulfils the terms of the agreement between the belligerents.

All weapon-related BCI and AB systems together with their associated weapons that are mobile in nature must be evacuated from the demilitarised zone before the agreement comes into effect. After the agreement has taken effect, any BCI- or AB-related weapons or other weapons that remain there must not be used either for hostile purposes or otherwise to support military operations. AB systems must be deactivated and must not be capable of self-reactivation. **5.156**

5.13 HUMANITARIAN RELIEF

5.157 Under Geneva Convention IV, States Parties 'shall allow the free passage of all consignments of medical and hospital stores and objects necessary for religious worship' and 'essential foodstuffs, clothing and tonics intended for children under fifteen, expectant mothers and maternity cases'.[141] This duty to allow free passage is, however, subject to the party allowing passage being 'satisfied that there are no serious reasons for fearing: (a) that the consignments may be diverted from their destination, (b) that the control may not be effective, or (c) that a definite advantage may accrue to the military efforts or economy of the enemy through the substitution of the abovementioned consignments for goods which would otherwise be provided or produced by the enemy or through the release of such material, services or facilities as would otherwise be required for the production of such goods'.[142] The consignments must be forwarded as rapidly as possible but the state permitting free passage has the right to 'prescribe the technical arrangements under which' that passage is permitted.[143]

5.158 API requires that where there is not adequate provision for the civilian population of listed items,[144] impartial humanitarian relief action shall be undertaken without any adverse distinction[145] subject to the agreement of the parties concerned. The parties to the conflict and States Parties generally must 'facilitate rapid and unimpeded passage of all relief consignments, equipment and personnel'.[146] Article 70(3) of API permits the parties allowing passage of these consignments to prescribe technical arrangements, including search, and prohibits their diversion or delay. The parties to the conflict must protect these relief consignments and must facilitate their rapid distribution.[147]

5.159 The obligation to allow free passage clearly implies an obligation not to attack the consignments of humanitarian relief supplies. Moreover, the principles

---

141 Geneva Convention (IV) relative to the Protection of Civilian Persons in Time of War, Geneva, 12 August 1949, 75 UNTS 287 (GCIV), Art.23(1).

142 GCIV, ibid, Art.23(2).

143 GCIV, ibid, Art.23(4).

144 Food, medical supplies, clothing, bedding, means of shelter, and other supplies essential for the survival of the civilian population, objects necessary for religious worship: API, n.5, Art.69(1).

145 Priority shall be given to persons such as children, expectant mothers, maternity cases and nursing mothers who, under GCIV or API, are to be accorded privileged treatment or special protection: API, n.5, Art.70(1), final sentence.

146 API, n.5, Art.70(2).

147 API, n.5, Art.70(4).

and rules of the law of targeting discussed in Chapter 4 must also be complied with.

Planners, commanders and operators involved in operations using BCI-enabled systems must therefore not direct attacks against such relief consignments and must allow their free passage. It will also be for those persons to consider whether the fears referred to in Geneva Convention IV (GCIV) Article 23(2) apply and if so what technical arrangements would be necessary and lawful. Where AB-enabled systems are being used by that party, it will, in the author's view, be for the planners, commanders and operators of operations involving such systems to ensure that the requirements set forth in this section are complied with. The provision of effective protection will be dependent on information as to the relief supplies and relief operations, their locations, numbers, the vehicles being employed, the routes being used, and any other relevant details being passed in a timely way to relevant personnel. **5.160**

5.14 DENIAL OF QUARTER AND PERSONS WHO ARE *HORS DE COMBAT*

'It is prohibited to order that there shall be no survivors, to threaten an adversary therewith or to conduct hostilities on this basis.'[148] Planners, commanders and operators involved in operations using BCI systems must comply with this rule, which reflects customary law and therefore binds all states in international and non-international armed conflicts. Compliance with the obligation will be the responsibility of those individuals, who must not engage in any activity, whether or not involving BCI-enabled technologies, in a manner that would breach this rule. Likewise, no AB system should be programmed so as to conduct military operations, including attacks, on the basis that is prohibited by the rule, and no AB system should be capable of issuing the threats prohibited by the rule. **5.161**

Article 41, API then further provides: 'A person who is recognized or who, in the circumstances, should be recognized to be *hors de combat* shall not be made the object of attack.'[149] The treaty then stipulates that '[a] person is *hors de combat* if: (a) he is in the power of an adverse Party; (b) he clearly expresses an intention to surrender; or (c) he has been rendered unconscious or is otherwise incapacitated by wounds or sickness, and therefore is incapable of defending **5.162**

148 API, n.5, Art.40.
149 API, n.5, Art.41(1).

himself; provided that in any of these cases he abstains from any hostile act and does not attempt to escape.'[150]

5.163 A combatant is entitled to continue fighting up to the time when they surrender. The fact that a soldier is wounded does not mean that the soldier is *hors de combat*. The wounded soldier only becomes *hors de combat*, and thus protected by this provision, either when they clearly express an intention to surrender or when they are unconscious or incapacitated by wounds or sickness and are thus incapable of defending themselves.[151]

5.164 Planners, commanders and operators involved in operations using BCI systems must actually recognise a person as being *hors de combat* in all situations where the person should be so recognised. Having recognized the individual as being *hors de combat*, they must not make the individual the object of attack. AB systems involved in deciding on attacks must also reliably and consistently recognise a person as being *hors de combat* in all circumstances in which the person should be so recognised. In the AB context, this means, in the author's view, that the AB system should reliably and consistently recognise the person as being *hors de combat* whenever the attendant circumstances are such that a human commander should so recognise the person. This implies that the AB system must reliably and consistently:

1. detect that a person is in the hands of any adverse party to the conflict;
2. detect that a person is clearly expressing an intention to surrender;
3. detect that a person is unconscious or incapacitated by wounds or sickness and thus incapable of defending themselves; and
4. if points 1 or 2 or 3 apply, refrain from making the person the object of attack.

5.165 Where the proviso to Article 41(2) is concerned, much will depend on whether the AB system is capable of detecting a hostile act or an attempt to escape. If it can do so consistently and reliably, it may be programmed to make the person the object of attack when either of those events is clearly and unambiguously occurring. If there is doubt as to whether a hostile act or an attempt to escape is taking place, the author takes the view that the AB must be programmed not to make the individual the object of attack. If the AB system

150 API, n.5, Art.41(2), UK Manual, n.31, para.5.6. The *hors de combat* rule applies to persons, that is to combatants and to civilians who have been taking a direct part in the hostilities; AMW Manual, n.48, Rule 15b, para.4. If a person does not indicate the intention to surrender in a way that the enemy can perceive and understand, they remain liable to be attacked: ibid, Rule 15b, para.5. The rule does not apply to AB systems that may have been rendered inoperative. This is because AB systems are not persons.

151 UK Manual, n.31, para.5.6.1.

cannot consistently and reliably detect that the person is undertaking a hostile act or attempting to escape, it must refrain from making any person to whom points 1, 2 or 3 apply the object of attack.

If other persons in the vicinity of the person who is *hors de combat* are continuing to fight, they may be made the object of attack. **5.166**

Scenario 14. State A's infantry patrol has an autonomous land roving vehicle which is equipped with an autonomous high velocity rifle system which is, in turn, controlled by AB technology. The system employs a target evaluation system which reliably detects when an opposing combatant is standing, kneeling or lying flat on the ground. It has been programmed to assume that any adversary personnel who are lying down on the ground are wounded to such a degree as to be incapable of defending themselves. The weapon system encounters an enemy soldier who has collapsed onto his knees and is propped up against a chainlink fence. The soldier cannot move because of his injuries, cannot therefore take hold of his rifle and is essentially defenceless. The AB classifies the enemy soldier as wounded but not defenceless and therefore fires upon him, killing him. This would be a breach of API Article 41. **5.167**

Scenario 15. A soldier from State A is attacked by enemy State B infantry personnel. He is badly wounded but let us assume that the State B personnel know that the soldier is equipped with a weapon that is BCI-controlled such that if he looks at the target and develops the relevant thought or intent, his weapon will be fired in the corresponding direction. The international law issue is whether the wounded soldier, who is still conscious and apparently alert, is *hors de combat*. The author believes the answer to that question will depend on whether the soldier has or has not been rendered defenceless by his injuries. If he has, he is *hors de combat* provided that he refrains from any hostile act and does not attempt to escape.[152] **5.168**

5.15 JOURNALISTS AND THEIR EQUIPMENT

Under Article 79(1) of API: '[j]ournalists engaged in dangerous professional missions in areas of armed conflict shall be considered as civilians within the meaning of Article 50, paragraph 1.' They are protected 'provided that they **5.169**

152 See the discussion of certain *hors de combat* and perfidy issues in N Lubell and K Al-Khateeb, 'Cyborg Soldiers: Military use of Brain-Computer Interfaces and the Law of Armed Conflict' (11 April 2022), later published in L A Dickinson and E Berg (eds), *Big Data and Armed Conflict: Legal Issues Above and Below the Armed Conflict Threshold* (Oxford University Press, 2024), 16–17.

take no action adversely affecting their status as civilians …'. This may cause confusion because taking a direct part in hostilities does not, as a consequence, cause a person to cease to be a civilian. Article 79(2) appears to be intended simply to point out that the protection of journalists, like that of other civilians, is subject to them not directly participating in the hostilities.

5.170 Accordingly, when BCI and AB systems are used in connection with attacks, the principle of distinction must be applied; they must not be made the object of attack; they must be included as civilians when the proportionality rule is being applied; and Article 57 precautions must be taken with a view to protecting them. The notion of journalist extends to reporters, camera personnel and sound recordists. Their cameras, recording, transmitting and other equipment will be classed as protected civilian objects.[153]

153 See Customary Law Study, n.1, pp.115–19.

6

WEAPONS LAW AND BRAIN TECHNOLOGIES

6.1 INTRODUCTION

The law that determines whether weapons, means or methods of warfare are prohibited by the law of armed conflict or are subject to restrictions on the circumstances in which they can lawfully be used is the subject of this chapter. There is an important distinction between the rules that regulate weapons as such, weapons law, and the law that deals with targeting, which is addressed **6.001** in Chapters 4 and 5. Whereas targeting law is concerned with the lawfulness of military operations against a specific target on a known occasion using a particular means or method of warfare, weapons law is concerned with the lawfulness of weapons per se and the legality of their employment in the general circumstances that are intended when they are acquired.

6.002 Before we get into the detail of that body of law, however, it is important that the terms used in the previous sentence be defined. The definitions that are discussed here take on a particular significance when brain technologies are being considered. If, for example, a brain-computer interface system (BCI) is being used to enable the direct control of a weapon, means or method of warfare from the mind of, say, a soldier, does such a process cause the soldier whose mind is employed in that way, or for that matter the mind itself, to become an integral part of the weapon system, or does the neurotechnological aspect actually make no difference for these purposes? This will be discussed in the next section.

6.003 The international law treaties that apply to armed conflict do not define the meaning of the word 'weapon'. Quoting, in part, Justin McLelland, the author has in the past suggested that a weapon: 'connotes an offensive capability that can be applied to a military object or enemy combatant. The means whereby this is achieved will involve a device, system, munition, implement, substance, object, or piece of equipment that is used, that it is intended to use, or that has been designed for use to apply the offensive capability, usually causing injury or damage to an adverse party to an armed conflict.'[1] A 'means of warfare' is also not defined in the treaties, but is generally understood to refer to weapons and weapon systems, that is 'all weapons, weapons platforms, and associated equipment used directly to deliver force during hostilities'.[2] When discussing the meaning of weapon, the HPCR Air and Missile Warfare Manual (AMW Manual) explains that a weapon also includes the integral equipment directly

1 J. McClelland, 'The Review of Weapons in Accordance with Article 36 of Additional Protocol 1' (2003) 850 IRRC 397; W H Boothby, *Weapons and the Law of Armed Conflict*, 2nd edn (Oxford University Press, 2016), 4 and see Program on Humanitarian Policy and Conflict Research at Harvard University (HPCR), *Manual on the International Law Applicable to Air and Missile Warfare* (March 2010) (AMW Manual), available at https://cdn.ca9.uscourts.gov/datastore/library/2013/09/06/Flores_Manual.pdf,(ff) Rule 1. See, with reference to human enhancements, the discussion in R Liivoja and L Chircop, 'Are Enhanced Warfighters Weapons, Means or Methods of Warfare?' (2018) 94 Int'l L Stud 161 173–8 and with reference to BCIs, N Lubell and K Al-Khateeb, 'Cyborg Soldiers: Military use of Brain-Computer Interfaces and the Law of Armed Conflict' (11 April 2022), later published in L A Dickinson and E Berg (eds), *Big Data and Armed Conflict: Legal Issues Above and Below the Armed Conflict Threshold* (Oxford University Press, 2024), 12–14.

2 Boothby, n.1, 5.

necessary to cause the force which launches the ammunition or munitions.[3] Methods of warfare 'consist of the various general categories of operations, such as bombing, as well as the specific tactics used for attack, such as high altitude bombing'.[4] Autonomous attack operations and the use of BCIs to undertake attacks would both be regarded as examples of methods of warfare.

6.2 APPLYING THE WEAPON NOTION TO BRAIN TECHNOLOGY

Taking the BCI example referred to in the previous section, a number of pertinent considerations arise. The first, and perhaps critical, issue is whether the brain is, by means of the BCI, being incorporated into the 'offensive capability' or does the brain remain distinct from that capability. This may be something that can only really be determined by reference to the particular kind of BCI and how that BCI interacts with the firing system. In most cases, the author would suggest that the brain will indeed remain distinct. In a sense, the only difference here between a conventional weapon and one that employs BCI in that manner is that the BCI is transmitting the operator's instruction directly from the brain to the firing system without the need for an intervening operator activity, such as pulling a trigger, pressing a firing button, or, at the more basic level, thrusting a bayonet. On this interpretation, the operator, and the brain of the operator, remain distinct from the firing system. While this interpretation would seem to follow from a clinical assessment of the processes involved, however, the author cannot be certain that states will view the matter in that way. **6.004**

A different situation arises if a BCI is used in order adversely to affect the cognition of an enemy combatant. In that example the BCI would, the author suggests, be characterised as a weapon if the effect on the enemy combatant can properly be described as an injury. If, however, the effect on the enemy combatant is, for example, to make that individual careless or to reduce the attentiveness with which they perform their duties, the question that then arises is whether that effect can properly be regarded as an injury. Arguably, if the effect that the BCI is intended to have does not amount to an injury, the BCI is not being used as a weapon. However, it is likely that the use of BCIs to create the effects discussed in this paragraph will in due time come to be regarded as methods of warfare with the important consequence that states **6.005**

3 AMW Manual, n.1, para.4 of the Commentary accompanying Rule 1(ff).

4 AMW Manual, n.1, Rule 1(v).

that are party to Additional Protocol I (API) will be required by Article 36 to review such methods before their adoption of them.[5]

6.006 Taking this part of the discussion one stage further, let us imagine a weapon system that involves an artificial brain (AB). For the purposes of the present paragraph, assume that the relevant artificial brain is based entirely on computer technology, that is that no biological brain material, whether taken from a human or produced synthetically, is involved. In this situation, the human being is being removed from the decision to apply the offensive capability. In a sense, such an arrangement will have significant similarities with a weapon system based on the more sophisticated levels of artificial intelligence (AI). Indeed, viewed literally, AI is exactly what such a system is designed to produce. While views may differ on this point, it would seem to the author that the commander or operator who initiates the military operation using a weapon system equipped with such AB computer technology remains distinct from the composite weapon system, and that the computer technology part of it does not stop the weapon system as a whole (including the computer-based AB) from being a tool that the operator or commander is deciding to use. The commander's or operator's decision whether to employ the weapon system will be based on their understanding of its capabilities and limitations, on what is known about the circumstances in which it is to be employed, and on other information available to that operator/commander.

6.007 The third circumstance to consider is a system employing an AB constructed in whole or in part using real or synthetic brain material. Arguably, similar considerations apply to those discussed in the previous paragraph. The operator or commander retains the ability to decide whether to employ the real or synthetic brain weapon system. The distinction between operator/commander and weapon system is thereby maintained. The real or synthetic brain itself, however, would, the author suggests, become part of the weapon system. On this view, it would only be when the decision to deploy the weapon system, that is to initiate the mission, is delegated to the brain element in the weapon system itself that the brain and any attached human being become part of that system. The essential notion here, as the author sees it, is the distinction between a system that is a tool in the hand of the operator/commander and a

5 Note, in S E White, 'Brave New World: Neurowarfare and the Limits of International Humanitarian Law' (2008) 41(1) *Cornell International Law Journal* 177, 190 the suggestion that 'international law most likely does not prohibit brain-machine interfaced weapons' and the associated reasoning at pp. 191 and 192.

situation in which the operator, through the integration of their brain in the weapon system, becomes an integral element in that weapon system.[6]

If the reader finds the above analysis to be persuasive, this may help when it comes to considering when, or if, certain technologies take on the characteristics of a human being and, in the reciprocal sense, whether those technologies have the effect that the human being becomes an integral element in a machine. The author stresses, however, that what is put forward in this section is only one interpretation and that what will matter is how states interpret these complex and very sensitive issues. It is entirely possible that states will view the distinction between man and machine differently. Considerations of public policy, ethical and moral concerns, and the precise capabilities of the particular systems and the ways in which they are intended to be used will all, among others, be important considerations. Indeed, state concerns about the ethical acceptability, or otherwise, of the use of these technologies in warfare are likely to influence how the technologies are classified for the purposes of current and future legal rules as well as the detail of any new rules that are negotiated and adopted. 6.008

At the time of writing, there is no provision of international law that specifically addresses the use of brain technology in warfare. This will cause the reader to wonder whether this results in a legal vacuum. The next section will explain why that is not the case. 6.009

6.3 THE MARTENS CLAUSE

In 1899,[7] and indeed earlier in the 19th century,[8] it was accepted as a principle of law that the right of the parties to an armed conflict to choose methods and means of warfare is not unlimited. That principle has been reflected somewhat more recently in Article 35(1) of API. It is a customary principle of weapons 6.010

6 Importantly, there is a distinction between a BCI enabling the operator to communicate their thought or intent directly to a weapon system and a situation in which the brain of the operator becomes a component in the weapon system. In the former situation, the weapon system is being employed by the operator; it is a tool in the operator's hands, so to speak. In a sense, in the latter situation, the weapon system is employing the brain of the person. The author stresses, however, that this is merely his interpretation, and readers will have their own views.

7 'The right of belligerents to adopt means of injuring the enemy is not unlimited': Regulations Concerning the Laws and Customs of War on Land, annexed to Convention (II) with Respect to the Laws and Customs of War on Land, The Hague, 29 July 1899 (Hague Convention II), Art.22.

8 Project of an International Declaration concerning the Laws and Customs of War, Brussels, 27 August 1874 (Brussels Declaration), Art.12: '[t]he laws of war do not recognize in belligerents an unlimited power in the adoption of means of injuring the enemy'.

law and is binding upon all states in both international and non-international armed conflicts. The effect of this principle is that there are limits on the kinds of weapons and methods of warfare that states are allowed to use in armed conflict hostilities. It is the remaining principles and rules of the law of armed conflict (LOAC) that prescribe what those limits consist of. The LOAC is not generally expressed in permissive terms, allowing the use of specific weapons. On the contrary, the principles and rules are expressed as prohibitions and restrictions, with the implicit understanding that if a specific use of a weapon is not prohibited, it is permitted.

6.011 This is the context in which an important preambular provision, dating from 1899, should be considered. Under this provision, the negotiators of Hague Convention II of that year pointed out that the absence of specific treaty or customary rules dealing with a particular weapon or associated technology should not be interpreted as meaning that no law applies. The 1899 version of that provision is as follows:

> Until a more complete code of the laws of war is issued, the High Contracting Parties think it right to declare that in cases not included in the Regulations adopted by them, populations and belligerents remain under the protection and empire of the principles of international law, as they result from the usages established between civilized nations, from the laws of humanity, and the requirements of the public conscience.[9]

6.012 Hague Convention II of 1899 was superseded by Hague Convention IV of 1907, which contained a corresponding preambular provision. Article 1(2) of API is the modern formulation and is as follows:

> In cases not covered by this Protocol or by other international agreements, civilians and combatants remain under the protection and authority of the principles of international law derived from established custom, from the principles of humanity and from the dictates of public conscience.

6.013 This preambular paragraph and its modern formulation, known as the Martens Clause, makes it clear that if circumstances arise in armed conflict for which there is no specific legal provision, the customary principles of the LOAC will apply, and combatants and civilians will be both constrained and protected by those principles. The idea of established usages can, in the modern context, be seen as referring to customary principles established by the general practice of states and humanity is, in its own right, a customary principle of the LOAC.[10]

---

9 Hague Convention II, n.7, Preamble.

10 The principle of humanity forbids the infliction of suffering, injury, or destruction not actually necessary for the accomplishment of legitimate military purposes. It therefore forms the basis of the prohibition of

As noted at the end of the previous section, the law of armed conflict contains no principles or rules that refer specifically to brain technologies. The legal situation described in the Martens Clause therefore applies and accordingly, in sections 6.4 and 6.5, the customary principles of weapons law are discussed. Thereafter, the customary and treaty rules of weapons law will be considered, noting the principles and rules that prohibit certain weapons and the rules that restrict the circumstances in which certain weapons can lawfully be employed. The aim is to determine whether each rule applies in the context of military operations involving brain technology. Finally, the legal obligations of states to determine whether new weapons comply with their legal obligations will be examined. **6.014**

6.4 SUPERFLUOUS INJURY OR UNNECESSARY SUFFERING

It has, since the middle of the 19th century, been accepted that the employment of weapons, projectiles and material and methods of warfare which are of a nature to cause superfluous injury or unnecessary suffering is prohibited. This notion was first expressed in the Preamble to the St Petersburg Declaration.[11] It is a customary principle that binds all states in relation to both international and non-international armed conflicts. The principle was described by the International Court of Justice as 'cardinal' and 'intransgressible'.[12] While the Hague Regulations of 1899 prohibited employing 'arms, projectiles or material of a nature to cause superfluous injury',[13] the formulation of the same rule in the 1907 Hague Regulations prohibits the employment of 'arms, projectiles or material calculated to cause unnecessary suffering'.[14] The modern articulation **6.015**

unnecessary suffering, the requirement of proportionality and the immunity of civilians and the civilian population from being made the object of attack: UK Manual, para.2.4.1.

11 Declaration renouncing the Use in Time of War of Explosive Projectiles under 400 grammes weight, St Petersburg, 29 November 11 December 1868, 138 CTS 297. The Preamble to that Treaty stated as follows: Considering that the process of civilization should have the effect of alleviating as much as possible the calamities of war; That the only legitimate object which states should endeavour to accomplish during war is to weaken the military forces of the enemy; That for this purpose it is sufficient to disable the greatest possible number of men; That this object would be exceeded by the employment of arms which uselessly aggravate the sufferings of disabled men, or render their death inevitable.

12 International Court of Justice, Advisory Opinion on the Legality of the Threat or Use of Nuclear Weapons [1996] ICJ Reports 226, 35 ILM 809 (ICJ Nuclear Weapons Advisory Opinion), paras 78 and 79 and International Committee of the Red Cross, *Customary International Humanitarian Law*, Vol.1 (J-M Henckaerts and L Doswald-Beck (eds), Cambridge University Press, 2005) (Customary Law Study), Vol 1, 237, Rule 70.

13 Regulations annexed to Hague Convention II, n.7, Art.23(e).

14 Regulations annexed to Hague Convention (IV) Respecting the Laws and Customs of War on Land, The Hague, 18 October 1907 (Hague Convention IV), Art.23(e).

of the principle in Article 35(2) of API is generally accepted by states[15] and prohibits the employment of 'weapons, projectiles and material and methods of warfare of a nature to cause superfluous injury or unnecessary suffering'.[16]

6.016 The essentially comparative words 'superfluous' and 'unnecessary' make it clear that the principle involves a comparison, but neither the Hague Regulations nor API specify what is to be compared with the injury and suffering. The obvious answer lies in the purpose for which weapons are normally used in hostilities, namely to cause injury or damage to enemy personnel or objects and thereby to achieve a military advantage. It is therefore clear that the superfluous injury/unnecessary suffering principle requires that the nature and scale of the generic military advantage to be anticipated from the weapon in the application(s) for which it is designed to be used be compared with the pattern of injury and suffering associated with the normal intended use of the weapon.[17]

6.017 While the principle is easy to state, the practical conduct of the required comparison is not so straightforward. Suffering and injury are not easy to measure[18] and military advantage is a fundamentally different notion. The fact that a weapon can be expected to cause severe injury or death will not, alone, cause the weapon to breach this principle. The legal issue is whether the very nature of the weapon is to cause injury or suffering which is greater than is required for the achievement of the generic military purpose in using the weapon. If the injury or suffering inevitably caused by the weapon in its normal or designed circumstances of use is disproportionate to its military purpose or utility the rule will be broken. In making that determination, a comparison will be made with weapons that are currently used to accomplish the same generic military purposes.

---

15 The US prefers the 'calculated to cause' formulation in the 1907 Regulations ibid: US DoD *Law of War Manual* (June 2015, as subsequently amended) (US DoD Manual), para.6.6.1. The author suggests, however, that the US would nevertheless find a weapon the very nature of which is to cause injury or suffering for which there is no corresponding military purpose to be legally unacceptable.

16 Protocol Additional to the Geneva Conventions of 12 August 1949, and Relating to the Protection of Victims of International Armed Conflicts, Geneva, 8 June 1977, 1125 UNTS 3 (Additional Protocol I or API), Art.35(2); Rome Statute of the International Criminal Court, Rome, 17 July 1998, Art.8(2)(b)(xx).

17 W J Fenrick, 'The Conventional Weapons Convention: A Modest but Useful Treaty' (1990) 279 IRRC 498, 500 and W Hays Parks, 'Means and Methods of Warfare', Symposium issued in Honour of Edward R Cummings (2006) 38 *George Washington International Law Review* 511, 536, n.25.

18 Statement concerning unnecessary suffering presented by the informal working group of medical experts to the Second Session of the Conference of Government Experts on the Use of Certain Conventional Weapons set forth in the International Committee of the Red Cross, *Commentary on the Additional Protocols of 8 June 1977* (Y Sandoz, C Swinarski and B Zimmermann (eds), 1987) (API Commentary), para.1429.

The focus of this principle is the effects of a weapon system on enemy combatants and directly participating civilians. It is unlikely to be relevant if the weapon system is designed for use against objects.[19] Moreover, the principle is likely to be of greatest relevance to the warhead or other injuring mechanism, as opposed to the neurotechnological aspect of the decision to undertake attacks. The principle will, nevertheless, be of great importance where, as will usually be the case, a weapon system that involves brain technology also has an injuring mechanism. **6.018**

Example 1. Consider, for example, a BCI-enabled laser weapon that is designed, as one of its combat functions, to target human weapon operators and to cause dazzling which in most cases will be permanent. Because the combat function is not to cause permanent blindness, Article 1 of Protocol IV to the Convention on Certain Conventional Weapons (CCW)[20] will not apply. Nevertheless, permanent dazzling is a serious injury and it will be for those undertaking the procurement and for the individual conducting the weapon review to determine whether the weapon in question, in its intended circumstances of use, is of a nature to inflict additional injury or suffering for which there is no corresponding military purpose. If that is considered to be the case, the weapon will breach the superfluous injury/unnecessary suffering principle. **6.019**

6.5 INDISCRIMINATE WEAPONS PRINCIPLE

This is a customary law principle that binds all states in relation to international and non-international armed conflicts. It is based on Article 51(4)(b) and (c) of API where the rule was explicitly stated as a rule of treaty law for the first time. The 1899 Hague Regulations had required the taking of 'all necessary steps ... to spare as far as possible' the buildings and places referred to in Article 27.[21] The Hague Draft Rules of Aerial Warfare were never adopted by states in treaty form. While they are not, therefore, a source of the law **6.020**

19 If, however, the impact of the weapon on the relevant object is intended to cause injury or suffering to persons, the principle should be considered.

20 The prohibition of blinding lasers is discussed in subsection 6.7.3 below.

21 Hague Regulations 1907, n.15, Art.27. The listed places are buildings dedicated to religion, art, science, or charitable purposes, historic monuments, hospitals and places where the sick and wounded are collected, provided they are not being used at the time for military purposes.

as such,[22] it is noteworthy that the drafters included a draft rule prohibiting indiscriminate attacks.[23]

6.021 So, while it can be argued that by 1923 international law recognised that indiscriminate attacks are prohibited, it was only with the adoption of API that a definition of such attacks that specifically prohibits indiscriminate weapons emerged.[24] In API, the meaning of indiscriminate attacks is as follows:

> (a) those which are not directed at a specific military objective;
> (b) those which employ a method or means of combat which cannot be directed at a specific military objective; or
> (c) those which employ a method or means of combat the effects of which cannot be limited as required by th[e] Protocol;
>
> and [which], consequently, in each such case, are of a nature to strike military objectives and civilians or civilian objects without distinction.

6.022 Subparagraph (a) is a targeting law provision and was discussed in Chapter 4. It is subparagraphs (b) and (c) that are the basis for the customary law prohibition of weapons and methods of warfare which are by nature indiscriminate. The principle means that a weapon or way of conducting hostilities will be unlawful if, when employed in the intended manner and in its normal or designed circumstances, it cannot be directed at a specific military objective, or if its effects cannot be reasonably restricted to the target, and if the consequence is that its nature is to strike lawful targets, whether in the form of objects or persons, and protected persons and objects without distinction.[25]

6.023 Systems that are to be used in the conduct of hostilities and that employ brain technologies will need to be carefully assessed. Factors to consider will include:

1. Whether the weapon system, including the brain technology, is robust against external interference.
2. Whether the weapon system, including the brain technology, will perform as intended.
3. Whether the weapon system, including the brain technology, is intended to perform in a way that it will not lead to indiscriminate attacks.
4. Whether risks that are known potentially to apply to the use of AI in connection with hostilities, including design and manufacturing faults, sycophancy,

---

22 Note Statute of the International Court of Justice, San Francisco, 26 June 1945, 33 UNTS 993, Art.38.

23 The Draft Hague Rules of Aerial Warfare, The Hague, December 1922 to February 1923, Art.24(3).

24 Note that neither Hague Regulations 1907, n.15, Art.27 nor Convention (IX) concerning Bombardment by Naval Forces in Time of War. The Hague, 18 October 1907 (Hague Convention IX), Article 5 makes specific reference to indiscriminate weapons.

25 This is what is meant by weapons that are indiscriminate by nature.

the misinterpretation by the system of the allocated task, deliberate deception by the AI system and bias that adversely affects the objectivity of decision-making have been reliably excluded.

5. Whether the way in which the weapon system, including the brain technology, performed in tests was satisfactory.
6. Whether the tests accurately reflected the circumstances in which the weapon systems are intended to be used and were sufficiently rigorous and numerous.
7. Whether there is sufficient understanding of how the brain technology aspect of the weapon system reaches its decisions, and whether this understanding promotes confidence that legally compliant performance in tests is not concealing some underlying system fault that can lead to subsequent decisions and action that would breach the principle.

Ensuring robustness of the computer element in a brain technology-enabled or enhanced weapon system against known hacking exploits may, in some cases, be a simple case of patching against detected vulnerabilities. It may, however, be a more complex task to ensure reasonable robustness of such systems against hacking activity or vulnerabilities that are not yet known. **6.024**

The key point is that weapon systems that are, for whatever reason, inherently indiscriminate are unlawful. **6.025**

Example 2. State A is considering the acquisition of a BCI-enabled weapon system that is mounted on a remotely guided land vehicle. The controller of the land vehicle would be located in a command facility far from the hostilities. The system is being tested at the procurement stage. The weapon system mounted on the vehicle consists of a small turret with twin high-velocity rifles pointing in opposite directions. The controller would use the BCI to aim one of the rifles at the chosen target and to fire the weapon. However, on numerous occasions during pre-procurement tests that replicate the intended circumstances of use, the weapon fires at an object that is not the operator's intended target. The test report concludes that the operator's intent is not being reliably transmitted to the weapon control system and that the weapon cannot therefore be reliably directed at an intended target. The weapon reviewer advises that the BCI weapon system is indiscriminate under Article 51(4)(b) of API and should not be procured. **6.026**

In an interesting analysis, Denise Koecke discusses the lawfulness of using a similar kind of weapon system in two hypothetical modes.[26] In the first, **6.027**

---

26 D Koecke, 'Merging Man and Machine: A Legal Assessment of Brain-computer Interfaces in Armed Conflict' (2025) 107 IRRC 176–99.

active BCI mode, the soldier actively imagines that they are physically initiating the firing mechanism, for example, by imagining that they are pushing a button. Ms Koecke concludes that this mode 'poses no issues of legality'. The author would agree that, subject to sufficiently reliable performance in tests and during operations, such a mode does not per se pose legal challenges. In the second, reactive BCI mode, the BCI recognises the neural signals evoked when the soldier subconsciously recognises a target, whereupon the BCI instantly instructs the weapon to fire. Having thoroughly considered applicable law and notions of meaningful human control, Ms Koecke concludes[27] that pre-deployment testing of such a system would be insufficient to ensure predictability, such that such a system should fail weapon review. The author would observe that the relevant legal criterion to be applied in weapon review is whether the weapon is indiscriminate by nature. The author's view is therefore that a BCI weapon in the reactive BCI mode would fail the indiscriminate weapon test if its reactive technology is such that it cannot, in such a mode, be directed at a military objective with an acceptable degree of reliability.

6.028 It will be for the designers, manufacturers, suppliers, testers, reviewers and procurers of weapon systems involving brain technologies to ensure that they do not breach the principle.

6.6 CUSTOMARY RULES

6.029 As the preceding sections of this chapter show, the customary principles of weapons law apply to weapon systems involving brain technology by virtue of the Martens Clause. Moreover, the International Court of Justice (ICJ) explained that the intrinsically humanitarian character of the principles of international humanitarian law (IHL) 'permeates the entire law of armed conflict and applies to all forms of warfare and to all kinds of weapons, those of the past, those of the present and those of the future'.[28] A reading of the relevant part of the ICJ Advisory Opinion on Nuclear Weapons leads the author to conclude that the ICJ would take the view that it is not just the customary principles that apply to all weapons but also the customary rules of IHL. Accordingly, in this section, the customary rules of weapons law that appear to be relevant to weapons involving the use of brain technologies will be summarised.

27 Koecke, n.26, 198.
28 ICJ Nuclear Weapons Advisory Opinion, n.12, para.86.

6.6.1 Incidental environmental damage

In customary law, the natural environment is, in principle, a civilian object.[29] Subjecting the natural environment to wanton destruction is also prohibited by customary law.[30] The combined effect of these rules is therefore to require all states, as a matter of customary law, to have due regard to the impact their weapons may be expected to have on the natural environment.[31] This customary rule must be taken into account by states when developing new weapons involving brain technologies, where the damaging element of the weapon may be expected to have an adverse impact on the natural environment. The rule applies to both international and non-international armed conflicts. **6.030**

6.6.2 Poison

There is a long-recognised customary rule prohibiting the use in warfare of poison and poisoned weapons. The Lieber Code,[32] the Brussels Declaration[33] and the Oxford Manual[34] all refer to the prohibition. The Hague Regulations of 1899 and of 1907[35] also state the prohibition. All states are therefore prohibited from using poison or poisoned weapons that employ brain technology, and this applies in both international and non-international armed conflicts. **6.031**

The expression 'poison or poisoned weapons' refers to weapons the primary or exclusive effect of which is to poison or asphyxiate.[36] The rule will therefore apply to a weapon the main effect of which is to poison but that may have another injuring mechanism, such as fragmentation. The rule also prohibits any substance that is used to aggravate a wound. Equally prohibited is the poisoning of wells, reservoirs and rivers that the enemy uses for water supplies.[37] **6.032**

---

29 Rome Statute, n.16, Art.8(2)(b)(iv) includes damage to the natural environment in the crime of disproportionate attack; Y Dinstein, *The Conduct of Hostilities under the Law of International Armed Conflict*, 4th edn (Cambridge University Press, 2022), 274.

30 AMW Manual, n.1, Rules 88 and 89; M N Schmitt (ed), *Tallinn Manual 2.0 on the International Law Applicable to Cyber Operations* (Cambridge University Press, 2017) (Tallinn Manual 2.0), para.4 of the Commentary to Rule 143. The US rejects Arts 35(3) and 55 of API and regards environmental damage as only prohibited when it breaches the proportionality rule; see US DoD Manual, n.15, para.6.10.3.1.

31 AMW Manual, n.1, Rule 89.

32 Instructions for the Government of Armies of the United States in the Field, 24 April 1863 (Lieber Code), Art.16.

33 Project of an International Declaration concerning the Laws and Customs of War, Brussels, 27 August 1874.

34 The Laws of War on Land, Oxford, 9 September 1880 (Oxford Manual), art. 8(a).

35 Hague Regulations 1907, n.15, Art.23(a).

36 ICJ Nuclear Weapons Advisory Opinion, n.12, para.111.

37 H Lauterpacht (ed), *Oppenheim's International Law*, Vol.II (Reissue of 1952 edn, Longmans, 1955), available at http://www.gutenburg.org/files/41047/41047-h/41047-h.htm, 340; Customary Law Study, n.12, 253 and API Commentary, n.18, para.1419.

Accordingly, if a computer-based AB system were to decide, for example, to cause a poisonous substance to enter the main water pipe that supplies drinking water to planning staff in a command headquarters building, the fact that AB technology had made the relevant decision would not excuse the decision; the rule would have been breached.

6.6.3 Expanding bullets in international armed conflicts

6.033 Hague Declaration 3 of 1899[38] prohibits 'the use of bullets which expand or flatten easily in the human body, such as bullets with a hard envelope which does not entirely cover the core or is pierced with incisions'. The Declaration reflects customary law and binds all states in relation to the conduct of hostilities in international armed conflicts. If, during an international armed conflict a soldier causes his thoughts about firing a round consisting of expanding ammunition to be translated by a BCI into corresponding action, the customary rule will have been broken. It will be for commanders to ensure that expanding ammunition is not made available during international armed conflicts and for those same commanders to ensure that compliant rounds are not adapted so as to expand or flatten easily.

6.6.4 Expanding bullets in non-international armed conflicts

6.034 The treaty law prohibition of the use of expanding bullets is based on Hague Declaration 3 of 1899, which only applies to international armed conflicts. The rule as to the use of expanding ammunition during non-international armed conflicts (NIACs) is based not on that Treaty, but on the superfluous injury/unnecessary suffering principle. This has the effect that using such ammunition during a NIAC is prohibited by customary law in most circumstances. However, let us consider a situation during a NIAC in which (a) hostages are taken, or (b) in which a targeted individual must be instantly disabled to prevent a mass attack on civilians, or (c) in which the use of a conventional high-velocity round poses the risk of ricochet putting nearby civilians in danger. The protection of innocent civilians in such circumstances may give an additional military advantage which may have the effect that using expanding ammunition becomes lawful. The important thing to consider here is whether using the expanding ammunition yields an additional military benefit beyond that to be expected from a conventional, high-velocity round. If that is the case,

38 Declaration Concerning Expanding Bullets, The Hague, 29 July 1899.

the additional injury inflicted by the expanding nature of the round would not breach the superfluous injury/unnecessary suffering principle.[39]

This means that when brain technology is employed in conjunction with a weapon system of this kind, the links back to the operator must be such as to enable that operator to determine whether, in a NIAC context: (1) a situation of the kind referred to in the previous paragraph is arising; or (2) whether for some other reason the use of expanding ammunition offers additional military utility; and (3) whether in the circumstances the superfluous injury/unnecessary suffering principle will be respected. If the brain technology consists of a BCI, it will in practice be the BCI operator who will make those determinations. If the brain technology consists of an AB system, the AB should be programmed to reach back to the operator or commander for a human assessment of whether the circumstances permit the use of expanding ammunition. **6.035**

6.6.5 Exploding bullets designed for anti-personnel use

The operative provision of the St Petersburg Declaration 1868 prohibits the use, during international armed conflict, of projectiles below 400g weight that are either explosive or charged with fulminating or inflammable substances. Recognising subsequent developments in technology, the 1923 draft Hague Rules of Aerial Warfare noted that the 400g limit had become obsolete.[40] Nevertheless, current customary law prohibits explosive or incendiary bullets that are designed solely for use against personnel.[41] The basis for this rule is that a solid round would achieve the relevant military purpose, which means that using an explosive round in such circumstances would simply cause increased injury for which there is no corresponding additional military purpose, thereby breaching the superfluous injury/unnecessary suffering principle. It would therefore be unlawful for any state to use brain technology to operate a weapon system that employs exploding bullets designed exclusively for anti-personnel use. **6.036**

39 UK Manual, n.10, para.6.9 and n.32. On 10 June 2010 the Kampala Review Conference for the Rome Statute of the International Criminal Court adopted Resolution RC/Res 5 at the 12th Plenary Meeting, making it clear that the crime of using expanding bullets in a non-international armed conflict is only committed 'if the perpetrator employs the bullets to uselessly aggravate suffering or the wounding effect upon the target of such bullets, as reflected in customary international law': preambular para.9.

40 Draft Hague Rules of Aerial Warfare, n.23, Art.18(2).

41 UK Manual, n.10, para.6.10.1.

6.6.6 Asphyxiating gas

6.037 '[T]he use in war of asphyxiating, poisonous or other gases, and of all analogous liquids, materials or devices' is prohibited.[42] This prohibition in the Geneva Gas Protocol 1925 was an obvious response to the great suffering that was caused by the use of chlorine and mustard gases on the Western Front during the First World War. The prohibition reflects customary law and binds all states during both international and non-international armed conflicts. It follows from this that the use of brain technology in any form to control an asphyxiating gas weapon or a weapon employing an analogous liquid, material or device that is designed to asphyxiate or to poison will be unlawful.[43]

6.6.7 Chemical weapons

6.038 As was noted in the previous section, the Geneva Gas Protocol 1925 prohibits the use of certain chemical weapons. However, it was only with the adoption of the Chemical Weapons Convention 1993[44] that a comprehensive prohibition of chemical weapons was achieved and that the development, production, acquisition, stockpiling, transfer and retention of such weapons was also prohibited. The general practice of states and their collective *opinio juris* indicate, in the author's view, that these Convention rules reflect customary law and are therefore binding on all states. States that are party to the Chemical Weapons Convention are also prohibited from preparing to use chemical weapons and must not assist, encourage or induce anyone to undertake such prohibited activities.[45] While assisting, encouraging or inducing the commission of acts that are, themselves, prohibited by customary law is also prohibited by customary law, the author is not sure that the same can be said of assistance, encouragement or inducement of preparation to use such weapons.

6.039 The Convention defines chemical weapons as toxic chemicals, their precursors and equipment and munitions connected with their use. However, the Treaty

42 Protocol for the Prohibition of the Use in War of Asphyxiating, Poisonous or Other Gases, and of Bacteriological Methods of Warfare, Geneva, 17 June 1925. See also M Bothe, 'The 1925 Geneva Protocol', in E P J Myjer and T Marauhn (eds), *Research Handbook on International Arms Control Law* (Edward Elgar Publishing, 2022), 251–8.

43 'Asphyxia' is defined as 'a condition arising when the body is deprived of oxygen, causing unconsciousness or death': *Concise Oxford English Dictionary*, 11 edn (Oxford University Press, 2006), 77.

44 Convention on the Prohibition of the Development, Production, Stockpiling and Use of Chemical Weapons and on Their Destruction, Paris, 13 January 1993, 1975 UNTS 3 (Chemical Weapons Convention).

45 Chemical Weapons Convention, n.44, Art.I(1). For a discussion of the Treaty, see R Trapp, 'The Chemical Weapons Convention', in E P J Myjer and T Marauhn (eds), *Research Handbook on International Arms Control Law* (Edward Elgar Publishing, 2022), 279–96.

prohibition, and the customary rule, do not apply to such substances if they are intended for purposes that the Convention does not prohibit, provided that the kinds of substance and the quantities are consistent with such non-prohibited purposes.[46] Toxic chemicals, for the purposes of the Convention, are any chemicals, whatever their origin and however or wherever produced which, through their chemical action on life processes can cause death, temporary incapacitation or permanent harm to humans or animals.[47] A precursor is any chemical reactant which takes part, at any stage, in the production, by whatever method, of a toxic chemical.[48] These definitions also, in the author's view, reflect customary law.

The non-prohibited purposes, referred to in the previous paragraph, are: industrial, agricultural, research, medical, pharmaceutical or other peaceful purposes; protective purposes, namely those purposes directly related to protection against toxic chemicals and to protection against chemical weapons; military purposes not connected with the use of chemical weapons and not dependent on the use of the toxic properties of chemicals as a method of warfare; and law enforcement, including domestic riot control purposes.[49] Law enforcement, in this context, refers to the enforcement of domestic law.[50] **6.040**

Riot control agents (RCAs) are the subject of specific rules under the Convention. RCAs are defined as 'chemicals not listed in a Schedule to the Treaty which can produce rapidly in humans sensory irritation or disabling physical effects which disappear within a short time following termination of exposure'.[51] The Convention prohibits the use of RCAs as a method of warfare but permits their use for law enforcement, including domestic riot-control purposes.[52] These rules also, the author believes, reflect customary law.[53] **6.041**

Because the Convention prohibits activities other than the use of chemical weapons, it is classed as an arms control treaty. Its provisions apply to **6.042**

---

46 For the precise definition see Chemical Weapons Convention, n.44, Art.II(1).

47 Chemical Weapons Convention, n.44, Art.II(2).

48 Chemical Weapons Convention, n.44, Art.II(3).

49 Chemical Weapons Convention, n.44, Art.II(9). As Liivoja and Chircop explain, as the Chemical Weapons Convention only prohibits the use of toxic chemicals in a weaponised manner, performance enhancing substances (which are discussed in Chapter 10 below) would not violate the Treaty even if under certain conditions they are toxic; Liivoja and Chircop, n.1, 173.

50 D P Fidler, 'The Meaning of Moscow: "Non-Lethal" Weapons and International Law in the 21st Century' (2005) 859 IRRC 525, 540–44.

51 Chemical Weapons Convention, n.44, Art.II(7).

52 Chemical Weapons Convention, n.44, Art.I(5).

53 Note that there are now 193 States Parties to the Chemical Weapons Convention, n.44: source www.icrc.org.

international and non-international armed conflicts[54] and there is an important verification annex.[55]

6.043 It is therefore clear that the use of a BCI to enable the direct brain control of a weapon that employs a toxic chemical will be prohibited to all states, including a state that is not party to the Convention. Equally prohibited will be the use of an AB technology, whether wholly computer-based or employing biological brain material, to control a weapon that employs toxic chemicals. Customary law will also prohibit the development, production, acquisition, stockpiling, transfer and retention of such artificial brain-controlled weapons; moreover, any activity to assist, encourage or induce another to develop, produce, acquire, stockpile, transfer or retain such an AB-controlled weapon will also be prohibited under customary law.

6.6.8 Biological weapons

6.044 The use of bacteriological methods of warfare was prohibited by the 1925 Geneva Gas Protocol. Under the Biological Weapons Convention[56] States Parties undertook: 'never in any circumstances to develop, produce, stockpile or otherwise acquire or retain: (1) Microbial or other biological agents or toxins whatever their origin or method of production, of types and in quantities that have no justification for prophylactic, protective or other peaceful purposes; (2) Weapons, equipment or means of delivery designed to use such agents or toxins for hostile purposes or in armed conflict.'[57] They also undertook not to transfer such agents, toxins, equipment or materials and not to assist, encourage or induce their manufacture or acquisition.[58]

6.045 Although use of such weapons is not referred to, states agreed at the Fourth Review Conference of the Biological Weapons Convention in 1996 that use is effectively prohibited by the Convention.[59] In the author's view, the general

54 The reference in Chemical Weapons Convention, n.44, Art.1 to 'never under any circumstances' engaging in the prohibited activities makes it clear that the Convention also applies in non-international conflicts.

55 The Chemical Weapons Convention, n.44, Annex on Implementation and Verification includes complex provisions as to national declarations and verification arrangements.

56 The Convention on the Prohibition of the Development, Production and Stockpiling of Bacteriological (Biological) and Toxin Weapons and on their Destruction, 10 April 1972, 1015 UNTS 163 (Biological Weapons Convention). For a discussion of the Treaty, see U Jakob, 'The Biological Weapons Convention', in E P J Myjer and T Marauhn (eds), *Research Handbook on International Arms Control Law* (Edward Elgar Publishing, 2022), 259–78.

57 Biological Weapons Convention, n.56, Art.I.

58 Biological Weapons Convention, n.56, Art.III.

59 States Parties to the Protocol for the Prohibition of the Use of Asphyxiating, Poisonous or Other Gases, and of Bacteriological Methods of Warfare, Geneva, 17 June 1925 (Geneva Gas Protocol) are prohibited

practice of states and their collective *opinio juris* establishes that all of the prohibitions in the Biological Weapons Convention are now reflective of customary law and therefore bind all states, including states that are not party to the Convention, in relation to both international and non-international armed conflicts. As the Biological Weapons Convention prohibits activities beyond actual use of the relevant weapons, it is an arms control treaty to which almost all militarily significant states are party.

It would not therefore be lawful for any state to use a BCI to enable the direct brain control of a weapon that employs a biological agent or toxin.[60] Equally prohibited will be the use of an AB technology, whether wholly computer-based or employing biological brain material, to control a weapon that employs a biological agent or toxin. Customary law will also prohibit the development, production, stockpiling, acquisition or retention of such weapons irrespective of their AB control facilities; moreover, any activity to assist, encourage or induce another to transfer such agents, toxins, equipment or materials or to assist, encourage or induce their manufacture or acquisition will also be prohibited. If brain-to-brain communication is indeed developed in the future, the use of such technology to assist, encourage or induce the manufacture or transfer of chemical or biological weapons would also be prohibited. **6.046**

It is therefore unlawful for any state, whether it is party to the Chemical and Biological Weapons Conventions or not, to equip itself for or undertake a chemical or biological attack. No state is permitted to develop, produce, stockpile, acquire, retain or use any kind of new technology that uses, or that in any way contributes to the use of, toxic chemicals or their precursors or microbial or other biological agents or toxins for hostile purposes or in an armed conflict. Likewise, it is prohibited to use synthetic biological substances, bacteria, viruses and incapacitating chemical substances in connection with armed conflict hostilities. **6.047**

---

from using bacteriological weapons by that provision anyway.

60 Patrick Lin and others have argued that bioenhanced warfighters and some biological enhancements amount to weapons that are prohibited by the Biological Weapons Convention: P Lin and others, Case Western Reserve University, Case Legal Studies Research Paper No. 2013-2 dated 13 February 2013 available at https://papers.ssrn.com/sol3/papers.cfm?abstract_id=2202982. 'Enhanced Warfighters: Risk, Ethics and Policy' (2013), 31–2. Rain Liivoja and Luke Chircop consider, rightly in the author's view, that such a contention 'fails to persuade', but point out, also correctly, that if, for example a person were to be infected with a biological agent with a view to spreading the infection, such an activity may come within Art.I(b) of the Convention: Liivoja and Chircop, n.1, 170. The author also agrees (Liivoja and Chircop, n.1, 172) that the Biological Weapons Convention is primarily about the weaponisation of microorganisms and toxins, further supporting the rejection of the approach proposed by Lin and others.

6.6.9 Protocol II and mines, booby-traps and other devices

6.048 There are three distinct weapons law treaties that deal with mines, booby-traps and other devices. In this subsection, the focus is on the provisions in the first of those treaties, namely the Second Protocol to the Conventional Weapons Convention.[61] This is because the prohibitions and restrictions set forth in that Protocol are generally accepted as reflecting established doctrine and are binding on all states as being reflective of customary law. The second treaty dealing with the use, in armed conflict, of mines, booby-traps and other devices is Amended Protocol II[62] to the Conventional Weapons Convention. The rules in Amended Protocol II bind the states that are party to that Treaty, as do the provisions of the Ottawa Convention.[63] The Ottawa Convention is an arms control treaty that prohibits anti-personnel landmines. The provisions of these two treaties will be discussed in subsections 6.7.5. and 6.7.6.

6.049 The Protocol II definition of a mine is 'any munition placed under, on or near the ground or other surface area and designed to be detonated or exploded by the presence, proximity or contact of a person or vehicle'. [64] Protocol II defines booby-traps as 'any device or material which is designed, constructed or adapted to kill or injure and which functions unexpectedly when a person disturbs or approaches an apparently harmless object or performs an apparently safe act'.[65] 'Other devices' are defined in the same Treaty as 'manually-emplaced munitions and devices designed to kill, injure or damage and which are actuated by remote control or automatically after a lapse of time'.[66]

6.050 Under Article 6 of Protocol II, it is prohibited to use 'any booby-trap in the form of an apparently harmless portable object which is specifically designed

---

61 Second Protocol to the Convention on the Prohibition of the Development, Production, Stockpiling and Use of Chemical Weapons and on Their Destruction, Geneva, 10 October 1980.

62 Protocol on Prohibitions or Restrictions on the Use of Mines, Booby-Traps and Other Devices as amended on 3 May 1996, Geneva, 3 May 1996.

63 Convention on the Prohibition of the Use, Stockpiling, Production and Transfer of Anti-Personnel Mines and on their Destruction, Oslo, 18 September 1997, 2056 UNTS 211 (Ottawa Convention). For a discussion of the Treaty, see S Casey-Maslen, 'The Convention on the Prohibition of the Use, Stockpiling, Production and Transfer of Anti-Personnel Mines and on Their Destruction', in E P J Myjer and T Marauhn (eds), *Research Handbook on International Arms Control Law* (Edward Elgar Publishing, 2022), 347–59.

64 Protocol II, Art.2(1), n.61. There are minor and relatively inconsequential amendments to the equivalent definition in Amended Protocol II, Art. 2(1), n.62.

65 Protocol II, Art.1(2), n.61.

66 Protocol II, Art.1(3), n.61. The Amended Protocol II definition of 'other devices' is: "Other devices means manually emplaced munitions and devices including improvised explosive devices designed to kill, injure or damage and which are actuated manually, by remote control or automatically after a lapse of time."; Amended Protocol II, Art. 2(5), n.62.

and constructed to contain explosive material and to detonate when it is disturbed or approached'.[67] Article 6 of Protocol II also prohibits the use of booby-traps

> which are in any way attached to or associated with:
>
> (i) internationally recognised protective emblems, signs or signals;
> (ii) sick, wounded or dead persons;
> (iii) burial or cremation sites or graves;
> (iv) medical facilities, medical equipment, medical supplies or medical transportation;
> (v) children's toys or other portable objects or products specially designed for the feeding, health, hygiene, clothing or education of children;
> (vi) food or drink;
> (vii) kitchen utensils or appliances except in military establishments, military locations or military supply depots;
> (viii) objects clearly of a religious nature;
> (ix) historic monuments, works of art or places of worship which constitute the cultural or spiritual heritage of peoples;
> (x) animals or their carcasses.[68]

These prohibitions apply also where any such weapons are used in association with any form of brain technology. 6.051

Example 3. An autonomous AB-enabled booby-trap deployment vehicle has been developed. The vehicle is equipped with a hydraulic arm and has been programmed not to apply the booby-traps to any of the objects on the list in Article 6 of Protocol II. The weapons testers select three items from the list and the AB system does not deploy the booby-trap on any of those three items. A report describing the tests is sent to the weapon reviewer who correctly replies insisting that the testers must assess whether the device will refrain from booby-trapping all of the classes of object on the list. Clearly, there is a problem here because it may not be feasible to test in relation, for example, to all types of food and drink, all items of a religious nature, all types of animal carcass, and so on. If thorough testing is not feasible, it may be that human decision-making will be required. 6.052

Protocol II also imposes certain weapons law restrictions on the use of mines, booby-traps and other devices. Where provisions merely restate targeting law rules these are not included here. It should be borne in mind that these restrictions reflect established doctrine and are customary in nature. 6.053

67 Protocol II, Art.6(1)(a), n.61.
68 Protocol II, Art.6(1), n.61; Amended Protocol II, n.62, Art.7(1).

6.054 Article 4 of Protocol II addresses the use of mines other than remotely delivered mines,[69] booby-traps and other devices in populated areas. It prohibits the use of such weapons: 'in any city, town, village or other area containing a similar concentration of civilians in which combat between ground forces is not taking place or does not appear to be imminent unless either: (a) they are placed on or in the close vicinity of a military objective belonging to or under the control of an adverse party; or (b) measures are taken to protect civilians from their effects, for example, the posting of warning-signs, the posting of sentries, the issue of warnings or the provision of fences.'

6.055 Article 5 of the same Protocol prohibits the use of remotely delivered mines: 'unless such mines are only used within an area which is itself a military objective or which contains military objectives and unless: (a) their location can be accurately recorded[70]... or (b) an effective neutralising mechanism is used on each such mine, that is to say, a self-actuating mechanism which is designed to render a mine harmless or cause it to destroy itself when it is anticipated that the mine will no longer serve the military purpose for which it was placed in position, or a remotely-controlled mechanism which is designed to render harmless or destroy a mine when the mine no longer serves the military purpose for which it was placed in position.'[71] If the use of such mines may affect the civilian population, effective warning must be given unless circumstances do not permit.[72] The prohibitions in this and the preceding paragraphs also apply to any such weapons that are used in association with any brain technology.

6.056 Article 7 of Protocol II requires that parties to the conflict record the location of all pre-planned minefields that they lay and of all areas in which they have made large-scale and pre-planned use of booby-traps.

69 Remotely-delivered mines' means, for the purposes of Protocol II, any mine delivered by artillery, rocket, mortar or similar means or dropped from an aircraft.

70 For the requirements as to recording, see Protocol II, Art.7.

71 Protocol II, Art.5(1).

72 Protocol II, Art.5(2).

6.7 NON-CUSTOMARY PROHIBITIONS AND RESTRICTIONS ON THE USE OF WEAPONS

6.7.1 Environmental modification

States that are party to the UN Environmental Modification Convention 1976 (ENMOD) must not 'engage in military or any other hostile use of environmental modification techniques having widespread, long-lasting or severe effects as the means of destruction, damage or injury to any other State party' to that Convention.[73] The term 'environmental modification techniques' is defined in the Convention and means 'any technique for changing – through the deliberate manipulation of natural processes – the dynamics, composition or structure of the Earth, including its biota, lithosphere, hydrosphere and atmosphere, or of outer space'.[74] For the Convention to be breached, all of the following must apply: 6.057

1. The dynamics, composition or structure of one of the listed items must be altered.
2. This effect must have been achieved by the manipulation of natural processes.
3. The manipulation of those natural processes must have been deliberate.
4. The employment of the environmental modification technique must be military or hostile in nature.
5. Either a widespread or a long-lasting or a severe effect must result.
6. The relevant effect(s) must be the means of causing destruction, damage or injury to another state.
7. Both the acting and the victim states must be parties to the Convention.

The effect of item 7 in the above list is that the Convention only effectively applies to international armed conflicts. The Convention does not, the author believes, reflect customary law but does, of course, bind states that are party to it. 6.058

Examples of modification of the environment will include changing weather patterns, for example by increasing or reducing rainfall, generating floods or 6.059

---

73 Convention on the Prohibition of Military or any Other Hostile Use of Environmental Modification Techniques, Geneva, 2 September 1976 (ENMOD) 1108 UNTS 151, Article I. For a discussion of the Treaty, see S Vöneky, 'The ENMOD Convention', in E P J Myjer and T Marauhn (eds), *Research Handbook on International Arms Control Law* (Edward Elgar Publishing, 2022), 360–77.

74 ENMOD, n.73, Art.II. The term 'widespread' has been interpreted as 'encompassing an area on the scale of several hundred square kilometres', while 'long-lasting' would involve 'lasting for a period of months, or approximately a season' and effects are 'severe' if they involve 'serious or significant disruption or harm to human life, natural and economic resources or other assets': Conference Understanding relating to Article I, available in the International Committee of the Red Cross (ICRC) treaty database at www.icrc.org.

drought,[75] initiating earthquakes and tsunamis, disturbing the ecological balance of a region, and altering climate patterns.[76] So if a State Party to the Convention uses any kind of brain technology in association with an environmental modification technique and thereby inflicts upon another State Party the effects referred to in Articles I and II, the Convention will have been breached.

6.7.2 Fragmentation weapons

6.060 Protocol 1 to the Conventional Weapons Convention[77] prohibits the 'use [of] any weapon the primary effect of which is to injure by fragments which in the human body escape detection by x-rays'. Injury by non-detectable fragments, not necessarily penetrating non-detectable fragments, must be the primary effect of the weapon. The prohibition is binding on the states that are party to the Protocol. If the nature of a weapon that comes within this definition is to cause injury or suffering that is, respectively, superfluous or unnecessary, the weapon will be prohibited to all states under that customary principle.

6.061 Accordingly, a weapon system that incorporates brain technology in its method of operation must not have as its injuring mechanism a warhead the primary effect of which breaches this provision.

6.7.3 Blinding laser weapons

6.062 Under Protocol IV to the Conventional Weapons Convention it is prohibited to use 'laser-weapons specifically designed, as their sole combat function or as one of their combat functions, to cause permanent blindness to unenhanced vision, that is, to the naked eye or to the eye with corrective eyesight devices'.[78] The way in which the Protocol is drafted draws a clear distinction between the prohibited laser weapons defined in the previous sentence, that is that are specifically designed as a combat function to cause permanent blindness, and '[b]linding as an incidental or collateral effect of the legitimate military employment of laser systems, including laser systems used against optical equipment'. This incidental or collateral kind of blinding 'is not covered by the

75 P J Rowe, *Defence, the Legal Implications* (Brassey's, 1987), 117.

76 Conference Understanding relating to Article II, available in the ICRC treaty database at www.icrc.org.

77 Convention on Prohibitions or Restrictions on the Use of Certain Conventional Weapons Which may be Deemed to be Excessively Injurious or to Have Indiscriminate Effects, Geneva, 10 October 1980 (CCW), Protocol on Non-Detectable Fragments, Geneva, 10 October 1980.

78 Convention on Prohibitions or Restrictions on the Use of Certain Conventional Weapons Which may be Deemed to be Excessively Injurious or to Have Indiscriminate Effects, Geneva, 10 October 1980 (CCW), Protocol on Blinding Laser Weapons, Geneva, 13 October 1995 (Protocol IV), Art.1.

prohibition of this Protocol'.[79] States that are bound by the Treaty must 'take all feasible precautions to avoid the incidence of permanent blindness to unenhanced vision' when using laser systems. Relevant precautions should include training and other practical measures.[80]

A laser weapon that causes incidental or collateral permanent blindness will not, therefore, necessarily be prohibited by the Protocol. Moreover, a laser weapon that is designed as a combat function to cause temporary blindness or to dazzle does not breach the Protocol. Laser or similar equipment designed to cause damage to other objects or vehicles or to perform measurement, range-finding or other military tasks but that has no combat function to cause permanent blindness is not prohibited by this treaty rule, but the precautionary measures mentioned in the previous paragraph should be taken. **6.063**

If a laser system is to be used in association with brain technology, it will be necessary for that brain-computer link to be so set up that a combat function to cause permanent blindness cannot be developed. It may be necessary to impose limits on the employment of a laser system that is brain technology-enabled or -enhanced in order to ensure that the precautionary obligations in the Treaty are honoured. **6.064**

6.7.4 Cluster munitions

A treaty adopted in Dublin in May 2008[81] requires that States Parties 'never under any circumstances ...: (a) use cluster munitions; (b) develop, produce, otherwise acquire, stockpile, retain or transfer to anyone, directly or indirectly, cluster munitions; (c) assist, encourage or induce anyone to engage' in any activity prohibited under the Convention.[82] This is an arms control treaty as it includes prohibited activities other than use. The Convention is binding on States Parties but does not reflect customary law. **6.065**

---

79 CCW, Protocol IV, n.78, Art.3. Consider, however, Shereshevsky's plea for an expansive interpretation of Art.1, n.12, 24–6: A Shereshevsky, Are all Soldiers created Equal? On the equal application of law to enhanced soldiers, 3 September 2020 available at https://papers.ssrn.com/sol3/papers.cfm?abstract_id=3684645, later published in the *Virginia Journal of International Law*. The author's view is that the reference to unenhanced vision in Art.1 is an essential element of the provision, and that a laser weapon that is designed to cause blindness to vision that is enhanced would be excluded from Art.1. The superfluous injury/unnecessary suffering principle and Arts 2 and 3 of the Treaty would both, however, need to be considered most carefully.

80 CCW, Protocol IV, n.78, Art.2.

81 Convention on Cluster Munitions, Dublin, 30 May 2008 (Cluster Munitions Convention) 2688 UNTS 39.

82 Cluster Munitions Convention, n.81, Art.1(1).

6.066 The term 'cluster munition' is defined in the Convention as 'a conventional munition that is designed to disperse or release explosive sub-munitions each weighing less than 20 kilograms and includes those explosive sub-munitions'. Certain kinds of munition are excluded from the definition, namely: munitions or sub-munitions designed to dispense flares, smoke, pyrotechnics or chaff; munitions designed exclusively for an air defence role; munitions or sub-munitions designed to produce electrical or electronic effects; and munitions that, in order to avoid indiscriminate area effects and the risks posed by unexploded sub-munitions, contain fewer than ten explosive sub-munitions each of which weighs more than 4kg, is designed to detect and engage a single target object, is equipped with an electronic self-destruction mechanism and is equipped with an electronic self-deactivating feature.[83]

6.067 The term 'explosive sub-munition' means 'a conventional munition that in order to perform its task is dispersed or released by a cluster munition and is designed to function by detonating an explosive charge prior to, on or after impact'.[84]

6.068 A key provision of the Convention is Article 21 which addresses relations between states that are party to the Treaty and those which are not. States that are party must encourage states that are not party to participate in the Convention, and they must notify the governments of states that are not party of their Convention obligations. States Parties and their military personnel or nationals are, however, permitted to 'engage in military cooperation and operations with States not party to th[e] Convention that might engage in activities prohibited to a State party'.[85] This provision does not permit a States Party itself to acquire, transfer or use cluster munitions; moreover, a States Party must not specifically request the use of cluster munitions where the choice of munitions used is within its exclusive control.[86]

6.069 This final provision can be interpreted as actually permitting the personnel of a State Party to request a non-party state to use cluster munitions provided that the final decision as to the nature of the weapons used rests with the non-party state.[87] A mental decision by a commander from a state that is party to

---

83 Cluster Munitions Convention, n.81, Art.2(2).

84 Cluster Munitions Convention, n.81, Art.2(3). The Treaty defines the notions of self-destruction and self-deactivation.

85 Cluster Munitions Convention, n.81, Art.21(3).

86 Cluster Munitions Convention, n.81, Art.21(4).

87 See for example Section 11(1)(b) of Canada's Prohibiting Cluster Munitions Act, S.C. 2014 c.27, available at https://laws-lois.justice.gc.ca/eng/acts/P-24.8/page-1.html.

the Treaty to formulate and communicate such a request entirely using brain technology, say by using a brain-to-brain interface (BBI), may well be interpreted as amounting to a request for the purposes of Article 21(4)(d). So, if the officer from the State Party communicates through a BBI a thought or intent amounting to a request for the use of a cluster munition and if the officer of the state not party to the Convention receives that thought or intent and then employs a cluster munition, provided it was the thought of the officer from the non-party state that constituted the final decision to use the cluster munition, that provision of Article 21 will have been complied with. More generally, cluster munitions of kinds that are covered by the Treaty, whether or not they involve brain technologies, should not be made available to the armed forces of states that are party to the Convention and it will be the responsibility of commanders to ensure this.

6.7.5 Non-customary prohibitions of mines, booby-traps and other devices

The provisions of Amended Protocol II do not yet reflect customary law, although the prohibitions of that Treaty that immediately follow are close to doing so and certainly reflect good practice. **6.070**

Amended Protocol II prohibits: **6.071**

- the use of 'mines, booby-traps or other devices which employ a mechanism or device specifically designed to detonate the munition by the presence of commonly available mine detectors as a result of their magnetic or other non-contact influence during normal use in detection operations';[88]
- the use of 'a self-deactivating mine equipped with an anti-handling device that is designed in such a manner that the anti-handling device is capable of functioning after the mine has ceased to be capable of functioning';[89]
- anti-personnel mines that do not 'incorporate in their construction a material or device that enables the mine to be detected by commonly-available technical mine detection equipment and that provides a response signal equivalent to a signal from 8 grammes or more of iron in a single coherent mass';[90]
- remotely delivered[91] anti-personnel mines which do not comply with specified self-destruction and self-deactivation requirements;[92]

---

88 Amended Protocol II, n.62, Art.3(5).

89 Amended Protocol II, n.62, Art.3(6).

90 Amended Protocol II, n.62, Art.4 and Technical Annex, para.2(a). This restriction applies to anti-personnel mines produced after 1 January 1997. Mines produced before that date must either incorporate into their construction or have attached prior to their emplacement in a manner that is not easily removable a material or device with identical characteristics: Amended Protocol II, n.62, Technical Annex, para.2(b).

91 For the definition of 'remotely-delivered', see Amended Protocol II, n.62, Art.2(1).

92 Amended Protocol II, n.62, Art.6(2). For the requirements, see Amended Protocol II, n.62, Technical Annex, para.3(a) taken with (b).

- remotely delivered mines other than anti-personnel mines 'unless, to the extent feasible, they are equipped with an effective self-destruction or self-neutralization mechanism and have a back-up self-deactivation feature, which is designed so that the mine will no longer function as a mine when the mine no longer serves the military purpose for which it was placed in position';[93]
- 'booby-traps or other devices in the form of apparently harmless portable objects which are specifically designed and constructed to contain explosive material'.[94]

6.072 Accordingly, the various kinds of weapons that are listed above, whether or not they involve brain technologies, should not be used by armed forces of states that are party to Amended Protocol II, should not be made available to the armed forces of such states, and it will be the responsibility of commanders to ensure that only lawful weapons are used. It will, furthermore, be the responsibility of those who procure weapons, review them and introduce them into service to ensure that the weapons that are supplied to the armed forces are lawful.

6.073 The Ottawa Convention prohibits anti-personnel landmines. It binds states that are party to the Convention in respect of international and non-international armed conflicts, but its provisions do not have customary law status and thus do not bind states that are not party. The term 'anti-personnel mine' for the purposes of the Convention refers to: 'a mine designed to be exploded by the presence, proximity or contact of a person and that will incapacitate, injure or kill one or more persons. Mines designed to be detonated by the presence, proximity or contact of a vehicle as opposed to a person, that are equipped with anti-handling devices, are not considered anti-personnel mines as a result of being so equipped.'[95]

6.074 The Ottawa Convention stipulates that States Parties must never use, develop, produce, otherwise acquire, stockpile, retain or transfer anti-personnel mines or assist, encourage or induce, in any way, anyone to do so.[96] By prohibiting activities in addition to use, the Convention is classed as an arms control treaty. The Convention makes detailed provision as to the destruction of anti-personnel mines in stockpiles[97] and in mined areas[98] and restricts the retention

---

93 Amended Protocol II, n.62, Art.6(3).
94 Amended Protocol II, n.62, Art.7(2).
95 Ottawa Convention, n.63, Art.2(1).
96 Ottawa Convention, n.63, Art.1(1).
97 Ottawa Convention, n.63, Art.4.
98 Ottawa Convention, n.63, Art.5.

of anti-personnel mines for training purposes.[99] The Convention also includes an extensive compliance regime.[100]

The brain technology implications of the provisions of the Ottawa Convention discussed in this section are clear. Use of antipersonnel landmines by means of brain technology systems is not permitted by states that are party to the Convention. **6.075**

6.7.6 Non-customary restrictions of mines, booby-traps and other devices

Amended Protocol II imposes the following weapons law restrictions on the use of mines, booby-traps and other devices. Where provisions in the Treaty merely restate principles or rules of general application or of targeting law, these are not included here. Amended Protocol II restrictions bind states that are party to the Protocol and may be applicable to other states as a matter of good practice. **6.076**

Article 3 of Amended Protocol II places upon a party to a conflict that employs mines, booby-traps or other devices responsibility for clearing, removing, destroying or maintaining those munitions in accordance with later provisions.[101] Article 5 prohibits the use of anti-personnel mines other than remotely-delivered mines[102] if they are not designed and constructed according to the specifications referred to in the Treaty.[103] **6.077**

There is a specific exemption in the Treaty for weapons that propel fragments in a horizontal arc of less than 90° and which are placed on or above the ground. However: the maximum permitted use of such weapons is 72 hours; they must be located in immediate proximity to the military unit that emplaced them; and the area must be monitored by military personnel to ensure the effective exclusion of civilians.[104] **6.078**

Remotely delivered mines must be 'recorded in accordance with' the Technical Annex.[105] Remotely delivered mines other than anti-personnel mines must, 'to the extent feasible, [be] equipped with an effective self-destruction or self-neutralisation mechanism and have a back-up self-deactivation feature which **6.079**

99 Ottawa Convention, n.63, Art.3(1), sentence 2.
100 See Ottawa Convention, n.63, Art.8.
101 Note also Amended Protocol II, n.62, Art.3(10).
102 'Remotely-delivered mine' is defined in Amended Protocol II, n.62, Art.2(2).
103 See Amended Protocol II, n.62, Technical Annex, para.3(a) and (b).
104 Amended Protocol II, n.62, Art.5(6).
105 Amended Protocol II, n.62, Art.6(1) and see Technical Annex, subpara.1(b).

is designed so that the mine will no longer function as a mine when the mine no longer serves the military purposes for which it was placed in position'.[106]

6.080 Article 7 of Amended Protocol II prohibits the use of booby-traps or other devices: 'in any city, town, village or other area containing a similar concentration of civilians and in which combat between ground forces is not taking place or does not appear to be imminent, unless either: (a) they are placed on or in the close vicinity of a military objective; or, (b) measures are taken to protect civilians from their effects, for example, the posting of warning sentries, the issuing of warnings or the provision of fences.'[107]

6.081 The brain technology implications for states that are party to Amended Protocol II of the rules in this section are simple, namely that the use of any weapon system of the kinds referred to here must be in accordance with the stated restrictions. The brain technology, such as a BCI or an AB facility, that is part of the weapon system as a whole in no way exempts the weapon system from the application of these restrictions. It will be for those designing such systems to ensure that they can only be used in accordance with the applicable restrictions, and it will be for all others in the supply chain to ensure that the relevant restrictions are made known to weapon users and for those users to ensure that the rules are complied with.

6.7.7 Incendiary weapons

6.082 For the purposes of Protocol III[108] to the Conventional Weapons Convention, incendiary weapon means 'any weapon or munition which is primarily designed to set fire to objects or to cause burn injury to persons through the action of flame, heat, or a combination thereof, produced by a chemical reaction of a substance delivered on the target'. The definition states that such weapons can take various forms, but they do not include '[m]unitions which may have incidental incendiary effects, such as illuminants or tracers, smoke or signaling systems'.[109] Similarly excluded from the definition are 'combined effects munitions in which the incendiary effect is not specifically designed to cause burn

106 Amended Protocol II, n.62, Art.6(3).

107 Amended Protocol II, n.62, Art.7(3).

108 Convention on Prohibitions or Restrictions on the Use of Certain Conventional Weapons Which may be Deemed to be Excessively Injurious or to Have Indiscriminate Effects, Geneva, 10 October 1980 (CCW), Protocol on Prohibitions or Restrictions on the Use of Incendiary Weapons (Protocol III), Geneva, 10 October 1980.

109 Protocol III, n.108, Art.1(1)(b)(i).

injury to persons, but to be used against military objectives, such as armoured vehicles, aircraft, and installations or facilities'.[110]

It is forbidden 'in all circumstances to make any military objective located within a concentration of civilians[111] the object of attack by air-delivered incendiary weapons'.[112] It is also: 'prohibited to make any military objective located within a concentration of civilians the object of attack by means of incendiary weapons other than air-delivered incendiary weapons, except when such military objective is clearly separated from the concentration of civilians and all feasible precautions are taken with a view to limiting the incendiary effects to the military objective and to avoiding, and in any event to minimizing, incidental loss of civilian life, injury to civilians and damage to civilian objects.'[113] **6.083**

Article 2(4) of the Protocol prohibits making 'forests or other kinds of plant cover' the object of attack using incendiary weapons 'except when such natural elements are used to cover, conceal or camouflage combatants or other military objectives, or are themselves military objectives'.[114] **6.084**

If a state is party to Protocol III and a munition comes within the definition in that Treaty and the munition is air-delivered, the prohibition in Article 2(2) of the Protocol will apply. If the first two conditions apply but the weapon is not air-delivered, the weapon can only be used against a military objective located within a concentration of civilians if the particular circumstances described in Article 2(3) apply and if the precautions required by that paragraph can be taken. Any state that is party to Protocol III may only use an incendiary weapon as defined in Article I of the Protocol subject to the restrictions set forth in Article 2. The brain technology component in the weapon system does not exempt it from these restrictions. **6.085**

Article 2(2) and (3) bind all states that are party to the Treaty, but these provisions may not yet reflect customary law. States that are not party to the Protocol will, nevertheless, be bound by the customary principle of distinction, by the customary prohibition of indiscriminate attacks, by the customary proportionality rule and by the requirement for attackers to take precautions. **6.086**

---

110 Protocol III, n.108, Art.1(1)(b)(ii).

111 A 'concentration of civilians' may be permanent or temporary, and can include inhabited parts of cities, towns, villages, camps, columns of refugees or groups of nomads: Protocol III, n.108, Art.1(2).

112 Protocol III, n.108, Art.2(2).

113 Protocol III, n.108, Art.2(3).

114 Protocol III, n.108, Art.2(4).

6.087 *Example 4.* A weapon reviewer from a state that is party to Protocol III receives a business case which discloses that one of the intended uses of a BCI-enabled, air-delivered incendiary weapon is against military facilities such as marshalling yards and logistics compounds. The reviewer includes in the review document a quote from Article 2(2) of the Protocol and explains that it would be prohibited to use the weapons against such targets if they are located in a concentration of civilians. The reviewer adds that the use of such a weapon would be lawful if there was no concentration of civilians in the area, for example because the civilian population has left. The advice might also usefully point out that operators of such a system should ensure that the BCI is deactivated during the search for and assessment of targets to exclude the possibility of inadvertent use against inappropriately positioned military objectives.

6.088 AB systems that are armed with weapons that come within the definition in Protocol III must be programmed in accordance with the Protocol. The programming for both air-delivered and non-air-delivered incendiaries must start by determining whether the target is located within a concentration of civilians. If it is and if the weapon is air-delivered, the AB must be programmed to refrain from attack. If the weapon is non-air-delivered, the AB system must be programmed to:

1. assess whether the military objective is clearly separated from the concentration of civilians;
2. assess whether the precautions that can be taken will limit the incendiary effects to the military objective; and
3. assess whether civilian deaths, injury and damage can be avoided or minimised.

6.089 If the AB system cannot do these things, the author suggests that the AB system should not be used in association with incendiary weapons.

6.8 NON-LETHAL WEAPONS

6.090 'Non-lethal' is a term that is not used in the LOAC. Moreover, when used in military doctrine it includes weapons that, depending on the manner of use, are capable of causing death. Weapons law applies equally to lethal and non-lethal weapons[115] and the same weapon review criteria must be applied to

115 'Non-lethal weapons are weapons which are explicitly designed and developed to incapacitate or repel personnel, with a low probability of fatality or permanent injury, or to disable equipment with minimal undesired damage or impact on the environment': NATO Policy on Non-Lethal Weapons (7 September 1999).

both classes of weapon. It is, however, correct to note that death or permanent injury should occur less frequently when non-lethal weapons are being used in the intended, designed manner.

6.9 NUCLEAR WEAPONS

The legal position of a state in relation to nuclear weapons depends on the treaties to which that state is party and on other factors, including a judgment issued by the International Court of Justice (ICJ) in the mid-1990s (discussed briefly below). States that are party to the Treaty on the Prohibition of Nuclear Weapons[116] (TPNW) must not 'develop, test, produce, manufacture, otherwise acquire, possess or stockpile nuclear weapons or other nuclear explosive devices', must not directly or indirectly transfer them or control over them to anyone, must not receive them, must not use or threaten to use them, must not assist, encourage or induce prohibited activities and must not permit the stationing, installation or deployment of nuclear weapons or nuclear explosive devices on their territory or in any place under their jurisdiction or control.[117] States that are party to this Treaty must submit declarations as to their ownership, possession or control of nuclear weapons, as to whether they host such weapons and as to their elimination of them.[118] Article 3 provides for a system of Safeguard Agreements between each States Party to the Treaty and the International Atomic Energy Agency. Article 4 deals with international verification of the elimination of nuclear weapons-related facilities. The Treaty entered into force on 22 January 2021.[119] As yet, none of the permanent members of the United Nations (UN) Security Council and no states that are currently known to possess nuclear weapons have become party to this Treaty, and in the author's opinion no such state is likely to do so for the foreseeable future. **6.091**

Subject to the TPNW and to regional nuclear weapon-free zone treaties,[120] there is in general international law no explicit prohibition or permission to **6.092**

116 Treaty on the Prohibition of Nuclear Weapons, New York, 7 July 2017 (TPNW).

117 TPNW, n.117, Art.1.

118 TPNW, n.117, Art.2.

119 There are, at the time of writing, 74 states that are party to the Treaty: source, the ICRC Treaty database at www.icrc.org.

120 Treaty for the Prohibition of Nuclear Weapons in Latin America and the Caribbean (Treaty of Tlatelolco), opened for signature at Mexico City 14 February 1967, entered into force for each state individually, 33 parties, Additional Protocol II, Art.3; South Pacific Nuclear-Free Zone Treaty (Treaty of Rarotonga), opened for signature at Rarotonga 6 August 1985, entered into force 11 December 1986, 13 parties, Protocol 2, Art.1; Treaty on the Southeast Asia Nuclear Weapon-Free Zone (Bangkok Treaty), opened

possess nuclear weapons. The general principles of international law and the rules of the LOAC will determine whether any such use is lawful.

6.093 In July 1996, over two decades before the adoption of TPNW, the ICJ addressed the legality or otherwise of the threat or use of nuclear weapons.[121] It concluded that there is in neither customary nor conventional international law any specific authorisation for threatening or using nuclear weapons and that there is in neither customary nor conventional international law any comprehensive or universal prohibition of the threat or use of nuclear weapons as such.[122] The Court noted that a threat to use, or use of, nuclear force that is contrary to Article 2(4) of the UN Charter and that fails to meet the requirements of Article 51 is unlawful and that such a threat or use should be compatible with the LOAC and with treaties and other undertakings dealing expressly with nuclear weapons. Having acknowledged that a threat or use of nuclear weapons would generally be contrary to the LOAC, the Court stated that it could not 'conclude definitively whether the threat or use of nuclear weapons would be lawful or unlawful in an extreme circumstance of self defence, in which the very survival of a state would be at stake'. [123]

6.094 Although this *non liquet* judgment by the Court has been the subject of considerable academic criticism,[124] it will remain the position adopted by the Court unless the issue comes back before it. Moreover, the practice of the numerous states that either possess nuclear weapons or that place security reliance on the nuclear weapon capability of an ally indicates that there is no general practice of states accepted as law in favour of a prohibition on the possession of nuclear weapons. This leads the author to conclude that there is in customary law no prohibition on the possession of nuclear weapons, with the consequent conclusion that, for states that are not party to TPNW or to a nuclear weapon free zone treaty, the possession of nuclear weapons as such does not breach any specific rule under the LOAC. States will, however, be required

---

for signature at Bangkok 15 December 1995, entered into force 27 March 1997, 10 parties, Protocol 1, Art.2; African Nuclear Weapon-Free Zone Treaty (Pelindaba Treaty) opened for signature at Cairo 11 April 1996, entered into force 15 July 2009, 43 parties; Treaty on a Nuclear Weapon-Free Zone in Central Asia (CANWFZ), opened for signature at Semipalatinsk 8 September 2006, entered into force 21 March 2009, 5 parties.

121 ICJ Nuclear Weapons Advisory Opinion, n.12.

122 ICJ Nuclear Weapons Advisory Opinion, n.12, para.105(1) and (2).

123 ICJ Nuclear Weapons Advisory Opinion, n.12, para.97.

124 See, for example, T L H McCormack, 'A Non Liquet on Nuclear Weapons – The ICJ Avoids the Application of General Principles of International Humanitarian Law' (1997) 316 IRRC 76; and see C Greenwood, 'The Advisory Opinion on Nuclear Weapons and the Contribution of the International Court to International Humanitarian Law' (1997) 316 IRRC 65, 73.

to comply with any other relevant treaties to which they may be party, such as the Nuclear Non-Proliferation Treaty and such as nuclear weapon free zone treaties.

Certain states made declarations with regard to nuclear weapons when they became party to API; in these declarations, they stated their understanding that the new rules introduced by that Treaty would not apply to nuclear weapons.[125] The states making these declarations did not mention in them which rules they considered to be covered by these statements on ratification, but they are generally recognised as including the environmental protection rules in Articles 35(3) and 55 and the prohibition on taking reprisals against civilians and civilian objects. It has been suggested that they also include the indiscriminate weapons principle[126] but the proportionality and discrimination rules[127] do apply to any use of nuclear weapons. The lawfulness of taking the reprisal action prohibited by API will depend on the position taken by the relevant state when ratifying that Treaty.[128] **6.095**

Article I of the Non-Proliferation Treaty prohibits states that have nuclear weapons from transferring to any recipient nuclear weapons or nuclear explosive devices and provides that nuclear weapon states must not assist non-nuclear weapon states to manufacture or otherwise acquire such weapons or devices. Under Article II of the same Treaty, states that do not have nuclear weapons must not receive the transfer of nuclear weapons or nuclear explosive devices or of control over them and must not seek or receive any assistance in the manufacture of such weapons or explosive devices.[129] **6.096**

'Nuclear weapons are the most awful kinds of weapon known to humankind. Their use would put at risk humanity's very existence and must, in most if not all circumstances, be seen as not only unlawful but also morally repugnant.' These sentiments appear in the opening lines of a book about nuclear weapons published by the present author with his good colleague, Professor Heintschel von Heinegg[130] and they continue to reflect the author's view. **6.097**

---

125 See, for example, statement (a) made by the UK on ratification of API on 28 January 1998, the first statement made by Belgium on ratification of API on 20 May 1986, the first statement by Italy on ratification of API on 27 February 1986, and statement 2 made by France on ratification of API on 11 April 2001.

126 F Kalshoven, 'Arms, Armaments and International Law' (1985-II) 191 RdC 183–341, 236 and 287.

127 API, n.16, Art.51(5)(b) and (4) respectively.

128 Consider in that regard the statement made by the UK on ratification of API on 28 January 1998, statement (m).

129 Treaty on the Non-Proliferation of Nuclear Weapons, New York, 1 July 1968.

130 W H Boothby and W Heintschel von Heinegg, *Nuclear Weapons Law: Where Are We Now?* (Cambridge University Press, 2022).

6.098 Any use of a nuclear weapon will inevitably unleash almost unimaginable degrees of death, injury and destruction, and everything possible must therefore be done to avoid their use. If brain technologies of any kind are to be used as part of the nuclear command, control and communications systems associated with nuclear weapons, those brain technologies must be so configured or programmed as to ensure that everything possible is indeed done to avoid the use of nuclear weapons. Decisions as to the use of nuclear weapons must, the author believes, be made by human beings and must only ever be made in the most exceptional and grave of circumstances, and only after every conceivable alternative course of action has been tried and has failed. Even then, every possible precaution must be taken to protect human life, and these considerations apply irrespective of whether it is a first or subsequent use of a nuclear weapon that is being contemplated. They also apply where brain technologies are used to support the human decision about nuclear weapon use.

6.10 THE LEGAL REVIEW OF NEW WEAPONS

6.099 All states are required by international law to consider whether the use of a new weapon or weapon technology that it is planning to acquire would, in some or all circumstances, breach the international law rules that apply to that state.[131] It cannot be said that this is a rule of customary law simply because too few states are known to have a systematic approach to the conduct of such weapon reviews. The obligation can, however, be deduced from a number of the rules of the LOAC.[132] These rules include the 1868 St Petersburg Declaration,[133] Article 1 of Hague Convention II of 1899 and Article 1 of Hague Convention IV of 1907.[134] Article 1 common to the Geneva Conventions 1949 requires

131 AMW Manual, n.1, Rule 9; Tallinn Manual 2.0, n.30, Rule 110(a), the Commentary to which cites Hague Convention IV, n.14, Art.1 and Geneva Conventions 1949, Art.1. Illustrating that this obligation has been recognised for some time, see the UK Manual, n.10, paras 6.20–6.20.1, the *United States Naval Commanders' Handbook on the Conduct of Naval Operations*, NWP 1–14, para.5.3.4; Canadian Department of National Defence, *Joint Doctrine Manual Law of Armed Conflict at the Operational and Tactical Levels* (13 August 2001), para.530 and Bundesministerium der Verteidigung, *Law of Armed Conflict Manual*, ZDv 15/2 (May 2013), para.405.

132 For the ICRC's recommended approach to weapon reviews, see ICRC, *A Guide to the Legal Review of New Weapons, Means and Methods of Warfare* (10 June 2020).

133 The final paragraph of the Declaration Renouncing the Use, in Time of War, of Explosive Projectiles Under 400 Grammes Weight, St Petersburg, 11 December 1868 (St Petersburg Declaration) 'reserve[s] to [States Parties] to come hereafter to an understanding whenever a precise proposition shall be drawn up in view of future improvements which science may effect in the armament of troops, in order to maintain the principles which they have established, and to conciliate the necessities of war with the laws of humanity'.

134 'The contracting Powers shall issue instructions to their armed land forces which shall be in conformity with the Regulations respecting the laws and customs of war on land, annexed to the present Convention.' Consider, for example, W Hays Parks, 'Conventional Weapons and Weapons Reviews' (2005) 8 *Yearbook*

states that are party to the Conventions to respect, and ensure respect, for them.[135] In addition, the wording of numerous weapons law treaties suggests an obligation for states to ensure that the weapons they acquire and use comply with the legal rules that bind them. The author would therefore describe the obligation as an implied rule which is nevertheless binding on all States.

States that are party to API are bound by Article 36 of that Treaty. The Article requires that: '[i]n the study, development, acquisition or adoption of a new weapon, means or method of warfare [they must] determine whether its employment would, in some or all circumstances, be prohibited by th[e] Protocol or by any other rule of international law applicable to the High Contracting Party.' This makes it clear that a state that is party to API must undertake a weapon review when a weapon or method of warfare[136] is being studied and when it is being developed. The 'study' requirement arises when the weaponisation of a technology is being considered, that is when the possibility of adapting or applying the technology so as to cause death, injury, damage or destruction in the context of an armed conflict is being considered. It follows that at the early, study stage the extent to which the weapon review can go into detail will depend on how much is then known about the exact nature of the science, the technology and the eventual weapon, about the uses for which it is thought potentially applicable, and about other relevant matters. 'Development' for the purposes of Article 36 can be taken to refer to the creation of a weapon and its improvement, refinement and testing. Weapons will be regarded as having been acquired if they are obtained from other states or a commercial undertaking, or if they are simply transferred or given. A method of warfare is adopted when a state decides to employ that method in military operations. The legal review of methods of warfare is therefore likely to require a legal assessment of evolving approaches to the conduct of warfare by a state, including the consideration of how the law impacts on emerging military concepts and doctrine. 6.100

Some of the brain technologies that are discussed in this book, such as BCI technologies, are already employed in the medical sphere, with the consequence that there is already in existence technological capability that a state 6.101

of International Humanitarian Law 55, 55–7 and note that an important state not party to API, the US, has for many years had a system for the legal review of new weapons that it acquires.

135 Note that API, n.16, Art.1(1) contains a similar provision.

136 A 'method of warfare' essentially consists of a way of conducting hostilities, such as aerial bombardment, the use of remotely controlled platforms such as aircraft or submersibles in attack, missile warfare and cyber operations. For a discussion of enhanced warfighters as a method of warfare, see Liivoja and Chircop, n.1, 183–4.

may, at some point, be expected to consider employing in a military way. As a state studies that possibility, the Article 36 weapon review obligation will apply. Other brain science, such as ABs and BBIs, has been the subject of much scientific research. Published, peer-reviewed scientific findings, to which reference is made throughout this book, show that these brain technology capabilities that are discussed in the book appear to be scientifically feasible. How long it will take for the published science to evolve into established technologies remains to be seen. Nevertheless, the publication of the relevant scientific discoveries demonstrates that there are feasible, probably likely, ways of conducting activities, including military activities, in non-traditional ways in the future. It is because such developments are foreseeable and perhaps probable, and because legal advisers may need to provide appropriate advice at relatively early stages in these processes, that it is thought to be both appropriate and useful to produce this book.

6.102 There are 17 States Parties to API[137] all of which must comply with Article 36.

6.10.1 The criteria to be applied in a weapon review

6.103 The lawfulness of a weapon must be determined by reference to the rules of international law as they exist at the time of review. The fact that a new weapon system may employ new technologies does not change this. Accordingly, the principles and rules that have been discussed in the preceding sections of this chapter will constitute the criteria that must be applied to determine whether the weapon system complies with the international law that binds the state. All states must apply the customary principles and rules, whilst also applying the treaty-based rules and restrictions to which a state is bound by treaty law, taking into account any reservations or declarations the state may have made when becoming party to the relevant treaty. Therefore, the following specific issues must be addressed in a weapon review:

1. Is the weapon system of a nature to cause superfluous injury or unnecessary suffering?
2. Is the weapon system indiscriminate by nature?
3. If the state is party to API, is the weapon system intended, or may it be expected, to cause widespread, long-term and severe damage to the natural environment?
4. Irrespective of whether the state is party to API, will using the weapon in its intended manner and circumstances of use breach the obligation to have due regard to the natural environment and to treat the natural environment as, in principle, a civilian object?

---

137 Source www.icrc.org.

5. For states that are party to ENMOD, will the intended manner and circumstances of use of the weapon involve environmental modification techniques, and should such use be expected to have the consequences that are prohibited by that Treaty?
6. Are there ad hoc weapons law rules that either prohibit the use of the weapon or limit its permitted circumstances of use?

While these are the six criteria which should, the author considers, be applied in a review of a conventional weapon, there is an additional criterion that the author believes should be applied if the weapon system or method of warfare excludes, limits or affects the degree of human involvement in targeting decision-making. This is likely to be the case with AB systems that enable autonomous attack decision-making where decisions about attack are made by the autonomous system and do not involve human decision-making or oversight. The legal assessment of systems that employ technologies of that kind will require the weapon reviewer to consider whether the rules relating to targeting will in fact be applied. This might be achieved by a human operator undertaking the relevant precautionary tasks before the mission takes place. Alternatively, it might involve a human operator supervising the weapon system as it makes its decisions with that human operator being in a position to intervene and stop action that would be illegal or that would breach the commander's intent. A third possibility is that the weapon system itself makes the decisions that targeting law requires of attackers. **6.104**

It is important to appreciate that the weapon review will not address whether a particular attack would be lawful. That determination will be the subject of targeting law advice, often provided to the commander by the deployed legal adviser. The weapon reviewer's task will be to consider whether the way in which the weapon system is designed to be used enables the decisions required by targeting law to be made. This will necessarily require the reviewer to address all required targeting law decisions that are relevant to the specific weapon system and the contexts in which it is intended to employ it. **6.105**

If the weapon system involves a BCI, the weapon reviewer must assess whether that interface is such as to enable the human user to exercise effective and reliable control over the weapon. This will involve assessing whether the information supplied to the human operator is sufficient and accurate, so that the thoughts or intent that they develop and which initiate the attack have been developed on the basis of an appropriately informed understanding of the factual circumstances. **6.106**

6.107 When reviewing the potential employment of certain brain technologies, such as a BCI or brain degradation system, another body of law will also need to be considered, namely human rights law. Human rights law issues were discussed in Chapter 3, section 3.13. The weapon review issues will now therefore be described succinctly. Applying the ICJ's formulation in the Palestinian Wall case, to which reference was made in that section, whether the right to life under the International Covenant on Civil and Political Rights (ICCPR) has been breached during the conduct of hostilities will usually fall to be considered by reference to the relevant rules of the LOAC. However, if military operations involving the use of a BCI are undertaken outside the scope of an armed conflict, or arguably during an armed conflict but not in connection with hostilities, the right to life under the ICCPR and other human rights provisions may need to be considered. In those circumstances it will be important to determine whether the relevant individual(s) are within the human rights law jurisdiction of the state. Much will also depend on how the BCI is intended to be used and in which kinds of circumstances. The important points are that the reviewer will need to consider those intended contexts and manners of use and then refer to the human rights that appear to be of relevance, citing the wording in the human rights law instruments by which the relevant state is bound.

6.10.2 The form, method and content of a weapon review

6.108 The treaties do not specify any particular form for a weapon review. If the review is addressing the intended acquisition of a complex weapon with multiple intended uses, a lengthy document will be required in which the law is explained in detail with regard to each such intended use and in which the idiosyncrasies of the particular weapon or method are discussed fully. On other occasions, a relatively brief piece of advice to the relevant commander or other decision-maker may suffice.

6.109 Article 36 also does not require that a set procedure be followed. While some states task individual reviewers from their defence departments with the review of specific weapons, other states, it is understood, appoint a special body or committee consisting of personnel from relevant departments. What is necessary is that the person or persons conducting the review receive sufficient input from specialists in the applicable disciplines so that the resulting document and opinion are appropriately informed.

6.10.3 Data required to support a weapon review

When reviewing any weapon or method involving the use of brain technology, a reviewer will need to receive the following information: **6.110**

1. a thorough technical description of the weapon or method, including its speed, range and shape; the materials used in its construction; the damage mechanism and how it works; the reliability of the weapon; its accuracy; the effect it is designed to have; and how the weapon is deployed to target;
2. the intended radius, or radii, of effect;
3. the nature of the wounding mechanism and the kinds of wounds to be expected from the normal, designed use of the weapon;
4. the intended or designed circumstances of the weapon's use and the way in which the weapon will be used;
5. the results of any tests as to weapon accuracy, reliability, performance, wounds, failure rates or other relevant matters;
6. the environmental impact of the weapon;
7. the exact role and functions of the brain technology component and how it interacts with the rest of the weapon system;
8. the reliability and accuracy with which the brain technology component performs that function and those interactions;
9. the tests that have been applied to the weapon system as a whole and to the brain technology component and the results of those tests;
10. the extent to which those tests were arranged to reflect all of the intended circumstances in which the weapon system will be used;
11. whether the way in which the brain technology component interacts with the rest of the weapon system is transparent to the operator and whether any fault in the performance of the brain technology component is notified to the operator and to the commander in a timely manner;
12. whether the weapon system as a whole, and the brain technology component in particular, is robust against external, not necessarily hostile, sources of interference, and whether there will be timely supply of updates to patch or take other effective defensive action against future potential cyber vulnerabilities;
13. whether the user can be confident that the weapon system, with its brain technology component, will promote compliance with targeting law rules;
14. whether any potential risks or vulnerabilities have not been addressed, and why; and
15. finally, and most importantly, whether any element of the technology associated with the weapon is subject to a weapons law prohibition or restriction on use.

This is an illustrative list of matters for the reviewer to consider. Depending on the nature of the weapon system and the intended applications of it, other issues may need to be added to the list. **6.111**

7

METHODS OF WARFARE AND BRAIN TECHNOLOGIES

7.1 INTRODUCTION

7.001 Methods of warfare are 'attacks and other activities designed to adversely affect the enemy's military operations or military capacity, as distinct from the means of warfare used during military operations, such as weapons'.[1] The AMW Manual refers to 'various general categories of operations, such as

1 Program on Humanitarian Policy and Conflict Research at Harvard University (HPCR), *Manual on the International Law Applicable to Air and Missile Warfare* (March 2010) (AMW Manual), available at https://cdn.ca9.uscourts.gov/datastore/library/2013/09/06/Flores_Manual.pdf, Rule 1(v).

bombing, as well as the specific tactics used for attack, such as high altitude bombing' as being methods of warfare.[2]

In Chapter 6 it was pointed out that the 175 states that are party to Additional Protocol I to the Geneva Conventions (API) are obliged by Article 36 legally to review not just new weapons, but also new methods of warfare that they are planning to adopt. 'The right of belligerents to adopt means of injuring the enemy is not unlimited.'[3] This proposition, dating from 1899, is, in current law, reflected in Article 35(1) of API as follows: 'In any armed conflict, the right of the parties to the conflict to choose methods or means of warfare is not unlimited.' The law does not just assert that there are limits on the methods of warfare that a party to the conflict can lawfully adopt; it also prescribes what those limits are. It is therefore sensible in this chapter to consider the methods of warfare that are the subject of specific rules of the law of armed conflict (LOAC). Accordingly, the chapter will explain the law applicable to each of the methods that seem to be potentially relevant where brain-computer interfaces (BCIs), artificial brains (ABs) and, to an extent, brain-to-brain interfaces (BBIs) are concerned. The purpose in doing so is to identify what effect the applicable law may be expected to have on the specific application of those technologies. If a particular method has already been discussed elsewhere, the treatment of it in the present chapter will be suitably brief. **7.002**

There are numerous examples of methods of warfare, not all of which are lawful. They include blockade, the use in warfare of unmanned systems, the participation by civilians in armed conflict hostilities, the use of human shields as a method of warfare, the use of riot control agents as a method of warfare, the employment of autonomous weapons in the conduct of hostilities, starvation, scorched earth policies, the targeting of cash and staple resources, the conduct of hostilities in outer space, the employment of ruses and, as the case may be, perfidy in connection with attacks and the use of certain emblems, insignia and uniforms in connection with hostilities. So, each of these methods will be considered in turn with a view to identifying which legal issues are raised by the application to them of brain technologies. **7.003**

2 AMW Manual, ibid.

3 Regulations Concerning the Laws and Customs of War on Land, annexed to Convention (II) with Respect to the Laws and Customs of War on Land, The Hague, 29 July 1899 (Hague Regulations 1899), Art.22.

7.2 BLOCKADE

7.004 Blockade is a lawful method of interfering with the enemy's trade, and thus with its economy.[4] There are, however, rules that apply to blockade.[5] In the maritime context, a blockade is defined as 'a belligerent operation intended to prevent vessel traffic from all States from entering or leaving specified coastal areas that are under the sovereignty, occupation, or control of an enemy. Such areas may include ports and harbors, the entire coastline, or parts of it'.[6] An aerial blockade is 'a belligerent operation to prevent aircraft including unmanned aircraft, whether weaponised or not, from entering or exiting specified airfields or coastal areas belonging to, occupied by, or under the control of the enemy'.[7]

7.005 The following rules apply to blockades.

7.006 1. *The blockade must be declared and notified.*[8] The notification should be by means of a notice to mariners in the case of a maritime blockade and a notice to airmen in the case of an air blockade[9] or by some other official method. All aspects of the blockade must be notified, including the geographic extent, date of commencement, and the 'general scope of measures employed'.[10] Appropriate methods should be chosen for the communication of the declaration and notification. Those methods might include the use of AB-enabled systems, provided that the declaration and notification are in fact communicated properly.

7.007 2. *A blockade must be effective.*[11] The Newport Manual explains that a naval 'blockade is effective if there is a sufficient probability that vessels breaching or attempting to breach the blockade are captured'. Where air blockades are concerned, this aspect will effectively require that the blockading party have a sufficient degree of air superiority.[12] Provided effectiveness is achieved, there

---

4 *Newport Manual on the Law of Naval Warfare*, 2nd Edn (2025) available at https://digital-commons.usnwc.edu/cgi/viewcontent.cgi?article=3106&context=ils (Newport Manual), para.7.4.

5 Newport Manual, ibid, para.7.4.

6 Newport Manual, ibid, para.7.4.1.

7 AMW Manual, n.1, rule 147 and see W Heintschel von Heinegg, 'Blockade', in R Wolfrum (ed), *Max Planck Encyclopaedia of Public International Law*, 2nd edn (Oxford University Press, 2012), 960, 961.

8 AMW Manual, n.1, Rule 148(a).

9 Newport Manual, n.4, para.7.4.2; AMW Manual, n.1, Rule 148(c).

10 Newport Manual, n.4, para.7.4.2 and see footnote 525 as to relevant state practice.

11 AMW Manual, n.1, Rule 151.

12 Newport Manual, n.4, para.7.4.3, citing Declaration Respecting Maritime Law, Paris, 16 April 1856, UK State Papers, Vol. LXI, pp.155–8 (Paris Declaration), 1856, Art.4; Declaration Concerning the Laws of Naval Warfare, London, 26 February 1909 (London Declaration), Arts 2–3; and AMW Manual, n.1,

is no requirement that the enforcing forces be any particular distance from the coast, nor that any particular enforcement method be used.[13] It is imaginable that AB systems might be employed to assist with detecting and arranging for the interception of vessels or aircraft seeking to breach the blockade. It is also imaginable that BCI systems may be employed if the use of force were to become necessary and appropriate in enforcement of the blockade. These and other kinds of technology, such as the use of drones, may enable lawful blockades to be lawfully enforced by platforms that are somewhat distant from the blockade line; '[a]ssuming that there is a sufficient degree of probability of capture, the distance of the blockading force from the coast is not relevant'.[14] A blockading state may lawfully make arrangements for humanitarian relief to a blockaded area.[15] Information relating to the movement of vessels or aircraft that are transporting relief supplies should be fed into AB systems involved in the enforcement of the blockade and those AB systems must be so programmed that the relevant vessels and/or aircraft will not be made the object of attack. If BCI systems are being used in connection with blockade enforcement, it will be planners, commanders and operators who will be responsible for ensuring that the humanitarian relief shipments or flights referred to earlier are not made the object of attack.

3. '*A blockade must be applied impartially to the ships of all nations.*'[16] It will be for planners, commanders and operators to ensure that BCI systems that are being used in connection with enforcement apply the relevant measures impartially. AB systems involved in the enforcement of the blockade must also do so impartially, meaning that they must not favour ships and/or aircraft of particular flag states. **7.008**

Scenario 1. Consider a situation in which State A decides to impose a blockade against, and during its armed conflict against, State B. State A exclusively uses Block 1 autonomous enforcement systems that are located on unmanned surface vessels to enforce the blockade. The Block 1 systems intrude into the navigation systems of ships that are about to cross the blockade line so as to cause **7.009**

Rules 151 and 154. The London Declaration was not ratified by any signatory, but the text tended to reflect established custom and national prize court decisions.

13 See AMW Manual, n.1, Rule 151, para.2.

14 Newport Manual, n.4, para.7.4.3; AMW Manual, n.1, Rule 152.

15 Indeed, the blockading party must provide for free passage of food or other supplies if the population in the blockaded area is inadequately provided with food or other objects indispensable for its survival, AMW Manual, n.1, Rule 158. This is subject to the right to require technical arrangements and to require that distribution be by an impartial humanitarian organisation.

16 London Declaration, 1909, n.12, Art.5; AMW Manual, n.1, Rule 155.

the vessel involuntarily to change course and to proceed away from the line of blockade. However, the vessels of neutral State C are equipped with a different navigation system which is unaffected by State A's Block 1 autonomous enforcement systems. State C's vessels are therefore able to cross the blockade line with impunity and do so regularly. The blockade is therefore unlawful because it is not effective and because it is not being enforced impartially.

7.010 4. *'The establishment of a blockade is prohibited if it is solely intended to starve the civilian population, or solely intended to deprive the civilian population of objects essential to its survival.'*[17] It will be a matter for technical and legal interpretation whether an AB system is capable of forming any intent. It is unlikely that an AB system will in practice make the decision to impose a blockade. That decision will almost certainly be made within government, probably at a high level by a government minister, probably the prime minister in consultation with the cabinet. However, an AB system might, in its role connected to the enforcement of such a blockade, decide on action that has the effect of starving the civilian population or of causing it to be deprived of objects essential for survival. If, in light of the capabilities of the AB system and evolving interpretations of law, it is determined that the specific AB system is indeed capable of forming an intent, this rule may become relevant. The rule may also become relevant if the planners, commander and/or operators involved in implementing the AB-assisted blockade were to develop such an intent and to cause the AB system, or indeed a BCI weapon system that is being used in connection with the enforcement of the blockade, to assist in realising that intended outcome.[18]

7.011 *Scenario 2.* State A has, as a result of the Scenario 1 situation, introduced multiple enforcement measures and the blockade is now lawful and entirely effective. State A has decided to extend the area of blockaded coastline and has included the important port at Bravo in the blockade. State B civilians are suffering inconvenience and while essential goods are still available, prices have risen. The rule reflected in para.4 has not been broken as starvation has not yet been caused and objects indispensable to the survival of the population are not being denied; if that were to happen, State B would be required to accept relief supplies.

---

17 Newport Manual, n.4, para.7.4.5; AMW Manual, n.1, Rule 157a.

18 The proportionality rule as set forth in the Protocol Additional to the Geneva Conventions of 12 August 1949, and Relating to the Protection of Victims of International Armed Conflicts, Geneva, 8 June 1977, 1125 UNTS 3 (Additional Protocol I or API), Arts 51(5)(b) and 57 does not apply to blockade; see Newport Manual, n.4, footnote 533.

5. *'A blockade must not bar access to neutral ports or coasts'*,[19] and similarly must not bar access 'to straits used for international navigation or archipelagic sea lanes, in neutral waters'.[20] It will be for planners, commanders and operators involved in the enforcement of the blockade to ensure that this requirement is satisfied where BCI-controlled systems are being employed. If an AB system is being used to achieve that enforcement, it will be necessary for that system to be programmed so that action that it decides upon and implements does not result in a breach of this requirement. **7.012**

Scenario 3. The border between State B and neutral State C reaches the coast only a mile beyond the port of Bravo. The extension of State A's blockade line has resulted in the blocking of the navigation channel which serves not just Bravo but also State C's port of Charlie. Ships destined for Charlie port must pass through the blockaded channel. State C protests to State A and the State A authorities adjust the blockade line so that access to Charlie is restored. Like any other change, this change to the blockade arrangements must be declared and notified. Moreover, the Block 1 autonomous enforcement systems will need to be reprogrammed to take account of the changes in the blockade line. **7.013**

The decision to apply a blockade, the determination of the required extent and duration of the blockade and the selection of the military systems that will be used for the enforcement of the blockade are all decisions that, in practice, will be made by politicians, human commanders and other human operators. Planners, commanders and operators of BCI systems that are involved in the enforcement of a blockade must have correct information as to the location and duration of the blockade, must have direct access to up-to-date information about vessels and/or aircraft that are in the vicinity of the blockade line, and must ensure that the requirements particularised above, and (so far as relevant) those set forth below in relation to AB operations, are satisfied. **7.014**

AB systems that will be used to enforce a blockade must be programmed with the exact co-ordinates of the blockade line and blockaded area as reflected in the declaration and notification. That data will need to be updated in a timely way to take account of any alteration of the details of the blockade or any termination of it. In particular, an AB system that is being used for the enforcement of a blockade must fulfil the following requirements. **7.015**

19 London Declaration, n.12, Art.18.

20 Newport Manual, n.4, para. 7.4.6; see also Y Dinstein, *The Conduct of Hostilities under the Law of International Armed Conflict*, 4th edn (Cambridge University Press, 2022), 298–9.

1. The decision to use the AB system in connection with blockade enforcement must be conducive to the effective enforcement of the blockade. This means that the AB system, with the assistance of any personnel who are intended to operate with it, must reliably, consistently and in a timely way detect all vessels or aircraft that are breaching, or are about to breach, the blockade.
2. Having detected such vessels or aircraft, the AB system must reliably and consistently take lawful action with a view to ensuring the effectiveness of the blockade.
3. The AB system, with the assistance of any personnel intended to operate with it, must reliably and consistently distinguish between vessels or aircraft that are breaching, or that are perceived as being about to breach, the blockade and vessels or aircraft that should lawfully be allowed through, for example because they are vessels or aircraft that are in distress or that are involved in permitted humanitarian relief operations.
4. The AB system must act impartially when assisting with the enforcement of a blockade, so careful action should be taken to remove relevant bias from the system.
5. The AB system must not be capable of forming an intent to starve the civilian population or to deprive it of objects that are essential to its survival.
6. The AB system must not be capable of barring entry to neutral ports, coasts or airfields.

7.016 If an AB system has a role in the navigation of neutral shipping or aircraft, it will need to have access to Notices to Mariners and to Airmen, and will need, reliably and consistently, to prevent the relevant neutral vessel or aircraft from crossing the blockade line, from being in the vicinity of the blockade line or from entering or being in the vicinity of a blockaded airfield.

7.3 UNMANNED WEAPON SYSTEMS

7.017 There are numerous kinds of weapon platforms, including aircraft, ground vehicles, surface or sub-surface vessels, that operate without a human being on board. So, for example, numerous states operate medium-altitude long-endurance armed drones.[21] Much work is also underway to develop and introduce into service unmanned ground vehicles,[22] and unmanned surface vessel devel-

21 Source: 'Which Countries have Armed Drones', *Drone Wars*, https://dronewars.net/which-countries-have-armed-drones/.

22 For details see '10 unmanned ground vehicles being developed around the world' *Mobility Engineering*, 1 April 2024, https://www.mobilityengineeringtech.com/component/content/article/50439-10-unmanned-ground-vehicles-being-developed-and-tested-around-the-world.

opment is underway in the US,[23] China,[24] Israel,[25] India[26] and elsewhere. Unmanned sub-surface vessels[27] have been demonstrated and there are associated projects around the world. These unmanned systems can be used in a wide range of military roles, including intelligence gathering, surveillance, the detection and acquisition of targets for attack, the conduct of attacks, the conduct of post-attack damage assessment, and so on. The LOAC does not prohibit the use of such systems, and air operations have employed such systems during the Russia-Ukraine war and in other conflicts.[28]

In the Israel-Gaza armed conflict, drone technology is being reportedly used in conjunction with artificial intelligence (AI). The AI is seemingly being used to learn to detect humans and the drone technology is used to operate underground in the tunnels.[29] There has also been extensive use of kamikaze or suicide drones in recent conflicts. These are unmanned aircraft that may be steered to target by a remotely located operator, but which are usually packed with explosives and are designed to be flown into the target on what is essentially a 'one-way' mission. The author would characterise such systems as cruise missiles because they differ from unmanned platforms, remotely piloted aircraft or drones. The intention, where the latter class of weapons is concerned, is that the unmanned aircraft on a ground attack mission fires its weapon at the target and then returns to base where it can be rearmed and used for further missions.[30] **7.018**

23 See CRS Report R45757 *Navy Large Unmanned Surface and Undersea Vehicles: Background and Issues for Congress* (19 December 2024), available at https://sgp.fas.org/crs/weapons/R45757.pdf.

24 H I Sutton, 'China Builds World's Largest Uncrewed Warship', available at http://www.hisutton.com/Chinese-JARI-USV-A.html.

25 Note, for example, the 'Katana USV system', *IAI*, https://www.iai.co.il/p/katana.

26 R Pandit, 'Indian Navy Steaming Ahead with Autonomous Unmanned Vessels', *Times of India*, 24 July 2023, available at https://timesofindia.indiatimes.com/india/indian-navy-steaming-ahead-with-autonomous-unmanned-vessels/articleshow/102064482.cms.

27 Consider, for example, the General Dynamics Bluefin-9 and Bluefin-12 referred to at https://gdmissionsystems.com/underwater-vehicles, the British Aerospace Herne extra-large autonomous underwater vehicle described at https://www.baesystems.com/en-uk/article/british-engineers-successfully-demonstrate-uk-s-first-autonomous-extra-large-submarine-for-military-use, and the Boeing Orca extra-large unmanned under sea vehicle, the potential capabilities of which include mine countermeasures, anti-surface warfare, electronic warfare and strike missions, described at https://www.naval-technology.com/projects/orca-xluuv/.

28 See K D Thompson, 'How the Drone War in Ukraine is Transforming Conflict', *Council on Foreign Relations*, 16 January 2024, available at https://www.cfr.org/article/how-drone-war-ukraine-transforming-conflict; W H Boothby, 'The Drone Threat, the Laser Response and the Law – Part I', *Articles of War*, 10 January 2025 available at https://lieber.westpoint.edu/drone-threat-laser-response-law-part-i/

29 AFP Report, 'Israel Deploys New Military AI in Gaza War', *France24*, 10 February 2024, available at https://www.france24.com/en/live-news/20240210-israel-deploys-new-military-ai-in-gaza-war.

30 See the discussion of these matters at Boothby, n.28.

7.019 The use of unmanned systems in the intelligence-gathering and surveillance roles is not prohibited by the LOAC. Indeed, Article 24 of the Hague Regulations of 1907 stipulates: 'Ruses of war and the employment of measures necessary for obtaining information about the enemy and the country are considered permissible.'[31] Moreover, if a system fulfilling such a role is operating in or over territory controlled by an adverse party while using properly marked platforms and if no other features would cause the operation to be described as 'clandestine or under false pretences', the relevant acts will not be classed as espionage under the LOAC.[32]

7.020 Human rights law may apply to the intelligence-gathering and surveillance operation if individuals affected by such operations are regarded as being within the jurisdiction of a state that is undertaking the operations. Therefore, if the operating state is performing the operations within its own territory, jurisdiction, and thus human rights law, will apply. The European Court of Human Rights (ECtHR) stated in the case of *Loizidou v Turkey (Preliminary Objections)*[33] that jurisdiction can apply if, through military action, a state exercises effective control of an area outside its national territory. Jurisprudence of the ECtHR[34] since *Loizidou* shows that if a state exercises authority and control over a person outside its national territory, that will cause the individual to be within its jurisdiction for human rights law purposes. Intelligence-gathering and surveillance operations alone, whether conducted inside or over enemy-held territory, will not, in the author's view, cause the individuals whose activities are being observed to be subject to the extra-territorial jurisdiction of the spying state for human rights law purposes. In this regard, and for completeness, it should be noted that Article 17 of the International Covenant on Civil and Political Rights[35] states: 'No one shall be subjected to arbitrary or unlawful interference with his privacy, family, home or correspondence ...'[36]

---

31 Regulations Respecting the Laws and Customs of War on Land annexed to Hague Convention (IV) Respecting the Laws and Customs of War on Land, The Hague, 18 October 1907 (Hague Regulations 1907), Art.24.

32 Hague Regulations 1907, ibid, Art.29.

33 *Loizidou v Turkey*, Application No.15318/89, Judgment on Preliminary Objections dated 23 March 1995, paras 56 and 62–4.

34 Note *Ocalan v Turkey*, Application No.46221/99, 12 May 2005; ECtHR, *Issa and Others v Turkey*, Application No.31821/96, 16 November 2004; ECtHR, *Al-Skeini and Others v United Kingdom*, Application No.55721/07, 7 July 2011; ECtHR, *Jaloud v The Netherlands*, Application No.47708/08, 20 November 2014.

35 UN General Assembly Resolution 2200A(XXI), 16 December 1966, International Covenant on Civil and Political Rights (ICCPR).

36 ICCPR, ibid, Art.17(1).

The principles and rules of targeting law, explained in Chapters 4 and 5, also apply to unmanned ground attack operations. Planners, commanders and operators employing BCI systems must therefore ensure that distinction, discrimination, proportionality and precautions principles and rules are adhered to if those systems are to be used for ground attack. If AB systems are used to control attacks using unmanned weapon systems or unmanned weapon-carrying platforms against ground targets, the principles and rules of the law of targeting will also apply. Accordingly, the AB systems, together with planners, commanders and operators to the extent that they are involved, must fulfil the detailed requirements listed in Chapters 4 and 5. This is so whether an aircraft, land vehicle, surface vessel or submarine is being employed in an attack that may affect civilians on land.[37] **7.021**

7.4 EMPLOYING CIVILIANS IN HOSTILITIES

Employing civilians to take a direct part in hostilities is not prohibited by the LOAC. There are, however, consequences for the civilians that do so. These are: that they lose their protection from being made the object of attack if, and for such time as, they take a direct part in the hostilities;[38] that they have no combatant immunity; and that they can therefore be prosecuted for their role in violent acts, including acts that may comply with the LOAC If they are captured by the enemy, such civilians who are not in the categories listed under Article 4A of Geneva Convention III (GCIII) will also not have prisoner of war status. **7.022**

There is no international agreement as to which activities are, and respectively are not, classed as direct participation. The International Committee of the Red Cross (ICRC) has published Interpretive Guidance[39] on the matter, but that Interpretive Guidance has not been generally agreed by states.[40] The author's view is reflected in the following ten propositions. **7.023**

A. Civilians are protected from attack provided that they abstain from taking a direct part in hostilities.[41] **7.024**

---

37 API, n.18, Art.49(3).

38 API, n.18, Art.51(3).

39 N Melzer, *Interpretive Guidance on the Notion of Direct Participation in Hostilities under International Humanitarian Law* (ICRC, 2009).

40 Criticisms of the *Interpretive Guidance* were addressed in (2010) 42 NYUJILP 3 and were summarised in W H Boothby, *The Law of Targeting* (Oxford University Press, 2012), Ch.8.

41 API, n.18, Arts 48 and 51(1), (2) and (3).

7.025 Planners, commanders and operators involved in BCI-enabled operations must therefore assess whether a person is a civilian. If so, they must decide whether that civilian is taking a direct part in hostilities. In particular, they must decide whether the civilian person retains protection or has forfeited civilian protection due to direct participation. They must also consider whether it is reasonable for them to make the determination on the basis of the information that is available to them.

7.026 If AB systems are being employed in connection with attack decisions, the AB system must reliably and consistently:

1. differentiate between combatants and civilians in connection with an international armed conflict, and between fighters and civilians in connection with a non-international armed conflict;
2. decide whether a civilian that the sensors are observing is taking a direct part in the hostilities, that is the AB system must decide whether the civilian is performing a specific act that constitutes direct participation, or is preparing to do so, or is deploying to a location in order to undertake the act of direct participation, or is returning to their normal peaceable location having performed the act of direct participation, or is, at that time, maintaining, storing, or concealing equipment with a view to its future use in connection with hostilities.

7.027 Each of these acts would amount to direct participation in the hostilities.

7.028 It may be difficult for the AB system to distinguish between peaceable acts, such as digging fence post holes, and acts of hostility, such as planting an improvised explosive device. Nevertheless, the AB system must have shown, in tests that adequately reflect operational reality, that it will make the required distinction with acceptable reliability.

7.029 B. Civilians supporting the war effort generally are to be distinguished from civilians taking a direct part in hostilities. Civilians who only give general support to the war effort are not directly involved in the hostilities and must not be individually targeted. Directly participating civilians may be individually targeted as long as their direct participation lasts.[42]

7.030 Where BCI-enabled operations are concerned, it will be for planners, commanders and operators to decide whether a civilian is giving general support to the war effort or is taking a direct part in hostilities. It is suggested that,

42 See Danish MOD Manual, Example 5.13 at 170 and Dinstein, n.20, 205.

where possible, the BCI system should be switched off until that decision has been made.

If an AB system is being used in support of attacks against persons where civilians are known to be present and if planners, commanders and operators cannot do this in advance of the mission, the AB system itself must: 7.031

1. have been programmed reliably and consistently to distinguish between combatants/fighters and civilians;
2. have been programmed reliably and consistently to distinguish between acts amounting to direct participation and those that do not;
3. have been programmed reliably and consistently not to make civilians the object of attack unless they are observed doing things that the AB system has been programmed to recognise as direct participation. In this regard, it should be borne in mind, for example, that ammunition factory workers are normally regarded as giving general support to the war effort and should not, therefore, on the basis of that work alone, be classed as direct participants. There are, of course, numerous other activities that constitute general support to the war effort, not direct participation. Test results may suggest that the AB system should only be permitted to recognise certain activities as amounting to direct participation.

C. The right to participate directly in the hostilities and the consequent immunity from prosecution for lawful acts undertaken as part of the hostilities are rights of war accorded only to combatants.[43] 7.032

Planners, commanders and operators of BCI-enabled systems used in connection with attacks will need to know and apply this proposition. This proposition does not have implications for AB systems other than those implications mentioned in the discussion of proposition A above. 7.033

D. If an organised armed group participates in the hostilities, those of its members who have a combat function, whether permanent, temporary, or contingent, are liable to be attacked throughout the period of their membership of the group. 7.034

Planners, commanders and operators of BCI-enabled systems employed in attacks will be responsible for applying this requirement. 7.035

If an AB system is being used in connection with attacks, it or, more likely, planners, commanders and operators involved in such missions will need to: 7.036

43 API, n.18, Art.43(2) and Hague Regulations 1907, n.31, Art.1.

1. decide whether the individual it observes is a member of an organised armed group. This may be achieved by the AB system recognising distinctive clothing or a fixed sign indicating membership of the group. If the organised armed group does not wear a uniform or mark to distinguish its members, there may need to be a different approach. One possibility is that the AB system is programmed to recognise specific individuals who are known to be members of the group;
2. decide whether the members of the organised armed group it observes have a combat function which may be permanent, temporary or contingent. This may imply only permitting the AB system to recognise, and thus to target, specific individuals previously identified by planners, commanders or operators as coming within paragraph D and whose details will have been fed in advance into that system. If the organised armed group exclusively consists of persons with combat functions, this may simplify the task of the AB system and associated personnel.[44] If the group includes individuals with exclusively diplomatic or other non-military roles, the AB system and/or associated personnel must ensure that they are not made the object of an attack.

7.037 E. The decisions under propositions A to D above must be made in good faith and on the basis of the attacker's interpretation of the information from all sources reasonably available to the attack decision-maker at the relevant time.[45]

7.038 Where BCI systems are being used in the conduct of attacks, it will be the good faith of planners, commanders and operators that will be germane. Those are the persons who must satisfy themselves that they have considered all available information in applying propositions A to D.

7.039 Where AB systems are being used in connection with attacks, those involved in setting up such systems along with planners, commanders and operators must, when performing their assigned tasks, act in good faith when arranging for the AB system to make the proposition A to D determinations. The AB system must be programmed to apply all relevant information when it makes its decisions and the associated personnel must do likewise. What this really means is that the decision-making processes that are programmed into the AB system must be designed to achieve assessments that are as objectively accurate as possible, based on all of the available information, giving each piece of information its due weight, ignoring irrelevant information and applying the law correctly.

---

44 But consider API, n.18, Art.41.

45 Note API, n.18, Arts 48 and 57(1).

F. Members of an organised armed group who have no combat function and who do not otherwise participate directly in hostilities retain civilian protection from attack.[46] **7.040**

Planners, commanders and operators involved in BCI operations will be responsible for ensuring that the BCI capability is not used to target members of the group who continue to be entitled to civilian protection on the basis that they have no combat role. The thought or intent that is used to trigger the firing of the BCI-enabled weapon must not be formed in respect of persons entitled to that protection. This again implies switching off the BCI system while these matters are being considered and only switching it on when a determination is made that the individual is indeed directly participating and, thus, has lost civilian protection. **7.041**

The implications for AB-linked weapon systems are similar, that is that the AB must be programmed to recognise the members of the group referred to in proposition F and must not make them the object of attack. It must do this consistently and reliably, an aspect that will need to be checked by appropriate testing. Achieving this requirement may involve feeding into the AB system details of the group members who are known not to have a combat function. If that is done, the issue then becomes whether the weapon system as a whole, including the AB element, will reliably and consistently recognise those persons and, having done so, refrain from attacking them. It should also be noted that the members of the group referred to in F must be counted as peaceable civilians in the proportionality evaluation. **7.042**

G. Members of an organised armed group who have a combat function and civilians who are not members of such a group but who participate repeatedly or regularly in hostilities, must clearly and adequately communicate an act of disengagement before they can resume civilian protection from attack. **7.043**

The corollary of this is that there must be information available for planners, commanders and operators involved in using BCI-enabled weapon systems as to which persons come within the first two lines of proposition G. It must also be possible for acts of disengagement to be recognised. This will involve the disengaging civilian making their intent clear and planners, commanders and operators detecting such acts of disengagement. **7.044**

46 Consider API, n.18, Art.50(1).

7.045 If AB-enabled weapon systems are being used, the AB system must be programmed to recognise acts of disengagement and, having done so, refrain from making the disengaging civilian the object of attack. The act of disengagement will be clear and adequate if it is made in an appropriately visible way such that it would be reasonable for the planner, commander or operator of the AB system to detect the act and appreciate what it conveys.

7.046 H. These principles apply also to employees of civilian contractors; if the employees are sufficiently involved in the conduct of the hostilities, they will be regarded as directly participating. While this will render them liable to be attacked lawfully, and liable to prosecution for their participation in hostilities, exercising jurisdiction may pose practical challenges.

7.047 The practical implications of this proposition have already been discussed in relation to previous propositions.

7.048 I. Civilians who participate directly in the hostilities repeatedly or on a regular basis are likely to be regarded as losing their protection on a continuous basis; civilians whose direct participation is sporadic or infrequent lose civilian protection while doing so, while preparing to do so, while deploying in order to do so, while returning having done so, and while maintaining, storing, or concealing equipment with a view to its future use in connection with hostilities.

7.049 Planners, commanders and operators involved in BCI operations will be responsible for the correct application of this proposition. Where AB systems are being used in connection with targeting, the AB system must reliably and consistently:

1. be fed with targeting instructions that correctly apply the direct participation rule as interpreted by the using state;
2. if the state regards repeated and regular participation as rendering the individual continuously targetable, be programmed to apply that state's interpretation of what repeated and regular participation amounts to;
3. detect whether an individual is directly participating on a repeated or regular basis.

7.050 J. There is no legal presumption that a civilian is not participating in hostilities. If BCI-enabled systems are being used in connection with attacks, planners, commanders and operators must therefore consider the available information and if there is doubt about whether an individual is directly participating, planners, commanders and operators must seek information to resolve that doubt. If no further information is available, planners, commanders and operators must consider the information that is available and must be guided by whether a reasonable military commander, having considered the information that they have, would proceed with the attack.

An AB system that is used in connection with attack operations must be programmed to recognise when uncertainty exists as to whether a civilian person is directly participating in the hostilities. The legally safer course is likely to be for the AB system, having determined that such doubt exists, to refer the matter to the operator for human decision-making. **7.051**

An AB system involved in the conduct of attack operations must be programmed to make reasonable judgements as specified in this section, taking into account all of the relevant information that is reasonably available to it at the relevant time. What is considered to be reasonable may be affected by numerous factors, and programming an autonomous AB-enabled system to make such assessments may therefore be challenging. **7.052**

7.5 HUMAN SHIELDS

The topic of human shields is discussed fully in Chapter 4, section 4.8 above. It is sufficient, for present purposes, to state that, in accordance with Article 51(7) of API, using human shields is a prohibited method of warfare, is also a war crime,[47] and is prohibited by customary law. All states are bound by the rule. However, if the rule is broken, that does not entitle the attacking state to ignore its obligations with regard to civilians, including the requirement to take precautions in attack.[48] **7.053**

Planners, commanders and operators using BCI-enabled weapon systems will be directly responsible for ensuring the rule in this section is complied with. The BCI system should therefore probably be switched off while the legal complexities, discussed below, arising from the presence of human shields are considered. Arguably, the system should only be switched on when the planners, commanders and operators have decided that the attack can lawfully take place. **7.054**

If an AB system is deciding upon an attack against a military objective in a location where civilians are present, the AB system must reliably and consistently: **7.055**

47 Rome Statute of the International Criminal Court, 17 July 1998 (Rome Statute), Art.8(2)(b)(xxiii).

48 API, n.18, Art.51(8).

1. detect the presence of the civilians;
2. distinguish between civilians who are present as human shields and civilians who are present for other, non-shielding reasons;
3. distinguish between human shields who are present voluntarily and those who are not;
4. if there is doubt, assume that a human shield is present involuntarily, and is thus entitled to the highest appropriate level of protection; and
5. apply the value to the human shields in the proportionality evaluation that accords with the attacking state's interpretation of the law relating to human shields.

7.056 If the AB system cannot fulfil these requirements, it must be programmed either to give the full peaceable civilian value to all of the human shields or to report to an operator for a human decision to be made.

7.6 USE OF RIOT CONTROL AGENTS

7.057 The Chemical Weapons Convention defines riot control agents as 'chemicals not listed in a Schedule to the Treaty which can produce rapidly in humans sensory irritation or disabling physical effects which disappear within a short time following termination of exposure'.[49] Such weapons can lawfully be used during an armed conflict for law enforcement, including domestic riot-control purposes; they must not be used as a method of warfare.[50]

7.058 Responsibility for ensuring that BCI-enabled riot control agents are not used as a method of warfare rests with planners, commanders and operators. If AB systems are controlling such weapons, the AB system must reliably and consistently distinguish between lawful law enforcement use and prohibited method of warfare use. If the AB system cannot reliably make that distinction and thus ensure its lawful use, an operator will need to be available to do so.

7.7 STARVATION AND OBJECTS INDISPENSABLE TO THE SURVIVAL OF THE CIVILIAN POPULATION

7.059 In Chapter 5, section 5.7 the prohibition of starvation of the civilian population as a method of warfare is set forth and discussed along with the

49 Convention on the Prohibition of the Development, Production, Stockpiling and Use of Chemical Weapons and on Their Destruction, Paris, 13 January 1993, 1975 UNTS 45 (Chemical Weapons Convention), Art.II(7).

50 Chemical Weapons Convention, ibid, Art.I(5).

provisions protecting objects that are indispensable to the survival of the civilian population.

7.8 SCORCHED EARTH POLICIES

This topic and its implications for the use of BCI and AB-related systems are discussed in Chapter 5, section 5.7 above. **7.060**

7.9 TERRORISING THE CIVILIAN POPULATION

Acts or threats of violence, the primary purpose of which is to spread terror among the civilian population are prohibited.[51] This prohibition applies irrespective of the method used. If a BCI system is being used in connection with attacks, the planner, commander and operator must not have the prohibited purpose when performing the act or making the threat. The incidental occasioning of terror where that was not the primary purpose of the act or threat will not cause the rule to be breached. **7.061**

Scenario 4. Imagine a situation in which State A is using an AB-controlled electronic information operations system to spread messages to the State B population via social media. The message tells the population that if the armed forces of State B do not lay down their weapons within the next 24 hours, poisoned gas will be released in the capital city and mass casualties can be expected. Article 51(2) of API will have been breached if at least one of the planners, commanders or operators who issued the message on social media had the required primary purpose in doing so. If those individuals had no such primary purpose, the issue then becomes whether the AB system is capable of forming its own purpose. The author doubts that this can be the case but believes that this is a technical issue which can only be determined by reference to the particular technology that is involved. **7.062**

51 API, n.18, Art.51(2), second sentence; Protocol Additional to the Geneva Conventions of 12 August 1949, and relating to the Protection of Victims of Non-International Armed Conflicts (Protocol II), 8 June 1977, 1125 UNTS 609 (APII), Art.13(2), second sentence. The rule applies in international and non-international armed conflicts.

7.10 WANTON DESTRUCTION

7.063 Under Article 23(g) of the Hague Regulations 1907 it is prohibited '[t]o destroy or seize the enemy's property, unless such destruction or seizure be imperatively demanded by the necessities of war'. This rule reflects customary law and binds all states. Breach of this provision constitutes a war crime.[52] Destruction or seizure of objects that are military objectives does not breach the rule but needless destruction and seizure of things that belong to the enemy is unlawful. Dinstein explains that the notion of 'the enemy's property' extends to both public and private enemy property and is construed broadly while 'necessities of war' also, inevitably, 'has a broad sweep'.[53]

7.064 If operators, commanders and planners undertaking operations using BCI systems take the precautions set forth in Chapter 4, they will thereby not only comply with the general targeting requirements to which those precautions relate but also satisfy the requirements of the rule referred to in the present section. Likewise, if an AB system is being used in connection with attacks, configuring it to comply with the requirements set forth in Chapter 4 will, at the same time, mean that it will not breach the obligation in the present rule.

7.11 DECEPTION OPERATIONS – PERFIDY

7.065 Deception is nothing new in warfare, but there are some kinds of deception that are unlawful. As Yoram Dinstein pointed out, it is the presence of foul play that distinguishes unlawful deception.[54] The Hague Regulations 1907 provide that it is prohibited to 'kill or wound treacherously[55] individuals belonging to the hostile nation or army'. This rule reflects customary law, therefore it binds all states and its breach constitutes a war crime.[56] API builds on this prohibition by adding capture to killing or wounding. The API provision also refers to perfidy as follows:

---

52 Rome Statute, n.47, Art.8(2)(b)(xiii).

53 Dinstein, n.20, 337. Consider also Geneva Convention IV relative to the Protection of Civilian Persons in Time of War, Geneva, 12 August 1949, 75 UNTS 287 (GCIV), Arts 53 and 147 and Rome Statute, n.47, Arts 8(2)(a)(iv) and 8(2)(e)(xii).

54 Dinstein, n.20, 303, noting that if effective protection under the law is to be achieved, a modicum of mutual trust is required.

55 Hague Regulations 1907, n.31, Art.23(b). Dinstein links the notion of treachery to the offer of a bounty or reward for the assassination of enemy personnel, distinguishing this from the targeting in wartime of specific individuals so long as treachery is not used; Dinstein, n.20, 304. Dinstein argues that treachery and perfidy are distinct but complementary notions, see ibid, 305.

56 Rome Statute, n.47, Art.8(2)(b)(xi).

> It is prohibited to kill, injure or capture an adversary by resort to perfidy. Acts inviting the confidence of an adversary to lead him to believe that he is entitled to, or is obliged to accord, protection under the rules of international law applicable in armed conflict, with intent to betray that confidence, shall constitute perfidy. The following acts are examples of perfidy:
>
> (a) the feigning of an intent to negotiate under a flag of truce or of a surrender;
> (b) the feigning of an incapacitation by wounds or sickness;
> (c) the feigning of civilian, non-combatant status; and
> (d) the feigning of protected status by the use of signs, emblems or uniforms of the United Nations or of neutral or other States not Parties to the conflict.[57]

The structure of this provision distinguishes between perfidy per se and the prohibited acts, namely killing, injuring or capture by means of perfidy. The way in which Article 37(1) is drafted clearly indicates that causing damage or destruction by resort to perfidy is not prohibited. However, section 7.13 below notes that the misuse of certain emblems, uniforms, and so on is prohibited under Articles 38 and 39 of API. **7.066**

The implications of this rule where the employment of BCI-enabled systems is concerned are straightforward. The BCI is merely a mechanism for translating the intent or wish of the operator directly into action triggered by the BCI system. It is the operator, and the associated planner and commander, who would form the intent or wish that is the subject of that translation process. It will therefore be the responsibility of the planner, commander and the operator to ensure that perfidy is not used to kill, injure or capture the enemy. Put another way, if planners, commanders and/or operators use BCI systems as part of an operation to deceive the enemy as to LOAC protected status and thereby kill, injure or capture the enemy, the fact that BCI was involved will not, per se, entitle them to be acquitted of the war crime. **7.067**

If an AB system is being used either by the attacking party or by the party that is being attacked, slightly more complex issues arise. If a planner, commander or operator were to set up an AB weapon system in order to perpetrate a perfidious act causing death, injury or capture of an adversary, this would breach the rule in API. But that is an easy case because the acting individual is using the AB system as their tool to perform the perfidious act. The more difficult scenario is where the AB system itself decides to deceive the adversary and then initiates the act of killing, injuring or capture. Can an AB system form the required intention to betray the confidence? The author believes the answer **7.068**

57 API, n.18, Art.37(1).

to that question will depend on the precise capabilities of the particular AB system.

7.069 An equally intriguing question arises if the AB system, instead of undertaking the act of deception, is instead being deceived.

7.070 *Scenario 5.* In this scenario, for example, an attacking party consisting of a platoon of infantry soldiers dressed in civilian clothing approaches an enemy encampment protected by AB-enabled weapon systems. The AB system has been programmed to detect civilian clothing and, having done so, not to fire the weapon. The attacking force, because it is dressed to look like protected civilians, is therefore able to gain access to the encampment where it kills and wounds some enemy soldiers. The first question that arises is whether the AB weapon system that was being used to secure the encampment can form a belief that it is required to accord LOAC protection to the attacking force that is masquerading as civilians. The second question is whether the AB system can develop confidence on the basis of which to form the relevant belief. In other words, are there emotive sensations associated with ideas of confidence and belief that are unique to the human mind and that AB systems are incapable of forming? One alternative approach would be to say that it was the personnel inside the encampment whose confidence and belief were being betrayed. A second alternative approach would simply say that no human being was being deceived, so the attack was lawful. It will be for states to take a view as to whether prohibited perfidy can only be perpetrated directly against persons. The author believes that the interpretation of these matters may be expected to change as AB technology evolves.

7.071 Perhaps the more likely situation is that a commander or operator is basing their decisions on the output of an AB system that has been deceived, say in the manner discussed in the previous paragraph. In that case, deception as to protection under LOAC is operating on the mind of that commander or operator and the consequent death, injury or capture would amount to unlawful perfidy.

7.12 DECEPTION OPERATIONS – RUSES

7.072 The term that is used to describe lawful ways of deceiving the enemy is ruses of war. Article 37(2) of API describes ruses as: 'acts which are intended to mislead an adversary or to induce him to act recklessly but which infringe no rule of international law applicable in armed conflict and which are not perfidious because they do not invite the confidence of an adversary with respect to protection under that law. The following are examples of such ruses: the use of camouflage, decoys, mock operations[58] and misinformation.'

If, therefore, operations that comply with Article 37(2) are undertaken using BCI technology, they will not be prohibited. Similarly, using AB systems to undertake a ruse will also be lawful. The relevant act must, however, comply with the LOAC and there must be no misrepresentation as to protection under the LOAC. It will be for planners, commanders and operators of both BCI- and AB-enabled operations to ensure that any deception activities fulfil the requirements of ruses. It will be for those responsible for programming AB systems to ensure that the system is not permitted to undertake acts that are perfidious or that breach the LOAC. **7.073**

7.13 DECEPTION OPERATIONS – EMBLEM MISUSE

Irrespective of the perfidy rule, misuse of certain emblems is prohibited. The rules prohibit the following acts: **7.074**

- making improper use of the distinctive emblems of the red cross, the red crescent and the red crystal, and misuse of 'other internationally recognized protective emblems, signs or signals', such as the cultural property emblem and the flag of truce;[59]
- using the UN emblem except as authorised by the UN;[60]
- using, in armed conflict, the flags, military emblems, insignia or uniforms of neutrals;[61] or
- using the flags, military emblems, insignia and uniforms of the enemy during an attack or to shield, favour or impede military operations.[62]

Planners, commanders and operators using BCI-enabled weapon systems will be responsible for ensuring that these provisions are not breached. This will involve ensuring that activity that would breach any of these provisions is not **7.075**

58 Consider Operation Mincemeat, 1943. The body of a deceased tramp was dressed in the uniform of a British Army captain. False correspondence between two army generals was placed on the body in which false plans were described to the effect that the Allies would invade Greece and Sardinia with only a minor feint being directed at Sicily: 'What was Operation Mincemeat', *Imperial War Museum*, available at https://www.iwm.org.uk/history/the-war-on-paper-operation-mincemeat.

59 API, n.18, Art.38(1).

60 API, n.18, Art.38(2).

61 API, n.18, Art.39(1).

62 API, n.18, Art.39(2).

the subject of thoughts or intentions that are communicated from the operator's brain to the relevant weapon system.

7.076 AB systems must also be prevented from breaching these rules. The application of markings and insignia to a physical object will usually be a human activity, and states will therefore be responsible for ensuring that all personnel involved in marking military objects, transports, facilities, and so on comply with these rules. If the AB system were to have the capability to apply markings, for example, to data, the programming of the AB system must ensure that prohibited markings or insignia are not applied. It is important to note that no particular purpose needs to be established for the rule to be breached.

7.14 OPERATIONS IN OUTER SPACE – THE APPLICABLE LAW

7.077 Sovereignty ceases where airspace ends and outer space begins, so there are no sovereign rights over outer space.[63] The division between airspace and outer space is imprecise and there is a lack of international agreement on the matter[64] but outer space can be regarded as being above the highest altitude at which an aircraft can derive lift from its interaction with the air and below the lowest possible perigee of an Earth satellite in orbit. This has the effect that anything in orbit or beyond is in outer space.[65]

7.078 Article III of the Outer Space Treaty states that 'activities in the exploration and use of outer space' must be 'in accordance with international law, including the Charter of the United Nations …'[66] API does not, however, make any specific reference to outer space, which causes one to wonder whether the targeting law provisions, Articles 48 to 67, would apply. However, the principle of distinction, the prohibition of indiscriminate attacks, the proportionality rule and the attacker's precautionary obligations are, as was noted in Chapter 4, generally accepted as customary, as are many of the rules giving effect to those

63 Treaty on principles governing the activities of States in the exploration and use of outer space, including the moon and other celestial bodies, 27 January 1967, 610 UNTS 205 (Outer Space Treaty), Art.II; Y Dinstein and A-W Dahl (eds), *Oslo Manual on Select Topics of the Law of Armed Conflict* (2020) (Oslo Manual), Rule 1(a)(ii).

64 J Beard and D Stephens (eds), *The Woomera Manual on the International Law of Military Space Operations* (Oxford University Press, 2024) (Woomera Manual), 26 and 27.

65 AMW Manual, n.1, Rule 1(a) and accompanying Commentary; Oslo Manual, n.63, Rule 1(a)(i) but see Woomera Manual, ibid, 28 and 29.

66 See Woomera Manual, n.64, 274, and note Oslo Manual, n.63, Rule 2, which adds that outer space operations are also governed by the applicable principles and rules of the LOAC. Paragraph 2 of the Commentary to Rule 2 suggests that 'the application or interpretation of LOAC in Outer Space may be subject to controversy'.

provisions. Interestingly, the Woomera Manual concludes that LOAC rules concerning attack, distinction, direct participation in hostilities, the notion of military objectives and protections associated with medical units and religious personnel all apply with regard to outer space military operations during armed conflict.[67] Rules regarding precautions in attack are also found, by the Woomera experts, to similarly apply, as is the constant care obligation and important rules dealing with means and methods of warfare.[68] Accordingly, hostilities using brain technologies that are conducted from, in or to outer space will also be regulated by the same principles and rules.

Article IV of the Outer Space Treaty forbids 'plac[ing] in orbit around the Earth any objects carrying nuclear weapons or any other kinds of weapons of mass destruction' and 'station[ing] such weapons in outer space in any other manner'.[69] The passage through outer space of an inter-continental ballistic missile carrying a weapon of mass destruction is not prohibited by Article IV[70] on the basis that the missile does not enter orbit.[71] Stationing conventional weapons in orbit is also not prohibited.[72] For Article IV purposes, weapons of mass destruction are, for practical purposes, biological and chemical weapons.[73] This means that the use of any method or system to place nuclear, chemical or biological weapons or weapons of comparable destructive effect in outer space is simply unlawful. Whether brain technologies have a role in the placement of such weapons is irrelevant. Article IV goes on to prohibit the establishment of military bases, installations and fortifications, the testing of any type of weapons and the conduct of military manoeuvres on the Moon and other celestial bodies. Conventional weapons and military space stations can **7.079**

67 Woomera Manual, n.64, Rules 31 to 35.

68 Woomera Manual, n.64, Rules 36 to 41, 46 and 42 to 45 respectively.

69 Outer Space Treaty, n.63, Art.IV(1) and Woomera Manual, n.64, Rule 5(a).

70 The term 'nuclear weapons' appears to include a laser weapon which uses a small nuclear explosion in outer space to generate the laser beam; M Bourbonnière and R J Lee, 'Legality of the Deployment of Conventional Weapons in Earth Orbit: Balancing Space Law and the Law of Armed Conflict' (2007) 18(5) EJIL 873, 881.

71 Woomera Manual, n.64, 72, para.2 but recall that the Chemical Weapons Convention, n.49 and the Convention on the Prohibition of the Development, Production and Stockpiling of Bacteriological (Biological) and Toxin Weapons and on their Destruction, 1972, 10 April 1972 (Biological Weapons Convention) prohibit a wide variety of activities associated with chemical and biological weapons, and that many of those prohibitions, including the ban on use, reflect customary law.

72 Bourbonnière and Lee, n.70, 888.

73 See the reference in the Woomera Manual to 'atomic explosive weapons, radio-active material weapons, lethal chemical and biological weapons, and any weapons developed in the future which have characteristics comparable in destructive effect to those of the atomic bomb or other weapons mentioned above': Woomera Manual, n.64, 73 citing a 1948 UN Security Council Commission for Conventional Armaments, 18 August 1948.

be placed in orbit and space-based exercises and weapons testing are permitted in outer space but not on celestial bodies.[74]

7.080 It follows from the points made in this section that planners, commanders and operators must ensure that their military outer space activities comply with international law in general and with the rules summarised in this section, irrespective of whether brain technologies are involved.

7.15 ANTI-SATELLITE ATTACK

7.081 The use of a satellite in orbit for military purposes will render it a military objective and thus a potential target for attack. This will remain the case even if it is also used for civilian purposes.[75] It is therefore foreseeable that during an armed conflict, parties to the conflict will wish to attack the satellites being used by the adversary for military purposes, irrespective of whether those satellites are also employed for civilian purposes.

7.082 The alternative methods of undertaking such attacks will have differing consequences. For example, a kinetic attack against a satellite, whether by colliding with it or by initiating an explosion in its vicinity, may be expected to create a cloud of debris with consequent potential dangers for other space vehicles.[76] An alternative method of attack might involve the use of a laser weapon to defeat the target satellite by burning a hole in it or by dazzling or destroying its sensors.[77] A third possibility would be to conduct a cyber operation to permanently or temporarily disable the satellite, or to adversely affect the specific transponder that is carrying the military traffic, or to enable the attacker to take control of the relevant satellite or transponder with a view to using it thereafter for their own purposes.[78] Other potential ways of defeating an

---

74 Outer Space Treaty, n.63, Art.IV, third sentence.

75 Woomera Manual, n.64, 321.

76 Consider the Chinese kinetic test on 11 January 2007 against its Fengyun-IC weather satellite using a SC-19 interceptor at an altitude of 860km. This test reportedly created 2,600 pieces of trackable debris and perhaps 150,000 smaller but hazardous fragments all in a swarm ranging from 200 to 2,300km in altitude; S Kan, CRS Report for Congress, *China's Anti-Satellite Weapon Test* (23 April 2007); 'US Satellites Dodge Chinese Missile Debris', *Washington Times,* 11 January 2008, A1. Note also, however, US destruction of a satellite at 247km approximate altitude – the hazardous fragments are assessed to have left orbit: Woomera Manual, n.64, 180 and 181. Consider also I Ali and S Gorman, 'Russian Anti-satellite Missile Test Endangers Space Station Crew – NASA', *Reuters,* 16 November 2021, available at https://www.reuters.com/world/us-military-reports-debris-generating-event-outer-space-2021-11-15/#:~:text=WASHINGTON%2C%20Nov%2015%20(Reuters),for%20years%2C%20U.S.%20officials%20sai.

77 Note, for example, Woomera Manual, n.64, 308.

78 Consider Woomera Manual, n.64, 303 to 306.

enemy satellite exist, including shadowing it or removing it from its intended orbit.

If a BCI-enabled weapon system were to be used to undertake anti-satellite operations, the planners, commanders and operators of the mission would be responsible for ensuring that the satellite to be targeted was a military objective and that the method of attack selected complied with applicable targeting law. **7.083**

Scenario 6. The use of an AB-enabled weapon system to undertake autonomous attack operations in outer space will raise some complex potential issues. Let us imagine that State A is involved in an armed conflict with State B. State A's Commander in Chief wishes to attack a satellite that is used by State B to collect intelligence imagery. He wishes to do this by means of a kinetic anti-satellite attack in which the attacking autonomous space vehicle uses AB technology to navigate to a position in the same orbit as the target satellite. The AB system then instructs State A's space vehicle to approach, and then collide with, State B's satellite causing it to break up and cease performing its intelligence-gathering role. Such an attack may be expected to cause a large cloud of potentially destructive space debris, the potentially damaging effects of which, for other space users, must be considered when applying the proportionality rule.[79] **7.084**

Scenario 7. To continue in the same scenario, State A's commander receives advice that the expected debris cloud's characteristics would cause the attack to breach the proportionality rule. He agrees to consider other possible methods for attacking the relevant satellite and opts in the end for a cyber operation in which the link that is used to transmit the relevant imagery is targeted, causing no space debris. **7.085**

If the AB system is designed to decide upon the target that is to be attacked and the method of attack that is to be chosen, that system will need to be able to apply the proportionality rule and to assess the factors discussed above in evaluating any kinetic option. In the author's view, if at all possible, non-kinetic methods of attack should generally be preferred. **7.086**

79 Woomera Manual, n.64, Rule 38. The Commentary to Rule 38 identifies the location of the target satellite, the anticipated spread of the debris field, how long the debris will remain in orbit, the quantity and size of the debris pieces and the feasibility of tracking them as matters to consider.

7.16 UNMANNED SURFACE AND SUB-SURFACE VESSELS

7.087 'Unmanned maritime systems (UMS) are: (i) self-propelled or remotely-navigated craft that are normally recoverable and designed to perform functions at sea by operating on the surface, semi-submerged or undersea; and (ii) either: a. are remotely operated, b. are remotely controlled, or c. perform their functions independently from a human controller or operator on board the craft.'[80]

7.088 Although this is not explicitly stated in the Oslo Manual Rule or in the associated Commentary, the inference is that the reference to being remotely operated is intended to refer to remote operation by a human operator. This would clearly include a situation in which a human operator is using a BCI system to convey their thought or intent to the control systems on the craft which are then programmed to act in accordance with the operator's thoughts, wishes and intent. The idea of performing functions independently of a human controller would include the use of both kinds of AB system (discussed in Chapters 2 and 3) to operate and control the craft. As is the case in relation to the other rules discussed in this book, the fact that one of the varieties of AB system may involve the use of biological brain material in its construction does not affect this interpretation. An AB system that includes biological brain material, whether synthetic or naturally generated, does not cause the system that is employing it to become a human being. The potential use of BBI technology will not have implications for this definition.

7.089 The Oslo Manual states that these kinds of craft 'may be employed for attacks and for the exercise of other belligerent rights if they: (a) are operated by the armed forces of a State; (b) bear the military markings of that State; and (c) are controlled or deployed by persons subject to regular armed forces discipline'.[81] The Manual observes that '[c]ontrol and deployment of UMS can include either direct control or the setting of mission conditions, objectives or parameters'.[82] So the Manual requires that persons subject to armed forces discipline either directly control the craft or set mission conditions, objectives or parameters. This seems to be a particularly loose interpretation of the notion of control. The BCI operator referred to earlier in this section is clearly controlling the craft because their thought, wish or intent is being translated by the BCI into corresponding action by the craft. Equally, if a BBI system is being used as the vehicle for command group discussion as to the action to be taken

---

80 Oslo Manual, n.64, Rule 46(a).

81 Oslo Manual, n.63, Rule 52.

82 Oslo Manual, n.63, para.2 of the Commentary accompanying Rule 52(c).

by the craft with the resulting decision being communicated to the craft's operating systems via a BCI, this will also represent actual operator control. If AB systems are being used, much will depend on how these are set up and, in particular, on the extent to which the AB is given discretion to make decisions that would lie outside the scope of any pre-set mission conditions, objectives or parameters.

In the Newport Manual, a warship is defined as a ship belonging to the armed forces of a state, bearing the external marks distinguishing such ships of its nationality, under the command of an officer duly commissioned by the government of the state and whose name appears in the appropriate service list or its equivalent and which is manned by a crew that is under regular armed forces discipline.[83] The Manual takes the position that '[w]arships include both manned and unmanned surface ships, submarines and other submersibles that have been designated as a warship by the flag State and are included in the respective State's list/registry of warships'.[84] **7.090**

The Manual states thereafter: 'There is no requirement that the commanding officer or crew be physically on board the warship. Warships may therefore be autonomous or remotely commanded, crewed, and operated by personnel ashore or on board a manned platform.'[85] The Manual later notes that the classic definition of warship is evolving in light of contemporary technologies.[86] It remains to be seen whether unmanned naval vessels, whether surface or sub-surface, will be controlled in future using BCI technology or will operate autonomously using AB technology. Were either possibility to materialise, both the Oslo Manual approach and that in the Newport Manual lead one to conclude that vessels employing either technology could properly be classified as warships. It will, however, be for states to indicate, probably through their practice, whether such an approach is indeed acceptable. The author suspects that it would be. If they are classified as warships, such vessels have belligerent rights. Whether so classified or not, such vessels may only be used in hostilities if they can conduct military operations in accordance with the law of naval warfare. **7.091**

---

83 The Manual cites numerous authorities in support of this formulation, including Convention (VII) relating to the Conversion of Merchant Ships into War-Ships, The Hague, 18 October 1907, Arts 1–4; Convention on the High Seas, 29 April 1958, 450 UNTS 11, Art.8; the United Nations Convention on the Law of the Sea (UNCLOS), 10 December 1982, 1833 UNTS 3, Art.29; UK Manual, para.13.5.n; and US DoD *Law of War Manual* (June 2015, as subsequently amended) (US DoD Manual), para.13.4.1.

84 Newport Manual, n.4, para.3.2.1, second paragraph.

85 Newport Manual, ibid, para.3.2.1.

86 Newport Manual, ibid, para.3.3.

7.17 CYBER OPERATIONS

7.092 Cyber operations were used in 2008 during the armed conflict between Russia and Georgia.[87] Cyber operations have also been a feature of the armed conflict between Russia and Ukraine.[88] The possibility that the brain technologies that are being discussed in this book might in the future be used in connection with cyber operations cannot be excluded. This brief section will therefore note the lack of conventional and customary law on cyber operations during warfare and will consider a few implications for the use of brain technologies in connection with those cyber operations.

7.093 There are no treaties that specifically address cyber hostilities during armed conflict. The conduct of cyber operations tends to be cloaked in secrecy and is frequently denied. As a result, the emergence of customary rules dealing specifically with cyber operations in warfare is likely to depend on the emergence of a consensus among states, most likely based on the written declarations of national legal understandings that individual states choose to issue. That is a process that is already under way and some states have published their national views;[89] customary law will only, however, crystallise if a sufficiently uniform and convincing body of state practice accompanied by *opinio juris* becomes evident. That has not yet occurred. Most states would probably agree that the principle of distinction will apply to cyber hostilities, but there is no uniform agreement among states as to the detailed rules that should be applied, nor as to the precise way in which such rules should be interpreted in the cyber context.

7.094 Computer-to-computer activity is likely to be a critically important component in the brain technologies being discussed in this book. Although, for the reasons given in the previous paragraph, there is no ad hoc customary law on that matter either, the Martens Clause, which is discussed in Chapter 6,

---

87 D J Smith, 'Russian Cyber Strategy and the War Against Georgia', *Atlantic Council*, 17 January 2014 available at https://www.atlanticcouncil.org/blogs/natosource/russian-cyber-policy-and-the-war-against-georgia/.

88 A Levite, 'Integrating Cyber into Warfighting: Some Early Takeaways from the Ukraine Conflict', *Carnegie*, 18 April 2023 available at https://carnegieendowment.org/research/2023/04/integrating-cyber-into-warfighting-some-early-takeaways-from-the-ukraine-conflict?lang=en.

89 Ministère des Armées, *Droit international appliqué aux les operations dans le cyberspace* (2019), available at https://www.defense.gouv.fr/sites/default/files/ema/Droit%20international%20appliqué%20aux%20opérations%20dans%20le%20cyberespace.pdf; *Australia's position on the application of international law to state conduct in cyberspace* (2017 with a 2019 supplement), available at https://www.dfat.gov.au/sites/default/files/application-of-international-law-to-cyberspace.pdf; UK Attorney-General's office, 'Cyber and International Law in the 21st Century', *Gov.UK*, 23 May 2018, available at https://www.gov.uk/government/speeches/cyber-and-international-law-in-the-21st-century.

section 6.3 makes it clear that, where circumstances arise in armed conflict for which no specific rules have been agreed by states, combatants and civilians benefit from, and are regulated by, the customary principles of law, including the principle of distinction. It can also be assumed that in addition to those customary principles, the customary rules of the LOAC will also apply and that is the approach taken in this book.[90] It will, moreover, be for each state to ensure that cyber operations are undertaken in accordance with the law as recognised by that state.

An International Group of Experts has produced the Tallinn Manual 2.0,[91] an international manual that demonstrates how the accepted principles and rules of law can be sensibly applied to cyber operations. In a different process under United Nations (UN) General Assembly auspices, a geographically balanced Group of Governmental Experts has been discussing what are termed Information and Communication Technologies (ICTs).[92] The groups have examined developments in the field of such technologies in the context of international security, and have produced reports in 2010,[93] 2013,[94] 2015[95] and 2021.[96] Some important progress has been made by the successive groups, for example agreement that the UN Charter applies to ICT activities.[97] However, detailed rules applicable to the conduct of cyber hostilities have not so far been agreed. **7.095**

90 Accordingly, in the discussion of the *jus in bello* in Chapters 4 to 6 and in the present chapter, rules that are considered to have customary law status are identified.

91 M N Schmitt (ed), *Tallinn Manual 2.0 on the International Law Applicable to Cyber Operations* (Cambridge University Press, 2017) (Tallinn Manual 2.0).

92 UN General Assembly Resolution 66/24 of 2012, para.4 and UN General Assembly Resolution 68/243 of 2014, para.4.

93 Group of Governmental Experts on Developments in the Field of Information and Telecommunications in the Context of International Security, A/65/201, 30 July 2010.

94 Group of Governmental Experts on Developments in the Field of Information and Telecommunications in the Context of International Security, A/68/98, 24 June 2013.

95 Group of Governmental Experts on Developments in the Field of Information and Telecommunications in the Context of International Security, A/70/174, 22 July 2015.

96 Group of Governmental Experts on Advancing Responsible State Behaviour in Cyberspace in the Context of International Security, A/76/135, 14 July 2021.

97 The Reports are expressed as a series of recommendations addressed to states and, in broad terms, set forth recommended norms, rules and principles for responsible state behaviour; recommendations on confidence-building measures and the exchange of information; recommendations on capacity-building measures, international co-operation and assistance in ICT security; and recommendations on how international law applies to the use of ICTs.

7.18 AUTONOMOUS ANTI-PERSONNEL ATTACK USING BIOMETRICS

7.096 When persons, as opposed to objects, are to be attacked, biometric technologies may have a role to play, particularly if specified individuals are the target. There are potential issues associated with the use of biometrics in targeting, but they lie outside the intended scope of this section. If BCI technology is employed in connection with an anti-personnel military operation, the operator's thought or intent will be the initiator, via the BCI, of the attack and therefore the same precautions should be taken to ensure the correctness of the biometric identification as would be done in the case of such an operation not involving the use of BCI. If an AB-enabled weapon system is tasked with using biometrics to recognise, and thereafter autonomously to target, a specific person,[98] additional issues specific to such a method of attack will be as follows.

1. Has the correct operation of the combined system, comprising AB, biometrics and sensors, been sufficiently tested in conditions that appropriately reflect the circumstances of the planned operation?
2. Has that testing shown that the AB, using the biometrics system together with the information derived, for example from the available sensors, will reliably and consistently identify the target individual in circumstances that include those which are anticipated?
3. Are there circumstances that would render the identification unreliable and will the operation reliably and consistently be called off, for example by the AB, if any such circumstance exists?
4. Will the AB system reliably and consistently apply the proportionality rule in Article 51(5)(b) of API by satisfying all of the requirements identified in Chapter 4, section 4.7?
5. Will the AB system reliably and consistently choose the attack method that minimises collateral damage while also complying with the proportionality rule?
6. Will a human operator be able to observe what is taking place and intervene to stop the attack if it becomes clear that, for a reason not necessarily detected by the AB system, the attack should not proceed?
7. Is there a way of verifying post-attack that the intended person was in fact attacked?

7.097 If BBI is to be used, for example, to facilitate communication between commanders, operators and other relevant staff during such an attack, it will be

---

98 Autonomous anti-personnel targeting using biometric techniques seems likely to become a significant method of warfare. Consider M Zwanenburg, 'Know Thy Enemy: The Use of Biometrics in Military Operations and International Humanitarian Law' (2021) 97 Int'l L Stud 1404, 1410–13.

operationally and legally important to seek to ensure that the system is operating correctly and that it has not been compromised.

7.19 ESPIONAGE AND INFORMATION GATHERING

7.19.1 Distinguishing espionage and information gathering

So far as relevant to the topic of this book, spies are defined by Article 29 of the Hague Regulations 1907 as follows: **7.098**

> A person can only be considered a spy when, acting clandestinely or on false pretences,[99] he obtains or endeavours to obtain information in the zone of operations of a belligerent,[100] with the intention of communicating it to the hostile party. Thus, soldiers not wearing a disguise who have penetrated into the zone of operations of the hostile army, for the purpose of obtaining information, are not considered spies.

This wording makes it clear that, for the purposes of the LOAC, espionage involves: an act committed in the zone of operations of a belligerent party;[101] the spy obtaining or trying to obtain information (or dispatches) for the enemy; and the act being carried out clandestinely or under false pretences.[102] The ordinary meaning[103] of 'clandestine' is 'kept secret or done secretively'[104] and of 'pretend' is 'make it appear that something is the case when in fact it is not'.[105] Use of a disguise, of a forged pass or of a uniform to which the spy is not entitled would indicate that false pretences are being used. **7.099**

The term 'zone of operations' includes occupied territory[106] and land, sea or airspace controlled by a party to the conflict. For an act to be espionage, the **7.100**

---

99 See K Ipsen, 'Combatants and Non-combatants', in D Fleck (ed), *The Handbook of International Humanitarian Law* (Oxford University Press, 2008), para.322; see International Committee of the Red Cross, *Commentary on the Additional Protocols of 8 June 1977* (Y Sandoz, C Swinarski and B Zimmermann (eds), 1987) (API Commentary), paras 1774–5, 1778 and note Lieber Code, Art.88 and Project of an International Declaration concerning the Laws and Customs of War, Brussels, 27 August 1874 (Brussels Declaration), Art.19.

100 US Navy, US Marine Corps, US Coast Guard, *The Commander's Handbook on the Law of Naval Operations* (March 2022) (NWP1-14M), para.12-8 requires the spy to be in territory under enemy control or the zone of operations of a belligerent force.

101 As Yoram Dinstein notes, the collector of the information, to be a spy, must be physically located in an area controlled by the enemy: Dinstein, n.20, 318.

102 Dinstein, ibid, 318.

103 Vienna Convention on the Law of Treaties, 23 May 1969, 1155 UNTS 331, Art.31(1).

104 *Compact Oxford English Dictionary*, 3rd edn (Oxford University Press, 2005), 175.

105 *Compact Oxford English Dictionary*, ibid, 806.

106 Territory is considered occupied when it is actually placed under the authority of the hostile army and extends only to places where such authority has been established and can be exercised: Hague Regulations 1907, n.31, Art.42.

spy must be physically present on land, sea or in airspace controlled by the adverse party.[107] Virtual presence is not sufficient. Espionage does not breach the LOAC[108] and spying is not a war crime. Acts undertaken by the spy to gain access to the desired information may, however, breach that law and be war crimes. While not breaching international law, espionage will almost certainly breach the domestic law of the state against which it is undertaken.[109]

7.101 *Scenario 8.* Imagine a situation in which State A uses BCI technology to control the movement of a miniature flying drone. Members of State A's armed forces remotely control the movements and activities of the drone from a facility located within State A's military headquarters. The miniature drone is flown into enemy-controlled airspace and uses televisual sensors and a miniature transmitter to film and send footage back to State A's military intelligence department showing enemy State B's preparations for an amphibious assault. Because the drone is launched from State A's territory and because the controllers of the drone remain throughout outside territory controlled by State B, the act of information gathering does not amount to espionage under the LOAC.

7.102 *Scenario 9.* Changing the facts slightly, imagine that the limited permitted range between the operator and the drone means that the operators need to enter State B territory. They conceal themselves in an apartment occupied by a sympathiser, but State B security personnel enter the flat while the drone operation is underway and arrest the drone operators. The physical presence of the operators within territory controlled by State B and the operators' concealment of themselves within the apartment means that their act of obtaining or endeavouring to obtain information with the appropriate intention amounts to espionage under the LOAC.

7.103 *Scenario 10.* Adjusting the facts a little further, imagine that the operators of the drone enter a rural part of State B territory wearing State A military uniform and use a disused barn from which to control the drone. Imagine also that the miniature drone, measuring 10cm from nose to tail, has State A's military markings painted on both sides of the fuselage. Arguably, the act of information gathering has not been undertaken clandestinely or by using false pretences, so the information gathering would not amount to LOAC espionage.

107 Tallinn Manual 2.0, n.91, Commentary accompanying Rule 89, para.8.
108 Tallinn Manual 2.0, n.91, Commentary accompanying Rule 89, para.5.
109 See Hague Regulations 1907, n.31, Art.24; API Commentary, n.99, para.1765 and UK Manual, n.83, para.4.9.3.

Scenario 11. Developing the scenario even further, imagine that AB technology is being employed whereby State A's aerial surveillance drone undertakes its information-gathering mission within State B airspace autonomously. Imagine that the endurance of the drone is such that it can be flown from and can return at the end of its mission to State A territory. No State A personnel enter State B territory with the consequence that the act does not constitute LOAC espionage. **7.104**

Espionage and information gathering may of course be perpetrated against the state using brain technologies. The use of cyber hacking tools would seem to be one, possibly likely, way of achieving this. **7.105**

Scenario 12. Imagine that State B decides to obtain information about the brain technology capabilities of State A and erode those capabilities. State B hackers operating from State B military headquarters use malware to gain access to the computers involved in the BCI control of State A's short-range missile system. Having achieved that access, State B is able to obtain information relating to the thought and intent stimuli that are required in order to fire the missiles. Because those cyber activities do not require the physical presence of the hackers in State A-controlled territory, that act also is not LOAC espionage. **7.106**

7.19.2 Information gathering

Article 24 of the Hague Regulations 1907 states: 'Ruses of war and the employment of measures necessary for obtaining information about the enemy and the country are considered permissible.'[110] So both information gathering and activities that fall within the narrow definition of espionage are permitted under the LOAC. Information gathering which does not require an individual's physical presence in enemy-controlled territory seems likely to be the option that states are more likely to choose in modern armed conflicts. If, however, information needs to be obtained from the enemy's closed systems that are not directly or indirectly linked to the internet, a close-access operation is likely to be needed and LOAC espionage involving clandestine or false pretence activity may well be the preferred approach. Much will depend on how the brain technologies evolve, but the computer and connectivity elements in BCIs, the computer and connectivity facilities that support AB systems and the numerous operator-computer linkages that are likely to be required for BBI systems to work will also render such systems vulnerable to external **7.107**

110 Hague Regulations 1907, n.31, Art.24.

interference. It is that interference that may take the form of virtual intrusion in order to identify vulnerabilities and assess optimal methods of attack.

7.108 In the brain technologies context, therefore, commanders will likely wish to have as much information as possible, including information on such matters as: which military BCI, AB and BBI systems an adversary has; which weapon systems employ BCIs; the precise nature of the computer connectivity in such systems; which functions the enemy will perform using BBI systems; the military capability requirements that are fulfilled by the enemy using AB systems; whether any of these systems are not closed-loop systems; and how access to each of them can most conveniently be achieved.

7.109 Parties to the conflict will also require information on many and varied matters, not least because attacks are also likely to be directed at various kinds of lawful targets. Commanders will be keen to receive information as to: where enemy commanders will be on specific dates/times; weapon production and delivery schedules; staffing and security arrangements; weapon research programmes and their levels of maturity; the financing of military equipment procurement; the locations of military bases and forward positions; the quality of enemy defences; opposing army strengths; the location of civilians; the identities and military activities of specified individuals; whether particular civilians are directly participating in the hostilities; whether civilians have remained in a village or fled; and the future intentions of the opposing commander. Commanders will also want to know about: where target individuals or groups are; the uses to which specific buildings or structures are put; the functions of buildings near to military objectives and the classes and numbers of persons who are in them; the materials and substances that are likely to be present in those buildings or places; the presence or absence of human shields; and whether any such human shields are there voluntarily or under duress. These are merely illustrative of the numerous types of data that a commander is likely to require.

7.19.3 Information gathering and espionage from the brain[111]

7.110 Rather than rely on what enemy personnel, captured or otherwise, may choose to say, rather than focus on the comments of captured soldiers about their commanders' priorities, a more reliable source of such intelligence would be likely to come from direct monitoring of the thoughts of the relevant personnel. The

111 This section draws on a chapter that the author has contributed to K Watkin (ed), *Intelligence Relating to Armed Conflict* (forthcoming).

question that now needs to be considered is what legal rules apply to information gathering if the technologies discussed in this book are employed. Each technology will be considered in turn, with more detail inevitably being devoted to the relatively more mature BCI technology.

7.19.4 Information gathering and espionage using BCIs

There are obvious applications for BCI technology in the obtaining of intelligence about an adversary. There are suggestions that the technology may have utility in lie and deception detection and perhaps in revealing subconscious brain information.[112] While Ienca and others suggest that the current state of the technology does not permit mind-steering or mind-reading,[113] it is certainly foreseeable that the development of such technologies to deal with particular medical problems may lead to such a capability in the medium to long term. **7.111**

The exact ways in which the technology will be used in the intelligence-gathering context are, at the time of writing, uncertain. However, it is thought that by considering the following four illustrative scenarios, the ways in which existing law may be expected to apply can be considered, and it is hoped that this approach to the subject of BCI-assisted information gathering will be helpful. **7.112**

Scenario 13. In the first scenario in the present subsection, State A is using BCI technology to control its weapon system. Enemy State B might choose to use a cyber capability to hack into the computer element of State A's BCI system in order to obtain information as to which units or operators are using the BCI system, as to which weapons the BCI is linked with, as to planned uses of the weapon, as to how the computer interacts respectively with the operator's brain and with the weapon, as to computer vulnerabilities and as to alternative courses of action either to degrade the performance of the system or to destroy it and, perhaps, its associated weapons. If such activity involved State B sending its hacker inside territory controlled by State A, for example because the BCI technology employs a closed loop system which can only be accessed from a State A computer terminal, and if the operator gathering the information operates secretively or, for example, feigns civilian, neutral or enemy status, the operation is likely to be classed as espionage under the LOAC. **7.113**

---

112 P R Roelfsema and others, 'Mind Reading and Writing: The Future of Neurotechnology' (2018) 22(7) Trends Cogn Sci 598–610.

113 M Ienca and others, 'Towards a Governance Framework for Brain Data' (2022) 15 *Neuroethics* 2.

7.114 *Scenario 14.* In the second scenario in this sub-section, State A might decide to use its BCI system to obtain information from the brain of one of State B's commanders. The reader is invited to suspend disbelief. What follows is a hypothetical the realism or otherwise of which does not really matter. It is the legal point that is being made that is more important. Let us imagine that an agent of State A who is a member of the catering staff at the residence of the State B Air Commander manages to introduce a minute electrode into the Air Commander's muesli. The electrode is designed to find its way into the Air Commander's bloodstream and thereby reach the outer surface of the cerebral cortex, within the cranium. The electrical activity that the electrode detects is translated by State A's computer system into intelligible information as to future military air operations. The act of the member of staff at the residence might be classed as espionage on the basis that it is a proximate act leading to the passage of the information to the enemy. If all of the State A personnel who were involved in the information gathering remained throughout outside State B controlled territory, their acts cannot be classed as espionage for LOAC purposes. However, their acts may well be classed as espionage under State B domestic law. If the relevant State A personnel were combatants, they would enjoy combatant immunity for their acts linked to the information gathering, it being borne in mind that information gathering and espionage do not breach the LOAC.

7.115 The focus will now shift to a rather different technique for obtaining information about the enemy.

7.116 *Scenario 15.* In the third scenario in this subsection, State A uses a BCI system to obtain information from combatants from enemy State B who have been captured during hostilities. The technique that is employed involves the wearing by the prisoner of an external headset. The prisoner is then asked a series of questions and their answers, together with the electrical brain activity as detected using the headset, are used to infer information which then informs targeting decisions.[114]

---

114 Note, for example, the iCognative device, the online advertising for which explains: 'Simply place the headset on the suspect's head and input a range of stimuli including pictures, words and phrases. As the suspect's brain involuntarily responds to these stimuli, the headset collects the brainwave responses, providing you with invaluable insight into their mind.' Applications suggested in the advertising material are uncovering: crime-related information in a suspect's brain; conceptual or experiential knowledge as to a crime; and hidden intentions: see https://www.brainwavescience.com/icognative-page/. There are, however, critics who call into question the reliability of this P300 brain fingerprinting technology; for a discussion of the pros and cons see D Cox, 'Can Your Brain Reveal You Are a Liar?', *BBC In Depth*, 25 January 2016, available at https://www.bbc.co.uk/future/article/20160125-is-it-wise-that-the-police-have-started-scanning-brains.

Under the LOAC, such activity will raise numerous issues. GCIII will apply to the prisoners[115] who will have prisoner of war (PW) rights which they cannot renounce under the Convention.[116] State A, as the capturing power, is responsible for the proper treatment of the prisoners. Article 13 of the Convention prohibits subjecting[117] PWs to 'physical mutilation or to medical or scientific experiments of any kind which are not justified by the medical, dental or hospital treatment of the prisoner concerned and carried out in his interest'.[118] It is a matter of interpretation whether the fitting of a headset in connection with the interrogation of a PW constitutes 'medical or scientific experiments'. The author suggests that, given the current limited understanding of brain activity and the equally limited understanding of the link between observed brain activity and specific thoughts, there is bound to be a degree of experimentation associated with the kind of procedure contemplated in this scenario. Most states are likely, in the author's view, to regard such activity as prohibited by Article 13(1), particularly as it would not be employed for therapeutic purposes.[119] It will also be for states to consider whether activity of the kind discussed in this scenario is consistent with the obligation to respect the persons and honour of PWs.[120] **7.117**

Of arguably greatest relevance are the duties under Article 17 of the Convention with regard to the questioning of PWs. The use of BCIs in connection with interrogation does not necessarily raise issues under Article 17(1), although one can imagine interrogators becoming tempted to use the BCI to facilitate the extraction from a PW of information other than their full name, rank, service number and date of birth.[121] Under GCIII: '[n]o physical or mental torture, nor any other form of coercion may be inflicted on prisoners of war to secure from them information of any kind whatever. Prisoners of war who refuse to answer may not be threatened, insulted, or exposed to any unpleasant or disadvantageous treatment of any kind.'[122] This makes it clear that unpleasant or disadvantageous treatment must not be applied, even for the purpose of securing the information a PW is obliged to give under Article 17(1) and (2). **7.118**

---

115 Geneva Convention III relative to the Treatment of Prisoners of War, Geneva, 12 August 1949, 75 UNTS 135 (GCIII), Art.4. Note also API, n.18, Arts 44 and 45.

116 GCIII, ibid, Art.7.

117 GCIII, ibid, Art.12(1).

118 GCIII, ibid, Art.13(1).

119 J S Pictet (Ed), *Commentary on Geneva Convention III relative to the Treatment of Prisoners of War*, ICRC, 1960 (Pictet Commentary to GCIII), 141.

120 GCIII, n.115, Art.14(1).

121 GCIII, ibid, Art.17(1).

122 GCIII, ibid, Art.17(4).

7.119 The key issue for the purposes of the present discussion is whether the use of a BCI in this scenario constitutes coercion or unpleasant or disadvantageous treatment. If, as seems entirely possible, the combination of the question posed and the electrical signals that are detected represents the involuntary provision by the PW of information, some would argue that such activity constitutes the employment of coercion. However, the dictionary definition of to coerce is: 'persuade an unwilling person to do something by using force or threats'.[123] It will be for states to interpret the application of their treaty obligations in these novel contexts and, in particular, to decide whether the described action of applying the headset constitutes the use of force or threats. It will also be for states to determine whether the application of the headset in association with the interrogation amounts to 'unpleasant or disadvantageous treatment'. While less pleasant and less advantageous treatment can certainly be imagined, that is not, the author suggests, determinative of this issue. If science demonstrates that the employment of these headsets has adverse potential medical consequences for the wearer, this may also determine whether the last two issues apply.

7.120 Under API, certain acts are prohibited, including 'outrages upon personal dignity, in particular humiliating, and degrading treatment ...'.[124] Inevitably, much will depend on exactly what is done to the prisoner, the circumstances in which the headset is applied and so on. The possibility that such a method of interrogation would be regarded as an outrage on personal dignity and as humiliating and degrading treatment can by no means be excluded.

7.121 Where the application of human rights law to activities of the kind discussed in *Scenario 15* is concerned, the rights under the ICCPR that seem to be of greatest relevance are Articles 7, 10(1), 17, 18 and 19. While derogation from certain ICCPR Articles is permitted '[i]n [a] time of [declared] public emergency which threatens the life of the nation', out of the listed Articles derogation from Articles 7 and 18 is not permitted.[125]

7.122 What this all means can only sensibly be considered in relation to individual rights. Article 7 states that nobody 'shall be subjected to torture or to cruel, inhuman or degrading treatment' and shall not be 'subjected without his free consent to medical or scientific experimentation'. The question here

---

123 *Compact Oxford English Dictionary*, n.104, 186. The origin is stated to be Latin, *coercere, to restrain.* It is sensible to conclude that the notion of coercion will also extend to persuading the unwilling person to refrain from performing some act.

124 API, n.18, Art.75(2)(b).

125 ICCPR, n.35, Art.4.

will be whether the way in which the BCI-assisted interrogation is conducted is degrading and whether it constitutes experimentation. The condition of capture and consequent detention will likely preclude the giving of free consent. The author believes that the conduct of such an interrogation method is likely to be regarded as degrading, because of the insight into the private thoughts of the detainee that the BCI is likely to give, but again much will depend on the specific facts.

Article 10(1) requires that '[a]ll persons deprived of their liberty shall be treated with humanity and with respect for the inherent dignity of the human person'. In circumstances in which free consent cannot be given, to connect a prisoner of war to a BCI system, even using an external headset, and then to monitor their innermost thoughts during interrogation is unlikely, the author believes, to be considered consistent with respect for the inherent dignity of the detained individual. It seems likely that a court would consider such action to be inconsistent with Article 10(1). **7.123**

Article 17 stipulates that '[n]o one shall be subjected to arbitrary or unlawful interference with his privacy …'.[126] It is hard to imagine anything that is more private to an individual than that person's thoughts.[127] The issues under this right are therefore likely to be whether there is a legal provision that permits the interference, whether that legal provision is fully complied with, and whether the interference is arbitrary. Action that complies with a legal provision that inadequately reflects the right might breach the right as being arbitrary. Arbitrariness suggests interference that is greater than that necessary to achieve a lawful purpose. It will be for a court to determine whether a BCI interrogation involving a headset would breach the right. The author rather suspects that it would. **7.124**

Article 18, from which no derogation can be made, grants, so far as strictly relevant, freedom of thought.[128] There is an obvious link between this freedom and Nita Farahany's persuasive and carefully argued plea for a 'right to **7.125**

126 ICCPR, ibid, Art.17(1).

127 In relation to the Convention for the Protection of Human Rights and Fundamental Freedoms, 4 November 1950, 213 UNTS 221 (European Convention on Human Rights (ECHR)), Art.8 protection of the right to respect for private and family life, home and correspondence, consider the views of the European Court of Human Rights as to the broad scope of the right, as reflected, for example, in *Antović and Mirković v Montenegro*, Application No.70838/13, ECtHR 365/2017, 28 November 2017; *Bărbulescu v Romania*, Application No.61496/08, ECtHR 268/2017, 5 September 2017; and *Z. v Finland*, Case No.22009/93, judgment dated 25 February 1997.

128 Note UN General Assembly, *Interim Report of the Special Rapporteur on freedom of religion or belief, Ahmed Shaheed, Freedom of thought*, A/76/380, 5 October 2021, available at https://docs.un.org/en/A/76/380.

cognitive liberty'.[129] Were a human rights challenge to be made on the basis of Article 18(1) against what might be termed BCI-enhanced interrogation, a respondent state might argue that the freedom of the individual to have thoughts is not being impaired. Rather, what is happening is the monitoring of those thoughts rather than interference with them. The author is not, however, confident that such an argument would necessarily prevail. The author is supported in that view by the relatively brief observation in ICCPR General Comment 22 that 'no-one can be compelled to reveal his thoughts'.[130] It will be a matter for interpretation whether the use of the relevant technology, the associated questioning and the prevailing circumstances, taken together, amounted to compulsion.

7.126 Article 19 of ICCPR provides that '[e]veryone shall have the right to hold opinions without interference'[131] and that '[e]veryone shall have the right to freedom of expression ...'.[132] It will be a question of fact whether BCI-enhanced interrogation, as practiced in the particular scenario, constitutes interference with the holding by the individual of a specific opinion. The author suggests this is unlikely to be the case. More likely is a challenge based on Article 19(2). Freedom of expression, it might be argued, necessarily implies the freedom not to express particular thoughts or opinions. To the extent that a BCI interrogation is undertaken in a manner that erodes or removes the ability of the individual to refrain from expressing a thought or opinion, it would seem that the individual's freedom of expression is being adversely interfered with.

7.127 *Scenario 16*. The final BCI scenario is similar to the third. State A again uses a BCI system to obtain information from combatants from enemy State B who have been captured during hostilities. In this scenario, the technique that is employed involves the surgical insertion of electrodes inside the cranium. The prisoner is then asked a series of questions and his answers, together with his electrical brain activity as detected using the electrodes, are used to infer information which is then used in order to inform targeting decisions. The LOAC will apply to such an activity and the provisions that were discussed in connection with the non-intrusive use of BCI will also apply to this scenario, but in subtly different ways. The author considers that the surgical process involved in the insertion of the electrodes coupled with the practical inability

---

129 N A Farahany, *The Battle for your Brain* (St Martin's Press, 2024), Chs 7 and 10, and 213 and 223–5.

130 ICCPR General Comment 22: Article 18 (Freedom of Thought, Conscience or Religion), CCPR/C/21/Rev.1/Add.4, para.3.

131 ICCPR, n.35, Art.19(1).

132 ICCPR, n.35, Art.18(2).

of the PW to give effective consent to the procedure means that all of the legal objections identified under *Scenario 15* will apply with even greater force under *Scenario 16*.

The reference in Article 13 of GCIII to 'physical mutilation or to medical or scientific experiments of any kind which are not justified by the medical, dental or hospital treatment of the prisoner concerned and carried out in his interest' will also apply. The insertion of the electrodes into the brain would at the least constitute mutilation and the activity is being carried out in the interest of the detaining power, not that of the PW. Moreover, the points made in this part of the *Scenario 15* discussion would apply equally in *Scenario 16*; and states are unlikely to consider the insertion of electrodes for these purposes as consistent with the obligation to respect the persons and honour of PWs.[133] 7.128

All of the points made in the *Scenario 15* discussion of Article 17 of GCIII apply also to the discussion of *Scenario 16*. However, the insertion of electrodes into the brain of the detainee without the detainee's consent, or in circumstances in which the detainee will be regarded as unable to give free consent, is almost certain to be regarded as the use of coercion to secure from them information, contrary to Article 17(4). One can imagine the circumstance in which a PW has previously been interrogated and has declined to give information, whether generally or in response to particular questioning. The threat to insert electrodes into that prisoner's brain for BCI interrogation purposes, when considered in association with the fear experienced by the prisoner, would certainly amount to 'unpleasant or disadvantageous treatment' for the purposes of Article 17(4). Actually carrying out the medical procedure to insert the electrodes and then undertaking the subsequent interrogation would simply be an even more serious breach of the rule. 7.129

The API prohibitions of mutilation and of 'outrages upon personal dignity, in particular humiliating, and degrading treatment …' will apply to *Scenario 16* activity.[134] It will, be regarded as an outrage on the personal dignity of the PW to insert electrodes into their brain and then use that technology to access that individual's private thoughts. 7.130

As was explained during the discussion of *Scenario 15*, human rights law may be expected to apply extra-territorially in favour of PWs because they will be regarded as within the jurisdiction of the state in whose control they find 7.131

---

133 GCIII, n.115, Art.14(1).

134 API, n.18, Art.75(2)(a)(iv) and (b).

themselves. The provisions of the ICCPR will therefore apply in favour of the prisoner referred to in *Scenario 16*. Both the insertion without effective consent of the electrodes into the brain and the subsequent interrogation are likely to be regarded as constituting inhuman or degrading treatment, and the two processes, taken together, are liable to be characterised as medical experimentation without consent. The point made under *Scenario 13* about insight into private thoughts will also apply here.

7.132 The *Scenario 16* procedure is highly unlikely to be regarded as consistent with the Article 10(1) requirement of treatment 'with humanity and with respect for the inherent dignity of the human person' and the ensuing interrogation will almost certainly be viewed by a court as subjecting the PW to 'arbitrary or unlawful interference with his privacy', and thus as breaching Article 17(1).[135] It will be recalled that arbitrariness involves interference that is greater than that necessary to achieve a lawful purpose, and while the application of non-intrusive electrodes may well be seen as going too far, the intrusive character of the electrodes in *Scenario 16* is likely to render such a process even less acceptable for the purposes of this provision.

7.133 If the right under Article 19(2) to freedom of expression is indeed understood as implying a freedom not to express particular thoughts or opinions, the application of intrusive electrodes to monitor the PW's thoughts during interrogation is likely to be seen as limiting or excluding the individual's right to refrain from stating an opinion or thought, and thus seen as limiting the PW's freedom of expression.

7.134 The discussion of the law applicable to *Scenarios 15* and *16* does not purport to consider all of the potentially relevant LOAC and human rights law provisions. Indeed, the human rights law discussion has been limited to the ICCPR and has deliberately omitted discussion of the European Convention on Human Rights and other regional human rights law documents. It is, however, felt that by focusing on GCIII, API and the ICCPR, the key legal considerations that must be borne in mind if BCI technologies are to be used in this way for intelligence-gathering purposes become clearer.

7.19.5 Information gathering and espionage using BBIs

7.135 The important feature of BBI systems where intelligence gathering is concerned will, the author suspects, be the computer system that links the respective

---

135 ICCPR, n.35, Art.17(1).

brains. While that computer process will be of critical importance to the correct performance of the BBI it will also be a key vulnerability of such a system. Adverse parties to the conflict and, perhaps, troublesome third parties may seek to gain access to the relevant computer links either simply to observe what is going on or to access the thoughts, intentions, plans and activities that are being undertaken or agreed there. Where the target BBI computer system is a closed system, a close access cyber operation is likely to be necessary in order to achieve the required access. The consequence of this is that a LOAC espionage mission is likely to be necessary. Similarly, adversaries and malicious third parties may seek to undertake cyber sabotage operations, for example to corrupt the processes and/or to insert false thoughts, intentions or plans with a view to misleading the opposing party or parties.

The party to the conflict that is relying on BBI systems will wish to ensure the robust security of the system. The degree of confidence that a state can have in the security and correct performance of its military BBI systems will depend on the characteristics of the particular BBI, on the care with which patches and other security measures are applied and taken, on the technical expertise of the adversary state and, no doubt, on other factors. It should be recalled that misinformation is specifically listed in Article 37(2) of API as a lawful ruse of war. Provided that the misinformation that is employed does not relate to protected status under the LOAC and does not otherwise breach that body of law, the act of misinformation will be a ruse and thus will not be unlawful. **7.136**

7.19.6 Information gathering and espionage using AB technology

While AB technologies would seem, at present, to be in the very early, theoretical stages of research, it is foreseeable that such systems might be developed to undertake the kinds of activity that are the current focus of AI initiatives. Imagine, for example, an AB system that has been developed by State A to be used to obtain information as to State B's invasion plans. Imagine that it does this by employing a cyber tool, controlled by the AB, to autonomously intrude into State B's military planning and military communications systems and acquire copies of all communications between State B's J2 staffs and its operational commander. This would, the author suggests, be classed as information gathering as opposed to LOAC espionage if, as seems likely, human planners, commanders and operators from State A who are involved in the conduct of the intelligence-gathering operation remain throughout outside the territory, as well as airspace, of State B. The sophistication of the AB system, even if it includes natural or synthetically developed brain material, will not cause the AB to be categorised as a human, so the presence of the AB system in the zone **7.137** of operations of the adverse party will not satisfy that aspect of the LOAC espionage definition.

7.138 It must, however, be stressed that these early technologies may include unforeseen features as particular applications develop, and it will be for legal advisers to consider carefully the features and implications of the specific system on which they are asked to advise. There is, so far as the author is aware, no legal rule that would prohibit the use of AB technology in the information-gathering or espionage roles.

7.20 BRIEF CONCLUDING REMARKS

7.139 While the precise ways in which the technologies discussed in this book will be used in future conflicts cannot be stated with any degree of certainty, it is necessary at this relatively early stage in their development to consider what the legal rules are, and how they can sensibly be interpreted in the context of emerging brain technologies. Discussion of these matters is also, of course, appropriate because states are required by Article 36 of API to consider how existing legal principles and rules by which they are bound apply to new methods of warfare. The author hopes that the observations in this chapter will be useful, perhaps as a basis on which states and others can develop an understanding of the law that should be applied to these novel and vitally important capabilities of the future.

8

BRAIN TECHNOLOGIES AND THE LAW OF NEUTRALITY

8.1 SCOPE OF NEUTRALITY LAW

The law of neutrality applies during an international armed conflict. However, 'the law of neutrality becomes inapplicable if the UN Security Council has either (i) identified one or more Belligerent Parties as responsible for an unlawful resort to armed force in breach of Article 2(4) of the UN Charter or (ii) if the UN Security Council has taken preventive or enforcement measures under Chapter VII of the UN Charter against that belligerent party or parties.'[1] In either of these cases, a state that is not a party to the conflict cannot argue that the law of neutrality permits it to undertake an act that is incompatible with its obligations under the United Nations (UN) Charter.[2] This means that if the UN Security Council determines under Article 39 of the UN Charter that there has been a threat to the peace, a breach of the peace or an act of aggression and then takes preventive or enforcement measures, a UN Security **8.001**

1 Program on Humanitarian Policy and Conflict Research at Harvard University (HPCR), *Manual on the International Law Applicable to Air and Missile Warfare* (March 2010) (AMW Manual), available at https://cdn.ca9.uscourts.gov/datastore/library/2013/09/06/Flores_Manual.pdf, Commentary accompanying Rule 1(aa), para.3.

2 AMW Manual, n.1, Commentary accompanying Rule 1(aa), para.3 and Rule 165 and consider US DoD *Law of War Manual* (June 2015, as subsequently amended) (US DoD Manual), para.15.2.3.

Council decision under Chapter VII binds Member States and takes priority over conflicting treaty provisions.[3] Accordingly, states that do not participate in the enforcement or preventive action must not hamper or impede action being taken in accordance with a binding UN Security Council decision and cannot rely on neutral impartiality.[4]

8.002 Some states support the doctrine of qualified neutrality under which a state that is not involved in an international armed conflict can take non-neutral action in support of a state that is the victim of an unlawful war of aggression.[5] The war between Russia and Ukraine has caused more attention to be focused on this aspect of neutrality law,[6] but many states consider themselves obliged to apply neutrality law fully when not involved in an international armed conflict.[7]

8.003 The rules discussed in this chapter do not apply to non-international armed conflicts.[8] In its Nuclear Weapons Advisory Opinion, the International Court of Justice stated that 'as in the case of the principles of humanitarian law applicable in armed conflict, international law leaves no doubt that the principle of neutrality, whatever its content, which is of a fundamental character similar to that of the humanitarian principles and rules, is applicable (subject to the relevant provisions of the United Nations Charter) to all international armed conflict, whatever type of weapons might be used.'[9] This observation makes it clear that neutrality law will apply to activities associated with brain-computer interface (BCI), artificial brain (AB) and brain-to-brain interface (BBI)

3 UN Charter, 26 June 1945, Article 103. Subject to Article 103, note that regional and collective self-defence agreements may affect the right of a state to maintain neutral status because the relevant state may be required to provide assistance or to take military action in collective self-defence: US DoD Manual, para.15.2.4.

4 AMW Manual, n.1, Commentary accompanying Rule 165, para.2.

5 See, for example, US DoD Manual, n.2, para.15.2.2; W Heintschel von Heinegg, 'Benevolent Third States in International Armed Conflicts: The Myth of the Irrelevance of the Law of Neutrality', in M Schmitt and J Pejic (eds), *International Law and Armed Conflicts: Exploring the Faultlines* (Brill, 2007), 543–68.

6 Note that countries recorded as having given military aid to Ukraine are, in the order of their contributions, as follows: the US, Germany, the UK, Denmark, the Netherlands, Norway, Poland, Canada, Sweden, Finland, Czech Republic, Estonia, Lithuania, Slovakia, Italy, France, Australia, Latvia, Spain, Belgium, Bulgaria, Croatia, Greece, Luxembourg, Portugal, Slovenia, New Zealand, Romania, Austria and South Korea: source: 'Ukraine Support Tracker', Kiel Institute, available at https://www.ifw-kiel.de/topics/war-against-ukraine/ukraine-support-tracker/.

7 Note, for example, US DoD Manual, n.2, para.15.3.2.1 citing Hague Convention (XIII) concerning the Rights and Duties of Neutral Powers in Naval War, The Hague, 18 October 1907 (Hague Convention XIII), Art.6.

8 AMW Manual, n.1, Commentary accompanying Section X, para.5.

9 International Criminal Court (ICJ) Nuclear Weapons Advisory Opinion on the Legality of the Threat or Use of Nuclear Weapons [1996] ICJ Reports 226, 35 ILM 809, paras 88–89.

technologies in connection with an international armed conflict. Accordingly, after summarising the sources of neutrality law and explaining a couple of key terms, this chapter will explain some of the obligations that neutrality law places upon parties to the armed conflict and neutrals and their implications in relation to the three listed technologies.

8.2 SOURCES OF NEUTRALITY LAW AND SOME PRELIMINARY TERMS

The main sources of neutrality law consist of Hague Conventions V and XIII of 1907 and customary law. As will be readily apparent, the treaties are old. Technology has advanced rapidly during the numerous intervening decades, so care is required in applying old law to new and emerging technologies and methods of warfare. The limited purpose of the chapter is to examine the rules that are thought to be of greatest relevance to military operations involving BCI, AB and BBI technologies; consequently, only certain aspects of neutrality law will be addressed. **8.004**

The term 'belligerent' refers to a state that is a party to an international armed conflict.[10] The term 'neutral' refers to a state that is not a belligerent party to the international armed conflict.[11] A state is permitted to assert its neutrality during an international armed conflict, but such an assertion is not required for its neutral status to be established.[12] It is the fact that the state is not a belligerent party to the international armed conflict that sufficiently demonstrates its neutral status.[13] **8.005**

Neutrality law governs the relationship between belligerents, their aircraft, their vessels, their outer space vehicles[14] and their people and neutrals together with their aircraft, vessels, outer space vehicles and people.[15] As will be shown below, belligerents and neutrals have distinct rights and responsibilities under the law of neutrality. The three main purposes of neutrality law are: to preserve friendly relations between belligerents and neutrals; to prevent additional **8.006**

10 Note US DoD Manual, n.2, para.15.1.2.1.

11 M N Schmitt, C H B Garraway and T Dinstein, *The Manual on the Law of Non-International Armed Conflict, With Commentary* (San Remo, International Institute of Humanitarian Law, 2006) (NIAC Manual), para.13(d).

12 US DoD Manual, n.2, para.15.2.1.4.

13 UK Manual, para.12.11.

14 For a brief discussion of relevant aspects of neutrality law in its application to outer space, see section 8.12 below.

15 US DoD Manual, n.2, para.15.1.1.

states being brought into the conflict; and to minimise the effects of the conflict on uninvolved states.[16]

8.3 NEUTRAL TERRITORY

8.007 Article 1 of Hague Convention V, 1907[17] states that '[t]he territory of neutral Powers is inviolable'. This means that 'any unauthorized entry into the territory of a neutral State, its territorial waters, or the airspace over such areas by armed forces or the instrumentalities of war' is prohibited.[18]

8.008 Hague Convention V deals with the law of neutrality as it applies on land whereas Hague Convention XIII[19] addresses neutrality law at sea. Article 1 of Hague Convention XIII states: 'Belligerents are bound to respect the sovereign rights of neutral Powers, and to abstain, in neutral territory or neutral waters, from any act which would, if knowingly permitted by any Power, constitute a violation of neutrality.'[20] Moreover, in customary law, hostilities between belligerents must not be conducted in or from neutral territory.[21]

8.009 Neutral territory means the 'land territory of neutral States, as well as waters subject to their territorial sovereignty (internal waters, territorial sea and, where applicable, archipelagic waters) and the airspace above those areas'.[22] Neutral territory does not include a state's Exclusive Economic Zone (EEZ). This means that a belligerent is permitted to conduct hostilities using BCI- or AB-enabled weapon systems, or to use BBI arrangements in connection with the planning of such hostilities, within a neutral state's EEZ and within the airspace above a neutral state's EEZ.[23] Belligerents must, however, pay due regard to the rights of coastal states (for example in respect of exploration and exploitation of the EEZ's economic resources and the protection of the marine

16 US DoD Manual, n.2, para.15.1.3.

17 Hague Convention (V) Respecting the Rights and Duties of Neutral Powers and Persons in Case of War on Land, The Hague, 18 October 1907 (Hague Convention V).

18 US DoD Manual, n.2, para.15.3.1.1.

19 Hague Convention (XIII) concerning the Rights and Duties of Neutral Powers in Naval War, The Hague, 18 October 1907 (Hague Convention XIII).

20 See also US DoD Manual, n.2, para.15.3.1.

21 Note US DoD Manual, n.2, paras 15.3.1.2 and 15.10.1.

22 M N Schmitt (ed), *Tallinn Manual 2.0 on the International Law Applicable to Cyber Operations* (Cambridge University Press, 2017) (Tallinn Manual 2.0), Commentary accompanying Part 20, para.2. See also AMW Manual, n.1, Commentary accompanying Rule 166, para.2; San Remo Manual on International Law Applicable to Armed Conflict at Sea, June 1994 (San Remo Manual), paras. 34, 35.

23 San Remo Manual, n.23, paras. 34, 35.

environment). Their obligation is to 'balance the military advantages anticipated as against any negative impact on the rights of Neutrals'.[24]

These rules mean that belligerents must not conduct hostilities, including the firing of weapons, in, from, to or through neutral territory. Accordingly: **8.010**

1. Planners, commanders and operators of BCI and AB weapon systems and methods must reliably and consistently be able to restrict where the weapon systems go and the locations in, from, to or through which they operate.
2. Planners, commanders and operators must clearly restrict the geographical areas in, from, to and through which BCI and AB weapon systems and methods are permitted to fire their weapons or otherwise conduct hostilities.
3. In the context of BCI systems, this means that operators must not develop thoughts or intent that would cause the weapon system to move to neutral territory, to undertake any act of hostility from neutral territory, to pass through or otherwise enter neutral territory (for example on its way to the theatre of operations) or to target any person or thing in neutral territory.
4. In the context of AB operations, this means that planners, commanders and operators must ensure that the mission plan reflects the prohibitions in points 1 to 3 above and that the AB system is not capable of acting in any way that is contrary to those prohibitions. The system must have been thoroughly tested so that planners, commanders and operators can be appropriately confident that the AB system will abide by the limitations that must be programmed into it.

Consider, for example, a situation in which a BCI- or AB-enabled weapon system enters neutral land territory, airspace or territorial waters, whether because of a programming error or because the operator of the BCI weapon or the AB system itself failed to comply with programmed instructions. In both cases, neutrality is breached. The belligerent and the neutral will not necessarily be aware of the neutrality breach. If and when the neutral becomes aware of the presence of the weapon system on neutral territory, it must do what it can to stop the violation of its neutrality. If and when the belligerent becomes aware that its weapon is present in neutral territory, airspace or waters, it must immediately move the weapon system outside such territory, airspace or waters. This suggests to the author that certain robust restrictions must be in place. The BCI- or AB-enabled weapon systems must be set up so that commanders and operators of the system know at all times where the weapon system is. AB systems must not be able to circumvent the relevant limitations placed by planners, programmers, commanders and operators. The AB system must also not be permitted to falsify its, or at least the weapon's, location. **8.011**

---

24 AMW Manual, n.1, Commentary accompanying Rule 166, para.3.

8.4 INVIOLABILITY OF NEUTRAL TERRITORY AND OTHER PROHIBITED ACTS IN NEUTRAL TERRITORY

8.012 Belligerent states must not conduct hostilities on neutral territory, in neutral airspace, in neutral internal waters or in neutral territorial seas and archipelagic seas.[25] It is also prohibited for belligerent states to fire weapons from those places, no matter where the intended target may be. This means that:

1. Belligerent State A in its international armed conflict with State B is not permitted, for example, to conduct a BCI-enabled mission from neutral State C's land territory. By way of another example, it must not initiate an AB-controlled mission from a vessel on an internal lake within neutral State C. A third example would be that it must not conduct a military operation which involves BBI interaction technology from an aircraft that is flying in neutral State C's airspace. It must be recalled that this prohibition does not extend to neutral State C's EEZ but State C's ability to explore and exploit that zone must not thereby be impeded and State A must pay due regard to State C's rights in the EEZ.
2. Initiating an AB-controlled mission will include programming the AB element of a weapon system to enter neutral State C's land territory, airspace or waters.
3. If any State A weapon enters neutral State C territory, it must not be permitted to launch or release any weapon or munition from neutral territory, waters or airspace. This aspect of the rule would also be breached if the AB technology were to decide autonomously to permit the weapon with which it is linked to be fired or released within neutral territory, airspace or waters.

8.013 Under Article 2 of Hague Convention V '[b]elligerents are forbidden to move troops or convoys of either munitions of war or supplies across the territory of a neutral power'. Article 3 adds that:

> Belligerents are likewise forbidden to:
>
> (a) Erect on the territory of a neutral Power a wireless telegraphy station or any apparatus for the purpose of communicating with belligerent forces on land or sea;
> (b) Use any installation of this kind established by them before the war on the territory of a neutral Power for purely military purposes, and which has not been opened for the service of public messages.

8.014 Continuing with the same example:

1. State A will not be permitted to move BCI- and AB-enabled weapons, associated military equipment (such as military BBI systems), ammunition and

---

25 Hague Convention V, n.17, Arts 1 to 3; Hague Convention XIII, n.19, Arts 2 and 5; The Hague Rules of Aerial Warfare, The Hague, November 1922 – February 1923 (Hague Draft Rules), Art.XXXIX; Tallinn Manual 2.0, n.22, Rule 151; note that the rule has customary law status.

supplies across neutral territory, airspace or waters. The logistical arrangements for the movement of all troops, weapons, munitions and military supplies must therefore ensure that neutral land, air and sea are avoided, subject to the right of innocent passage in the law of the sea,[26] and AB systems must be prevented from undertaking movement in breach of this rule.

2. State A must also not establish or use in neutral State C territory, whether land, airspace or waters, a system for communicating with land or sea forces. Unsurprisingly given the year of their adoption, in these provisions no mention was made of air forces. However, erecting and using such communications facilities within neutral land, sea or airspace territory would breach State C's neutrality and thus would be prohibited.
3. Article 3(b) makes it clear that if, before the international armed conflict commenced, State A had set up any purely military communications facility in neutral State C, and if that communications facility remains purely military in nature, State A cannot use it during the international armed conflict.

It will be for states to interpret their international law obligations. However, the reference to 'forces on land or sea' in Article 3(a) would seem to apply also to air forces, and the notion of communicating would also seem, on the same basis, to extend to communication with BCI- and AB-enabled weapon systems. An interesting question is whether the provisions in Articles 2 and 3 should also be interpreted as extending to BBI communication facilities. The mere fact of these interpretation difficulties, caused as they are by the extreme age of the treaty provisions, amply illustrates the urgent need for an updating of the law. The considerable mutual antipathy and suspicion between the major states of the world at the time of writing, however, make such a revision and updating of the law unlikely. It will therefore be for states to interpret their legal obligations, preferably sensibly. **8.015**

It is prohibited for belligerent states to attack targets located on or in neutral land, airspace or waters, and neutral land, airspace and waters must not be used as a base from which to undertake military operations, including attacks, no matter where the targets of the attacks may be.[27] The AMW Manual stipulates that belligerent parties must not commit the following acts: '(a) Attack on or capture of persons or objects located in neutral airspace. (b) Use of neutral territory or airspace as a base of operations – for attack, targeting or intelligence purposes – against enemy targets in the air, on land or on water outside that territory. (c) Conducting interception, inspection, diversion or capture of **8.016**

26 Hague Convention XIII, n.19, Art.10.
27 Hague Convention V, n.17, Arts 1 and 5; Hague Convention XIII, n.19, Arts 1 and 5 and US DoD Manual, n.2, para.15.5.

vessels or aircraft in neutral territory. (d) Any other activity involving the use of military force or contributing to the war-fighting effort, including the transmission of data or combat search-and-rescue operations in neutral territory.'[28]

8.017 What amounts to contributing to the war-fighting effort of a belligerent has become a key issue in relation to the ongoing war between Russia and Ukraine in light of the extensive support to the key belligerents by third states.[29] Questions such as whether it makes a legal difference if the support is being given to a state that is perceived (at least by the assisting state) as the victim of aggression and whether indeed the law of neutrality remains relevant in a war of aggression are being debated.[30] Recent scholarship has also explored the point at which the provision of support renders the supporting state a party to the pre-existing armed conflict.[31] Hague Convention V provides that a 'neutral Power is not called upon to prevent the export or transport, on behalf of one or other of the belligerents, of arms, munitions of war, or, in general, of anything which can be of use to an army or a fleet'.[32] Article 6 of Hague Convention XIII states: 'The supply, in any manner, directly or indirectly, by a neutral Power to a belligerent Power, of warships, ammunition or war material of any kind whatever, is forbidden.' Article 7 of the same Treaty then states: 'A neutral power is not bound to prevent the export or transit, for the use of either belligerent, of arms, ammunition, or, in general, of anything which could be of use to an army or fleet.'

8.018 The Hague Draft Rules, dating from 1923, add that a neutral 'is not bound to prevent the export or transit on behalf of a belligerent of aircraft, parts of aircraft, or material, supplies or munitions for aircraft'.[33] A neutral is, however, 'bound to use the means at its disposal: (1) to prevent the departure from its jurisdiction of an aircraft in a condition to make a hostile attack against a belligerent Power …'.[34] Basing itself on this provision and on Article 7 of both Hague Convention V and Hague Convention XIII of 1907, the AMW

---

28 AMW Manual, n.1, Rules 171(a), (b), (c), (d).

29 G Bartolini, 'The Law of Neutrality and the Russian/Ukrainian Conflict: Looking at State Practice', *EjilTalk*, 11 April 2023, available at https://www.ejiltalk.org/the-law-of-neutrality-and-the-russian-ukrainian-conflict-looking-at-state-practice/.

30 See for example N Zugliani, 'The Supply of Weapons to Victims of Aggression: The Law of Neutrality in Light of the Conflict in Ukraine' (2024) 35(2) EJIL 389–410.

31 A Wentker, *Party Status to Armed Conflict in International Law* (Oxford University Press, 2025).

32 Hague Convention V, n.17, Art.7. It must also be noted that '[e]very measure of restriction or prohibition taken by a neutral Power' under this provision 'must be impartially applied by it to both belligerents': Hague Convention V, n.17, Art.9(1).

33 Draft Hague Rules of Aerial Warfare, Art.XLV.

34 Ibid, Art.46(1).

Manual stipulates as follows: 'A Neutral is not bound to prevent the private export or transit on behalf of a Belligerent Party of aircraft, parts of aircraft, or material, supplies or munitions for aircraft.'[35] The AMW Manual goes on to state: 'However a Neutral is bound to use the means at its disposal: (a) To prevent the departure from its jurisdiction of an aircraft in a condition to make a hostile attack against a Belligerent Party, if there is reason to believe that such aircraft is destined for such use. (b) To prevent the departure from its jurisdiction of the crews of military aircraft, as well as passengers and crews of civilian aircraft, who are members of the armed forces of a Belligerent Party.[36] The Commentary to the first sentence of Rule 173 makes it clear that this rule applies exclusively to private activities, not to activities of governments. Accordingly, '[t]he supply in any manner, directly or indirectly, by a neutral government to a Belligerent power of aircraft, parts of aircraft, or material, supplies or munitions required for aircraft is forbidden'.[37]

To continue with the example discussed earlier in this chapter, the effect of the foregoing is: **8.019**

1. Neutral State C is prohibited from supplying military equipment, platforms, weapons and supplies to either of belligerent States A or B.
2. Neutral State C does not have to prevent the export or transportation by or on behalf of States A or B of arms, munitions of war and military equipment.
3. The items referred to in point 2 above would include weapons, systems and equipment associated with the conduct of BCI, AB and BBI activities concerning hostilities. This only applies if it is State A or B that is doing the exporting or the transiting of the items through neutral State C territory. If that is the case, State C's neutrality is not breached.
4. Neutral State C would breach Article 6 of Hague Convention XIII if it supplied 'ammunition or war material of any kind'. So the key distinction seems to be between a belligerent purchasing weapons, arms, ammunition, and so on under commercial arrangements from companies or individuals that are based in neutral territory (which does not breach neutrality law) and the belligerent buying the same weapons, arms, ammunition, and so on from neutral State C.

The inviolability of neutrals also prohibits the armed forces of a belligerent using military bases located within the neutral state, even if such forces may be present on neutral territory pursuant to an established inter-state agreement. **8.020**

35 AMW Manual, n.1, Rule 173, first sentence.
36 AMW Manual, n.1, Rule 173, second sentence.
37 Hague Draft Rules, Art.44 and AMW Manual, n.1, Commentary to Rule 173, para.2.

8.5 OTHER ACTIVITIES

8.021 The provision by third states of military intelligence to a belligerent may also, it seems, conflict with the duty of a neutral 'to refrain from placing its various governmental agencies at the disposal of a belligerent in such a way as to aid it directly or indirectly in the prosecution of the war'.[38] That said, certain Western states have been sharing military intelligence with Ukraine during its war with Russia.[39] This may be indicative of the exercise of a qualified neutrality policy of the sort briefly discussed in section 8.1.

8.022 Particular neutrality issues may arise if a belligerent state receives advanced weapon systems, such as those employing the technologies discussed in this book, but lacks the expertise required to operate them correctly and efficiently. The temptation will be to obtain assistance from the supplying state, or from some other neutral state that operates the relevant systems.

8.023 Continuing, therefore, with the example that we have been using in this chapter, belligerent State A has purchased from neutral State C a new missile system that uses BCI technology (1) to fire the weapon, and (2) in connection with target selection. State A does not have personnel who are familiar with the operation of BCI systems, and neutral State C makes a team of technicians available to help with the firing and directing of the missiles. This would constitute non-neutral activity by State C. It would, arguably, be different if State A were to contract privately with a commercial supplier, perhaps a company registered in neutral State C, for the purchase of the equipment and for the provision by the supplying company of personnel with the required skillset. Neutrality law would require that neutral State C should decline any request that it receives from belligerent State A (or indeed from belligerent State B) for the supply by State C of such assistance.

8.024 Certain activities do not constitute a breach of neutrality, such as publicly expressing sympathy for one belligerent or disapproval of the other,[40] the provision of humanitarian assistance, or taking on the role of a Protecting Power.[41]

---

38 US DoD Manual, n.2, para.15.3.2.1.

39 Note for example N Robertson, 'US Agrees to Resume Military Aid, Intel Sharing with Ukraine', *Defense News*, 11 March 2025, available at https://www.defensenews.com/global/europe/2025/03/11/us-agrees-to-resume-military-aid-intel-sharing-with-ukraine/; A Mackinnon and others, 'Europe Scrambles to Aid Ukraine After US Intelligence Cutoff', *Politico*, 3 August 2025, available at https://www.politico.com/news/2025/03/08/europe-scrambles-to-aid-ukraine-after-us-intelligence-cutoff-00219678.

40 US DoD Manual, n.2, para.15.3.2.3.

41 US DoD Manual, n.2, para.15.3.2.4.

8.6 NEUTRALITY LAW AND MARITIME OPERATIONS

Neutral waters consist of 'the internal waters, territorial sea, and, where applicable, the archipelagic waters, of neutral States'.[42] Hague Convention XIII provides that '[a]ny act of hostility … committed by belligerent warships in the territorial waters of a neutral Power, constitutes a violation of neutrality and is strictly forbidden'.[43] Paragraph 15 of the San Remo Manual confirms that: 'Within and over neutral waters, including neutral waters comprising an international strait and waters in which the right of archipelagic sea lanes passage may be exercised, hostile actions by belligerent forces are forbidden.' The same Manual goes on to state that hostile actions include: '(a) attack on or capture of persons or objects located in, on or over neutral waters or territory; (b) use as a base of operations, including attack on or capture of persons or objects located outside neutral waters, if the attack or seizure is conducted by belligerent forces located in, on or over neutral waters; (c) laying of mines; or (d) visit, search, diversion or capture.'[44] This makes it clear that using any of the technologies discussed in this book to target any person or object that is located in neutral waters is prohibited as is using neutral territory or waters as a base from which to conduct BCI, AB or BBI operations against targets inside or outside neutral waters. It will be for states to interpret how these provisions apply to modern military operations using the three kinds of technology. A sensible reading of the provisions may lead to the conclusion that the idea of a base of operations would include a facility from which autonomously operating AB-enabled craft are deployed and to which they periodically return, irrespective of whether the relevant base is manned or unmanned. That will, however, be a matter for individual national interpretation. **8.025**

Continuing with the example we have been using, Belligerent States A and B will therefore need to program their AB systems with the exact co-ordinates of neutral waters and will need to ensure that individual operations comply with these rules. State A must not, for example, use: **8.026**

1. a BCI-enabled weapon system to undertake attacks against targets on land in neutral State C;
2. an AB-enabled weapon system to attack State B's warship while it is engaged in innocent passage through neutral State C's territorial sea;

---

42 San Remo Manual, n.23, para.14.

43 Hague Convention XIII, n.19, Art.2; San Remo Manual, n.23, para.15, which goes on to refer to the neutral's obligation to undertake surveillance, to the extent the means at its disposal allow, to prevent the violation of its neutrality.

44 San Remo Manual, n.23, para.16.

3. a floating base of operations in neutral State C's territorial sea to undertake attack operations against belligerent State B's naval vessels via its fleet of autonomous AB-enabled craft;
4. visit and search, diversion or capture activities within State C's neutral waters.

8.027 'Belligerents are forbidden to use neutral ports and waters as a base of naval operations against their adversaries, and in particular to erect wireless telegraphy stations or any apparatus for the purpose of communicating with the belligerent forces on land or sea.'[45] Belligerent warships may continue to exercise the right of innocent passage in neutral territorial seas, but this does not permit the launching, landing or taking on board of any aircraft or of any military device.[46]

8.028 Continuing with our example, belligerent State A's aircraft carrier is exercising its right of innocent passage through neutral State C's territorial waters while carrying a squadron of combat aircraft and several unmanned sub-surface vessels which are capable of undertaking autonomous attack operations against enemy warships. All of the aircraft and submersibles must remain on board the aircraft carrier while the innocent passage continues, but when the aircraft carrier leaves neutral territorial waters and enters the EEZ, the aircraft may take off and the submersibles may be launched.

8.029 The use by a party to an international armed conflict of a public, internationally and openly accessible network such as the internet for military purposes does not breach neutrality, even if part of this infrastructure is situated within the territories of neutrals.[47]

8.030 The San Remo Manual explains the position that arises if a belligerent's naval operations are breaching a state's neutrality. The neutral must: 'take the measures necessary to terminate the violation. If the neutral State fails to terminate the violation of its neutral waters by a belligerent, the opposing belligerent must so notify the neutral State and give that neutral State a reasonable time to terminate the violation by the belligerent. If the violation of the neutrality of the State by the belligerent constitutes a serious and immediate threat to the security of the opposing belligerent and the violation is not terminated,

45 Hague Convention XIII, n.19, Art.5.

46 United Nations Convention on the Law of the Sea (UNCLOS), 10 December 1982, 1833 UNTS 397, Art.19(2).

47 Consider Hague Convention V, n.17, Art.8. It must also be noted that '[e]very measure of restriction or prohibition taken by a neutral Power' under this provision 'must be impartially applied by it to both belligerents': Hague Convention V, n.17, Art.9(1).

then that belligerent may, in the absence of any feasible and timely alternative, use such force as is strictly necessary to respond to the threat posed by the violation.'[48]

Consider the following scenarios. Belligerent State A positions its aircraft carrier within neutral State C's territorial waters. Unmanned aircraft are flown from the carrier on autonomous missions in which the AB technology with which they are equipped selects and engages belligerent State B's unmanned submersibles while they are on the surface of the sea as they approach the entry to a nearby port on State B's coastline. Such activity breaches State C's neutrality. Belligerent State B protests to neutral State C's government demanding immediate action to stop the breaches, but neutral State C does nothing and ignores the protests. Belligerent State B therefore sends formal notification via diplomatic and military communication systems to neutral State C specifying the neutrality breaches and giving State C 24 hours in which to stop the breaches. Neutral State C assesses the 24-hour period to be reasonable given the serious military consequences of the neutrality breach. If neutral State C continues to do nothing to bring the breaches of its neutrality to an end, and if there is no other feasible and timely alternative, belligerent State B may use what force is strictly necessary to put an end to the violation and to the threat it poses. The degree of force that is used must be carefully judged. **8.031**

'Merchant vessels flying the flag of neutral States may not be attacked unless' specific circumstances listed in para. 67 of the San Remo Manual apply.[49] Operators using BCI-enabled weapon systems must therefore be able to distinguish vessels to which the rule applies and must refrain from forming the intent or wish to attack them unless the exceptions specified in Rule 67 apply. AB systems must be programmed reliably and consistently: **8.032**

1. to identify merchant vessels;
2. to identify that a merchant vessel is flying a neutral flag;
3. to make the identifications in points 1 and 2 and determine whether the circumstances in para.67 of the San Remo Manual apply;
4. to decide to attack the vessel only if point 3 is answered in the affirmative; and

48 San Remo Manual, n.23, para.22 and see section 11.8 below.

49 These are that the vessel is: 'believed on reasonable grounds to be carrying contraband or breaching a blockade, and after prior warning [it] intentionally and clearly refuse[s] to stop, or intentionally and clearly resist[s] visit, search or capture; (b) engage[s] in belligerent acts on behalf of the enemy; (c) act[s] as [an auxiliary] to the enemy's armed forces; (d) [is] incorporated into or assist[s] the enemy's intelligence system; (e) sail[s] under convoy of enemy warships or military aircraft; or (f) otherwise make[s] an effective contribution to the enemy's military action … and it is not feasible for the attacking forces to first place passengers and crew into a place of safety … ' (San Remo Manual, n.23, para.67).

5. if there is any difficulty in addressing points 1 to 4, to either programme the AB system above, to refrain from attacking the vessel or refer the matter to a human operator.

8.033 The San Remo Manual explains that '[i]n carrying out operations in areas where neutral States enjoy sovereign rights, jurisdiction, or other rights under general international law, belligerents shall have due regard for the legitimate rights and duties of those neutral States'.

8.034 If operations are to be undertaken involving the employment of BCI, AB or BBI technologies, it will be for planners, commanders and operators to take the necessary steps to ensure that this obligation is complied with. Those individuals will therefore need to consider whether the kind of activity that is being planned or, in the case of AB operations, that it is foreseeable that the system may, in the anticipated circumstances, decide to undertake, will affect the relevant rights. If the assessment is that it may do so, it will be for planners, commanders and operators to take such action as the obligation to have due regard implies. An example might be that the AB may, foreseeably, decide to take action that is likely to affect the neutral state's, in our example State C's, access to and management of natural resources in its EEZ.[50]

8.7 NEUTRALITY LAW AND AIR OPERATIONS

8.035 There are no treaty rules dealing specifically with neutrality in airspace. Under the Hague Draft Rules[51] '[b]elligerent aircraft are bound to respect the rights of neutral Powers and to abstain within the jurisdiction of a neutral State from the commission of any act which it is the duty of that State to prevent'[52] and '[b]elligerent military aircraft are forbidden to penetrate into the jurisdiction of a neutral State'.[53] Moreover, '[a] neutral government is bound to use the means at its disposal to prevent belligerent military aircraft from entering its jurisdiction and to compel them to land or to alight on water if they have

50 Consider UNCLOS, n.46, Art.56.

51 The Hague Rules of Aerial Warfare, The Hague, November 1922 – February 1923 (Hague Draft Rules), available at https://ihl-databases.icrc.org/en/ihl-treaties/hague-rules-1923/article-47?activeTab=. The Draft Rules were prepared by jurists but were never formally adopted by states in treaty form. They are not, as such, a source of international law but are seen as an authoritative statement of the relevant law as then understood by reference to technology as it then existed.

52 Hague Draft Rules, ibid, Art.39.

53 Hague Draft Rules, ibid, Art.40; San Remo Manual, n.23, para.18; and US DoD Manual, n.2, para.15.10.2.

penetrated therein'.[54] Article 42 also requires the neutral state to intern any belligerent military aircraft, crew and passengers that enter its jurisdiction.[55] The Hague Draft Rules go on to stipulate that a: 'neutral State is bound to take the measures at its disposal to prevent aerial observations of the movements, operations and defense works of a belligerent from being made within its jurisdiction for the purpose of giving information to the other belligerent. This rule also applies to a belligerent military aircraft on board a warship.'[56]

The Draft Rules would therefore prohibit a military aircraft operated by a belligerent, in our example by either State A or State B, from entering neutral State C's airspace, and this would include an aircraft that may be employing BCI, AB or BBI technologies in any of its functions. The rule will apply equally to manned and unmanned aircraft, including aircraft that are remotely piloted and ones that are operating autonomously. It is the military character of the aircraft and its operation by a belligerent that are the key features here. If, therefore, belligerent State A has military aircraft which are unmanned and which navigate autonomously, they must be programmed in such a way that they will not enter neutral airspace, such as the airspace of State C. **8.036**

The corresponding duty of the neutral state, that is State C, is not to permit belligerent military aircraft, in the example military aircraft of either belligerent State A or belligerent State B, to enter its airspace. Neutral State C must not permit such entry and must 'take the measures at its disposal' to prevent belligerent military aircraft from entering its airspace. If, despite those measures, a military aircraft of, say, belligerent State A were to enter State C airspace, State C must compel, that is force, it to land and must intern the aircraft, crew and passengers. **8.037**

Under Article 47 of the Draft Rules, it would breach neutrality law if neutral State C were to allow either belligerent state A or belligerent State B to fly any aircraft within its, State C's, neutral airspace in order to observe military activities over the border inside the other belligerent states. Neutral State C must take such action as it is able to prevent or, as the case may be, stop such activity. **8.038**

54 Hague Draft Rules, ibid, Art.42.
55 San Remo Manual, n.23, para.18.
56 Hague Draft Rules, n.51, Art.47.

8.039 It follows from this that it would (subject to what is discussed later about the enforcement of neutrality) be a clear breach of neutrality law if a belligerent state were to use any of the technologies discussed in this book:

1. to attack, destroy or capture an enemy aircraft in neutral airspace or at an airfield on neutral territory;
2. to attack, destroy or capture an enemy vessel in neutral waters or at a neutral port.

8.040 Additionally, if a belligerent state were to use an airfield on neutral territory as a base for aircraft that are undertaking ground attack operations using any of the technologies discussed in this book, or if it were to use a neutral seaport as the base from which any vessel employing such technologies operates, this would breach neutrality law.

8.041 Flying any belligerent military aircraft through neutral airspace breaches neutrality, whether the aircraft is unmanned or manned, and whether it is autonomously navigating or remotely piloted. Therefore, in our example, if an unmanned military aircraft belonging to belligerent State A is navigating autonomously using AB technology through the airspace of neutral State C, the neutrality of State C is being breached. It does not matter in this regard whether State C did or did not give permission for the flight, and the purpose of the flight is similarly irrelevant.[57] If a belligerent military aircraft, manned or unmanned, enters neutral airspace (other than the airspace superjacent to straits used for international navigation or archipelagic sea lanes), the neutral state must do everything in its power to prevent or terminate the violation of its neutrality.[58] If forcing it to land is not possible, it may be shot down.

8.8 DUTIES OF NEUTRALS UNDER NEUTRALITY LAW

8.042 Article 5 of Hague Convention V, Article 42 of the Draft Hague Rules of Aerial Warfare and customary international law all indicate that a neutral state

57 'Belligerent military aircraft in distress may be permitted to enter neutral airspace and to land in neutral territory under such safeguards as the Neutral may wish to impose. The Neutral is obligated to require such aircraft to land and to intern the aircraft and their crews': AMW Manual, n.1, Rule 172(a)(i). 'The Neutral may permit Belligerent military aircraft to enter for purposes of capitulation': AMW Manual, n.1, Rule 172(a)(iii). The capitulating military aircraft and its crew must likewise be interned for the duration of the conflict. If the belligerent military aircraft commits 'hostile acts, or should it fail to follow the instructions to land, it may be attacked without further notice': AMW Manual, n.1, Rule 172(b).

58 Hague Convention XIII, n.19, Art.25; Hague Draft Rules, n.51, Arts 42, 47; AMW Manual, n.1, Rule 170(c).

must not allow the breaches of neutrality law referred to earlier in this chapter to take place on its territory and must do everything in its power to prevent such activities.[59] Benefiting from the advantages and protections that the law of neutrality affords to a neutral requires that the neutral must not allow belligerents to misuse its territory. It follows from this that the neutral must use the capabilities at its disposal to monitor activities that are taking place on its territory, including its internal waters, territorial sea and airspace, because only by doing so can it become aware of neutrality breaches.[60] So, applying our example, neutral State C must use the equipment, technology and human skills that it has or can reasonably access in order to detect breaches of its neutrality. It must do all that it can to become aware of such breaches.

If a neutral state becomes aware of a neutrality breach by a belligerent state, it must then use the means available to it to stop that breach.[61] If the neutral state becomes aware of a potential future breach of its neutrality, the duty of that neutral state is to take action to prevent the breach.[62] The circumstances will determine the nature of the action that is required and appropriate. If force is deemed to be necessary and therefore appropriate, the force used should be limited to that which is required to 'repel the incursion and maintain its neutrality'.[63] Where a neutral uses force in such circumstances, the force used cannot be characterised as a hostile act[64] and force used in defence of neutrality cannot be an armed attack for the purposes of Article 51 of the UN Charter, so the affected belligerent has no right to use force in self-defence. This paragraph reflects customary law. In the author's opinion, it will be for the human planners, commanders and operators of neutral states to devise and implement the precautionary and response measures that are necessary to comply with the requirements discussed in this section. **8.043**

As for the belligerent states, it will be for planners, commanders and operators to ensure that BCI-enabled systems are not used in any manner that would breach neutrality. Planners, commanders, operators, programmers and others associated with the use of AB systems in connection with hostilities must **8.044**

---

59 Note, for example, San Remo Manual, n.23, para.22.

60 AMW Manual, n.1, Rule 170(b) and the accompanying Commentary.

61 See US DoD Manual, n.2, para.15.4.3.

62 Hague Convention XIII, n.19, Art.8; Hague Draft Rules, n.51, Arts 42, 47.

63 AMW Manual, n.1, Rule 169. If the neutral uses force that exceeds what is required to terminate the violation of its neutrality, the affected belligerent may take countermeasures; see AMW Manual, n.1, Commentary accompanying Rule 169, para.2.

64 Hague Convention V, n.17, Art.10; Hague Convention XIII, n.19, Art.26; Hague Draft Rules, n.51, Art.48.

ensure that the AB-enabled platform or weapon system is not permitted to act in breach of neutrality. If those persons cannot be sure that the system will be prevented from breaching neutrality, the system should not be used.

8.045 To apply the example we have been using to the situations discussed in the last three paragraphs, imagine that neutral State C's radar system detects a group of belligerent State B military aircraft, some of which are manned while others are unmanned and are evidently using AB technology in order to operate autonomously. The detected aircraft are approaching neutral State C's airspace with the evident intention that they will transit that airspace on their way to undertake ground attacks in belligerent State A. Neutral State C scrambles combat aircraft and the intruders are intercepted near the border between States B and C. Neutral armed forces members make unsuccessful attempts to communicate with the pilots of the manned aircraft. When State C's combat aircraft achieve the intercept, the manned aircraft from State B alter course and return to State B airspace. Two unmanned aircraft bearing State B military markings maintain course into neutral State C airspace where the intercepting State C aircraft shoot them both down. This would be a legally justifiable use of the force that was necessary to repel the incursion and to enforce State C's inviolability as a neutral.[65] It is likely that human judgement would be required to determine what force was justifiable in the relevant circumstances.

8.046 The obligation in Article 5 of Hague Convention XIII was cited and explained in section 8.6 above. Article 25 of the same treaty requires the neutral power to exercise such surveillance as the means at its disposal allow to prevent any violation 'occurring in its ports, or roadsteads or in its waters'. This surveillance might of course be provided or assisted by appropriately programmed AB systems.

8.9 NEUTRAL STATE UNABLE OR UNWILLING TO ACT

8.047 If a neutral state is either unwilling or unable to take the required action to stop a violation of its neutrality, the aggrieved belligerent 'may, in the absence of any feasible and timely alternative, use such force as is necessary to terminate the violation of neutrality'.[66] The AMW Manual makes it clear, however, that this only applies if the use of neutral territory or airspace by the

65 San Remo Manual, n.23, para.18.

66 AMW Manual, n.1, Rule 168(b). UK Manual, n.13, para.1.43a; see San Remo Manual, n.23, para.22 and US DoD Manual, n.2, paras 15.3.1.2 and 15.4.2.

belligerent constitutes a serious violation.[67] The AMW Manual explains that, where feasible, a prior warning must be given and a reasonable time limit must be given to the neutral to terminate the violation.[68] If the force that is used by the belligerent is that which is necessary to terminate the violation, the force in question cannot be regarded as an armed attack for the purposes of Article 51 of the UN Charter, so the neutral has no right of self-defence against the belligerent.[69]

8.10 HARMFUL EFFECTS OF HOSTILITIES ON NEUTRAL TERRITORY

Belligerents must take all practicable or practically possible measures, taking **8.048** into account military and humanitarian considerations, with a view to avoiding the harmful effects of the hostilities spreading to neutral territory. This proposition is not reflected in either of the 1907 Treaties, but it follows from the general obligation to refrain from activities violating the sovereign rights of other states and from the Article 1, Hague Convention V stipulation as to the inviolability of neutral territory. The former notion protects the territorial integrity of neutral states against the harmful effects of hostilities. This is not an absolute duty, and the circumstances that apply at the relevant time will determine what measures are, indeed, practicable, and thus required.

8.11 NEUTRALITY LAW IN CYBERSPACE

The Tallinn Manual experts agreed that the law of neutrality applies to cyber **8.049** operations. It will be appreciated that computer systems are intrinsically involved in all three of the main technologies discussed in this book, so it is clear that those experts would support the view that the rules of neutrality law discussed in this chapter will apply to BCI, AB and BBI technologies when used in warfare. The Tallinn Manual describes neutral cyber infrastructure as 'public or private cyber infrastructure that is located within neutral territory (including civilian cyber infrastructure owned by a party to the conflict or nationals of that party) or that has the nationality of a neutral State (and is located outside belligerent territory)'.[70]

---

67 AMW Manual, n.1.

68 AMW Manual, n.1, Commentary accompanying Rule 168(b), para.1.

69 AMW Manual, n.1, Commentary accompanying Rule 168(b), para.2.

70 Tallinn Manual 2.0, n.22, 553.

8.050 The effects of belligerent cyber operations can frequently spill over into private or public neutral cyber infrastructure, and belligerents will likely be unable to prevent cyber packages from passing through neutral computer facilities such as servers, cabling, and so on. However, the Tallinn Manual experts recognised that exercising belligerent rights by cyber means directed against neutral cyber infrastructure and exercising belligerent rights by cyber means in neutral territory are both prohibited.[71] Applying our example, it would therefore be unlawful for a belligerent State A operator of a BCI-enabled weapon system to develop a thought or intent to attack neutral State C cyber infrastructure, whether with the intent to corrupt or delete the data on which it relies or with a view to causing physical damage to that neutral cyber system. Likewise, it would not be lawful, for example, for belligerent State A to use an AB system that it has concealed in neutral State C territory to direct cyber operations against belligerent State B's military computer-based communication systems. Equally, it would not be lawful for operators, planners and commanders of belligerent State A, when consulting together by means of a BBI system, to plan and then execute an offensive cyber operation against neutral facilities or to use a cyber capability in neutral territory to undertake cyber attacks against belligerent State B. The author takes the view that this rule would also prohibit belligerent State A both from taking control of computer facilities in neutral State C and from then using those facilities to undertake attacks against belligerent State B.

8.051 The Tallinn Manual explains that a neutral state may not knowingly allow the exercise of belligerent rights by the parties to the conflict from cyber infrastructure located in its neutral territory or under its exclusive control.[72] As to the meaning of 'knowingly', the relevant Commentary states that the 'neutral State has actual knowledge if its organs have detected a cyber operation conducted by a party to the conflict originating from its territory or if the aggrieved party to the conflict has credibly informed the neutral State that a cyber operation has been initiated from its territory'. Constructive knowledge, according to the Commentary, exists when the state should in the circumstances reasonably have known of the activity.[73]

8.052 Imagine that the armed forces of neutral State C receive intelligence from an informant located within belligerent State B that State B is using neutral State C's servers to conduct offensive cyber operations against belligerent State A

71 Tallinn Manual 2.0, n.22, Rules 150 and 151.

72 Tallinn Manual 2.0, n.22, Rule 152.

73 Tallinn Manual 2.0, n.22, Commentary accompanying Rule 152, para.5.

using AB technologies. A suite of malware tools is stored in neutral State C servers and is accessed by belligerent State B's AB system which chooses the particular malware it requires once the AB system has identified its intended target. Neutral State C is obliged to take the necessary action to prevent and stop this use of its servers by belligerent State B. Equally, imagine that a belligerent State B operator of a BCI system that enables offensive cyber operations has formed a wish or intent to use similarly-located cyber malware against a previously selected target in belligerent State A. The selection by the State B AB system of the malware stored in the State C server and its use against the target in State A would breach this rule of neutrality law.

Neutral states are obliged to take practically possible measures to bring the **8.053** relevant use of their servers, or indeed of other elements of their neutral cyber infrastructure, to an end. The technical facilities that are available to a neutral state will determine the action that it is practically possible for it to take.[74] If a neutral state lacks the required capabilities, it may be appropriate for it to request assistance from other, more technically capable states. Similar considerations apply if a belligerent is conducting cyber operations using neutral cyber facilities located on a vessel in international waters if the vessel is flagged to a neutral state. The Tallinn Manual experts took the same position as that reflected in section 8.8 above, that is that if a neutral state fails to terminate the exercise of belligerent rights on its territory, 'the aggrieved party to the conflict may take such steps, including by cyber operations, as are necessary to counter that conduct'.[75] Accordingly, if any of the circumstances discussed in the previous paragraph apply, the belligerent that is adversely affected has the right to take the action that is necessary to put an end to the opposing belligerent's breach of the law of neutrality. For the associated action to be lawful it must be necessary, that is there is no practically possible and timely alternative to taking action on neutral territory and the action that is being taken by the other belligerent must constitute 'an immediate threat to the security of the aggrieved party'.[76]

74 Consider Tallinn Manual 2.0, n.22, Commentary accompanying Rule 152, para.6.
75 Tallinn Manual 2.0, n.22, Rule 153.
76 Tallinn Manual 2.0, n.22, Commentary accompanying Rule 153, para.4, citing San Remo Manual, n.23, Rule 22.

8.12 NEUTRALITY AND OUTER SPACE OPERATIONS

8.054 Two relatively recently published international manuals have come to somewhat differently expressed conclusions as to the application of neutrality law in the outer space context. The earlier of these manuals, the Oslo Manual, asserts that, 'as a general principle, neutral States must not knowingly allow space systems and assets for which they are responsible to be used by Belligerent States in Outer Space Operations related to armed conflict'.[77] The Oslo Manual experts stated that the concept of neutrality extends to outer space operations, but acknowledged that applying existing legal rules as to neutrality to space operations involved the use of analogy.[78] They accordingly took the position that belligerent states are forbidden to erect on neutral territory communication installations for satellites operated by their armed forces and that employing, in neutral territory, ground stations for communication between a spacecraft and ground systems for the execution of belligerent acts would breach neutrality.[79]

8.055 Applying this view, if belligerent State B uses a satellite control and communications facility located in neutral State C to communicate with its, State B's, surveillance satellite instructing the satellite to observe belligerent State A military activities, the neutrality of State C would be breached. Likewise, if belligerent State A, with or without the knowledge or permission of neutral State C, inserts a communication facility into State C's space communication and control facility so that, using that link, belligerent State A personnel can communicate with State A-operated satellites, such action would also breach neutrality law.[80]

8.056 The Oslo Manual experts then found a series of rules, clearly based on the established neutrality law rules discussed earlier in this chapter, to be applicable to space operations in connection with international armed conflicts. Those rules include the following:

> 8 A Neutral State may not launch military satellites on behalf of a Belligerent Party. Nor may it provide any services to a Belligerent Party military satellite already in orbit.
>
> 9 A Neutral State may not sell or otherwise transfer a satellite for military uses by a Belligerent Party.

---

77 Y Dinstein and A-W Dahl (eds), *Oslo Manual on Select Topics of the Law of Armed Conflict* (2020) (Oslo Manual), Rule 18.

78 Oslo Manual, ibid, Commentary accompanying Rule 18, paras 1 and 3.

79 Oslo Manual, ibid, Commentary accompanying Rule 18, paras 5 and 7.

80 Oslo Manual, ibid, Commentary accompanying Rule 18, para.7.

> 10 However, commercial and trade activities by neutral companies or individuals with a Belligerent State are not prohibited.
> 11 The use by a Belligerent State of telecommunication satellites owned by or under the exclusive control of a Neutral State is not a violation of neutrality …
> 14 The necessary use of force by a Neutral State to prevent its Outer Space assets from being used by a Belligerent State to commit a belligerent act is not a violation of neutrality.[81]
>
> …
>
> As a general principle, Belligerent States must conduct their Outer Space operations with due regard for the rights of Neutral States.[82]

The explanations given with regard to each rule earlier in this chapter would apply similarly in respect of its outer space application. **8.057**

The Woomera Manual takes a more cautious, caveated position by stating that, 'to the extent that any general international law exists on neutrality, it is applicable to space via art. III of the [Outer Space Treaty]'.[83] The Woomera Manual experts, however, emphasised the lack of state practice and associated *opinio juris* on how the law of neutrality applies in space.[84] They therefore limited themselves to noting that the general principles of neutrality law 'would require belligerents to refrain from attacking neutral states, persons, and property in space, to respect the rights of neutrals in areas outside the jurisdiction of any state (including rights under the OST), and to spare them the consequences of hostilities, to the extent feasible'. The Woomera Manual goes on to note the obligation of a neutral to remain impartial, to refrain from non-neutral activities and to 'take certain actions to end or prevent belligerent military activities that would violate its neutrality'.[85] **8.058**

Acknowledging the relative lack of state practice and of associated *opinio juris*, the author suggests that a sensible approach would be for belligerents and neutrals to apply, during international armed conflict hostilities in outer space, the rules discussed in this chapter, to the extent that they make sense in that environment. There is, of course, a similar lack of state practice and *opinio juris* as to the application of neutrality law to the employment of brain technologies in international armed conflict. However, the author reminds readers of the **8.059**

---

81 Oslo Manual, ibid, Commentary accompanying Rule 18, paras 8, 9, 10, 11 and 14.

82 Oslo Manual, ibid, Rule 19.

83 J Beard and D Stephens (eds), *The Woomera Manual on the International Law of Military Space Operations* (Oxford University Press, 2024) (Woomera Manual), 400, n.393.

84 Woomera Manual, ibid, 401.

85 Woomera Manual, ibid, 400 and 401.

position taken by the International Court of Justice in the Nuclear Weapons Advisory opinion, noted in section 8.1 above. If neutrality principles truly are fundamental and applicable to all kinds of weapons, those principles, as explained throughout this chapter, apply to the use of weapons in outer space and should be implemented by belligerents and neutrals alike.

9

BRAIN TECHNOLOGIES AND THE *JUS AD BELLUM*

9.1 INTRODUCTION

This chapter deals with the implications of the law on the resort to the use of force for the employment of brain-computer interface (BCI), artificial brain (AB) and brain-to-brain interface (BBI) technologies. The rules of the *jus ad bellum*, as this body of law is also called, are largely to be found in the United Nations (UN) Charter and in associated customary law provisions. There is an important distinction between the *jus ad bellum*, with its prohibition of the resort to the use of force, and the law dealing with the conduct of hostilities during an armed conflict, otherwise known as the *jus in bello*. They are two distinct bodies of law, but there is a relationship between them. An important aspect of that relationship is the principle of the equal application of *jus in bello* to the parties to an international armed conflict.[1] The effect of that principle is that, irrespective of which party may have breached the *jus ad bellum* and thus initiated the international armed conflict, the rights and duties set forth in the **9.001**

1 M Sassóli, '*Ius ad Bellum* and *Ius in Bello* – the Separation of the Legality of the Use of Force and Humanitarian Rules to be Respected in Warfare – Crucial or Outdated', in M N Schmitt and J Pejic (eds), *International Law and Armed Conflict: Exploring the Faultlines – Essays in Honour of Yoram Dinstein* (Martinus Nijhoff Publishers/Brill, 2007), 241–64; A Roberts, 'The Equal Application of the Laws of War: A Principle Under Pressure' (2008) 90 IRRC 872, 931–62.

jus in bello (discussed in Chapters 4 to 7) and the law of neutrality (referred to in Chapter 8) apply to all parties to the conflict equally.[2]

9.2 PROHIBITION OF THE THREAT OR USE OF FORCE

9.002 Article 2(4) of the UN Charter provides: 'All Members shall refrain in their international relations from the threat or use of force against the territorial integrity or political independence of any state, or in any other manner inconsistent with the purposes of the United Nations.' This is a rule of customary international law which therefore binds all states.[3] Its effect is to protect states against any use or threat of force by another state. So, if, for example, State A armed forces forcibly enter State B territory without the consent of State B, this will be contrary to the territorial integrity of State B and will be a use of force. To take another example, if State A uses BCI technology to direct a missile into State B territory and causes it to detonate there, giving rise to damage and casualties, this will also breach State B's territorial integrity and will be a use of force. If, to give another example, State A threatens to program an AB-enabled missile system to target a cultural object in State B territory if State B fails to enter into a new, disadvantageous trade agreement, this would be contrary to State B's political independence and would be an unlawful threat of force. All states have the right to apply their own domestic and international political processes and to make their own political decisions free from external interference.

9.003 Article 2(4) refers to the purposes of the UN and these are set forth in Article 1 of the UN Charter. Key among them is the maintenance of international peace and security,[4] so any use or threat of force that is in any way inconsistent with the purposes listed in Article 1 breaches Article 2(4).

---

2 Protocol Additional to the Geneva Conventions of 12 August 1949, and Relating to the Protection of Victims of International Armed Conflicts, Geneva, 8 June 1977, 1125 UNTS 3 (Additional Protocol I or API), Preamble, para.5; Geneva Conventions, 12 August 1949, common Art.2; UK Manual, paras 3.12, 3.12.1.

3 ICJ, Military and Paramilitary Activities in and against Nicaragua (Nicaragua v. United States of America), Judgment, 26 November 1984 [1984] ICJ Reports 392, paras 188–91 and 196–7; UN General Assembly Resolution 2625(XXV), 24 October 1970.

4 Charter of the United Nations and Statute of the International Court of Justice (UN Charter), 1 UNTS XVI, Art.1(1).

The rule is directed at the actions of states.[5] A use of force that is attributable to a state will therefore breach the rule, and the acts of organs of the state[6] are always attributable to it.[7] If a public corporation, semi-public entity, public agency or even a private contractor is empowered by law to exercise public functions of the state, for example by operating AB-enabled systems that perform those public functions, the act of that corporation, entity, agency or company will become the action of the state.[8] The significance of attribution is that the act of the individual or group becomes the act of the relevant state. **9.004**

The International Court of Justice (ICJ) has stated that Article 2(4) of the UN Charter applies to 'any use of force, regardless of the weapons employed'.[9] It is therefore safe to conclude that the prohibition applies to any use of the technologies discussed in this book that amounts to a threat or use of force. The meaning of those terms will now be briefly discussed. **9.005**

Although the UN Charter does not define use of force, Article 2(4) will certainly apply to the use of armed force. Economic or political pressure will not be sufficient to constitute a use or threat of force.[10] Activity that is designed to cause, or that results in, death, injury, damage or destruction will so qualify.[11] This of course raises the interesting question, designed by whom or what? If a BCI is being used in conjunction with a weapon system to perpetrate the relevant act, it will, the author suggests, be the purpose of the operator and/or commander in conducting/ordering the operation that will be relevant. If the act is perpetrated by a weapon system that employs AB technology, it will be important to know whether that technology has the capability to form a design purpose. If it does, it will then be necessary to find out whether it did in fact form a design purpose that breaches the rule on the occasion in question. It **9.006**

---

5 It is states that are the Members of the UN to which reference is made in Art.2(4).

6 The notion of an organ of a state 'covers all the individual or collective entities which make up the organization of the State and act on its behalf. It includes an organ of any territorial governmental entity within the State on the same basis as the central governmental organs of that State': para. 1 of the Commentary to Art. 4 of the Articles on State Responsibility. Draft Articles on Responsibility of States for Internationally Wrongful Acts, with commentaries, 2001 available at https://legal.un.org/ilc/texts/instruments/english/commentaries/9_6_2001.pdf. The organ must be acting in that capacity: ibid, para.3. The rule applies to organs whether they exercise judicial, legislative, executive or other functions.

7 Articles on State Responsibility, ibid, Art.4.

8 Articles on State Responsibility, ibid, para.2 of the Commentary to Art.5.

9 ICJ, Nuclear Weapons Advisory Opinion on the Legality of the Threat or Use of Nuclear Weapons (Nuclear Weapons Advisory Opinion) [1996] ICJ Reports 226, para.39.

10 See M N Schmitt (ed), *Tallinn Manual 1.0 on the International Law Applicable to Cyber Warfare* (Cambridge University Press, 2013), Commentary accompanying Rule 11, para.2.

11 M N Schmitt (ed), *Tallinn Manual 2.0 on the International Law Applicable to Cyber Operations* (Cambridge University Press, 2017) (Tallinn Manual 2.0), Commentary accompanying Rule 69, para.8.

is, of course, possible that the AB system was set up in such a way as merely to implement the design purpose formed by the commander or operator or, perhaps, the operational planners. However, it may not be possible to work out after the event where the design purpose was formed.

9.007 The use of BBI technology in making *ad bellum* decisions may be expected to raise additional and complex issues. A state that is seeking to apply pressure against another state will, it is assumed, wish to avoid any suggestion that it is acting in breach of Article 2(4). This implies that its acts will need to be calibrated most carefully. Any use of technology that may precipitate the use of unlawful force will need to be avoided, and only technologies that are so mature that the state can have confidence that they will perform exactly as intended will be contemplated. States against which such acts are being contemplated or undertaken may hesitate to use these technologies for similar reasons. Victim states will wish to be sure that all senior military personnel, politicians and advisers who are involved in deciding whether the victim state should respond to the initiating act, and if so how, are properly 'linked-in'. That means both that all participants in the BBI process must receive the input of all others involved in making the relevant decisions while at the same time each participant in the BBI process must have confidence that their contribution is being accurately received by all other participants that need to receive it.

9.008 All involved participants must also be justifiably confident that all links are completely secure. It means being confident that all information that is necessary to support a proper decision is available to all those in the network of links who need access to it. It presupposes that, if the integrity of the links or if the security of the system is for any reason compromised, this will be made known immediately to those who need to know it. Face-to-face meetings to discuss these, and other similarly important kinds of issues may well sometimes be far from perfect. To put it bluntly, the loud but less reflective participants may drown out the more withdrawn but thoughtful. The point being made here is that unavoidable imperfections of that kind do not need to be added to by systemic issues.

9.009 Activity the aim of which is to disable key elements of the victim state's national defence infrastructure will generally be seen as amounting to a use of force. If a state were to become involved in some way in an ongoing non-international armed conflict (NIAC) that is taking place in another state, arming the organised armed group involved in the NIAC and providing it with military training might qualify as a use of force by the assisting state, particularly if other significant assistance is being given.[12] This is likely to be particularly significant in the context of the technologies discussed in this book because, in addition to the relevant equipment, the supplying state may also be supplying experts to ensure that the equipment is set up and then operated correctly. So imagine, for example, that State N supplies a weapon system that is BCI-enabled to Belligerent State A. Imagine that State N also sends a group of BCI experts to help State A to operate the weapons properly. This may, depending on the relevant facts, be classed as a use of force by State N. Policy decisions on how far to go in assisting another state are likely to be made by senior politicians, not, it is suggested, by brain technology systems. Care will be needed to ensure that the extent and nature of such assistance does not cause the assisting state to breach Article 2(4).

For an act to constitute a use of force, the operation must cross an international border or must be intended to do so.[13] If, for example, a military operator of State A's BCI-enabled missile system forms the intent or wish to fire a missile against a target in State B and if the BCI translates that wish into the corresponding act, the fact that the missile crosses the border into State B will satisfy this requirement. A more difficult scenario would involve the use of a BCI in which the State A operator is in State A territory but the missile is actually launched from a firing unit located inside State B. The very provisional view is that under the law as currently understood the fact that the intent or wish has crossed the border may not be sufficient for these purposes such that the event would not be regarded as a use of force or, for that matter, an armed attack. Imagine a different scenario in which an AB-enabled weapon system is launched by State A from State A territory. The AB facility within the weapon system decides to enter State B territory and while it is located in that territory the AB system makes a further decision to attack a building in State B causing damage and casualties. The author takes the view that the cross-border requirement is satisfied even though it was the AB system that decided to take that action without human input. **9.010**

The points made so far in this section deal with the important factors that determine whether an event is capable at law of being a use of force. A discrete issue is whether the victim state will choose to so characterise an act that satisfies those factors. In deciding whether to do so, a victim state is likely to be **9.011**

12 ICJ Nicaragua Judgment, n.3, para.228.

13 See UN General Assembly Resolution on the Definition of Aggression (A/RES/3314(XXV)), 14 December 1974 and ICJ Nicaragua Judgment, n.3, para.195.

influenced by disparate matters, including things lying outside the scope of this book.

9.012 Uses of force in necessary and proportionate self-defence or when authorised by the UN Security Council will not breach Article 2(4). A use of force may also be rendered lawful by the consent of the territorial state.

9.3 THREATS TO USE FORCE

9.013 If threatened forceful action, were it to be carried out, would breach Article 2(4), the threat itself will also be unlawful. Equally, if the threatened force would be lawful, for example, in necessary and proportionate self-defence, the threat to use that force will also be lawful. A threat necessarily requires the statement of an intention.[14] The Tallinn Manual experts considered that the 'essence of a threat is that it is explicitly or impliedly communicative in nature'.[15] Imagine that State A obtains BCI technology and the Minister of Defence of State A calls a press conference at which she announces that the BCI technology will be integrated to heavy machine-gun installations at various locations along its border with State B. During the press conference, the Minister is asked: 'So would you be planning to use these weapons?' and she answers: 'We are going to fire these things every time that State B's government says something we consider to be disrespectful about our country.' Those words amount to a clearly communicated threat to use armed force and making disrespectful remarks does not justify the use of force, so the Defence Minister's statements amount to an unlawful threat to use force.

9.014 Adjusting the scenario slightly, imagine that the heavy machine gun installations are put in place in secret. Thereafter, an AB system employed by State A detects that derogatory remarks about State A have been made by the State B Minister of Defence. The AB system therefore prepares a statement which purports to be a press release from the Prime Minister's office announcing that the weapons will be used in future every time that State B Ministers make disrespectful remarks about State A. The issue is whether it makes a difference that the purported press release was issued by an AB system. Clearly, it would be open to State A to dissociate itself from the false press release. If, however, for whatever reason it does not do so, the question is whether a use of force has

---

14 Award in the Arbitration regarding the Delimitation of the Maritime Boundary between Guyana and Suriname (Guyana v Suriname), Award of 17 September 2007, *Reports of the International Arbitral Awards*, Vol.XXX, 1, para.439. (Guyana v Suriname Award).

15 Tallinn Manual 2.0, n.11, Commentary accompanying Rule 70, para.4.

in fact been threatened. It will be for states to consider that issue. However, this point does rather demonstrate the importance of applying careful constraints on such systems, constraints the AB system is not able to circumvent.

A threatening statement will be communicative in nature if the words used are explicitly directed at a specific state or states, or if the acts constituting the threat show that the threatened unlawful force will be directed at a specific state or states. Actions, such as State A massing its troops on its border with State B in circumstances that make it clear that military action is being threatened against State B, are likely to satisfy this aspect of the rule.[16] **9.015**

A threat directed against a specific state or states to use unlawful force breaches Article 2(4) irrespective of whether it is accompanied by a coercive demand. **9.016**

9.4 ARMED ATTACK AND SELF-DEFENCE

Article 51 of the UN Charter is as follows: 'Nothing in the present Charter shall impair the inherent right of individual or collective self-defence if an armed attack occurs against a Member of the United Nations, until the Security Council has taken measures necessary to maintain international peace and security. Measures taken by Members in the exercise of this right of self-defence shall be immediately reported to the Security Council and shall not in any way affect the authority and responsibility of the Security Council under the present Charter to take at any time such action as it deems necessary in order to maintain or restore international peace and security.' **9.017**

An armed attack is occurring if the effects are being experienced, for example, if an explosion is occurring or injury, damage or destruction is being caused. An armed attack is also occurring if, for example, the munition carrying the warhead has been launched, fired or dropped but has yet to reach the target. Indeed, once the firing process, that is the sequence of actions that must, in the ordinary course of events, be completed as part of the firing of the weapon, that is that form an integral part of that firing process, is underway, the armed attack is taking place. **9.018**

Where an armed attack using a BCI-enabled weapon system is concerned, the author suspects that most states will regard the firing procedure as commencing for these purposes with the activation of the BCI link. States that take a **9.019**

16 Consider the massing of Russian armed forces on the border with Ukraine during January and the first three-and-a-half weeks of February 2022.

more restrictive view of the matter are likely to argue that the armed attack commences with the communication by the BCI operator of the thought or intent that causes the weapon to fire. Where an AB system is to be used for the armed attack, the armed attack will probably be interpreted by states as commencing when the AB system commences the process of locking onto its chosen target.

9.020 The important distinction will be between a preparatory act and the actual commencement of the attack process. This may well prove to be a difficult distinction to apply in the context of the technologies discussed in this book. If loading target data into a guidance system, for example, is an integral element of the actual firing of the weapon, that action arguably also becomes part of the actual conduct of the armed attack. This might lead to the conclusion that loading mission requirements and constraints into the mission control system of an AB-enabled weapon system would also be seen as part of the conduct of the subsequent attack, as opposed to mere preparation. The author is deliberately approaching these issues with hesitation. They are matters on which emerging state practice will be of critical importance. Maintaining system readiness is not part of the conduct of an attack because such maintenance constitutes preparation, not the conduct of an attack; maintenance of readiness would not therefore justify forceful self-defence action.

9.021 States also have a customary law right to use necessary and proportionate force in self-defence in response to an armed attack. This, of course, begs the question that we have been discussing, namely what constitutes an armed attack. The first point to make is that if the cross-border element discussed in section 9.2 is absent, that is if the attack is conducted entirely from within the target state, the forceful event cannot be an armed attack. The comments the author made in section 9.2 in relation to the use of AB technology within the victim state apply equally to armed attack.

9.022 The ICJ noted in its Nuclear Weapons Advisory Opinion that the prohibition of the use of force in Article 2(4) of the UN Charter, the inherent right of individual or collective self-defence in Article 51 and the lawful use of force envisaged in Article 42 apply 'to any use of force, regardless of the weapons employed'.[17] The use, therefore, of BCI, AB or BBI technology in connection with a use of force will not affect its potential classification also as an armed attack. The ICJ's observation does not suggest that a weapon must be used,

---

17 ICJ Nuclear Weapons Advisory Opinion, n.9, paras 38 and 39.

although a weapon or weapons of some kind are likely to be involved in the armed attack.

The effects caused by the attack will be an important factor in determining whether an armed attack has occurred. Whether novel or traditional weapon systems and methods are used, to be classed as an armed attack, the effects of the attack must reach the level that would normally be classed as an armed attack. So if State A's operator of a BCI-enabled missile system forms the intent to fire the missile at a civilian residential area, it will be the fact that the missile hits a medium-sized apartment block in a densely populated civilian area causing the collapse of the building and numerous deaths and injuries that would, the author believes, cause the event to be classed as an armed attack. **9.023**

The author takes the position that not all uses of force contrary to Article 2(4) rise to the level of an armed attack.[18] The scale and effects of the event[19] will be greater for armed attacks than for uses of force that are not armed attacks. This matters because victim states are only permitted to use force in self-defence in response to an armed attack. The ICJ discussed 'scale and effects' in its Nicaragua judgment and distinguished 'the most grave forms of the use of force (those constituting an armed attack) from other less grave forms'.[20] **9.024**

This causes one to wonder what grave scale and effects might look like. While the ICJ has not given detailed guidance on the matter, it has indicated that an attack on a single military platform or installation might qualify as an armed attack.[21] States will therefore wish to ensure that AB weapon systems that they operate in peacetime are reliably and consistently prevented from targeting platforms and that they are not able to circumvent that prohibition. The ICJ has also explained that the supply of arms and other support to armed bands and mere frontier incidents would be insufficient.[22] It has, however, been suggested that serious injury to, or death of, a number of persons or significant damage to, or destruction of, property would satisfy the requirement.[23] **9.025**

---

18 ICJ Nicaragua Judgment, n.3, para.191.
19 ICJ Nicaragua Judgment, ibid, para.195.
20 ICJ Nicaragua Judgment, ibid, para.191.
21 ICJ, Oil Platforms (Islamic Republic of Iran v. United States of America), Judgment, 6 November 2003 [2003] ICJ Reports 161, paras 57 and 61.
22 ICJ Nicaragua Judgment, n.3, paras 247 and 195 respectively.
23 Tallinn Manual 2.0, n.11, Commentary accompanying Rule 71, para.8.

9.026 A series of sufficiently related attacks which, individually, would not meet the armed attack threshold, might be considered cumulatively as having the required scale and effects.[24]

9.027 It will, in practice, be for the victim state to assess how to treat an event that, at law, is capable of being classed as an armed attack. In making this assessment, the state will no doubt take into account the severity of the consequences and a number of other relevant considerations, including the political and diplomatic context, the strategic position of the victim state, the relevant rhetoric of military and political leaders, the events leading up to the event being assessed, and the type of target that has been attacked and, perhaps, the nature and technological sophistication of the systems employed. It is an open question whether the use of brain technology to undertake an attack would render it more or less likely that the event would be classed as meeting the gravity required for an armed attack. What is being offered here is not a legal rule. It is merely a discussion of some of the things that a victim state may be expected to think about when deciding whether to treat as an armed attack an event that can legally be so classified. It must be stressed that the applicable international law, as discussed in this section, will determine whether an event is in fact an armed attack, and therefore whether the use of force in self-defence is a lawful option. It will, moreover, be for human decision-makers, almost certainly at the highest level of government, to determine whether an event amounts to an armed attack.

9.028 If an operation against the victim state causes no injury or damage but renders essential parts of its critical national infrastructure inoperable, this may, perhaps depending on which element of critical national infrastructure is affected and in exactly what way, be interpreted by the victim state as constituting an armed attack.[25] Victim states may well assume that the perpetrator intended to cause the damage and casualties arising from a violent act and will act accordingly. If it becomes clear that the relevant event was not intended, for example because it was a mistake, forceful action in self-defence would be prohibited as being unnecessary.[26] The classic examples of this would be:

1. a BCI operation in which the BCI misinterprets the intent or wish of the operator; and

---

24 Consider, in this regard, International Law Commission, *Responsibility of States for Internationally Wrongful Acts*, Annex to UN General Assembly Resolution 56/83, 12 December 2001, Article 15 (Breach consisting of a composite act).

25 Consider Tallinn Manual 2.0, n.11, Commentary accompanying Rule 71, para.12.

26 Note ICJ Oil Platforms Judgment, n.21, para.64.

2. an AB-enabled operation in which the AB goes outside its programmed constraints.

In each of these cases, if force is used that would satisfy the scale and effects and gravity requirements for an armed attack, the danger is that the victim state will use force in self-defence thereby unnecessarily triggering an international armed conflict the origin of which lies in an error. **9.029**

The actions of a non-state actor may constitute an armed attack. The activities of a private individual, of a contractor's employee or of members of an armed group can be attributed to a state, thereby becoming the acts of that state, if the individual, employee or group was sent by or on behalf of the state to undertake those activities. Attribution can also apply if the state is substantially involved in the activities.[27] Imagine, for example, State A has recently acquired BCI-enabled weapon systems but lacks the trained personnel to use them. It therefore contracts with a private citizen who is gifted in the use of BCI technology. The citizen is instructed to use the weapon to target a specific building in belligerent State B's territory, causing extensive damage and a large number of casualties. The attack would be attributable to State A and would have sufficiently grave consequences to constitute an armed attack.[28] **9.030**

Numerous states take the view that an attack undertaken by an armed group, without any participation by a state, can constitute an armed attack for the purposes of Article 51 and the customary law right to use force in self-defence. Some other states believe, however, that the notion of armed attack applies only in the case of a state-on-state activity and that violent acts by non-state actors are matters for law enforcement only, even where a cross-border element is present.[29] In considering these differing views, it is worth remembering that the Security Council has characterised terrorist acts by non-state actors as being capable of amounting to a threat to international peace. However, a number of states consider themselves entitled to resort to extra-territorial self-defence against non-state actors that have committed armed attacks against them or their allies.[30] In this context, reference should also be made to the **9.031**

27 ICJ Nicaragua Judgment, n.3, para.195; and UN General Assembly Resolution 3314(XXIX), 14 December 1974, Definition of Aggression, Annex, Art.3(g).

28 Tallinn Manual 2.0, n.11, Commentary accompanying Rule 71, para.17.

29 ICJ, Advisory Opinion on the Legal Consequences of the Construction of a Wall in the Occupied Palestinian Territory, 9 July 2004, [2004] ICJ Reports 136, 136, 139 (ICJ Palestine Wall Advisory Opinion).

30 State practice indicates the assertion by states of the right to take forceful action in self-defence in response to armed attacks by terrorist and other armed groups operating across borders when the government of the state where the threat is located is unwilling or unable to prevent the use of its territory for such attacks.

allied military activities against the so-called Islamic State in Syria in response to that group's armed attacks against Iraq.[31]

9.032 The sovereignty of the state from which the armed group operated must be properly respected, for example by giving that state a proper opportunity to deal with the matter by taking steps to prevent a repetition. Accordingly, the victim state must instruct the territorial state to stop the acts constituting the armed attack and must give it time in which to do so. This will reduce the risk of erroneous action in self-defence. However, the situation may be so clear, serious and urgent that it is unrealistic to expect the victim state to delay acting after issuing such an instruction.

9.033 Imagine that State A receives reliable intelligence from a source it has used in the past on several occasions indicating that State B has deployed an AB weapon system with a biological material in the warhead. The human source has told his State A handlers that the active agent in the biological weapon consists of a virus which will spread uncontrollably within populated areas, that the virus is fatal in most cases and that there is no known antidote. Another human intelligence (humint) source confirms this information and explains that the weapon will be fired at State A's capital city within the next couple of days. The urgency of the situation and the severity of the consequences of a successful use of the weapon are such that State A can use force in self-defence without having to issue a prior demand. Sometimes it will be necessary to take suitable precautions to confirm the veracity of the intelligence. In the circumstances described in the scenario, this may be unnecessary. The obligation is to consider carefully the information reasonably available to decision-makers at the relevant time; information that is only available after the event is irrelevant.

9.034 Views differ as to the action a victim state can lawfully take if the state from which the armed group operated is unable or unwilling to take effective preventive measures. Some states contend the victim state has the right to use

---

See UN Security Council documents: S/2014/695, dated 23 September 2014 (United States); S/2015/221, dated 31 March 2015 (Canada); S/2015/693, dated 9 September 2015 (Australia); S/2014/851, dated 26 November 2014 (UK); S/2015/688, dated 8 September 2015 (UK); S/2015/745, dated 9 September 2015 (France); S/2015/928, dated 3 December 2015 (UK); S/2015/946, dated 10 December 2015 (Germany); S/2016/34, dated 13 January 2016 (Denmark); S/2016/132, dated 10 February 2016 (The Netherlands); S/2016/513, dated 3 June 2016 (Norway); and S/2016/523, dated 9 June 2016 (Belgium).

31 Note that the terrorist attacks of 11 September 2001 in the US resulted in an activation of Article V of the North Atlantic Treaty, 4 April 1949, 34 UNTS 243, and terrorist attacks in Paris in November 2015 were considered armed attacks triggering the application of the common defence clause in Article 42(7) of the Treaty on European Union (Consolidated Version of the Treaty on European Union [2012] OJ C326/13). Consider also action against Kurdish fighters in Northern Iraq and in Syria by the Turkish armed forces and the recognition of Israel's right of self-defence in response to the Hamas attacks of 7 October 2023.

necessary and proportionate force in extra-territorial self-defence.[32] Other states object that this approach unacceptably loosens the prohibition of the use of force. A self-defence operation involving activity in a state to which the armed attack cannot be attributed can, however, be undertaken if that state consents.[33] It will, the author suggests, be a matter for human judgement whether the state that is hosting the group is indeed unable or unwilling and even if unwillingness or inability has been established, it will be for commanders or members of government at suitable levels of seniority to decide whether forceful defensive action is appropriate.

Imagine that a group of civilian brain technology and artificial intelligence (AI) specialists employed in State A by a research company decides to use an AB-enabled weapon system to target a radar early warning facility in State B, destroying the radar installation and causing numerous deaths and injuries among personnel in another co-located military facility. State A authorities were not aware in advance of the actions taken by the group. State A is disputing with State B sovereignty over a piece of land at the border between the two countries. When State B authorities inform State A's government of what has happened and demand that they take appropriate preventive action within the next seven days, the State A official government spokesman says: 'That's all too bad but it ain't our problem. No, we ain't doing nothing.' The attack cannot be attributed to State A. The authorities of State A have been given a suitable opportunity to take required preventive action but have declined to do so. Some states, such as the US, say State B has the legal right to use necessary and proportionate force against the group on State A territory in self-defence. Other states disagree. **9.035**

The author believes that if an individual or small group of individuals were to perpetrate an attack with the kind of consequence discussed in this section, a law enforcement approach is the more likely response.[34] **9.036**

Attacks targeting, for example, government employees and personnel or governmental non-commercial facilities, that are located outside the territory of the victim state are, depending on the extent of the damage caused, the status **9.037**

32 Consider the 'Bethlehem Principles': see Daniel Bethlehem, 'Principles Relevant to the Scope of a State's Right of Self-Defense Against an Imminent or Actual Armed Attack by Non-State Actors' (2012) 106 *American Journal of International Law* 1.

33 The primary legal justification for the use of force would be the territorial state's consent, not self-defence.

34 Consider Tallinn Manual 2.0, n.11, para.20, 346.

of the targeted individuals, and any political motive, capable of being armed attacks against that state.[35]

9.038 The Article 51 right of a victim state of an armed attack to use force in self-defence applies until the Security Council has taken the measures that would render the use of force in self-defence unnecessary. The ICJ has stated that the reporting obligation in the second sentence of Article 51 does not exist in customary law[36] but has implied that a failure to make the required report may call into question whether the state was in fact acting in self-defence.[37]

9.039 The ICJ has described armed attacks as 'the most grave forms of the use of force'.[38] This leads to the conclusion that, while any armed attack conducted by or attributable to a state will constitute a use of force, not all uses of force will amount to an armed attack. However, the US considers that any unlawful use of force is capable of being regarded as an armed attack triggering the right of the victim state to use force in self-defence.[39] The author rejects that approach.

9.040 The ICJ has stated that Article 51 of the UN Charter applies to 'any use of force, regardless of the weapons employed'.[40] This leads to the conclusion that the legal position set forth in this section also applies to the threat or use of force involving any of the technologies that are discussed in this book.

9.041 It is unlikely that a responsible victim state would entrust to an AB system the assessment of whether a use of force satisfies the 'most grave' criterion. This is peculiarly a matter for human decision-making at the senior, that is strategic, level.

9.5 IMMINENT ARMED ATTACK

9.042 Article 51 refers to 'if an armed attack occurs' but also mentions the inherent nature of a state's right to use force in self-defence in such circumstances. The key question that then arises is whether a state must wait until a weapon's firing procedure has been commenced before it is permitted to use self-defence force. It must be remembered that the inherent customary right of states to use force

---

35 Tallinn Manual 2.0, n.11, Commentary accompanying Rule 71, para.22.

36 ICJ Nicaragua Judgment, n.3, para.235.

37 ICJ Nicaragua Judgment, n.3, para.265.

38 ICJ Nicaragua Judgment, n.3, para.191.

39 Consider US DoD, *Law of War Manual* (June 2015, as subsequently amended), para.1.11.5.2; A D Sofaer, 'International Law and the *Use of Force*' (1988) 82 *Proceedings of the ASIL Annual Meeting* 420, 422.

40 ICJ Nuclear Weapons Advisory Opinion, n.9, para.39.

in self-defence against an armed attack is independent of Article 51. Common sense suggests that if waiting until an armed attack actually commences will preclude the taking of effective action to prevent its grave consequences, limiting the defensive right in that way would be inconsistent with the inherent nature of the right of forceful defence. The author's view, therefore, is that there is indeed an inherent right of states to use necessary and proportionate force in self-defence if an armed attack is imminent.[41] However, there is an alternative view that the use of force in self-defence is only permissible if an armed attack has actually been initiated.[42] Maybe the development in recent years of increasingly rapid forms of attack, such as cyber attacks and the use of hypersonic missiles, in which states are given very little practical time for defensive response, will cause most states to reject the alternative, more restrictive view. That speed factor may also cause states to rely on BCI, AB and BBI technologies to enable timely decisions and action. While humans may be making the ultimate decisions, they will rely on the technology, which must therefore be robust against external interference, must reliably perform its tasks with accuracy and must be free from bias.

Any discussion of imminence must take into account the core purpose of the UN, namely the maintenance of international peace and security. An exces- **9.043**
sively liberal interpretation of imminence may prejudice that core purpose by permitting the use of force in too great a set of circumstances. An excessively restrictive interpretation may be seen by states as prejudicing their national security. It has been suggested that forceful action in self-defence should be lawful if 'the attacker is clearly committed to launching an armed attack and the victim State will lose its opportunity to effectively defend itself unless it acts'.[43] This 'last window of opportunity' may be when an attack is about to be launched or may come earlier. It would reflect the urgency of the need for effective action to be taken, while also recognising that, the longer the time interval before the armed attack is expected to occur, the more likely it is that this is not the last window of opportunity. Was it therefore reasonable for the victim state to conclude that it was indeed acting during that last window? If AB systems are supporting human decisions, is the input from those systems reliable and accurate? If BBI systems are being used to facilitate the human decisions, are those systems operating properly and, if that is not the case, is

41 Indeed, this is arguably implicit in the correspondence between Lord Ashburton and Daniel Webster arising from the Caroline incident and is reinforced by state practice.

42 Consider Tallinn Manual 2.0, n.11, Commentary accompanying Rule 73, para.3, citing I Brownlie, *International Law and the Use of Force by States* (Oxford University Press, 1963), 275–8.

43 Tallinn Manual 2.0, n.11, Commentary accompanying Rule 73, para.4.

the supported human decision-maker made aware of the deterioration in the provided support? These are among the matters that need to be considered.

9.6 NECESSITY AND PROPORTIONALITY

9.044 Customary law provides that a state acting in self-defence may only use the force that is necessary and proportionate.[44] As to necessity, force must be needed 'to successfully repel an imminent armed attack or defeat one that is under way'.[45] Non-forceful measures may also be employed, but if force is to be used in self-defence, the necessity element in the rule requires that non-forceful measures alone will not be enough to deal with the situation.

9.045 Consequently, if the assessment is that non-forceful measures can prevent or stop the imminent armed attack, using force in self-defence would not comply with the necessity requirement. In the famous letter of 1842 from Daniel Webster, the US Secretary of State, to his British opposite number, Lord Ashburton, Webster associated the right of self-defence with 'the necessity of self-defense, instant, overwhelming, leaving no choice of means, and no moment for deliberation'. He added that 'the act justified by the necessity of self-defense must be limited by that necessity, and kept clearly within it'.[46] It will be for the victim state to perceive whether forceful action in self-defence is necessary. It will base its assessment on the information that is reasonably available to it and must act reasonably when deciding whether force is required.

9.046 Imagine a situation in which televisual sensors on drones operated by State A have shown that State B is moving a BCI-enabled inter-continental ballistic missile to its launch facility. Human intelligence from within State B's military HQ states that a launch of the missile is timed for the following day and that a university campus within State A is to be the target. State A comes to the reasonable conclusion that non-forceful measures will not be sufficient to prevent the launch. This means that the use of force by State A to stop the armed attack will meet the requirement of necessity. This is a judgement that State A can only make on the basis of the information at its disposal at the time when it makes that decision.

---

44 ICJ Nicaragua Judgment, n.3, 176, 194; ICJ Nuclear Weapons Advisory Opinion, n.9, para.41; ICJ Oil Platforms Judgment, n.21, paras 43, 73–4, 76.

45 Tallinn Manual 2.0, n.11, Commentary accompanying Rule 72, para.2.

46 Letter dated 27 July 1842, from Daniel Webster to Lord Ashburton, *British & Foreign State Papers* Brit. & For. State Papers, Vol.XXX, 193–4 (1841–42).

If the necessity criterion is satisfied, the force actually used must not exceed in extent, duration and degree that which is needed to stop the armed attack or prevent the imminent armed attack. How much force is required will depend on the circumstances and will not be determined by the degree of force used in the armed attack; neither will the kind of force used in self-defence be dictated by that used in the armed attack. Accordingly, while the armed attack may have involved the use of BCI-enabled weapons, the force used in self-defence may well employ more traditional weapon systems. **9.047**

The victim state's assessment of the kind and degree of force that is required in self-defence will necessarily be subjective based on information that was reasonably available at the time of the decision. Information that only becomes available later will not affect the lawfulness of the decision to use the relevant amount of force. **9.048**

9.7 IMMEDIACY

The circumstances may be such that a victim state requires time in order to be able to take forceful action in self-defence. It may be unclear which state perpetrated the armed attack; it may take time to determine which targets should be attacked in self-defence; the units to be used for the defensive use of force may need time to prepare; and achieving ministerial agreement on the action to be taken may take time. **9.049**

An important factor to consider will be the extent of the resulting delay between the armed attack and the forceful action in self-defence. If a substantial period of time elapses after the armed attack, the immediacy requirement[47] may not be satisfied with the result that a subsequent use of force in self-defence may be unlawful. Much will depend on what is occurring during the period of delay. If there are continuing threats or acts by the aggressor state showing that a further attack can be anticipated, the use of force in self-defence is likely to be lawful. Inevitably, however, much will depend on the particular circumstances and on the reasonableness of the victim state's conclusion that further attacks are likely to follow. Planners, commanders and operators that are involved in deciding on or implementing self-defence action will need to be sensitive to the immediacy requirement. It may be obvious to human decision-makers at **9.050**

47 See Tallinn Manual 2.0, n.11, Rule 73, paras 12 and 13; T D Gill, *Legal Basis of the Right of Self-defence Under the UN Charter and Under Customary International Law* (University of Amsterdam Digital Academic Repository, 2015), 223.

an early stage that an event the consequences of which rise to the level of an armed attack has occurred. What may be less obvious is whether a state or armed group was responsible, and if so, which one. The technologies discussed in this book may facilitate the making of timely assessments.

9.8 COLLECTIVE SELF-DEFENCE

9.051 Article 51 of the UN Charter and customary law also provide for the inherent right of collective self-defence if a state that is the victim of an armed attack requests assistance from another state. The request for assistance must have been made by the state that is the victim of an armed attack to the assisting state before the latter is permitted to come to its aid by using force.[48] Each state involved in a collective self-defence operation must satisfy itself that the right to use force in collective self-defence applies in the prevailing circumstances.

9.052 It has been suggested that the force used by the assisting state must comply with any restrictions specified by the victim state.[49] There is limited authority for that view.

9.053 States may develop a collective self-defence arrangement to provide for potential future armed attacks against one or more participants. For example, Article 5 of the North Atlantic Treaty states that 'an armed attack against one or more of them in Europe or North America shall be considered an attack against them all and consequently they agree that, if such an armed attack occurs, each of them, in exercise of the right of individual or collective self-defence recognized by Article 51 of the Charter of the United Nations, will assist the Party or Parties so attacked'.[50] Once it has been established that a relevant armed attack has occurred, consultations among the participants will determine what assistance each will give. The requirements as to necessity, proportionality, immediacy, and the obligation to report to the UN Security Council also apply to collective self-defence. The potential use by the victim or assisting states of the technologies discussed in this book does not affect the points made in this section. Moreover, the issuing of a request for assistance, the decision of a state as to whether to provide such assistance and consideration by the victim state of possible limitations to impose on action in collective self-defence are all, in the opinion of the author, matters that are likely

---

48 ICJ Nicaragua Judgment, n.3, para.199 and customary law.

49 See Tallinn Manual 2.0, n.11, Commentary accompanying Rule 74, para.3.

50 North Atlantic Treaty, 4 April 1949, 34 UNTS 243, Art.5.

to require human decision-making at a senior level in the governments of the respective states.

9.9 REPORTING SELF-DEFENCE ACTION TO THE UN SECURITY COUNCIL

The second element of Article 51 of the UN Charter stipulates that a state **9.054** that exercises the right to use force in self-defence must immediately report the measures taken to the UN Security Council. The requirement here is to inform, and there is no stipulation as to the mechanism that must be used to convey the relevant information. If BCI technology were to be incorporated into a state's diplomatic communications system so that the thought or intent of a suitably senior official of the state could be translated into a textual communication to the Security Council containing the required information, this would, in principle, fulfil the obligation in the second part of Article 51. Equally, State B's strategic defence system might include an AB system which is programmed to initiate forceful action in self-defence if, say, neighbouring State A were to take specified action that the AB system has been trained to recognise as amounting to an armed attack, for example a military invasion on its northern border. That programming might sensibly include an instruction to the AB system to send the required notification to the Security Council, and the author suggests that could, if suitably expressed, satisfy the Article 51 obligation.

The Security Council retains the authority and responsibility to take the action **9.055** it deems necessary for the maintenance or restoration of international peace and security. This reporting rule does not reflect customary law.[51] When individual or collective self-defence measures are taken, the obligation to report arises. A failure to report once forceful self-defence action has been taken breaches Article 51 but does not per se render the defensive action unlawful. Notwithstanding such failure, the victim state may continue to take self-defence action that complies with the necessity, proportionality, imminence and immediacy requirements set forth above. The potential use by the victim or assisting states of the technologies discussed in this book does not affect the notification obligation discussed in this section.

51 ICJ Nicaragua Judgment, n.3, para.235.

9.10 UN SECURITY COUNCIL ACTION

9.056 The UN Security Council has the responsibility under Article 39 of the UN Charter to determine if there has been a threat to the peace, a breach of the peace or an act of aggression.[52] If the Security Council makes such a determination, it may, under Article 41 of the UN Charter: 'decide what measures not involving the use of armed force are to be employed to give effect to its decisions, and it may call upon the Members of the United Nations to apply such measures. These may include complete or partial interruption of economic relations and of rail, sea, air, postal, telegraphic, radio, and other means of communication, and the severance of diplomatic relations.'

9.057 If, therefore, an operator uses a BCI-enabled weapon system to perpetrate what the UN Security Council judges to be a breach of the peace, threat to the peace or act of aggression, the fact that the weapon system involved BCI technology will not prevent the UN Security Council from making a determination under Article 39. An interesting question would be at what stage the act of an operator of a BCI system becomes a threat to the peace. Does this arise, for example, when the thought or intent of the operator is formed? Alternatively, is there a threat to the peace when an operator switches on a BCI system that is linked to a weapon system, or to a weapon system of a specified kind? Similarly, does the deployment of an AB system that is equipped with a particular kind of weapon constitute a threat to the peace or is some further action of a threatening nature required? These are all matters that the UN Security Council may need to consider. It will be for the Security Council to make the relevant determinations.

9.058 Having made the Article 39 determination, the Security Council may take appropriate action as it sees fit under either Article 41 or Article 42. If the aggressor state were to use BBI technology in the decision-making process that leads to the activity that triggered the Article 39 determination, this will be equally irrelevant to the powers of the Security Council. It will be for the Security Council to judge whether activities involving the technologies discussed in this book constitute a threat to the peace, breach of the peace or an act of aggression. Self-evidently, it will be important for states carefully to control activities involving BCI- and AB-enabled weapon systems and carefully to ensure that BBI decision-making is properly conducted, in all three

52 Article 39 states: 'The Security Council shall determine the existence of any threat to the peace, breach of the peace, or act of aggression and shall make recommendations, or decide what measures shall be taken in accordance with Articles 41 and 42, to maintain or restore international peace and security.'

cases with a view to preventing breaches of or threats to the peace and events capable of interpretation as acts of aggression.

It should be emphasised that the list of measures under Article 41 is illustrative, not exhaustive. Other categories of non-forceful action might be decided upon by the Security Council. As the technologies discussed in this book mature, it will become clear whether they will facilitate the employment of the non-forceful measures that would be relevant under Article 41. In principle, it would seem likely that AB-controlled systems could, for example, be used to interrupt communication systems, such as cyber, postal, air and maritime communications and transport systems. However, a more specific discussion of this topic should wait until the relevant applications of the technologies have been demonstrated. The Security Council will choose the measures it thinks to be suitable for dealing effectively with the relevant situation. **9.059**

While 'Members of the United Nations agree to accept and carry out the decisions of the Security Council in accordance with the present Charter',[53] the manner of implementing the Security Council's decisions is a matter for national discretion, to be decided upon in light of the attendant circumstances. Legislation, regulations, instructions, military orders and other measures may be required, and the use of the technologies discussed in this book cannot, the author suggests, be ruled out. **9.060**

9.11 FORCEFUL ACTION BY THE UN SECURITY COUNCIL

Article 42 of the UN Charter states: 'Should the Security Council consider that measures provided for in Article 41 would be inadequate or have proved to be inadequate, it may take such action by air, sea, or land forces as may be necessary to maintain or restore international peace and security. Such action may include demonstrations, blockade, and other operations by air, sea, or land forces of Members of the United Nations.' **9.061**

The process therefore starts with the Security Council determining under Article 39 the existence of a threat to the peace, a breach of the peace or an act of aggression. If it makes that determination, the Security Council must then decide whether non-forceful measures would be inadequate to deal in an effective way with the situation, or, if they have been tried, whether they have proved to be inadequate. If it considers that non-forceful measures will not **9.062**

53 UN Charter, n.4, Art.25.

be effective in maintaining or restoring international peace and security, the Security Council may authorise the use of force.

9.063 Imagine a situation in which States A and B are involved in a border dispute. State A's Prime Minister has issued threatening statements and State B has deployed some additional armed forces units to border areas. Violent demonstrations are taking place in the capital cities of States A and B and State B's Minister of Defence has discussed a possible incursion into State A territory while being interviewed on national television. If the Security Council determines that the situation constitutes a threat to the peace and concludes that forceful measures are required, it would likely issue a Resolution in suitable terms. Such Resolutions often refer to the taking of 'all necessary measures' or 'all necessary means' (usually understood as permitting the use of armed force)[54] and will generally specify the purpose to be achieved. If such a resolution is issued, the author suggests that all necessary measures/means would be interpreted as potentially including BCI- and AB-enabled systems. It will be for the states acting under the resolution to determine what systems they need to use to give effect to the terms of the resolution.

9.064 As noted earlier, if a state concludes that UN Security Council-authorised forceful action under Article 42 is failing to protect it from unlawful aggression, it retains the right to take forceful action in self-defence.

9.065 Article 103 of the UN Charter states: 'In the event of a conflict between the obligations of the Members of the United Nations under the present Charter and their obligations under any other international agreement, their obligations under the present Charter shall prevail.' While the Security Council cannot deviate from *jus cogens* rules,[55] it need not consider states' obligations under other legal instruments when deciding on Article 42 action. Moreover, a state may only disregard its duties under other international agreements if there is an actual conflict with its UN Charter duties, and even then only for so long as such conflict continues.

9.066 Article 53(1) of the UN Charter provides: 'The Security Council shall, where appropriate, utilize ... regional arrangements or agencies for enforcement action under its authority. But no enforcement action shall be taken under

---

54 UN Security Council Resolution 678/1990, 29 November 1990; UN Security Council Resolution 1973/2011, 17 March 2011. Bearing in mind the current political and diplomatic frictions between major states, the author suggests that it is unlikely, but not impossible, that such a resolution will be issued in the foreseeable future.

55 Tallinn Manual 2.0, n.11, Commentary accompanying Rule 76, para.9.

regional arrangements or by regional agencies without the authorization of the Security Council …' Clearly, authorisation from the Security Council must come first before enforcement action under Articles 41 or 42 by a regional arrangement or agency can take place. Article 48 of the Charter specifies that 'action required to carry out the decisions of the Security Council for the maintenance of international peace and security shall be taken by all the Members of the United Nations or by some of them, as the Security Council may determine'[56] and that '[s]uch decisions shall be carried out by the Members of the United Nations directly and through their action in the appropriate international agencies of which they are members'.[57] So any group of states can be authorised by the Security Council to take Article 41 or 42 enforcement action.

56 UN Charter, n.4, Art.48(1).
57 Ibid, Art.48(2).

10

HUMAN BRAIN ENHANCEMENT

10.1 INTRODUCTION

10.001 In this chapter we take a brief look at technologies that are intended to enhance the performance of the human brain. At the commencement of this discussion, it is important to distinguish between, respectively, treating and enhancing the brain. Treatment for the purposes of this book consists of addressing a deficit in performance that may have been caused by injury, illness, birth defect or some other adverse cause. The treatment may include the curing of the illness, the healing or repairing of defects or wounds, including wounds to the brain and nervous system, and other action to restore cognitive performance to pre-existing or normal, healthy levels. Brain enhancement, in contrast, is what this chapter is about and consists, for the purposes of the following discussion, of the use of substances, systems or processes to increase the cognitive performance of the relevant individual above levels that would normally be expected of such an individual in a healthy condition.[1]

1 See I M Puscas, 'Military Human Enhancement', in W H Boothby (ed), *New Technology and the Law in War and Peace* (Cambridge University Press, 2019), 182, 187. 'Those enhanced abilities are also often above the level that the said individual could achieve by rigorous training alone': Puscas, ibid. As to the notion of human enhancement, see R Liivoja, *Being More than You Can Be: Enhancement of Warfighters and the Law of*

It is fair to say that there are, as shall be demonstrated, potential risks and benefits associated with brain enhancement techniques. Enhancing cognitive performance may enable tired, distracted or over-worked combatants to continue to make carefully considered decisions for longer, more protracted periods of time or in more difficult circumstances thus potentially promoting, rather than degrading, compliance with the law of armed conflict (LOAC). Such techniques may also improve the judgement that decision-makers employ in combat. They may improve the alertness of combatants, enhance their resistance to stress and fatigue, help to reduce mistakes, promote concentration on the task in hand and enable war fighters to control aggression. These would all seem to be positive possibilities. Whether they will materialise will, of course, depend on numerous factors, notably the characteristics of the specific enhancement technology and its effects on particular individuals. As Xiaolong Sun and Hua Yuan point out, military personnel need to be able to process complex environments and multiple critical events concurrently and over extended periods. Enhancing cognitive performance is therefore of paramount importance, 'enabling them to execute tasks and endure life-threatening situations successfully'.[2] **10.002**

There are, however, risks associated with brain enhancement, and the acceptability of a particular technology will require a careful assessment of the technology itself, its effects on individuals and their performance, on the long-term implications for such individuals, and on a consideration of the relationship between what are considered to be the likely benefits of the technique and the risks associated with its employment.[3] **10.003**

A further but important preliminary issue is how to classify brain enhancement technologies. In 2016, Heather Harrison Dinnis and Jann Kleffner identified the crossroads at which a person becomes a weapon by virtue of enhancement as being the point where 'enhancement technologies transmute humans into mere objects for the purpose of the law of armed conflict'.[4] The author consid- **10.004**

Armed Conflict, Law and the Future of War Research Paper, University of Queensland Law School (April 2020), 3–6, available at https://papers.ssrn.com/sol3/papers.cfm?abstract_id=3738499.

2 X Sun and H Yuan, 'Promising Applications of Non-invasive Brain Stimulation on Military Cognition Enhancement: A Long Way To Go' (2023) 36(5) Gen. Psychiatr e101264, available at https://pmc.ncbi.nlm.nih.gov/articles/PMC10618962/.

3 In this regard, it is important to note that the employment of an enhancement that diminishes the ability to comply with the LOAC is likely to be unlawful. Note Rain Liivoja's discussion of this issue: n.1, 13, citing the supply to combatants of drugs that increase the likelihood of infringements as an example that would conflict with that requirement of the LOAC.

4 H A Harrison Dinniss and J K Kleffner, 'Soldier 2.0: Military Human Enhancement Technologies' (2016) 92 International Law Studies 432, 438.

ers that none of the substances discussed in section 10.2 below have that effect. Where the technologies discussed in section 10.3 are concerned, the judgment will, in practice, need to be made by reference to the specific technology. However, to the extent that the human being determines the action that is to be taken and is merely assisted by the enhancement, the individual will not become a weapon or part of a weapon.

10.005 The author takes the view that if the enhancement integrates the human being with a weapon in such a way that the human enhancement renders the human being part of the firing mechanism[5] of a weapon, this would cause the human being to become part of that weapon system. In the different situation in which the human being is merely enabled by the enhancement to think clearly for longer periods, to restrain their aggression, cope with stress or identify targets more reliably, this will not, in the author's view, cause the individual to become part of the weapon system. The linked but distinct question of at what point an enhancement represents a method of warfare is discussed in sections 10.2 and 10.3 by reference to each category of enhancement technology.[6]

10.006 The status of a new substance or technology under the LOAC as weapon, means or method of warfare has obvious importance because these are the three things that trigger the obligation to conduct a legal review under Article 36 of Additional Protocol I to the Geneva Conventions 1949 (API). The author would, however, point out that under common Article 1 to the Geneva Conventions 1949, under Article 1(1) of API and, arguably, under the Martens Clause, there is the more general duty on all states to respect and to ensure respect for the Conventions, for the Protocol and, arguably, for international law in general. There is, therefore, an obligation on all states to satisfy themselves that, by adopting a particular brain enhancement technology, they are not breaching the international law rules that bind them. It is on this general assumption that the following sections of this chapter are based.

10.007 Another classification issue arises when one considers that the technologies discussed in this chapter are likely to have the effect of causing an individual who appears to be a normal combatant with normal combatant's capabilities and limitations to become an individual who is able to outperform unenhanced persons in what may prove to be key respects. From the perspective of the adverse party, there may be an element of deception inherent in this, and the

---

5 A distinction must be made between a BCI which is translating the thought or intent of the operator into action by the platform or weapon and the actual incorporation of the human into the firing mechanism.

6 Note the discussion in Liivoja, n.1, 9–11.

issue becomes how that deception should be classified. Perfidy is not involved here so long as there is no misrepresentation as to protected status under the LOAC.[7] Enhancements that promote concentration, endurance, decision-making skills, wakefulness and so on do not, per se, involve misrepresentation as to LOAC protected status. An enhanced soldier might of course make such a misrepresentation, but that is a different matter. Accordingly, and because they also do not, as such, breach LOAC, the enhancements discussed in this chapter will generally be classed, for these purposes, as ruses of war.[8] Ruses of war are not prohibited.[9]

10.2 ALCOHOL AND DRUGS

The idea of enhancing neural capabilities for military purposes is nothing new. **10.008**
Ioana Maria Puscas traces that history from the Napoleonic Wars to more recent times, showing that alcohol and drugs have been employed, with varying levels of effectiveness, to promote, for example, aggressiveness, endurance and efficiency.[10] During the Vietnam War, some US armed forces members, for example some air crew, used stimulants in the form of dextroamphetamines, such as Dexedrine,[11] to counteract the effects of sleep deprivation and promote alertness.[12] Modafinil has also been shown to have beneficial effects on spatial planning,[13] working memory, cognitive performance, alertness and vigilance.[14] There are, however, indications that while Modafinil may

7 Consider Protocol Additional to the Geneva Conventions of 12 August 1949, and Relating to the Protection of Victims of International Armed Conflicts, Geneva, 8 June 1977, 1125 UNTS 3 (Additional Protocol I or API), Art.37(1).

8 Consider API, ibid, Art.37(2).

9 API, ibid, but see other legal considerations discussed in the following sections of the chapter.

10 Puscas, n.1, 187–90. See also H Goodley, *Pharmacological Performance Enhancement and the Military* (Chatham House, 11 November 2020), available at https://www.chathamhouse.org/2020/11/pharmacological-performance-enhancement-and-military/02-brief-history, Ch.2.

11 Ł Kamieński, *Shooting Up. A History of Drugs and War* (Oxford University Press, 2016), 189.

12 P Lin and others, *Enhanced warfighters: Risk, Ethics and Policy*, Report prepared for the Greenwall Foundation (13 January 2013), available at https://case.edu/law/sites/default/files/2021-01/mehlman%20CLE%202-2021.pdf, 6 and A Estrada, 'Modafinil as a Replacement for Dextroamphetamine for Sustaining Alertness in Military Helicopter Pilots' (2012) 83(6) *Aviation, Space and Environmental Medicine* 557.

13 D Turner and others, 'Cognitive Enhancing Effects of Modafinil in Healthy Volunteers' (2003) 165 *Psychopharmacology* 260–69; as to effects on memory, see U Müller and others, 'Effects of Modafinil on Working Memory Processes in Humans' (2004) 177 *Psychopharmacology* 161–9. Note also Y Shereshevsky, *Are All Soldiers Created Equal? – On the Equal Application of the Law to Enhanced Soldiers* (3 September 2020), available at https://papers.ssrn.com/sol3/papers.cfm?abstract_id=3684645, later published in the *Virginia Journal of International Law*, 7.

14 J K Walsh and others, 'Modafinil Improves Alertness, Vigilance, and Executive Function During Simulated Night Shifts' (2004) 27(3) *Sleep* 434–9. 'Nootropics may also have negative effects, such as

increase the quantity of cognitive work it may decrease its quality,[15] which rather supports the need, identified in section 10.1, for a careful analysis of both perceived benefits and linked risks before the use of brain enhancement techniques is decided upon.

10.009 It will also be important to consider whether there has been sufficient research into the potential side-effects of a specific brain enhancement substance or technique. At the risk of stating the obvious, if there has been inadequate research into the risks associated with taking a substance, or if the potential adverse consequences that may follow a brain enhancement procedure have been inadequately tested and evaluated, it will not be possible properly to brief the soldier in advance of the commencement of the enhancement procedure with the consequence that any consent thereto given by that soldier is likely to be under-informed and therefore invalid. This is a most important point because a review of the literature suggests that research on these matters is somewhat lacking.

10.010 The Australian Alcohol and Drug Foundation describes cognitive enhancers, also known as nootropics, as drugs used in an attempt to improve memory, increase mental alertness and concentration and boost energy levels and wakefulness. 'Claims that nootropics improve a healthy person's cognitive processes and performance are weak whereas the side-effects do pose health risks.'[16] It would seem to the author that this assessment should be considered with great care by anyone tasked with giving legal advice as to the acceptability of such substances. Of course, the focus of any such advice will be on the particular substance or product, and on the data derived from testing and evaluation of it, but maybe some scepticism will be called for.

10.011 Drugs might also be used to reduce the physiological response to stress associated with military operations by seeking to prevent excessively aggressive

---

long-term cognitive decline, reduced learning ability or addiction': J Berry, 'What Are Nootropics or "'Smart Drugs"', *Medical News Today*, 25 October 2024, available at https://www.medicalnewstoday.com/articles/326379; see also F Schifano and others, 'Benefits and Harms of "Smart Drugs" (Nootropics) in Healthy Individuals' (2022) 82(6) *Drugs* 633–47, available at https://pubmed.ncbi.nlm.nih.gov/35366192/.

15 E Bowman and others, 'Not So Smart? Smart Drugs Increase the Level but Decrease the Quality of Cognitive Effort' (2023) 9 Sci. Adv. eadd4165.

16 'What Are Nootropics?', *Alcohol and Drug Foundation*, 11 February 2025, available at https://adf.org.au/drug-facts/cognitive-enhancers/#:~:text=Nootropic%20also%20known%20as%20'cognitive,boost%20energy%20levels%20and%20wakefulness. Note also, as Shereshevsky points out, the possibility that a pharmaceutical enhancement affects the mental state of the enhanced soldier 'to a degree that poses questions regarding their criminal culpability': Shereshevsky, n.13, 11.

reactions.[17] Other substances, such as oxytocin, that tend to promote trust and social bonding, might be employed to promote unit cohesion.[18] Another substance, propranolol, could reduce the mental casualties of war, thereby making war more humane.[19] It will, the author suggests, be important for anyone giving advice on such a procurement to consider the immediate consequences for the individual of the substance, that is the short-term effects. Where, as is likely, it is uncertain whether known side-effects will affect a specific individual, it will be necessary for safeguards to be in place so that if adverse reactions to the drug materialise, these can be dealt with promptly. Advisers will wish to know that there are techniques in place for dealing satisfactorily with such adverse reactions in a timely way. Such advisers will also need to receive authoritative data on the long-term medical and psychological consequences of taking such substances and of ceasing to take them, particularly after they have been taken for a protracted period. Measures that are available to mitigate any such adverse consequences together with information as to their effectiveness will also be important considerations.

The application of drugs to a combatant to enable them to perform better or for longer periods does not, per se, amount to a weapon.[20] Specifically, the mere fact that a soldier's cognitive performance has been enhanced, either generally or in specific conditions, does not cause the relevant soldier to become part of a weapon system. Harrison Dinniss and Kleffner consider that human enhancement technology can be classified as a method of warfare 'if and when their use constitutes an integral part of offensive activities at the strategic and tactical levels'.[21] On balance, the author takes the view that the use of the stimulant drug is facilitating a military activity, that is the method, rather than a method of warfare per se. However, a State Party to API that considers that the use of a particular enhancement technology that it is acquiring constitutes a method of warfare[22] would be required by Article 36 of API to conduct a weapon review. It would be necessary for the state to consider whether any of **10.012**

17 See the brief discussion of drugs such as propranolol in Y Adleff-Genot, 'Enhanced Soldiers and the Dehumanization of War', *AOAV*, 31 January 2025, available at https://aoav.org.uk/2025/enhanced-soldiers-and-the-dehumanisation-of-war/.

18 Adleff-Genot, ibid.

19 Goodley, n.10, Ch.4. As Goodley points out, 'this blunting of the senses in war could have damaging potential for the honourable conduct of soldiers': ibid.

20 Harrison Dinniss and Kleffner, n.4, 438. Harrison Dinniss and Kleffner express the view that a BCI that is the interface through which a weapon is operated is likely to form, as a result, a part of the weapon system. The reader is referred to section 6.2 for a discussion of whether a human brain, by virtue of the use of brain technology, becomes part of a weapon or weapon system.

21 Harrison Dinniss and Kleffner, ibid, 439.

22 On that issue, see the discussion in section 10.11 below.

the international law rules by which it is bound either prohibit the employment of the substance or restrict its lawful circumstances of use. The recognised criteria that are usually applied in weapon reviews and which are discussed in Chapter 6 would be of limited relevance. Drug-induced enhancements would not directly influence the injury or suffering to which enemy combatants are being exposed. They would also not, per se, necessarily render attack operations by the enhanced personnel indiscriminate by nature – indeed, they might, in some contexts, have the opposite effect. There are no environmental protection implications and there are no specific rules of the LOAC that prohibit or restrict the use of such substances by the combatant personnel belonging to a party to an armed conflict.

10.013 The more general duty on parties to armed conflicts to comply with the LOAC has already been pointed out. On a separate point, members of the armed forces are required to comply with lawful orders.[23] They have the right to refuse to take specific medication, including performance-enhancing drugs,[24] but can lawfully be ordered to participate in military operations the safety and successful performance of which may be enhanced if they were to take the drugs in question. The consent that a soldier gives to the taking of a drug should be informed consent.[25] The soldier should therefore understand the beneficial effects from operational and personal perspectives that taking the drug will yield, the known side-effects, together with the likelihood of each of them occurring, and the relevant matters concerning the particular drug that are either not known or not currently understood. The consent must be freely given, an aspect that must be addressed with care, particularly in the military sphere where discipline and obedience to orders are reinforced in regular training. In the author's view, the perception and reality must be that no adverse consequences will follow for personnel who choose not to take the relevant drug.

10.014 There are other concerns associated with the use of drugs to enhance performance. As with any medication, there is the danger associated with side-effects, a danger that may be more pronounced in the case of performance-enhancing

---

23 In relation to the UK, see, for example, Armed Forces Act 2006, s.12.

24 Informed consent is an ethical and legal requirement in most states. Where the UK is concerned, consider the Department of Health, *Reference Guide to Consent for Examination or Treatment*, 2nd edn (2009), available at https://assets.publishing.service.gov.uk/media/5a7abdcee5274a34770e6cdb/dh_103653__1_.pdf. Also with regard to the UK position see, for example, P Shah and others, 'Informed Consent', *National Library of Medicine*, 24 November 2024, available at https://www.ncbi.nlm.nih.gov/books/NBK430827/.

25 For a discussion of a number of the challenges in the military context associated with this requirement, see Goodley, n.10, Ch.7.

substances. There is then the issue of the psychological response when the substance is withdrawn. Important considerations will be the period during which the drug has been applied and how much is known about the psychological consequences of withdrawing the particular drug. As Adleff-Genot points out, 'the transition from chemically augmented hyper-awareness to ordinary existence could be profoundly destabilising'.[26] While the degree of psychological suffering associated with the removal of the enhancing substance may vary as between individuals and may be alleviated to a degree by human support and care, one wonders whether such support and care will, in practice, be available in the military sphere, particularly during hostilities.

In summary, there is no provision in the LOAC that prohibits or restricts the taking of drugs by combatants in an attempt to enhance cognitive performance. Military operations undertaken by drug-enhanced personnel must, however, comply with distinction, discrimination, proportionality and precautionary rules. National law and ethical practice will usually require that the free and informed consent of the relevant armed forces members be obtained before the drug is taken, and common sense indicates that if the affected individuals are seen to be suffering adverse effects or if their performance is seen to become less satisfactory, that they stop taking the drugs immediately and receive appropriate care. **10.015**

10.3 ENHANCEMENT USING BRAIN TECHNOLOGY

In modern warfare, reasons for brain enhancement will include sustaining high levels of performance over protracted periods without rest, enhancing attentiveness, increasing productivity and learning skills, limiting post-traumatic stress caused by distressing events[27] and improving the performance of particular tasks. It is now clear that other methods not involving the use of medication can be used to influence the performance of the human brain. The purpose of this section is to look at the legal implications of those techniques. This will be a relatively succinct discussion in which sample methods are chosen and in which enough is said about the applicable law to show where some, at least, of the legal challenges may lie. **10.016**

26 Adleff-Genot, n.17.

27 See R K Pitman, K M Sanders, R M Zusman and others, 'Pilot Study of Secondary Prevention of Posttraumatic Stress Disorder With Propranolol' (2002) 51(2) *Biological Psychiatry* 189–92.

10.017 The dictionary definition of cognition is 'the process of obtaining knowledge through thought, experience, and the senses'.[28] Arguably a more useful understanding of the notion, developed by Cambridge Cognition, is: 'the mental processes relating to the input and storage of information and how that information is then used to guide your behavior. It is in essence, the ability to perceive and react, process and understand, store and retrieve information, make decisions and produce appropriate responses.'[29] Enhancing cognition will, accordingly, be of potentially great significance in the military context and this section will briefly discuss the enhancement of cognition using brain-computer interfaces (BCIs).[30] This is a potentially very broad topic. A distinction must be made between enhancing cognition and monitoring the cognitive state of an individual. Consider, for example, the use of a sensor, to be worn by pilots beneath their helmets, which 'employs functional Near-Infrared Spectroscopy (fNIRS), a non-invasive optical imaging technique that uses near-infrared light to analyze tissue properties and evaluate brain activity'. The purpose is to monitor the neural status of the pilot and their operational readiness.[31] The distinction here is between monitoring performance and enhancing it. The focus of this section, and indeed chapter, is specifically on enhancement.

10.018 While BCI technology already exists, and while transcranial stimulation technology has already been demonstrated, there are nevertheless two key challenges associated with BCI devices, including the technologies for brain treatment and enhancement discussed later in this chapter. They are the difficulty in identifying a signal in the brain to give insight into when and where brain activity is taking place and demonstrating the ability to record that signal through the skin and skull of the person.[32] Researchers at Johns Hopkins University, pursuant to a Defense Advanced Research Projects Agency (DARPA) programme, have demonstrated that neural tissue deformations may provide a novel signal for brain activity which might be employed in future BCI devices. This could significantly improve non-surgical BCI. The Johns Hopkins research opens new possibilities for optical recording of brain

---

28 *Compact Oxford English Dictionary*, 3rd edn (Oxford University Press, 2005), 186.

29 'What is Cognition', *Cambridge Cognition*, 19 August 2015, available at https://cambridgecognition.com/what-is-cognition/.

30 See, for example, A M Gielas, 'Soldier Enhancement Through Brain-computer Interfaces', *RUSI*, 19 February 2025, available at https://www.rusi.org/explore-our-research/publications/rusi-journal/soldier-enhancement-through-brain-computer-interfaces, 1–4.

31 J Saballa, 'US Firm Wins Military Contract for Pilot Neuro-cognitive Monitoring Tech', *Defense Post*, 16 January 2025, available at https://thedefensepost.com/2025/01/16/us-military-pilot-monitoring/.

32 Johns Hopkins Applied Physics Laboratory Press Release, 'A New Path to Non-invasive Brain Computer Interface', 14 November 2024, available at https://www.jhuapl.edu/news/news-releases/241114-noninvasive-brain-computer-interface.

function by employing digital holographic imaging as a non-invasive method that is capable of high resolution recording.[33]

10.3.1 Transcranial direct current stimulation

Transcranial direct-current stimulation (tDCS) has been described as a portable and wearable technique for brain stimulation in which a low electric current is delivered to the scalp. Usually, the current is fixed at between 1 and 2mA. The technique applies a positive (anodal) or negative (cathodal) current using electrodes.[34] It is a technique for neuromodulation which results in immediate and lasting changes in the functioning of the brain. The anode and cathode electrodes are positioned on the head so as to set flows of current to specific regions of the brain.[35] 'The current delivered by tDCS is NOT[36] strong enough to trigger an action potential in a neuron; instead its "sub-threshold" changes the pattern of already active neurons. Think of the brain as active, trying to do or learn something, and tDCS coming along to boost this ongoing activity.'[37] The Neuromedec description explains that, when viewed at the level of cells, tDCS alters the firing of neurons and strengthens the synaptic transmission between neurons by augmenting synaptic plasticity. This is, at the level of cells, the basis of learning, so: 'tDCS is often combined with training. Training in itself produces learning (synaptic plasticity), and concurrent tDCS amplifies these effects (enhances synaptic plasticity).'[38] tDCS is being considered for the treatment of a variety of conditions such as depression, schizophrenia, addiction and epilepsy and has non-medical applications such as accelerated learning and focus.[39] **10.019**

In 2014 Nelson and others reported that '[b]ehavioural measures showed a significant improvement in target detection with tDCS'. They concluded that 'tDCS may be well suited to mitigate performance degradation in work settings requiring sustained attention ...'.[40] The use of tDCS in a virtual reality **10.020**

33 Johns Hopkins, ibid.
34 The description in this paragraph is based on that given at 'What is Transcranial Direct Current Stimulation?', *Neuromedec*, 2024, available at https://neuromodec.org/what-is-transcranial-direct-current-stimulation-tdcs/.
35 Neuromedec, ibid.
36 Emphasis in original text.
37 Neuromedec, n.34.
38 Neuromedec, ibid.
39 Neuromedec, ibid.
40 J T Nelson and others, 'Enhancing Vigilance in Operators With Pre-frontal Cortex Transcranial Direct Current Stimulation', *National Library of Medicine*, 15 January 2014, available at https://pubmed.ncbi.nlm.nih.gov/23235272/.

context to enhance skills in identifying threat-related objects was reported in November 2010[41] and Preston and others reported its use to enhance working memory in 2017.[42] It therefore seems sensible to assume that the military applications of tDCS may include the improvement and acceleration of military training; ensuring the development and maintenance of focus on specific military tasks, for example those requiring concentration over protracted periods; target identification and detection. Davis and Smith suggest tDCS may also be useful in promoting war fighter survivability and in enhancing quality of cognition in support of command and control. Specifically, they refer to the improvement of the attainment and maintenance of situational awareness and 'improvement of a number of aspects of cognition relevant to the formulation of intent, including planning, problem solving, probabilistic assessment, and acceptance of risk'.[43] tDCS has also shown potential in both the formation and communication of intent.[44] While short-term side effects are reportedly relatively mild, Davis and Smith point out the relative novelty of the technology, the perhaps relatively greater risks associated with employing home-made devices and uncertainties about longer-term and other effects.

10.3.2 Transcranial alternating current stimulation

10.021 Transcranial alternating current stimulation is a non-invasive brain stimulation technique that modulates cortical oscillations and influences behaviour. In experimentation, it has been shown to have the potential, as a non-invasive treatment, to address balance and gait disorders associated with cerebellar disfunction.[45] Transcranial random noise stimulation (tRNS) involves the use of a weak alternating current oscillating at random frequencies that is delivered through a pair of electrodes located on the scalp. Studies on perceptual or sensory processing showed that high frequency tRNS (hf-tRNS): 'can improve visual detection or discrimination and can enhance the perception of facial identity and facial expression of emotions … Findings on cognitive

---

41 V P Clark and others, 'TCDS Guided Using fMRI Significantly Accelerates Learning to Identify Concealed Objects', *National Library of Medicine*, 2 January 2013, available at https://pmc.ncbi.nlm.nih.gov/articles/PMC3387543/.

42 G Preston and others, 'Effects of 10Hz rTMS on the Neural Efficiency of Working Memory', *National Library of Medicine*, 17 November 2017, available at https://pmc.ncbi.nlm.nih.gov/articles/PMC5691603/.

43 S E Davis and G A Smith, 'Transcranial Direct Current Stimulation Use in Warfighting: Benefits, Risks and Future Prospects', *National Library of Medicine*, 18 April 2019, available at https://pubmed.ncbi.nlm.nih.gov/31105538/.

44 Davis and Smith, ibid.

45 V Sveva and others, 'Effects of Cerebellar Transcranial Alternating Current Stimulation on Balance and Gait in Healthy Subjects', *National Library of Medicine*, 28 March 2025, available at https://pubmed.ncbi.nlm.nih.gov/40180842/.

abilities revealed that hf-tRNS is even able to enhance arithmetic skills and calculation.'[46]

10.3.3 Repetitive transcranial magnetic stimulation

Repetitive transcranial magnetic stimulation (rTMS) can be used for the treatment of depression, obsessive-compulsive disorder, migraines and to help people stop smoking. Potential use for the treatment of epilepsy is also being assessed.[47] The procedure employs magnetic fields to stimulate nerve cells within the brain and thus improve symptoms of major depression.[48] It is a non-invasive procedure involving the application of a magnetic coil to the scalp. The coil delivers magnetic pulses that stimulate nerve cells in the part of the brain involved in mood control.[49] Deep TMS stimulates deeper and wider areas of the brain.[50] **10.022**

Where the safety of transcranial direct current stimulation and transcranial magnetic stimulation is concerned, Xiaolong Sun and Hua Yuan explain that most users display good tolerance with only a few users reporting sensations of burning, itching or headaches. They note, however, the lack of close medical supervision and evaluation of such uses in military contexts and suggest that enhancements in one cognitive function may be accompanied by reductions in others 'leading to unpredictable cognitive deficits that pose a greater risk'.[51] Dangers to third parties, the risk of addiction, and whether results obtained in computer simulations can be replicated in practical military settings are identified as key issues. Further research in these and other respects is clearly required.[52] It is clear from the literature relating to both tDCS, rTMS and tRNS that the precise functioning and effects of these technologies are not fully understood and this is an important factor to consider when assessing their acceptability for military use. **10.023**

---

46 B Moret and others, 'Transcranial Random Noise Stimulation: A Wide Range of Frequencies is Needed for Increasing Cortical Excitability', *Nature, Scientific Reports*, 22 October 2019, available at https://www.nature.com/articles/s41598-019-51553-7#:~:text=Transcranial%20random%20noise%20stimulation%20(tRNS)%20is%20a%20non%2Dinvasive,using%20a%20pair%20of%20electrodes.

47 'Transcranial Magnetic Stimulation', *Mayo Clinic*, 7 April 2023, available at https://www.mayoclinic.org/tests-procedures/transcranial-magnetic-stimulation/about/pac-20384625.

48 Mayo Clinic, ibid.

49 For the commercial marketing of such technologies, see, for example, https://www.flowneuroscience.com.

50 Mayo Clinic, ibid.

51 Sun and Yuan, n.2.

52 Sun and Yuan, n.2.

10.3.4 Vagus nerve stimulation

10.024 Vagus nerve stimulation involves sending electrical impulses to the main nerve that controls digestion, heart rate and other important functions. The result is to send electrical impulses to areas of the brain, thereby changing brain activity. The technique can be used to treat epilepsy and depression by sending impulses to areas of the brain that cause seizures and affect mood.[53] Transcutaneous vagus nerve stimulation (tVNS) involves stimulating the vagus nerve non-invasively with minimal side-effects[54] and such stimulation has been shown to improve performance across a range of learning tasks.[55] 'Based on the current and the previous findings supporting tVNS' efficacy on performance, training enhancement, and fatigue mitigation, we believe [transcranial cervical vagus nerve stimulation] to be an effective learning acceleration tool that can be utilized at language-teaching and other institutions focused on intensive training of cognitive skills.'[56] The rapid mastering of language skills has an obvious potential military application as does the speedy acquisition of other cognitive skills. Where side-effects are concerned, Redgrave and others concluded that 'tVNS is safe and well tolerated at the doses tested in research studies to date'.[57] This rather suggests that, in the military context, careful control will be required of the doses that are applied. As with all of the substances and technologies discussed in this chapter, it will be necessary to determine, through research and testing, the short-, medium- and long-term consequences of the use of tVNS, so that the consent that is a necessary precursor to its use is a fully informed consent, and indeed so that an informed decision can be taken as to whether to acquire the capability in the first place.

10.3.5 Genetic enhancement of the brain

10.025 Clustered Regularly Interspaced Short Palindromic Repeats (CRISPR): 'is a component of bacterial immune systems that can cut DNA, and has been repurposed as a gene editing tool. It acts as a precise pair of molecular scissors

---

53 'Vagus Nerve Stimulation', *Mayo Clinic*, 20 December 2024, available at https://www.mayoclinic.org/tests-procedures/vagus-nerve-stimulation/about/pac-20384565#:~:text=Vagus%20nerve%20stimulation%20involves%20using,to%20areas%20of%20the%20brain.

54 J Redgrave and others, 'Safety and Tolerability of Transcutaneous Vagus Nerve Stimulation in Humans: A Systematic Review' (2018) 11 Brain Stimul. 1225–38.

55 T Miyatsu and others, 'Transcutaneous Cervical Vagus Nerve Stimulation Enhances Second-language Vocabulary Acquisition While Simultaneously Mitigating Fatigue and Promoting Focus', *Nature Scientific Reports*, 26 July 2024, available at https://www.nature.com/articles/s41598-024-68015-4.

56 Miyatsu and others, ibid.

57 Redgrave and others, n.54.

that can cut a target DNA sequence, directed by a customizable guide.'[58] This technique, and developments of it, are being used in ongoing research that aims to develop new gene-editing treatments to correct genetic alterations underlying rare neurological disorders.[59] Consider, for example, the gene-editing technology that uses base editing to make a single letter change in DNA, thereby reducing levels of disease-causing prion in the brain. 'There is currently no cure for prion disease, and the new approach could be an important step towards treatments that prevent the disease or slow its progression in patients who have already developed symptoms. A base-editing approach could also likely be a one-time treatment for all prion disease patients regardless of the genetic mutation causing their disease.'[60] There are also suggestions that 'brain-wide neuroregenerative gene therapy may provide a viable strategy for the treatment of [Alzheimer's disease] and other brain disorders associated with massive neuronal loss'.[61] This is another technological field that is the subject of much current research. The focus of that research, as the limited number of cited sources indicates, is again in the medical therapeutic sphere; treating patients with deficits the causes of which may be genetic, illness, accident or some other factor. It remains to be seen how exactly such technology may be applied in the military sphere and what, if any, application it may have in warfare. There are, for example, reports that Chinese military researchers are starting to explore the potential use of CRISPR to increase human capabilities in the battlefield setting and that China has been undertaking human testing of such techniques involving members of the People's Liberation Army.[62] However, developments in the military sphere involving these technologies are likely to be highly classified and open-source information is somewhat sparse and often unconfirmed.

---

58 'What is CRISPR: The Ultimate Guide to CRISPR Mechanisms, Applications, Methods and More', *Synthego*, 2025, available at https://www.synthego.com/learn/crispr. There are reports that researchers at the University of Sydney have developed a gene editing tool that is more accurate than CRISPR.

59 See, for example, I Backman, 'The Future of Gene-editing Treatments for Rare Diseases', *Yale School of Medicine*, 17 February 2025, available at https://medicine.yale.edu/news-article/the-future-of-gene-editing-treatments-for-rare-diseases/.

60 A DiCorato, 'Gene Editing Extends Lifespan in Mouse Model of Prion Disease', *Broad Institute*, 14 January 2025, available at https://www.broadinstitute.org/news/gene-editing-extends-lifespan-mouse-model-prion-disease.

61 Z Wu and others, 'Brain-wide Neuroregenerative Gene Therapy Improves Cognition in a Mouse Model of Alzheimer's Disease' (2025) 12 *Wiley Advanced Science* 14.

62 K Dilanian, 'China Has Done Human Testing to Create Biologically Enhanced Super Soldiers, Says Top U.S. Official', *NBC News*, 3 December 2020, available at https://www.nbcnews.com/politics/national-security/china-has-done-human-testing-create-biologically-enhanced-super-soldiers-n1249914 and Adleff-Genot, n.17, where Russian and European attitudes are also briefly discussed.

10.026 Legal advice as to the acceptability of brain enhancements based on genetic processes of the sort discussed in this section will need to examine the possible side-effects in the short, medium and long term for the affected individuals. It will need to consider the requirement for free and informed consent and how that requirement can be fulfilled in the military, orders-based context. It will have to take into account the maturity, or otherwise, of research in this area, and will have to take into account gaps in contemporary understanding as well as the most recent findings derived from ongoing research and evolving military experience.

10.4 SCIENTIFIC REVIEWS OF RECENT DEVELOPMENTS

10.027 In a review of recent developments in this field, Violante and Okyere note that 'evidence for clear cognitive enhancement via non-invasive brain stimulation or machine-based interfaces is modest and it is still unclear whether long-term benefits that provide competitive advantages in ecological settings can be achieved'. They suggest that progress 'is expected to come through technologies that can make use of closed-loop approaches that can "read" and influence brain activity associated with the cognitive function to be enhanced' but 'the biggest challenge lies in the intrinsic complexity of the neural mechanisms underlying cognition'.[63]

10.028 Onno van der Groen and others reviewed studies published between 2019 and 2024 in which the effects of electrical stimulation (ES) on cognitive performance in military personnel and tasks were assessed: 'We focused on whether the studies addressed key questions about the generalizability of lab findings to military tasks, the frequency and intensity of adverse effects, the impact of repeated ES administration, and the ethical and regulatory considerations for its use in potentially vulnerable military populations.'[64] Most of the studies that met the inclusion criteria revealed low to some concern with two indicating a high risk of bias. Transcranial electrical stimulation and transcutaneous vagus nerve stimulation 'showed some promise for enhancing multitasking and visual search performance' but 'the results were mixed, with no reliable

63 I R Violante and P Okyere, 'Can Neurotechnology Revolutionize Cognitive Enhancement?' (2024) 22(10) *PLOS Biology* e3002831, available at https://journals.plos.org/plosbiology/article?id=10.1371/journal.pbio.3002831.

64 O van der Groen and others, 'Transcutaneous and Transcranial Electrical Stimulation for Enhancing Military Performance: an Update and Systematic Review', *National Library of Medicine*, 3 March 2025, available at https://pubmed.ncbi.nlm.nih.gov/40098747/.

effects on vigilance tasks'.[65] Van der Groen and colleagues note the need for better understanding of ES mechanisms, optimal stimulation parameters and individual differences in response to such stimulation. They highlight the need for research into efficacy, safety and ethical aspects in the military context and the long-term impacts of repeated use.[66]

In somewhat more optimistic terms, Xiaolong Sun and Hua Yuan conclude that: 'non-invasive brain stimulation (NIBS), such as transcranial direct current stimulation (tDCS) and transcranial magnetic stimulation (TMS), has demonstrated efficacy and precision in modulating neuroplasticity through direct brain stimulation. It offers the potential to augment cognitive function, that is, neuroenhancement.'[67] **10.029**

10.5 RISKS

Mention was made earlier in the chapter of Modafinil. The comments made by Evans, Hereth, Gross and Moreno are indicative of some of the risks associated with human enhancement technologies that need to be considered. They note as follows: 'The result is that while we know modafinil works, we do not know how, why, for what, or to what degree. We have some knowledge of the efficacy of modafinil, but not enough. We have little knowledge of its interaction with other enhancements and other therapies. And we have little knowledge of its long-term effects. Modafinil remains authorized by the Food and Drug Administration for its therapeutic properties in treating conditions such as narcolepsy and shift work sleep disorder, but *as an enhancement* it is still somewhat of a black box.'[68] **10.030**

There are, therefore, a multiplicity of issues to consider. The first, as reflected in much of the available literature, is that too little is known about the technologies discussed in this chapter; about how and why they work; about the reliability with which they work; about the short-, medium- and long-term side-effects they may have; about the likelihood of those side-effects **10.031**

65 O van der Groen and others, ibid.

66 O van der Groen and others, ibid.

67 Sun and Yuan, n.2. Note also DARPA Future Program Announcement Special Notice DARPA-SN-25-43, February 2025: 'RESTORE will test the potential for recent advancements in non-invasive neuromodulation technologies and understanding of the importance of sleep micro-architectures to increase sleep efficiency for maintenance of cognitive performance under sleep-restricted conditions commonly faced by warfighters.'

68 N G Evans and others, 'How Do We Justify Research into Enhanced Warfighters? (2024) 11(2) J Law Biosci lsae023, available at https://pmc.ncbi.nlm.nih.gov/articles/PMC11528700/.

materialising in particular individuals; about whether effects demonstrated in the medical therapeutic context translate across into the fundamentally different military enhancement sphere; and about how drug or neurotechnology enhancements may be affected by other drugs, medications or enhancements being taken by an individual. These and other relevant factors need to be the subject of further research. That very research may, however, raise ethical concerns of its own, not least in terms of the way in which the research should be conducted.[69] There is, however, the likely concern of an emerging capability imbalance if, as seems likely, other states with different cultural and legal approaches to these matters press ahead with research and, in due course no doubt, with the introduction of enhancements. While the temptation may be to cut corners and to proceed despite ethical and legal concerns, adhering to established legal and ethical approaches is the right approach, including from a military capability perspective.

10.6 THE LEGAL ASSESSMENT OF BRAIN ENHANCEMENT TECHNOLOGIES

10.032 It is an open question whether the insertion of electrodes into a combatant's brain, or the use by a combatant of a transcranial headset, in each case in order to enable them to perceive risk more rapidly, to assess military opportunities more accurately, to learn more speedily and effectively, or to perform other military tasks more efficiently amounts to a method of warfare. This was discussed in section 10.2. The position taken in this book is that the use of drugs for the kinds of purposes listed in the first sentence of this section does not amount to a method of warfare. Logic would therefore imply that the use of neurotechnology to achieve like effects also should not amount to a method of warfare. Methods of warfare, the argument would go, consist of ways of conducting hostilities, not techniques to enable one to undertake the associated tasks with greater efficiency. On that very provisional basis it is concluded that the techniques discussed in this chapter that are employed for that efficiency purpose do not generally amount to methods of warfare. In that respect, distinguish the use of BCI or artificial brain (AB) systems in connection, for example, with the firing of a weapon. That activity would amount to a method of warfare and, as mentioned earlier, if the precise nature of the link means that the human becomes part of the firing mechanism, would cause the human to become part of the weapon system.

69 Evans and others, ibid.

Similarly, the mere fact that neurotechnology has been used to enhance a soldier's cognitive performance does not cause the relevant soldier to become part of a weapon system. A state that is intending to enhance some of its combatants in such a way is not, therefore, obliged to conduct a legal review under Article 36 of API or under the implied rule mentioned in Chapter 6. That state is, however, bound by common Article 1 to the Geneva Conventions 1949 and, if a party thereto, by Article 1(1) of API to 'respect and to ensure respect' for the Conventions and Protocol. The Martens Clause also makes it clear that the employment of novel technologies such as these that are not the subject of specific LOAC provision is, nevertheless, regulated by the customary principles of that body of law. While states that agree with the analysis in this chapter will conclude that most human enhancement technologies do not therefore require legal review, those states will also need to consider whether a particular enhancement facilitates or impedes compliance with international law in general, in particular the law of targeting. This suggested requirement is distinct from the targeting law obligation that specific military operations be conducted in accordance with the LOAC. **10.033**

This obligation will require commanders to determine whether the specific military operations and attacks to be undertaken by the enhanced personnel are lawful.[70] The rights of the affected members of the armed forces must also be protected. The observations made in section 10.2 with regard to free and informed consent apply with equal force here. Moreover, to the extent that the intended procedures are experimental in nature, the provision in the International Covenant on Civil and Political Rights should be borne in mind: 'In particular, no one shall be subjected without his free consent to medical or scientific experimentation.'[71] **10.034**

It follows from the discussion in this chapter that legal advisers tasked with advising on the proposed introduction of brain enhancement systems, whether in the form of drugs or other systems, would be well advised to approach the task sequentially. The first issue will be to check whether all appropriate information has been received. The information that will be required to support properly informed legal advice will include: full details of the enhancement; its chemical structure (if applicable); the intended effects on the subject **10.035**

70 Note, inter alia, API, n.7, Arts 82, 85, 86 and 87.

71 International Covenant on Civil and Political Rights, adopted on 16 December 1966 by UN General Assembly Resolution 2200A (XXI), Art.7, sentence 2.

individuals;[72] the known side-effects and the probability of each such side-effect after short-, medium- and long-term use; the nature and extent of testing, the test results and the identity of the tester(s); details of relevant matters that have not been tested, that are not known, that are imperfectly understood or that are considered impossible to test, together with reasons; the nature of the individuals it is planned to enhance; the planned arrangements for obtaining their consent, including what they will be told; the planned arrangements for dealing with enhanced individuals who exhibit side-effects, including procedures for reporting the side-effects; planned arrangements for the removal of the enhancement; and scientific and other information as to the psychological and other effects of the removal of the particular enhancement, including its removal after short-, medium- and long-term use.

10.036 Legal advisers will wish to consider human rights law provisions that apply to the relevant state as well as applicable domestic law. As has been noted throughout the chapter, the obtaining of free, informed consent before enhancement commences will be important. That consent should be recorded, preferably in writing, and should, inter alia, specify the nature of the enhancement to which consent is being given. It would be prudent, when advising on matters of this nature, to explain the need for further advice as experience is gained as to the military performance of the enhancement, its side-effects and other relevant factors. It would also be prudent to make the point that the advice is particular to the specific enhancement. Separate legal advice should be obtained in respect of each form or type of enhancement. It would, for the avoidance of doubt, not be appropriate to seek to provide legal advice on enhancements in general. It is the legal acceptability of a particular enhancement when used in accordance with specific design parameters that will be the focus of the legal adviser.

10.7 CAPTURED ENHANCED INDIVIDUALS

10.037 Brief mention should be made of potentially complex issues that may arise if an enhanced individual is captured by an adverse party. If the enhancement consists of drugs, and if the prisoner will suffer adverse reactions, for example if the drug suddenly becomes unavailable to them, the capturing state will be

---

72 As Rain Liivoja notes, a normal intended use of an enhancement, for example, to cause the enhanced combatant to inflict unnecessarily gruesome injuries, say with their bare hands, will require careful consideration under the superfluous injury/unnecessary suffering principle, discussed in Chapter 6, section 6.4; Liivoja, n.1, 11.

obliged to ensure that the prisoner is treated humanely[73] and is not subjected to violence to their life, health or physical or mental well-being.[74] While the state to which the prisoner belongs may be hesitant to make known to its adversary the nature of enhancement technologies that it employs, it may be necessary in particular circumstances for such information to be made available to a capturing state to enable that state to comply with its Article 75 and customary law obligations. If the enhancement involved the employment of brain enhancement technologies other than drugs, or if the suffering of drug-enhanced soldiers cannot be addressed by the capturing state, other measures, such as a prisoner swap, may be necessary by arrangement between the parties to the conflict. The detail of the relevant obligations will depend on the precise status of the prisoner and more detail on this aspect lies outside the intended scope of this book.

10.8 BRIEF CONCLUDING REMARKS

As this chapter has shown, there are numerous legal complications associated **10.038** with brain enhancement in its various forms. These complications are made more difficult by the rapidly developing nature of these technologies and by the evolving understanding of them, of how they work and of their effects, intended and otherwise. It is plain that current understanding of these matters is less than complete, which complicates the obtaining of consent in the ways that have been explained. It also complicates the provision of accurate legal advice, and advisers should therefore be correspondingly cautious in formulating their assessments. As the chapter has shown, optimistic claims have been made by some researchers with positive assessments concerning the advances they have made. Other scientists express more sanguine views. At this, still early, stage in the development of these technologies, legal advice will be required and will need to present a balanced view, reflecting appropriately the state of understanding as it exists at the relevant time.

73 API, n.7, Art.75(1) and customary law.

74 API, n.7, Art.75(2)(a). Shereshevsky considers the issues arising from the capture of enhanced soldiers at some length. The conclusion is reached that captured enhanced soldiers 'could not be legally subject to harsher treatment than unenhanced soldiers': see Shereshevsky, n.13, 28–42.

11

HUMAN BRAIN DEGRADATION

11.1 DEFINING TERMS

11.001 Harry Aitken and Hitoshi Nasu define degradation, in the context of weapon technologies, as follows: 'A weapon will be degrading where it interferes with one or more of the human sensory systems with a view to reducing or eliminating the ability of an individual to respond to a situation as he or she ordinarily would by producing an automatic motor response (in the immediate term) or an involuntary behaviour (over the long term).'[1] To the extent that human degradation technology is interfering with the normal functioning of the brain, perhaps through the nervous system, in order to produce a desired effect on the behaviour of the affected person(s), the use of that technology will, for the purposes of this chapter, constitute human brain degradation. Aitken and Nasu identify two key elements, namely: 1. the intended outcome on the target, that

1 H Aitken and H Nasu, 'Human Degradation Technologies and International Law', in W H Boothby (ed), *New Technologies and the Law in War and Peace* (Cambridge University Press, 2019), 258, at 260. Note The Royal Society, 'Brain Wave Module 3: Neuroscience, conflict and security', February 2012 noting the military application of neuroscience in order to diminish enemy performance.

is automatic motor response or involuntary behaviour, and 2. the method of interference, that is sensory interference.[2]

Interference with the sensory-motor functions of an individual can be achieved by various means, including the use of riot control agents (RCAs), tasers, malodorants and incapacitants, acoustic waves, sonic attacks, active denial technology in the form of high-power microwave or millimetre waves and even loud rock music.[3] All of the listed technologies target the senses and, through their effect on them, cause the affected individuals to act in the desired way. In a sense, they can perhaps best be understood as systems that harness the normal functioning of the human brain and use that normal functioning for the purposes of the party to the conflict employing the technology. Purists might wonder whether this process really amounts to brain degradation. To the extent that the relevant interference overrides the preferred action of the affected individual and thus adversely affects that individual's intended use of their brain, one can perhaps interpret this as degradation, even if in some cases this is only temporary in nature. **11.002**

Each of the listed technologies is regulated, or not, according to the effect it has on the relevant senses and on the human body. Consider, for example, RCAs, malodorants and incapacitants; they would need to be assessed under the Chemical Weapons Convention[4] (and in the unlikely event that it is relevant, the Biological Weapons Convention[5]). The lawfulness of any of the listed systems would also need to be assessed by reference to the superfluous injury/unnecessary suffering principle,[6] the prohibition of indiscriminate weapons[7] and the other rules of weapons law. These technologies all potentially come within the notion of human brain degradation in the sense that an aspect of the normal functioning of the human brain, that is the translating of the will of the individual into action, is being affected by the particular technology. Another way of interpreting what is happening is that it is the affected individual's original will or intent that is being overridden by a more pressing desire induced by the particular technology. Either interpretation leads to the conclusion that each of the technologies comes within a broad interpretation **11.003**

2 Aitken and Nasu, ibid, 261.

3 Aitken and Nasu, ibid, 262–9.

4 Convention on the Prohibition of the Development, Production, Stockpiling and Use of Chemical Weapons and on their Destruction, Paris, 13 January 1993, 1975 UNTS 3.

5 Convention on the Prohibition of the Development, Production and Stockpiling of Bacteriological (Biological) and Toxin Weapons and on their Destruction, Geneva, 10 April 1972, 1015 UNTS 163.

6 Discussed in Chapter 6, section 6.4 above.

7 Discussed in Chapter 6, section 6.5 above.

of human brain degradation. The technologies will therefore be considered briefly and in turn in section 11.2.

11.004 The other kind of human brain degradation consists of activity that is intended directly to degrade the performance of the human brain, not so much by overloading the senses to produce a reaction but rather by having a direct effect on the brain itself and on its functioning. This will be addressed in sections 11.3, 11.4, 11.5 and 11.6. Some concluding remarks will be offered in section 11.7.

11.005 In some of the following sections, scenarios will be offered in an attempt to clarify the points that are being made. The novel nature of some of the concepts being discussed and their somewhat provisional basis in scientific experimentation make it inevitable that the scenarios are futuristic and theoretical in nature. The reader is nevertheless asked to suspend disbelief as the author feels that the scenarios will help to explain what, on the basis of current rather limited understanding, appear to be the potential uses of such technologies. The purpose in doing so is to try to provide a sensible basis for explaining the applicable law.

11.2 INTERFERENCE WITH SENSORY-MOTOR FUNCTIONS

11.006 In this section, the technologies listed in the second paragraph of section 11.1 will be considered in turn. In each case, the nature of the technology will be described, its effects on the targeted individual and on the individual's brain function will be stated and the applicable law will be explained. While a number of these technologies are used in law enforcement, this section is only concerned with, and will only discuss, their potential use in warfare.

11.2.1 Riot control agents (RCAs)

11.007 RCAs are defined in the Chemical Weapons Convention[8] as 'any weapon not listed in a Schedule[9] which can produce rapidly in humans sensory irritation or disabling physical effects which disappear within a short time following termination of exposure'.[10] RCAs therefore include, but are not necessarily limited to, *o*-chlorobenzylidene malononitrile (North Atlantic Treaty Organization (NATO) code CS), 1-chloroacetophenone (NATO code CN),

8 Convention on the Prohibition of the Development, Production, Stockpiling and Use of Chemical Weapons and on their Destruction, Paris, 13 January 1993, 1975 UNTS 3.

9 Schedules to the Chemical Weapons Convention list certain toxic chemicals and their precursors.

10 Chemical Weapons Convention, n.8, Art.II(7).

oleoresin capsicum (NATO code OC, or pepper spray), chloropicrin (PS) and dibenz(b,f)(1,4)oxozepine (NATO code CR). The important factors for the purposes of this book are that, to be an RCA, the substance must produce its effects on humans rapidly, that the effects must comprise sensory irritation or disabling physical effects and that these effects must disappear a short time after exposure ends. They do not actually alter the functioning of the brain. Rather, their effects on the senses cause the individual to wish to cease exposure. The effect of these substances is on the senses, not directly on the brain. It is the effect on the senses that essentially diverts attention from the originally planned activity.

The use of RCAs would be unlikely to breach the superfluous injury/unnecessary suffering[11] and indiscriminate weapons[12] principles, but that is somewhat academic because their use as a method of warfare is prohibited.[13] Law enforcement, including domestic riot control is a purpose that is not prohibited by the Convention.[14] **11.008**

11.2.2 Malodorants

Malodorants are military systems that produce an intense unpleasant smell, the intensity and nastiness of which are such that affected persons are compelled to leave the area immediately.[15] If the effects of the substance could properly be described as sensory irritation or as disabling physical effects, and if these effects manifested rapidly and disappeared shortly after exposure ceased, it would be classed as RCAs and the discussion in subsection 11.2.1 would apply. It is the sense of smell that is being affected so the key question is whether the effect on that sense can properly be described as irritation. If so, and if the RCA definition therefore applies, that would mean that malodorants could **11.009**

11 Protocol Additional to the Geneva Conventions of 12 August 1949, and Relating to the Protection of Victims of International Armed Conflicts, Geneva, 8 June 1977, 1125 UNTS 3 (Additional Protocol I or API), Art.35(2).

12 API, n.11, Art.51(4)(b) and (c). The issue to consider would be whether the use of such an agent constitutes an attack. Applying the API, Art.49(1) definition of attack, widely accepted as reflecting customary law, the issue becomes whether the use of an RCA constitutes an act of violence. In the context of cyber operations, acts of violence have been interpreted as encompassing acts that have violent consequences, which in turn have been understood as consisting of death, injury, damage or destruction; see M N Schmitt (ed), *Tallinn Manual 2.0 on the International Law applicable to Cyber Operations* (Cambridge University Press, 2017), Rule 92 and paras 3 and 4 of the Commentary thereto.

13 Chemical Weapons Convention, n.8, Art.I(5). Note that, at the time of writing, there are 193 states that are party to the Convention: source: treaty database at www.icrc.org.

14 Chemical Weapons Convention, n.8, Art.II(1) and (9).

15 See D Hambling, 'US Military Malodorant Missiles Kick Up a Stink', *New Scientist*, 30 May 2012, available at https://www.newscientist.com/article/mg21428676-800-us-military-malodorant-missiles-kick-up-a-stink/.

not be used as a method of warfare, but could be used in domestic riot control. If the substance cannot be classed as an RCA but comes within the Chemical Weapons Convention definition of toxic chemical,[16] its use will, in all circumstances, be prohibited. A possibility that it will cause temporary incapacitation or permanent harm is enough for classification as a toxic chemical.

11.010 If it is determined that the particular substance does not constitute an RCA and is not a toxic chemical, the superfluous injury/unnecessary suffering principle requires an assessment of the generic military advantage that it is expected to yield when employed in the intended circumstances and in the designed manner. That generic military advantage or purpose should then be compared with the degree of injury or suffering that enemy combatants could be expected to experience. Only if the injury or suffering exceeds the generic military benefit is the principle breached. This issue, and the question of whether the weapon is capable of being directed at a specific military objective and of reasonably limiting its effects thereto, can only be determined by reference to a particular weapon system. It is emphasised that it is the characteristics of the particular substance that will be determinative.

11.2.3 Incapacitating agents

11.011 NATO defines an incapacitating agent as: '[a] chemical agent which produces temporary disabling conditions which (unlike those caused by riot control agents) can be physical or mental and persist for hours or days after exposure to the agent has ceased. Medical treatment, while not usually required, facilitates a more rapid recovery.'[17] Substances in this category will include anaesthetic agents, skeletal muscle relaxants, opioid analgesics, anxiolytics, antipsychotics, antidepressants, and sedative hypnotic agents.[18] It will immediately be seen that these are substances that fall outside the Chemical Weapons Convention's definition of RCAs because of the longer time that it takes the disabling condition to cease after exposure. They are substances that will fall inside the Chemical Weapons Convention definition of toxic chemical[19] because of the temporary incapacitation that the substance causes. Such

---

16 '"Toxic chemical" means any chemical which through its chemical action on life processes can cause death, temporary incapacitation or permanent harm to humans or animals. This includes all such chemicals, regardless of their origin or of their method of production, and regardless of whether they are produced in facilities, in munitions or elsewhere': Chemical Weapons Convention, n.8, Art.II(2).

17 *NATO Glossary of Terms and Definitions*, 2013 edn, AAP-06(2013).

18 S Casey-Maslen, 'Non-Kinetic-Energy Weapons Termed Non-lethal', Geneva Academy of International Humanitarian Law and Human Rights, October 2012, 38, 46–9.

19 See definition in n.16 above.

substances are therefore prohibited under the Chemical Weapons Convention. Although somewhat academic, determining the compliance or otherwise of such substances by reference to the superfluous injury/unnecessary suffering principle would involve applying the considerations briefly discussed in subsection 11.2.2 above. If the method of delivery is capable of being directed at a military objective and of reasonably limiting its effects thereto, it would not breach the indiscriminate weapons prohibition.

11.2.4 Acoustic or sonic weapons, long-range acoustic devices and loud rock music

The reported functions of sonic or acoustic weapons and long-range acoustic devices (LRAD) are to broadcast sound messages over long distances and to emit pain-inducing deterrent tones.[20] The broadcast function will not be considered further. The emission of pain-inducing deterrent tones is a potential function that is common to each of the technologies discussed in this subsection. As with RCAs and malodorants, the effect on the senses is designed to cause the affected persons to move away. The potential effects of LRAD may include discomfort, inability to move away from the path of the sound and permanent hearing loss depending on the volume of sound at the location of the affected individual.[21] **11.012**

Assessing the lawfulness of using a particular weapon employing such a technology in warfare will require careful consideration of the features and intended circumstances of use of the particular weapon by reference to the principles and rules of weapons law, discussed in Chapter 6. The author is not aware of any rule of the law of armed conflict (LOAC) specifically addressing these technologies. Much will turn on whether the specific use of the technology amounts to an attack,[22] on whether the weapon can be directed at a specific military objective and whether it can reasonably limit its effects to that target. **11.013**

20 See G Thomas, Sonic device deployed in London during Olympics, BBC, 12 May 2012 available at https://www.bbc.co.uk/news/uk-england-london-18042528. For a discussion of the use of these technologies in the maritime context, see M D Montazzoli and J C Tramazzo, 'International Law and Acoustic Antagonism in East Asian Waters' (2024) 103 *International Law Studies* 112.

21 See R Baldwin, 'What is the LRAD Sound Cannon?', *Gizmodo*, 14 April 2014, available at https://gizmodo.com/what-is-the-lrad-sound-cannon-5860592.

22 As to this issue, see n.12 above.

11.2.5 Tasers

11.014 Tasers are battery-operated, hand-held pistol-like conducted energy devices used to manage violent and aggressive people. Introduced into UK policing in 2005, they deliver brief pulses of electricity into the body and can be operated in two modes: probe mode and drive-stun mode. In probe mode, darts that are connected to fine insulating wires are fired and remain embedded in clothing or skin. In drive-stun mode electrodes located at the front of the taser are directly applied to the clothing or skin. Most firings are in probe mode, which: 'produces a generalised, intense, pain sensation and disrupts voluntary movement. Observed clinical effects include localised burns and erythema,[23] dart penetration injuries, musculoskeletal injury due to intense muscle contraction, epileptic seizures, cardiac and breathing effects.'[24]

11.015 Tasers are generally used in the law enforcement role. A legal review of their potential use during armed conflict would likely conclude that the injuries that the employment of tasers may cause would lead to them being classed as weapons. The review would therefore start by considering the superfluous injury/unnecessary suffering principle,[25] and would note that any use of tasers would likely be as an alternative to the use of some other, potentially more injurious form of force, such as lethal force. The conclusion would likely be reached that tasers are not, per se, of a nature to breach that principle. The ability to aim the weapon at a specific individual means that they are also not indiscriminate by nature.[26] There is no specific rule of the LOAC of which the author is aware prohibiting or restricting their use, and their employment would have no significant impact on the natural environment.

11.016 Similarly to the other technologies discussed in this section, tasers do not target or degrade the brain or nervous system as such. Rather, voluntary movement is rendered difficult or impossible due to the involuntary contraction of muscles referred to above.

---

23 Erythema means any abnormal redness of the skin.

24 This paragraph is based on Faculty of Forensic and Legal Medicine, *Taser: Clinical Effects and Management of Those Subjected to Taser Discharge* (December 2017), available at https://fflm.ac.uk/wp-content/uploads/2020/03/Effects-and-management-of-TASER-discharge-Dr-J-Payne-James-and-Dr-B-Sheridan-Dec-2017.pdf.

25 Discussed in section 6.4.

26 The indiscriminate weapons principle is discussed in section 6.5.

11.2.6 High-power microwave or millimetre wave technology

Active denial technology (ADT) employs a focused beam of directed energy 'to stop, deter and turn back suspicious individuals with minimal risk of injury'.[27] 'Traveling at the speed of light, an invisible DE beam of radio frequency millimeter waves engages the subject, penetrating skin to a depth of only about 1/64th of an inch – the equivalent of three sheets of printer paper. This repel effect produces an intolerable heating sensation, compelling the targeted individual to instinctively move. It ceases immediately after the individual moves out of the beam or when the operator turns off the ADT system. There is minimal risk of injury due to the shallow energy penetration of the skin, normal human instinctive reactions, and system engineering controls.'[28] **11.017**

A legal review of an ADT system with a view to its potential use during armed conflict would likely conclude that the minimal risk of injury results in the system not being classified as a weapon. This is, however, a determination that can only properly be made by reference to the particular version of ADT that is being employed and taking into account the effects that such a system has demonstrated in tests. If the conclusion is that the particular ADT is not a weapon, the issue would then be whether it is a method of warfare. That will be determined by reference to the ways in which it is intended to use the particular system, as revealed no doubt in the business case. The use of such a system, for example, in arrangements to secure objects and/or locations of military importance in anticipation of enemy interference or attack during hostilities would amount to a method of warfare and would therefore require legal review under Article 36 of Additional Protocol I to the Geneva Conventions 1949 (API). **11.018**

Such a legal review would consider the superfluous injury/unnecessary suffering principle,[29] noting that the principle is only breached if the system inflicts injury or suffering for which there is no corresponding military purpose. That may be unlikely but would be considered by reference to the specific system that is being reviewed. The description of the technology indicates that a focused beam is employed. If that beam can be directed at a military objective, or if persons coming within the focus of a fixed beam have rendered themselves military objectives by virtue of their presence in the location irradiated by the **11.019**

---

27 US Joint Intermediate Force Capabilities Office Factsheet, 'Active Denial Technology', 11 May 2020, available at https://jifco.defense.gov/Press-Room/Fact-Sheets/Article-View-Fact-sheets/Article/577989/active-denial-technology/.

28 US Joint Intermediate Force Factsheet, ibid.

29 Discussed in section 6.4.

fixed beam, then the technology is unlikely to be regarded as indiscriminate by nature.[30] There is no specific rule of the LOAC of which the author is aware prohibiting or restricting the use of ADT and its employment would have no significant impact on the natural environment.

11.020 It appears that ADT does not target or degrade the brain or nervous system as such. Rather, by heating the skin, it induces an instinctive reaction to move away from the relevant location.

11.3 DIRECT DEGRADATION OF THE BRAIN/NERVOUS SYSTEM USING CHEMICALS

11.021 In this section, the potential use of chemical substances having a direct and degrading effect on the functioning of the human brain is discussed. The section will start by considering some of the substances that might be used for that purpose.[31]

11.022 Cassandra Granlund has undertaken a thorough study of the use of chemicals in cognitive warfare.[32] Among the categories of chemical that are identified as potentially capable of such use are the following:

- Anticholinergics, which include atropine, scopolamine, tricyclic antidepressants and antipsychotics. Their effects or side-effects are stated to include memory problems, confusion, less ability to concentrate, blurry vision and rapid heart rate.
- Calmatives and depressants, which include sedative-hypnotic agents (for example, benzodiazepines, barbiturates), anaesthetic agents, skeletal muscle relaxants, opioid analgesics, antipsychotics, antidepressants and anxiolytics. Their various effects or side-effects are stated to include deep sedation, hypnosis and lethal overdose.
- Hallucinogens, psychedelics and neuroleptic anaesthetics. These are stated to include LSD, psilocybin, peyote, DMT, dissociative agents (PCP, ketamine), NPS and salvia. Their effects or side-effects are stated to include profound changes in auditory and visual perception, the experience of time or space, moods, thoughts, judgement, memory and other mental states. They can also cause paranoia, psychosis, disorientation, memory loss, seizures and depression.
- Psychotomimetics, examples of which are cannabis and BZ. The effects or side-effects, depending on dose, are stated to include a psychosis or schizophrenia-like

---

30 The indiscriminate weapons principle is discussed in section 6.5.

31 The status of such substances under the Chemical Weapons Convention, n.8, is considered later in the section.

32 C Granlund, *Chemicals in Cognitive Warfare: A Peek Inside the Mind-modifying Arsenal* (NATO Science and Technology Organisation), STO-MP-HFM-361.

illness, often including hallucinations and delusions in normal individuals. Implicit in this term is a mimicking of naturally occurring psychosis.

- Neurotoxic compounds, examples of which are organophosphate pesticides, heavy metals, DDT, ethanol, PCBs, mercury/methylmercury, lead, fluoride, arsenic, polychlorinated biphenyls, PAHs and flame retardants. Their effects or side-effects are stated to include long-term adverse health effects, including neurological and psychiatric disorders affecting attention, memory, developmental malformation and endocrine disruption.

The list[33] also includes human enhancement drugs and RCAs, a category discussed earlier in this chapter. The possibility should be borne in mind that such substances might be re-engineered for human, including cognitive, degradation, purposes. Granlund makes specific mention of emerging psychoactive substances such as synthetic cannabinoids which 'at higher doses can induce auditory/visual hallucinations, intense paranoia, and suicidal thoughts … New synthetic opioids can trigger mood elevation, dysphoria, dissociation, and profound Sedation … Phencyclidine (PCP or "angel dust") can cause acute psychopathological symptoms, including memory impairments, reduced processing speed, anxiety, psychosis, and aggressive behaviour.'[34] **11.023**

Pitschmann and Hon point out that drugs are often capable of use both as a chemical weapon and for beneficial treatment effects.[35] No doubt a number of the substances that were discussed in the previous chapter as cognition enhancers are also capable of weaponisation as degraders of cognitive performance. The author considers that it is not feasible to provide legal advice on the general notion of human degradation using drugs as such. Rather, any legal opinion should consider the specific substance about which advice is required, its intended manner and circumstances of use, the chemical composition of the substance, the medical effects that it is capable of having on humans and animals and all other relevant data. **11.024**

The focus of this book is on activities undertaken during warfare. As Chapter 6 discloses, there are numerous principles and rules to be considered when determining whether a weapon system is lawful in the intended manner and circumstances of use. However, a key treaty to consider in relation to brain degradation using drugs is the Chemical Weapons Convention. That Convention prohibits the possession and use (and other activities relating to) **11.025**

---

33 The list is based on Granlund, ibid, Table 1.

34 Granlund, ibid.

35 V Pitschmann and Z Hon, 'Drugs as Chemical Weapons: Past and Perspectives', (2023) 11(1) Toxics 52, available at https://pmc.ncbi.nlm.nih.gov/articles/PMC9866636/.

chemical weapons which are defined in Article II(1) to include toxic chemicals and their precursors. Toxic chemical is then defined and 'means any chemical which through its chemical action on life processes can cause death, temporary incapacitation or permanent harm to humans or animals. This includes all such chemicals, regardless of their origin or of their method of production, and regardless of whether they are produced in facilities, in munitions or elsewhere.'[36]

11.026 The key question, therefore, during any legal review of a drug for use in a brain degradation role is whether the substance is capable of causing death, temporary incapacitation or permanent harm to either humans or animals. Answering this question will require careful testing and evaluation of the substance. Toxic chemicals that are intended for purposes that are not prohibited under the Convention are not classed as prohibited chemical weapons.[37] Those non-prohibited purposes are industrial, agricultural, research, medical, pharmaceutical, or other peaceful purposes; protective purposes, namely those purposes directly related to protection against toxic chemicals and to protection against chemical weapons; military purposes not connected with the use of chemical weapons and not dependent on the use of the toxic properties of chemicals as a method of warfare; and law enforcement, including domestic riot control purposes.[38] Such substances are not classed as chemical weapons provided that the types and quantities of the substance are consistent with those purposes.[39]

11.027 The likelihood is that either the intended degradation effect, or another effect that the substance is capable of generating, will either amount to temporary incapacitation[40] or to permanent harm. This would be enough to bring the substance within the definition of toxic chemicals. It is unlikely that the substance that is intended to cause the degradation effect will come within the non-prohibited purpose exclusion, but this is nevertheless a matter that should be considered. Moreover, in conducting a legal evaluation of such a system, the other principles and rules of weapons law, referred to in Chapter 6, should also be considered.

---

36 Chemical Weapons Convention, n.8, Art.II(2).
37 Chemical Weapons Convention, n.8, Art.II(1)(a).
38 Chemical Weapons Convention, n.8, Art.II(9).
39 Chemical Weapons Convention, n.8, Art.II(1)(a).
40 Incapacity is defined, so far as relevant, as '1 inability to do something or to function normally': *Compact Oxford English Dictionary*, 3rd edn (Oxford University Press, 2005), 510.

11.4 DIRECT DEGRADATION OF THE BRAIN USING BRAIN-COMPUTER INTERFACES (BCIs)

A BCI can potentially be used to connect an operator with any kind of weapon system, the purpose being that the thought or intent of the operator will be translated by the BCI into the firing or release of the relevant weapon in the manner and against the target intended, or thought about, by the operator. If the intent of the operator is that the weapon will adversely affect the brain functioning of a targeted individual, this will be an activity that comes within this section. The use of a BCI system to cause the firing of any weapon that is prohibited by international law will be an unlawful act. Therefore, for example, using a BCI system to fire a chemical weapon will breach the Chemical Weapons Convention. This will be the case if the weapon is delivered, for example, by bomb, missile or drone and is intended to cause, or is capable of causing, temporary incapacitation, illness, injury or death to person(s). It will also be unlawful to deliver a substance constituting a chemical weapon by microencapsulation against a specific individual. It is the categorisation of the substance as a chemical weapon that renders the operation unlawful, irrespective of the chosen method of delivery. **11.028**

If a BCI system is used to fire a weapon that complies with weapons law (see Chapter 6) and if the principles and rules of the law of targeting are complied with (see Chapters 4, 5 and 7), the facts that it is a BCI system that is being used and that the purpose of the attack is to degrade adversary brain performance will not per se render the operation unlawful. Moreover, to the extent that the activity for which the brain degradation technology is being used amounts to espionage, it should be recalled, when considering the following scenarios, that espionage does not per se breach international law.[41] **11.029**

The other aspect that should be considered is the carrying out of a cognitive attack against the operator of a BCI system. At this point, a series of scenarios are considered and legal points in relation to each will be briefly summarised. **11.030**

Scenario 1. An armed conflict is underway. Imagine, for example, that State A has been using a BCI system to control kamikaze or suicide drones that are being employed to target critical national infrastructure targets in State B. The authorities in State B have decided to respond by targeting the operators **11.031**

41 Note that Art.24 of the Regulations annexed to Hague Convention (IV), 18 October 1907, Respecting the Laws and Customs of War on Land, The Hague, 18 October 1907, provides that 'the employment of measures necessary for obtaining information about the enemy and the country are considered permissible'.

of these BCI-controlled drones. State B hackers have gained access to the computer links used by the State A operators to control their drones. After monitoring those and other communications, they have identified the personal details and locations of the operators. State B then fires BCI-enabled weapons which target those controllers with a substance that will cause the operators to become inoperative for a period of 12 hours following first exposure. The substance has no other side-effects; the operators return to their normal state after the 12-hour period.

11.032 While all of the principles and rules of weapons law should be addressed in any legal assessment of State B's BCI-enabled weapon, the key legal point in this scenario is that the incapacitating effect of the weapon brings it within the definition of toxic chemical and thus renders it a prohibited chemical weapon under the Chemical Weapons Convention.

11.033 *Scenario 2* is still an armed conflict situation; changing the *Scenario 1* facts a little, imagine that State B has decided to respond by targeting the operators of these BCI-controlled drones using their own BCI capabilities. The access that State B hackers have obtained to State A BCI computer links enables State B operatives to further access the link between those computers and the electrodes that are either implanted in State A operators' brains or that are worn by them as part of the State A BCI system. State B operatives are able to use State A's BCIs to influence the cognition of State A operators, for example by simply disabling them for particular periods or perhaps by influencing their thought processes in a manner that degrades performance of their military duties.

11.034 So what would the principles and rules of international law have to say about this? The answer is not a lot. Let us start with the armed conflict context. The technology is unlikely to be of a nature to cause injury or suffering for which there is no corresponding military purpose, so the superfluous injury/unnecessary suffering principle is unlikely to be breached. The military priority for State B is likely to be to ensure that the capability can be directed at targeted individuals in a reliable way, so the indiscriminate weapons principle is also unlikely to be breached. There are no environmental consequences arising from the BCI aspect of the capability and there are no relevant ad hoc law provisions. Such a capability would probably therefore pass weapon review for use in armed conflict, it being recognised that the characteristics of a specific weapon system would be determinative in that regard.

11.035 It will be recalled that ruses of war are: 'acts which are intended to mislead an adversary or to induce him to act recklessly but which infringe no rule of international law applicable in armed conflict and which are not perfidious because they do not invite the confidence of an adversary with respect to protection under that law'.[42] The examples that are given in Article 37 are the use of camouflage, decoys, mock operations and misinformation. Influencing thought processes, as mentioned in *Scenario 2*, and adversely affecting cognition would amount to ruses, and would thus not be prohibited, provided that no representation as to protected status under the LOAC is being made and provided that the rules of the LOAC are not otherwise breached.

Scenario 3. Imagine that there is as yet no armed conflict between States A and B but State A operators are using BCI systems to control information-gathering operations within State B airspace using unmanned aircraft. State B is aware that these operations are taking place and civilian hackers operating from State B have obtained access to the State A BCI computer links. The civilian hackers from State B use that access to adversely affect State A's operators' cognition, for example by reducing their attentiveness, causing them to lose focus for significant periods and by rendering them careless. Imagine that the intended result of this is to degrade the operators' control over the unmanned aircraft so that the onboard sensors do not observe the relevant locations. The result is that the intended intelligence is not obtained and that the raw intelligence that is submitted to intelligence analysts is less useful. **11.036**

A state of international armed conflict between States A and B will, arguably, not be initiated by the activities described in the previous paragraph because no declaration of war has been made,[43] because there has been no resort to the use of armed force by either State A or State B[44] and because there has been no intervention into the dispute by the armed forces.[45] As no armed conflict is under way, the applicable law will be the domestic law of the relevant state and, to the extent that it applies, human rights law. The operations by State A are taking place in State B airspace and let us assume that State A has no effective control of that part of State B territory. The affected persons within State B would only be regarded as coming within the human rights law jurisdiction **11.037**

42 API, n.11, Art.37(2).

43 See Geneva Conventions 1949, common Art.2.

44 International Criminal Tribunal for the Former Yugoslavia, *Prosecutor v Duško Tadić*, Case IT-94-1-A (Decision on the Defence Motion for Interlocutory Appeal on Jurisdiction of 2 October 1995) (Tadić Decision on Interlocutory Appeal on Jurisdiction), 70.

45 International Committee of the Red Cross, *Commentary on the Additional Protocols of 8 June 1977* (Y Sandoz, C Swinarski and B Zimmermann (eds), 1987) (API Commentary), para.236.

of State A if organs of State A exercise authority and control over them.[46] The author considers it highly unlikely that the facts discussed in this scenario would cause State A to have human rights law jurisdiction in respect of any persons within State B territory. It also seems unlikely that, in the scenario as described, the civilian hackers' activities and their effect on State A's operators' cognition would be sufficient to cause those operators to be under the effective control, and thus human rights jurisdiction, of State B.

11.5 BRAIN DEGRADATION USING ARTIFICIAL BRAINS (ABs)

11.038 In this section, we consider the potential use of AB technology to degrade cognitive performance of adversary personnel. It seems likely that states will be keen to develop such capabilities, and while much of the published scientific experimentation in this field will have a medical/therapeutic focus, the discussion of potential military applications will likely be classified. The approach in this book is, therefore, to seek to identify what he considers to be potentially relevant scientific developments and then to consider a potential and, as in the case of previous scenarios, entirely hypothetical military application as a basis for identifying where legal issues may arise.

11.039 The idea of using ABs to undertake attacks on the cognition of adversary personnel or, for that matter, to undertake attacks on the cognition of adversary ABs, seems far-fetched, and yet it is the logical projection from the technologies that we have been discussing in this book. One can imagine that AB technology and artificial intelligence (AI) techniques will be harnessed to enable enemy cognition in both natural and synthetic forms to be attacked, deceived, manipulated, influenced, mimicked and generally interfered with. The aim will be to affect or replace the perspectives, intentions and decisions of adversaries at all levels. Causing an adversary political leader to decide not to take contemplated strategic action, for example, the launching of an invasion or the firing of a strategic weapon, may well be a purpose of the utmost importance. Eroding cohesion in a potential enemy that is believed to be about to take such action by causing senior military leaders of the adverse party to contest, ignore, misrepresent or misinterpret political-level instructions can also have beneficial effects by sowing the seeds of mistrust at the highest levels in the

46 Consider, for example, ECtHR, *Ocalan v Turkey*, Application No.46221/99, 12 May 2005; ECtHR, *Issa and Others v Turkey*, Application No.31821/96, 16 November 2004; ECtHR, *Al-Skeini and Others v United Kingdom*, Application No.55721/07, 7 July 2011; ECtHR, *Jaloud v The Netherlands*, Application No.47708/08, 20 November 2014.

adversary state. Causing mid-level commanders to decide to act in a way that renders compliance with orders difficult or impossible and causing personnel at lower levels to decide to impede rather than support their state's military action can all have a profound effect on the outcome of crises and conflicts. If AB systems could be used to alter the perceptions and intentions of the adversary in this way, the benefits for the user state might, depending on the factual circumstances, be considerable.

Scenario 4. An armed conflict is not yet underway. Consider a situation in which an AB system operated by State A is being used to co-ordinate the activities of sensors on board autonomous drones, and the drones themselves. Those sensors are gathering intelligence in territory controlled by State B. A situation of tension falling short of armed conflict exists between States A and B. The tension is caused because the President of State A has been making public statements suggesting he would like to acquire sovereignty of State B, if necessary by military means. State B's political leadership is confident that the State B population will not wish to become citizens of State A. The strategic priority for State B is therefore to dissuade military action and a multifaceted operation is pursued to that end. That operation includes the tasking by State B of an AB system to develop and implement an information warfare campaign to convince the State A leadership and population that such military action would, for whatever reason, be foolish. Such an AB-enabled campaign might be accompanied by BCI operations of the kind discussed in *Scenario 3* above as well, no doubt, as other activities. So long as the multifaceted operation does not include a resort by State B to the use of force and does not involve an intervention into the dispute by the armed forces, no state of armed conflict will be triggered by that operation. If, for the reasons discussed in relation to *Scenario 3*, human rights law jurisdiction also does not apply, it will be applicable domestic law that will determine the lawfulness of the action taken pursuant to the operation. **11.040**

Scenario 5. Varying the facts somewhat, imagine that State A had two AB systems. AB System 2 was the one being used to co-ordinate the activities of the drones and the sensors. AB System 1 had been given the task of devising the intelligence-gathering operation, and the instruction to AB System 2 to undertake the operation had come from AB System 1. State B hackers gain access to the computers that control AB System 1 and cause it to instruct AB System 2 to cease intelligence gathering. The legal position discussed in the previous paragraph would continue to apply, and the *Scenario 5* activity would, the author suggests, amount to misinformation of a kind that is not prohibited **11.041** by international law and would be classed, were an armed conflict to be taking place, as a lawful ruse.

11.042 There are, of course, numerous other examples of potential activity that would involve the use of AB technology to degrade enemy cognition. For example, it is foreseeable that the technologies discussed in this book might be used in conjunction with one another for such a purpose. AB technology might, for example, be used in conjunction with a BCI system to gain direct access to the thoughts of adversary personnel with a view either to altering those thoughts or intent, or to causing the thoughts or intent of the adversary to be overridden by alternative thoughts or intent formed by the hacking party. This possibility is explained further in *Scenario 6* below.

11.043 *Scenario 6*. Building on the facts of *Scenario 4*, imagine that State B decides to use an AB system to identify a way of introducing microcapsules into the bodies of strategic policy personnel in State A, say by finding a way of placing the microcapsules in food to be consumed by the relevant personnel.[47] Imagine that the microcapsules contain electrodes and are designed to pass through the bloodstream and then to lodge in the desired locations within the brains of the State A personnel. It might be the AB system that identifies the preferred way of getting the microcapsules into the bodies of these people; it might then be a BCI-controlled device that performs the task of getting the microcapsules into the appropriate food, or indeed some other method might be chosen, for example a human operative might perform that task covertly.

11.044 The law that would apply comprises applicable domestic law and human rights law, subject to the jurisdiction issue discussed under *Scenario 3*. The targeted State A individuals are unlikely to be within the human rights law jurisdiction of State B, so in practice it will only be domestic law that applies. This continues to assume that the effects of the cognitive operations by State B, or for that matter the effects of State A's activities, do not themselves precipitate an international armed conflict.

11.045 Activities that comply with the law as outlined in this book will not be rendered unlawful by the mere fact of being undertaken by either a BCI-enabled

---

47 Consider K B Ramadi and others, 'Bioinspired, Ingestible Electroceutical Capsules for Hunger-regulating Hormone Modulation' (2023) 8(77) *Science Robotics*, available at https://www.science.org/doi/full/10.1126/scirobotics.ade9676; and more particularly B T Lobel and others, 'Current Challenges in Microcapsule Designs and Microencapsulation Processes: An Overview' (2024) 16(31) *ACS Applied Materials and Interfaces* 40326, available at https://pubs.acs.org/doi/10.1021/acsami.4c02462.

system or by an AB system against another AB system or against an adversary's natural brain.

11.6 BRAIN DEGRADATION USING BRAIN-TO-BRAIN INTERFACES (BBIs)

It will be recalled that: 'Direct brain to brain interfaces (BBIs) in humans are interfaces which combine neuroimaging and neurostimulation methods to extract and deliver information between brains, allowing direct brain-to-brain communication. A BBI extracts specific content from the neural signals from a "sender" brain, digitizes it, and delivers it to a "receiver" brain.'[48] It was therefore noted in Chapter 2 that BBIs are: 'made up of two parts known as the brain-computer interface part which reads a sender's brain activity and digitalizes it, and the computer-brain interface part, which writes the delivered brain activity to a receiving brain.'[49] **11.046**

BBI experimentation is in its infancy, and so the development of techniques for accessing an adversary's BBI and then using that BBI to erode cognitive performance is also likely to lie somewhat in the future. Military work in this field is likely to be classified and there is little in the literature on the topic at the time of writing. It is, however, sensible to imagine that the BCI elements of a BBI system would be subject to the kinds of potential vulnerability discussed earlier in this chapter. Expressed more specifically, perhaps that potential vulnerability would also apply to the BCIs that are used, respectively, to extract content from the sender brain and to deliver the 'message' to the receiver brain. The computer or computers that are used to achieve the BBI connectivity could, in principle, simply be hacked, thereby granting the hacker access to the respective BCI systems. It would therefore be important, if the integrity of the BBI were to be maintained, for that computer or those computers to be suitably patched and for other appropriate measures to be taken to ensure cyber security. **11.047**

The comments made above regarding the law applicable to the peacetime employment of BCIs for brain degradation operations apply equally in connection with such operations against BBIs. Where their use during armed **11.048**

48 L Jiang and others, 'BrainNet: A Multi-person Brain-to-brain Interface for Direct Collaboration Between Brains', *Nature Scientific Reports*, 16 April 2019 available at https://www.nature.com/articles/s41598-019-41895-7.

49 P Vakilipour and S Fekrvand, 'Brain-to-Brain Interface Technology: A Brief History, Current State and Future Goals' (2024) 84(5) Int J Dev Neurosci 351–67.

conflict is concerned, much will depend on the relevant facts. However, the principles and rules of targeting law, as discussed in Chapters 4 and 5, the principles and rules of weapons law as discussed in Chapter 6, the rules as to methods of warfare explained in Chapter 7 and the law of neutrality rules set forth in Chapter 8 will all apply. BBIs that are used for military purposes will, by virtue of such use, be military objectives, will be lawful targets for attack and, thus, also for manipulation. In the unlikely event that a BBI system is used for both civilian and military purposes, it will be a military objective on the basis of that military use.

11.7 BRAINWASHING

11.049 Nita Farahany refers to 1953 reports of brainwashing activities associated with the Korean War and applied against US prisoners of war. She also describes the Central Intelligence Agency's (CIA's) top secret MK-Ultra programme as involving the infliction of 'electroshock therapy, hypnosis, polygraphs, radiation, drugs, toxins and chemicals on willing and unwilling subjects alike … CIA officers in Europe and Asia used these techniques on captured spies'.[50]

11.050 The process of brainwashing involves the application of one or more of a variety of techniques, including violence, torture, drugs, sleep deprivation, indoctrination, repeated instruction, and other methods. The purpose is to erode the resistance of the individual, to cause him or her to abandon political, religious, legal, societal or other views and beliefs, and instead to become a loyal adherent to the views and beliefs that are advanced by those applying the brainwashing.[51]

11.051 The application of such activities against prisoners of war will generally be prohibited by the provisions of Geneva Convention III[52] and Article 75 of API.[53]

---

50 N A Farahany, *The Battle for Your Brain* (St Martin's Press, 2024), 174–6. See also a document issued under freedom of information arrangements on 3 April 2018, *Project MK-Ultra (15545700),* available at https://www.theguardian.com/world/2021/jan/12/uighur-xinjiang-re-education-camp-china-gulbahar-haitiwaji; and L J Meier, 'Mind Control: Past and Future', Harvard University Kennedy School, Carr Centre Discussion Paper, Spring 2025, 1–8.

51 This informal description is considered to be sufficient for the purposes of the current brief discussion. See, for example, G Haitiwaji and R Morgat, '"Our Souls Are Dead": How I Survived a Chinese Re-education Camp for Uyghurs', *The Guardian,* 12 January 2021, available at https://www.theguardian.com/world/2021/jan/12/uighur-xinjiang-re-education-camp-china-gulbahar-haitiwaji.

52 Consider, for example, Geneva Convention (III) relative to the Treatment of Prisoners of War, Geneva, 12 August 1949, 75 UNTS 135 (GCIII), Arts 13, 14, 17, 22 and, indeed, the Convention as a whole.

53 While Art.75 is set within a Treaty that addresses the protection of victims of international armed conflicts, the Article is widely accepted as providing fundamental guarantees that protect persons detained in

The application of such techniques against enemy civilians to whom Geneva Convention IV applies will also generally be unlawful.[54]

During non-international armed conflicts, the persons against whom brainwashing techniques might be applied will generally come within the categories of individuals described in paras 1 and 2 of common Article 3 to the Geneva Conventions 1949. Depending on exactly what is done, such brainwashing is likely, the author believes, to breach subparas (a) or (c) of common Article 3(1). **11.052**

The employment of such techniques outside the context of an international armed conflict will breach core principles of human rights law and, depending on what is done, may well breach the prohibition of torture.[55] By virtue of the presence of the relevant individual in the territory of the state or the application to that individual of the authority and control of agents of the state, human rights law jurisdiction will apply. In this regard, it should be recalled that under the International Covenant on Civil and Political Rights[56] derogation cannot be made from Articles 6 (Right to life), 7 (Torture, cruel, inhuman or degrading treatment or punishment), 8(1) and (2) (Slavery and servitude), and 18 (Freedom of thought, conscience and religion). **11.053**

The use of such techniques outside the scope of international armed conflict will also be regulated by the domestic law of the relevant state. However, if it is agents of that state that are applying the relevant techniques, the applicability of these bodies of law may do little to secure day-to-day protection for the victims of such activities. **11.054**

The intended focus of this book is the application of brain technologies in warfare, and the topic of this section lies at the margins, arguably beyond the margins, of that topic and will not therefore be discussed further, save to point out that, depending on the technology that is applied and the manner of such application, the legal prohibitions and restrictions discussed elsewhere in the book will also apply. **11.055**

---

connection with all armed conflicts as a matter of customary law.

54 Consider, for example, Geneva Convention (IV) relative to the Protection of Civilian Persons in Time of War, Geneva, 12 August 1949, 75 UNTS 287 (GCIV), Arts 27, 29, 31, 32, 33 and 34. Again, however, the whole of the Convention must be complied with.

55 Consider the discussion in Chapter 3, and in particular section 3.13. Note also the Convention against Torture and other Cruel, Inhuman or Degrading Treatment or Punishment, New York, 10 December 1984, 1465 UNTS 85.

56 International Covenant on Civil and Political Rights, adopted on 16 December 1966 by UN General Assembly Resolution 2200A (XXI), Art.4.

12

POSITIONS TAKEN BY STATES AND INTERNATIONAL BODIES

12.001 The purpose of this chapter is to set forth the positions that states and relevant international institutions have taken with regard to the development and use of neurotechnologies. The author is by no means certain that he has identified all such provisions. It is, moreover, not thought appropriate to comment on the documents that states and international institutions have issued. They should, it is thought, speak for themselves. Some provisions are directly quoted while other texts, or elements of texts, are summarised. It is hoped that the resulting summary of what is 'out there' at the time of writing is useful.

12.002 Another brief preliminary observation should be made. It is clear that extensive research is currently underway in the field of neurotechnology in all its forms. Any such research that involves human participants should be conducted in accordance with the Helsinki Declaration.[1]

1 World Medical Association Declaration of Helsinki – Ethical Principles for Medical Research involving Human Participants, first established in 1964; its most recent iteration was adopted by the 75th World Medical Association General Assembly, Helsinki, Finland, October 2024, available at https://www.wma.net/policies-post/wma-declaration-of-helsinki/.

12.1 POSITIONS TAKEN BY STATES

12.1.1 China

In February 2024, the Ministry of Science and Technology (MoST) of China issued *Guidelines for Research Ethics in Brain-computer Interface based on the principles set forth in the 2008 Declaration of Helsinki on 'Ethical Principles for Medical Research Involving Human Subjects'*.[2] The goal of these guidelines is to clarify the ethical norms for brain-computer interface (BCI) research and application, and to promote the sustainable development of BCI technology that enables monitoring, decoding and manipulating of human brain activity. A published report explains the scope and content of the guidelines in the following terms. **12.003**

> The guidelines announced by the Psychiatry Society of China are extensive in coverage and depth. Participating experts involved in formulating these guidelines also came from diverse disciplines, including neuroscience, psychiatry, neurosurgery, medical engineering, computer and information science, ethics, philosophy of science and technology, psychology and law. Six proposed criteria for ethical practices of BCI-related research and therapeutic application are briefly summarized below.
>
> - Scientific soundness—fully consider available scientific evidence, have scientifically sound and rigorous research protocols, ensure benefit to the subject and, in the absence of expected benefit to the subject, ensure sufficient social benefit with minimal risk to the human subject.
> - Beneficence—yield the maximal benefit in the diagnosis, intervention or rehabilitation of brain disorders, under the consideration of risk/benefit balance and the overall consideration of the benefit to the individual and general public.
> - Autonomy—protect the right to know and the decision of the subject or guardian, strictly follow the right-to-know procedure without deception, inducement or coercion and allow the subject or guardian to withdraw at any stage of the study.
> - Minimum harm—assess the short- and long-term benefits for the subject and control potential risk such as the biocompatibility of the implanted material, with non-invasive overriding invasive approaches and personal safety/health benefits overriding scientific/social benefit considerations.
> - Privacy—establish normalized regulations for data collection, technical standards for anonymization and de-identification, including general information and data on brain structure and functional activity.
> - Fairness and justice—adhere to unbiased selection, enrolment and exclusion of treatment subjects and distribution of research benefit, risk and burden.
>
> As BCI technology further develops and becomes widely applied, a more difficult ethical issue is its use for augmenting normal brain functions rather than for therapeutic purposes, applications such as non-invasive neuromodulation of sleep/wakefulness, attention, emotion, as well as learning and memory functions. The MoST guidelines include specific requirements from this aspect, including thorough risk–benefit assessment and more strict

2 These guidelines were preceded by an announcement in October 2023 by the Psychiatry Society of China on 'Ethics governance of brain-computer interface research in mental disorders'.

control of its use, in order to minimize addiction, adverse effects on human reasoning, decision-making and cognitive behaviours, and negative impacts on social fairness and individual autonomy.

We are only at the beginning of understanding how the human brain works, how to decode brain signals, what goes wrong in various brain disorders and what will be the consequence of manipulating brain activity. In fact, most BCI applications for therapeutic purposes are currently practiced without solid scientific basis in terms of understanding the most relevant brain targets and the long-term effects of BCI on the brain. Advances in BCI technology thus need to be aligned better with our understanding of the brain. It is often cutting-edge progress in frontier areas that calls for new regulatory guidelines and the updating of guidelines is required as the frontier expands. In the case of BCI, advances in basic brain science must play an important role in setting future guidelines for BCI. We look forward to evolving new guidelines that help to shape BCI development towards the ever-changing needs of our society.[3]

12.1.2 France

12.004 In 2022 the French Ministry of Higher Education adopted the French Charter for the Responsible Development of Neurotechnologies. It aims to protect patients and consumers from the potentially harmful applications of neurotechnologies for both medical and non-medical purposes. Acknowledging the therapeutic hopes associated with such technologies, the Charter notes that their 'ability to probe and interfere with an individual's brain activity call into question the notions of identity, physical and mental integrity as well as individual autonomy'. The stated aims of the Charter are to: 'promote the responsible development of neural technologies for medical and non-medical applications by strengthening the trust between all actors. It also aims to protect patients and consumers against potentially abusive and malicious uses leading to loss of cognitive freedom or a breach of confidentiality of the personal brain-data collected.'[4] The Charter is available for signature by the public and private sector in France. The undertakings in the Charter are as follows:

1 To protect personal Brain data by committing to
  - Provide patients and users with clear, accessible and rigorous information on the collection, processing and use of personal brain data as well as on the storage, dissemination and sharing of such data. Sharing needed to meet the requirements of open science will only occur with fully anonymized data and taking all reasonably practicable measures to prevent malicious re-identification.

---

3 Mu-ming Poo, 'China's New Ethical Guidelines for the Use of Brain-computer Interfaces', Editorial (2024) Nat Sci Rev 4.

4 France's Charter for the Responsible Development of Neurotechnologies, 2022, available at https://www.enseignementsup-recherche.gouv.fr/sites/default/files/2023-04/french-charter-for-the-responsible-development-of-neurotechnologies-27500.pdf, preambular paras 2 and 3.

- Recognize the patient's and the user's right to refuse the sharing of their personal brain data and reinforce the quality of information and the terms of consent, prior to data collection.
- Use all means available to delete or modify, upon request, the personal brain data collected, with the exception of data collected and already used for research purposes, and which has been anonymized and shared with the scientific community.

2 To ensure reliability, safety and security of medical and non-medical devices by committing to

- Guarantee the use of all available means to protect the devices from external intrusion.
- Demonstrate, outside of clinical studies, the effectiveness of the devices, products and services for the proposed non-medical applications.
- Use all available means to ensure the reversibility of implantable devices and avoid adverse carryover effects.
- Seek and take into account feedbacks and comments from patients and users.

3 To develop an ethical and deontological communication, by committing to

- Make every effort to avoid raising unrealistic expectations or, conversely, unfounded fears concerning neurotechnologies.
- Provide users of commercial devices with scientific evidence of the expected risks and benefits.
- Ensure transparency about the use of algorithms, and even their content.

4 To prevent misuse, malicious applications and manipulation, by committing to

- Oppose applications that result in any intrusive surveillance and/or evaluation of a person without prior consent, in the abusive manipulation of the brain state or functioning, cognitive functions or behaviours of an individual, a patient and a user.
- Desist from developing and implementing applications and uses of neurotechnologies if these are likely to harm the human person.
- Anticipate and block activities intended to influence the decision-making processes of individuals or groups by deliberately limiting freedom and self-determination.
- Oppose applications that result in any intrusive surveillance and/or evaluation of a person without prior consent, in the abusive manipulation of the brain state or functioning, cognitive functions or behaviours of an individual, a patient and a user.
- Desist from developing and implementing applications and uses of neurotechnologies if these are likely to harm the human person.
- Anticipate and block activities intended to influence the decision-making processes of individuals or groups by deliberately limiting freedom and self-determination.

5 To take into account societal expectations by committing to

- Question, in the design phase, the concept of reflectivity inviting to respond to the real needs of society, and the concept of inclusiveness which does not limit the stake of an activity solely to the simple producer-consumer relationship.
- Exercise special vigilance to detect applications leading to discrimination and communicate on the means implemented to prevent them.

- Participate in societal dialogue as much as possible.
- Ensure that as many people as possible have access to the products and services developed.
- Recognise, in the design phase, the need to anticipate potential abuses and apply *ethics by design* procedures as early as possible.
- Foster the development of neurotechnologies, particularly in the mental health area.[5]

12.1.3 UK

12.005 The UK Regulatory Horizons Council issued a report in 2022 that focused on neurotechnology regulation.[6] The report made numerous recommendations, some of which can be summarised as follows:

- That there should be an enhanced culture of dialogue between regulators (the Medical and Healthcare Regulatory Agency – MHRA) and innovators.
- That the MHRA should supplement existing guidance on medical device regulation to incorporate specific neurotechnology challenges.
- That a dedicated subgroup of specialists should be established to advise on future regulatory adaptation to address neurotechnologies.
- That the MHRA should consider options for facilitating the generation and presentation of clinical evidence.
- That all brain and neural tissue modulation devices (invasive and non-invasive) should be regulated under the medical devices framework irrespective of the purpose for which they are marketed.
- That non-invasive devices that merely record neural information for non-medical purposes should not be regulated by the MHRA but should comply with consumer protection, security, product safety, privacy and sectoral regulations according to their use cases.
- That the Information Commissioner's Office should clarify how the data protection framework would apply to neurodata.
- That the relevant government department should consider establishing a new, special category for neurodata so that its processing is limited under Article 9 of the General Data Protection Regulation (GDPR)[7] and should assess whether existing protections are proportionate to the risks posed by different kinds of neurodata.
- That the requirement for manufacturers to implement a post-market surveillance and vigilance system be clarified and strengthened (to consider requiring manufacturers to present a plan describing how they intend to manage long-term implants installed in patients).

---

5 French Charter, ibid.

6 Regulatory Horizons Council, *Neurotechnology Regulation* (November 2022), available at https://assets.publishing.service.gov.uk/media/63e9e8f88fa8f5050ee37d10/rhc-neurotechnology-regulation.pdf.

7 For the UK equivalent of Article 9 of the European Union's General Data Protection Regulations, as it is applied in UK following the British withdrawal from the European Union, see the relevant UK legislation at https://www.legislation.gov.uk/eur/2016/679/article/9.

- That there is a need to co-ordinate and drive forward thinking on neurotechnology regulation across government and to proactively collaborate with other countries to develop an international governance framework.[8]

The detailed response to the report from the then UK Government was published on 4 April 2024.[9] The UK Information Commissioner's Office's approach to regulatory issues concerning neurodata is available on that Office's website.[10] **12.006**

12.1.4 Chile – constitutional amendments

Chile has embraced the notion of neuroprivacy and was the first country to amend its constitution to protect mental integrity and neurodata. This was achieved by modifying Number 1 of Article 19 of the Political Constitution of the Republic by adding a new final paragraph as follows: **12.007**

> Scientific and technological development will be at the service of people and will be carried out with respect for life and physical and mental integrity. The law will regulate the requirements, conditions and restrictions for its use by people, and must especially protect brain activity as well as the information from it;[11]

It is also worthy of note that on 9 August 2023 the Chilean Supreme Court upheld the rights of a former Senator by requiring a neurotechnology company, Emotiv, to delete brain data it had collected.[12] **12.008**

12.1.5 Spain

In 2021 the Government of Spain adopted what is described as a reference framework to guarantee citizens' rights in the new digital age.[13] The Charter stipulates that human rights provided for in the Spanish Constitution, and in international treaties and covenants to which Spain is party, apply also in the **12.009**

8 Regulatory Horizons Council, ibid.

9 That response is available at https://assets.publishing.service.gov.uk/media/660e661075831500114a49f4/rhc_report_on_the_regulation_of_neurotechnology_government_response.pdf.

10 Information Commissioner's Office, 'Neurotechnology – Regulatory Issues', available at https://ico.org.uk/about-the-ico/research-reports-impact-and-evaluation/research-and-reports/technology-and-innovation/ico-tech-futures-neurotechnology/regulatory-issues/.

11 *Official Journal of the Republic of Chile*, Section I, General Norms, Ministry of Science, Technology, Knowledge, and Innovation, Law Number 21.383, 25 October 2021.

12 See S Spichak, The controversial push for new brain and neurorights, 27 J Med Internet Res (2025) 25 February 2025 available at https://www.jmir.org/2025/1/e72270.

13 Spain's Charter of Digital Rights, adopted 14 July 2021, available at https://espanadigital.gob.es/sites/espanadigital/files/2022-10/Carta%20de%20Derechos%20Digitales_0.pdf. An English translation is available at https://portal.mineco.gob.es/RecursosArticulo/mineco/ministerio/participacion_publica/audiencia/ficheros/Charter%20of%20Digital%20Rights.pdf.

digital environment.[14] Every person's right to the protection of personal data relating to them is stated.[15] The right to identity is recognised in Article III: 'One's identity may not be altered, controlled, or manipulated by third parties against one's will.' Moreover, '[g]uarantees shall be established to enable the preservation and control of one's identity in the digital environment'.[16] The right not to be traced and profiled is expressed in the following terms: 'The right to free individual self-determination and the guarantee of freedoms implies the right not to be traced nor to be subjected to personality or behavioural analyses involving the profiling of a person.'[17] Such processing must be with data subject consent or in accordance with law.[18]

12.010 Numerous other rights in the digital environment are set forth in the Spanish Charter, some of which may be applicable in particular neurotechnology-related circumstances. An example would be Article XIX's right of access to data for scientific research, innovation, and development purposes. There are, however, three Charter provisions that are of particular relevance to neurotechnologies and which will be stated verbatim. The first of these, which is an element of the Right to Health Protection in the Digital Environment, is expressed as follows:

> 5. Digital health environments shall guarantee full respect for patients' fundamental rights, and in particular for their right to receive information and give consent with regard to the processing of their personal data for research purposes and to the transfer to third parties of said data when consent is required.[19]

12.011 The Charter rights as regards artificial intelligence (AI) consist of the following:

> 1. In the development and life cycle of AI systems:
>   a) The right to algorithmic non-discrimination shall be guaranteed, regardless of the origin, cause or nature of the bias, with regard to decisions and processes based on algorithms.
>   b) Transparency, auditability, explainability and traceability shall be ensured.
>   c) Accessibility, usability and reliability shall be guaranteed.
> 2. Persons have the right not to be subject to a decision based solely on automated decision-making processes, including those that use AI procedures, produce legal effects, or significantly affect them in a similar manner, except in the cases provided for by law. In such cases, the following rights are recognized:

---

14 Spanish Charter, ibid, Art.I(1).

15 Spanish Charter, ibid, Art.II(1). The requirement for consent or a similar basis for fair processing of personal data is reflected in Art.II(2).

16 Spanish Charter, ibid, Art.III.

17 Spanish Charter, ibid, Art.V(1).

18 Spanish Charter, ibid, Art.V(2).

19 Spanish Charter, ibid, Art.XXI(5).

a) The right to request human supervision and intervention.
b) The right to challenge automated or algorithmic decisions.

3. Persons shall be informed of the use of AI systems that communicate with human beings using natural language in all its forms. In all cases, assistance from a human being at the request of the interested party shall be guaranteed.
4. The use of AI systems aimed at psychologically manipulating or disturbing persons, in any aspect affecting fundamental rights, is prohibited.[20]

Then, in the following Article, there are specific digital rights in the use of neurotechnologies. These comprise: **12.012**

1. The conditions, limits and safeguards for the implantation and use in humans of neurotechnologies shall be regulated by law, for the purpose of:
   a) Preserving individual identity as a person's sense of self.
   b) Guaranteeing individual self-determination, sovereignty, and freedom in decision-making.
   c) Safeguarding the confidentiality and security of data obtained or regarding their brain processes, and full control over them.
   d) Regulating the use of human-machine interfaces which could affect physical or psychological integrity.
   e) Ensuring that decisions and processes based on neurotechnologies are not conditioned by the provision of data, programs, or information that are incomplete, undesired, unknown, or biased, or by interference with neuronal connections.
2. To guarantee the dignity of the person, equality, and non-discrimination, in accordance, when appropriate, with international treaties and conventions, the law shall regulate those situations and conditions for the use of neurotechnologies which, beyond their therapeutic application, are aimed at mental augmentation or the stimulation or enhancement of human capabilities.[21]

The Charter guarantees a person's rights in the digital environment in Article XXVI. This includes the right to judicial and administrative redress and the possibility of invoking such guarantees if the violation or damage occurs in Spanish territory.[22] **12.013**

12.1.6 Australia

In March 2024 the Australian Human Rights Commission published a lengthy report[23] which starts by noting the very considerable global investments being made in the development of neurotechnologies. The report draws particular attention to BCIs and highlights the combination of BCIs with AI **12.014**

20 Spanish Charter, ibid, Art.XXIII.
21 Spanish Charter, ibid, Art.XXIV.
22 Spanish Charter, ibid, Art.XXIV(1) and (2).
23 Australian Human Rights Commission, *Protecting Cognition: Background Paper on Neurotechnology* (March 2024), available at https://humanrights.gov.au/our-work/technology-and-human-rights/publications/protecting-cognition-background-paper (Australia Report).

as an emerging area. Acknowledging the potential benefits of neurotechnological advance, the report notes also human rights implications, focusing on the need to protect the human mind and discussing the notion of neurorights. The report recognises the danger of 'rights inflation' if new neurorights are devised[24] and examines the degree to which mental privacy and mental integrity issues are addressed under current human rights instruments. Specific human rights that are considered in the report by reference to existing human rights instruments are the right to privacy, the right to freedom of thought, conscience, religion or belief and the right to equality and non-discrimination. Again acknowledging the potential benefits of some neurotechnology advances, notably in the medical sphere, the report points out the wide-ranging risks of invasions of privacy, safety and security for people[25] while noting potential military applications of such technologies.[26]

12.015 This comprehensive report also considers neurotechnology implications for the workplace and issues arising under Australia's domestic law. Among the many useful highlights in the report is the recognition of the benefits and drawbacks, respectively, of ad hoc neurorights and revised interpretation of how existing human rights apply in the neurotechnology era.

12.2 DECLARED POSITIONS OF INTERNATIONAL INSTITUTIONS

12.2.1 European Union

12.016 Under European Union (EU) law, medical devices are regulated by the Medical Device Regulation (MDR).[27] In general terms, research devices are not included as medical devices for these purposes.[28] Non-medical devices are addressed in Annex XVI of the MDR. Two implementing regulations were adopted by the European Commission dealing with certain devices, including non-invasive brain stimulation devices, that do not have a specific medical purpose. Technology-specific regulations were issued for non-invasive brain stimulation devices. Medical devices can enter the EU market if the

24 Australia Report, ibid, 9.

25 Australia Report, ibid, 24.

26 Australia Report, ibid, Section 4.4.

27 Regulation (EU) 2017/745 of the European Parliament and of the Council of 5 April 2017 on medical devices, amending Directive 2001/83/EC, Regulation (EC) No 178/2002 and Regulation (EC) No 1223/2009 and repealing Council Directives 90/385/EEC and 93/42/EEC [2017] OJ L 117/1 (MDR), which came into effect in 2021.

28 See Court of Justice of the European Union, *Brain Products GmbH v BioSemi VOF* (C-219/11) EU:C:2012:742, Judgment, 22 November 2012.

therapeutic benefits outweigh the risks.[29] For non-medical devices, clinical benefit is interpreted in terms of the demonstrated performance of the device; as to safety, the device, when used as intended, must present either no risk or 'a risk that is no more than the maximum acceptable risk related to the product's use which is consistent with a high level of protection for the safety and health of persons'.[30] Accordingly, the use of non-invasive brain stimulation devices must not present a risk that exceeds the maximum acceptable risk threshold. Manufacturer risk management obligations for medical devices are set forth in the MDR.[31] Where non-medical devices are concerned, risks must be eliminated or reduced as far as possible using control measures. Manufacturers of such non-medical devices must have risk management systems that involve risk planning, identification, evaluation, control, review and surveillance.[32]

Annex VII of EU Regulation 2022/2346 addresses, inter alia, brain stimulation devices 'that apply electrical currents or magnetic or electromagnetic fields that penetrate the cranium to modify neuronal activity in the brain'. The Annex does not apply to invasive devices.[33] The Annex imposes detailed requirements dealing with risk management, listing particular risks in Section 3 and required risk control measures in Section 4. Requirements as to the provision of information and of instructions for use are set forth in Sections 5–7. **12.017**

While the MDR applies to medical devices, it is understood that non-medical non-invasive brain stimulation devices will be placed in the highest risk category, Class III, because of the possible side-effects, including atypical brain development, abnormal patterns of brain activity, increased metabolic **12.018**

29 MDR, n.27, Art.1, Chapter 1, Annex 1.

30 MDR, n.27, Annex I, Art.9 and Art.61 para.9.

31 MDR, n.27, Recital 33 and Annex I, Chapter 1.

32 Commission Implementing Regulation (EU) 2022/2346 of 1 December 2022 laying down common specifications for the groups of products without an intended medical purpose listed in Annex XVI to Regulation (EU) 2017/745 of the European Parliament and of the Council on medical devices [2022] OJ L 311/60, Art.2.2, Annex I. Manufacturers must record how they evaluate residual risk and determine its acceptability: Art.3.2, Annex I, ibid. While all risks must be eliminated or minimised, the threshold of acceptable residual risk is defined in Art.3.3, Annex I, ibid. Note that this, and much of the rest of this section is based on the helpful explanation in C Bublitz and S Ligthart, 'The New Regulation of Non-medical Neurotechnologies in the European Union: Overview and Reflection' (2024) 11(2) J Law Biosci 1–15. See Section III.b of Bublitz and Ligthart, ibid, for a criticism of certain aspects of the definition of acceptable residual risk.

33 EU Regulation 2022/2346, ibid, Annex VII, Section 1.

consumption, fatigue, anxiety, irritability and headaches.[34] Accordingly, such devices will be subject to the most stringent requirements.[35]

12.2.2 Organisation for Economic Co-operation and Development (OECD)

12.019 In 2019 the Council of the OECD issued a Recommendation on Responsible Innovation in Neurotechnology.[36] The agreed purpose of the recommendation is to achieve responsible innovation in neurotechnology for health. This suggests that applications of such technologies other than for health are not addressed in this document. All actors are called upon to promote and implement, according to their roles, listed principles. The nine principles, each of which is accompanied by listed actions that relevant actors should take, are:

- Promote responsible innovation in neurotechnology to address health challenges.
- Prioritise assessing safety in the development and use of neurotechnology.
- Promote the inclusivity of neurotechnology for health.
- Foster scientific collaboration in neurotechnology innovation across countries, sectors and disciplines.
- Enable societal deliberation on neurotechnology.
- Enable the capacity of oversight and advisory bodies to address novel issues in neurotechnology.
- Safeguard personal brain data and other information gained through neurotechnology.
- Promote cultures of stewardship and trust in neurotechnology across the public and private sectors.
- Anticipate and monitor the potential unintended use and/or misuse of neurotechnology.[37]

12.2.3 Organization of American States

12.020 In March 2023, the Juridical Committee of the Organization of American States approved a Declaration of Inter-American Principles on Neurosciences,

34 Commission Implementing Regulation (EU) 2022/2347 of 1 December 2022 laying down rules for the application of Regulation (EU) 2017/745 of the European Parliament and of the Council as regards reclassification of groups of certain active products without an intended medical purpose [2022] OJ L 311/94, Recital 7.

35 That is, assessing the conformity of such appliances with safety and performance requirements will require the involvement of a notified body which will also monitor the elimination or required minimisation of risks; clinical investigations and trials will be required: see EU Regulation 2022/2346, n.32, Recital 11; EU Regulation 2022/2347, ibid, Recital 8 and MDR, n.27, Art.61.4.

36 OECD, Recommendation of the Council on Responsible Innovation in Neurotechnology, adopted 11 December 2019, Reference C(2019)/159/Rev.1.

37 OECD Recommendation, ibid.

Neurotechnologies and Human Rights.[38] The Declaration lists ten principles as follows:

> Principle 1: Identity, autonomy, and privacy of neural activity. The development and use of neurotechnologies will seek to contribute to the right of every person to enjoy a dignified life, together with the benefits of scientific and technological progress, preserving the rights of identity, autonomy, and the free development of personality. Neural activity generates the totality of the mental and cognitive activities of human beings, and therefore forms part of the essence of a person's very being, identity and privacy, and is therefore protected by human rights norms. It is essential to preserve and guarantee each person's control over his or her own individual identity, as well as to ensure people's self-determination and freedom of thought.
>
> Principle 2: Protection of Human Rights in the design of neurotechnologies. States shall promote a human rights-based approach in the development of neurotechnologies, seeking to ensure comprehensive protection and respect for human rights in the design of neurotechnologies, their research methods, as well as in their implementation, commercialization, evaluation, and use.
>
> Principle 3: Neural data are sensitive personal data. Neural data are highly sensitive personal data. Those responsible for the processing and use of neural data must adopt enhanced privacy and security measures and ensure limits on the use of decoding techniques that allow a person to be identified or made identifiable, especially with databases or sets of information that are shared with third parties. States shall foster measures to ensure control, security, confidentiality, and integrity of neural data.
>
> Principle 4: Express and informed consent regarding neural data. The consent of the person to whom the neural data belongs is a prerequisite for access to the collection of brain information. It is vital to guarantee free, informed, express, specific, unequivocal, and flawless consent when it comes to access to or processing of neural activity. The consent given must be revocable at any time. Special protection is required in the case of children and adolescents, as well as persons with disabilities, older persons, and persons deprived of liberty.
>
> Principle 5: Equality, Non-Discrimination, and Equal Access to Neurotechnologies. The goal is to promote the development and use of neurotechnologies, accessible to all people in accordance with the characteristics of the generation concerned based on the principle of equality and non-discrimination. States shall guarantee equitable access to neurotechnologies, while respecting customs and traditions, and to develop public policies for responsible innovation, seeking to narrow inequality and discrimination gaps, especially with respect to the most vulnerable groups.
>
> Principle 6: Exclusive therapeutic application with respect to the enhancement of cognitive abilities. The main purpose of these scientific and technological developments in medical assistance is to preserve or improve people's autonomy and thus promote their overall wellbeing, helping them to lead a dignified, healthy, productive, and autonomous

38 Published with annotations under the reference CJI/RES.281 (CII-0/23) corr.1, available at https://www.oas.org/en/sla/iajc/docs/CJI-RES_281_CII-O-23_corr1_ENG.pdf.

life. States shall endeavor to exercise particular caution in regulating the use of neurotechnologies to increase the cognitive abilities of individuals, and shall establish clear limits and enhanced control, while taking special care and precautions with provisions that, apart from their therapeutic or health application, seek to study neurotechnologies and use them to enhance or improve cognitive skills for other purposes.

Principle 7: Neurocognitive integrity. It is essential to guarantee protection of the neurocognitive integrity of all persons and to prevent the use of neurotechnologies for malicious purposes that could result in procedures aimed at harming or impairing brain activity or impairing the exercise of human rights. Access to brain activity may never impair freedom of thought and conscience, making a person dependent on a third party, affecting her or his ideas, security, and independence. Every person has the right not to suffer violations, alterations, manipulations, and/or modifications of his or her neurocognitive integrity and intimacy that jeopardize or impair personal integrity; clauses ruling out or limiting liability shall not be permitted. The protection of neurocognitive integrity is guaranteed in neurotechnological treatments; compulsive or forced application mechanisms, as well as their use as a method of torture or cruel, inhuman, or degrading treatment, are prohibited.

Principle 8: Transparent governance of neurotechnologies. States shall ensure that all state and non-state actors involved in the development, use, and/or marketing of neurotechnologies guarantee the transparency of neurotechnological advances. This encompasses not only the way in which neurotechnologies are studied, developed, and applied, and the way they function, but also the impact they have on human rights and the accountability of all actors involved for the use made of neural data in their possession.

Principle 9: Supervision and control of neurotechnologies. It is incumbent upon States to exercise a supervisory/oversight role by establishing a competent, technically specialized, financially autonomous, and independent national authority to ensure that neurotechnologies are used and applied in accordance with international human rights standards, so as to avoid and prevent risks and negative impacts on people's rights and pay special attention to the rights of children and adolescents, persons with disabilities, and persons deprived of liberty.

Principle 10: Access to effective protection and access to remedies associated with the development and use of neurotechnologies. States shall promote and ensure mechanisms for the effective protection of the rights associated with the development and use of neurotechnologies. It is also necessary to ensure access to judicial remedies and comprehensive reparation in the case of human rights violations, in order to promote effective protection of these guarantees, in accordance with these Principles.[39]

12.2.4 United Nations Human Rights Council

12.021 The Advisory Committee of the Human Rights Council (HRC) issued a report on these matters in August 2024.[40] Noting the beneficial health, welfare,

---

39 Organization of American States Declaration, ibid.

40 HRC, *Impact, opportunities and challenges of neurotechnology with regard to the promotion and protection of all human rights*, A/HRC/57/61, 8 August 2024, available at https://digitallibrary.un.org/record/4060417?ln=en&v=pdf (HRC Report).

education and well-being applications of such technologies, the report also points to the requirement for direct access of such devices to a person's brain activity and that there are associated profound human rights concerns.[41] The report explains that the 'particularity of neurotechnologies is that they allow a direct connection to be established between the human brain and external devices and thus provide a gateway to interfere with mental and cognitive functions'.[42]

The report points out the need, in the context of the foundational notion of human dignity, to consider the potential for neurotechnologies to impact 'the constitutive elements of the person: the individual's personhood, mental capacities and personality; considering whether their application contributes to the objectification and instrumentalization of individuals; whether autonomy may be neglected by altering the foundation of their mental processes and states; and assessing if they hinder individuals' capacity for self-determination'.[43] A human rights-based approach requires limitation of applications that are unable to comply with this foundational principle, the report notes. Specific human rights are then considered. **12.022**

Freedom of thought

Under Article 18 of the International Covenant of Civil and Political Rights,[44] everyone has the right to develop their thoughts autonomously, free from impermissible external interference. It therefore protects: 'the *forum internum*, that is the inner psychological realm of the person, where thoughts and convictions are formed. It is also at the origin of rights linked to the *forum externum* (i.e. freedom of opinion and expression), which relate to the manifestation of thoughts.'[45] In the same paragraph, the report describes freedom of thought as an absolute right permitting of no external interference. Pointing out that individuals have the right not to reveal their thoughts, the report points to the potential use of neurotechnologies in association with AI to: 'elaborate sophisticated individualized psychological profiles and use them to predict individuals' behaviour or intentions or to infer their mental characteristics or **12.023**

41 HRC Report, ibid, paras 1 and 2.

42 HRC Report, ibid, para.5. The report describes these technologies as disruptive, noting, inter alia, that they 'generally enable the exposition of cognitive processes, the direct alteration of a person's mental processes and thoughts, the bypassing of an individual's conscious control or awareness, non-consensual external access to thoughts, emotions and mental states and collect, analyse and process large personal datasets of a highly sensitive nature': HRC Report, ibid, para.5.

43 HRC Report, ibid, para.17.

44 International Covenant on Civil and Political Rights, 19 December 1966, 999 UNTS 171.

45 HRC Report, ibid, para.18.

predispositions. Based on those inferences, neurotechnology devices may also intervene to modify thoughts.' The report asserts the need for adequate safety, security and regulatory arrangements.[46] The criminalisation of mere thought and punishment of unexpressed thoughts, for example in the counterterrorism context, raises concerns where law enforcement and national security exemptions from relevant legislation are concerned.[47] Linked concerns include the potential manipulation of individuals, the influencing of consumer behaviour, for example neuromarketing and political campaigning, and behavioural modification in general.[48]

Privacy rights

12.024 The HRC report explains that as neurotechnologies 'gain access to people's minds to collect and record personal information they have the capacity to affect their physical and mental privacy by exposing individuals' private space and integrity. They may also interfere with the right to make autonomous life choices without outside interference or intimidation (decisional privacy), as well as affect informational privacy through unauthorized uses of the personal information collected.'[49]

12.025 The identity and personality aspects might include sexual orientation, personality traits, cognitive performance, intentions, beliefs and emotions; the HRC report acknowledges that the wide deployment of BCIs, involving the accumulation of large amounts of personal data, means that the risks of data misuse, of repurposing, of predatory practices and of hacking will become significant. There is, moreover, a concern that existing privacy protection frameworks may not be adequate and that consent-specific standards dealing with non-consensual intrusions may potentially be necessary. [50]

Right to personal integrity

12.026 Paragraph 27 of the report asserts that neurotechnology can lead to violation of the right to personal integrity through physical and mental harm and adverse effects on mental integrity; the right is stated to be incorporated in other rights. Meaningful and effective free and informed consent is stated to be indispensable, and effective measures to protect vulnerable persons from coercion should be adopted. 'In contexts characterised by power asymmetries,

46 HRC Report, ibid, para.19.
47 HRC Report, ibid, para.20.
48 HRC Report, ibid, para.21.
49 HRC Report, ibid, para.23.
50 HRC Report, ibid, paras 24 and 25.

for example in the military domain, human rights concerns may arise with regard to interventions for enhancement purposes. Coercive uses of neurotechnologies to augment resilience on the battlefield (i.e. to reduce emotions, empathy or the need for sleep) should be prohibited, while non-coercive uses may require limitations.'[51] The report recognises it is hard to see how informed consent can be given when the long-term consequences of neurotechnologies are unknown.[52]

Right to the enjoyment of the highest attainable standard of physical and mental health

Recognising the capacity for neurotechnology to protect mental health and to grant personal autonomy, the largely unknown long-term effects and the risk of health harm may be less acceptable in consumer than in health applications. However, '[w]hen safe, effective, secure and human-rights compliant neurotechnology products do exist, access becomes a key element of the right to health'.[53] **12.027**

Prohibition of torture, cruel, inhuman or degrading treatment or punishment

The report takes the position that 'Article 7 of the International Covenant on Civil and Political Rights provides offenders with protection against brain-reading and brain-writing techniques, particularly "neurocorrectives", which constitute an inherently degrading treatment in all circumstances', and asserts that '[m]edical, scientific or biological experimentation without the free consent of the person concerned is prohibited under international human rights law'.[54] **12.028**

Right to a fair trial and essential procedural guarantees

'The presumption of innocence and the right not to testify against oneself require that no direct or indirect physical or undue psychological pressure be exerted by the authorities on the accused to confess or testify. Subjecting detained or imprisoned persons to "brain-reading" techniques is clearly a form of prohibited pressure.'[55] **12.029**

The report considers persons in vulnerable situations, particularly disabled persons, children and older persons, and specific settings, namely the workplace, **12.030**

51 HRC Report, ibid, paras 28 and 29.
52 HRC Report, ibid, para.30.
53 HRC Report, ibid, para.32 and see para.33 as to the need for safeguards and for non-discriminatory access.
54 HRC Report, ibid, para.34.
55 HRC Report, ibid, para.36.

criminal justice and military settings. In the military domain, the use of brain stimulation to modulate cognitive functions (for example memory and learning), physical or cognitive augmentation of soldiers' combat capabilities (for example heightened awareness and control of emotions) and the neural control of weapons are all mentioned.[56] 'The identification of applicable standards to limit uses contrary to international law, including human rights and international humanitarian law, seems to be critical.'[57]

12.031 Issues associated with cognitive augmentation are noted, as are approaches to addressing the challenges while maximising the opportunities associated with these technologies.[58]

12.2.5 United Nations Educational, Scientific and Cultural Organization (UNESCO)

12.032 At a General Conference in Samarkand, Uzbekistan, UNESCO has adopted a global framework on neurotechnology ethics. The framework entered into force on 12 November 2025.[59]

12.2.6 European Parliament

12.033 In 2024 the European Parliament produced a paper in which options are identified for policy approaches to deal with neurotechnologies.[60] The options that are discussed are: the laissez-faire non-interference option; a blanket prohibition of neurotechnologies; and a set of orchestrated steps to prevent the European market from being dominated by non-European neurotech agents.

12.034 Other documents worthy of note include the European Charter for the Responsible Development of Neurotechnologies issued by the European Brain

56 HRC Report, ibid, para.50.

57 HRC Report, ibid, para.51.

58 HRC Report, ibid, paras 52–75.

59 A Smedley, UNESCO adopts first global framework on neurotechnology ethics, UNESCO, 18 November 2025 available at https://unesco.org.uk/news/unesco-adopts-first-global-framework-on-neurotechnology-ethics. The text of the recommendation that was adopted by UNESCO's General Conference is available here: https://unesdoc.unesco.org/ark:/48223/pf0000394866.

60 European Parliament STOA Options Brief, 'The Protection of Mental Privacy in the Area of Neuroscience: Societal, Legal and Ethical Challenges', 2024, available at https://www.europarl.europa.eu/RegData/etudes/STUD/2024/757807/EPRS_STU(2024)757807(ANN01)_EN.pdf.

Council[61] and a publication issued by the United Nations Children's Fund (UNICEF) addressing children's rights in the field of neurotechnologies.[62]

61 European Brain Council, *European Charter for the Responsible Development of Neurotechnologies* (April 2025), available at https://www.braincouncil.eu/wp-content/uploads/2025/04/European-Charter-for-the-Responsible-Development-of-NeuroTechnologies-FINAL.pdf.

62 UNICEF, *Neurotechnology and Children's Rights – Preparing for the Future* (July 2025), available at https://www.unicef.org/innocenti/media/11426/file/UNICEF-Innocenti-Neurotech-Childrens-rights-Report-2025.pdf.

13

BRAIN TECHNOLOGIES AND INTERNATIONAL CRIMINAL LAW

13.1 INTRODUCTION

13.001 It is not controversial to assert that international criminal law will apply to military operations conducted during an international or non-international armed conflict in which brain technologies are employed. It would, indeed, be strange if the criminal law ceased to apply just because a particular, novel technology was being used. As the following pages will show, the difficult issue is not whether specific crimes are capable of commission using brain technologies but, rather, how the provisions of international criminal law will apply.

13.002 Most offences that breach the domestic laws of states involve two important constituent parts. The first part of an offence comprises what, in Latin, is termed the *actus reus*. This term refers to the action, or inaction, that constitutes the crime. So in relation to the crime of theft, for example, the *actus reus* is the thief's action in taking away the object, such as a purse, belonging to the victim. The second part of the offence of theft, the *mens rea*, consists of the mental element which, in the case of theft, is the intention permanently to deprive the owner of the object, the purse. That intention will have been formed by the thief. So it is when the prosecution proves that the thief undertook that *actus reus* and that they did so with the required *mens rea* that the charge will be proved. International criminal law will also, as we shall see, require that the act constituting the international crime has occurred and that the perpetrator has committed the relevant act with the required mental element.

The brain technologies that we have discussed in this book raise a number of complex criminal law problems. In the international criminal law context, it will be for the international courts and tribunals, and perhaps for states by means of international agreements and/or state practice, to interpret the law or, in the latter case, to develop new law. These are some of the pertinent issues and reflections on each are offered as follows: **13.003**

1. Can a human being be guilty of an international crime if a brain technology was used in connection with the relevant act? The short answer is yes, provided that the human being can be shown to have performed an act, or failed to act, in a manner reflecting the *actus reus* and provided that that individual had the requisite *mens rea*.[1]
2. Specifically, do certain brain technologies have the effect of depriving the affected individual of the intent and knowledge that must be present to establish guilt in most cases under the Rome Statute?[2] The answer to this question will inevitably depend on the specificities of the particular technology, the way in which it is being applied and on the facts of a particular case. It seems that some brain technologies in some contexts may indeed deprive the relevant individual(s) of intent and knowledge.[3] An example might be if a brain-computer interface (BCI) is being used to target a person in a manner that so adversely affects the operating individual's cognition as to deprive the individual of the ability to form the requisite intent.
3. Can a brain technology itself be guilty of an international crime? At the time of writing, international criminal law focuses on the acts, or inactions, of persons. It remains to be seen whether, over time and as neurotechnologies acquire increasing levels of sentience, a point may be reached in which it becomes illogical to ignore the criminal nature of decisions that are, essentially, made by

---

1 This somewhat simplistic observation does, however, require some qualification, as reflected in, for example, D Mehta, 'Brain-computer Interface Tool Use and the Contemplation Conundrum: A Blueprint of Mental Action, Agency and Control' (2025) 4 *Oxford Open Neuroscience* (11 June 2025), available at https://pubmed.ncbi.nlm.nih.gov/40575493/.

2 Consider H Goodley, *Pharmacological Performance Enhancement and the Military* (Chatham House, 11 November 2020), available at https://www.chathamhouse.org/2020/11/pharmacological-performance-enhancement-and-military/05-soldier-and-state-responsibility, Ch.5.

3 See the discussion of this aspect in S E White, 'Brave New World: Neurowarfare and the Limits of International Humanitarian Law' (2008) 41(1) *Cornell International Law Journal* 177, 199 noting the potential, for example, for a BCI weapon to circumvent the operator's normal volitional processing signals and rely solely on a recognition activity, thus rendering it impossible for courts to determine whether a volitional act occurred before targeting.

systems that are neurotechnological in nature. Perhaps we are not quite at that point, but it may not be as far off as some of us might wish.

4. Can an intent formed by a brain technology be imputed to a human actor for the purpose of establishing guilt? While all of the issues posed in this series of questions are difficult, this one is particularly so. One suspects that the relevant imputation will normally be of the individual's intent to the act performed by the BCI- or artificial brain (AB)-enabled weapon system. However, if neurotechnology enables the device or system to form an intent, the issue then becomes whether the individual had a role in the formation of that intent or whether the intent was entirely generated within the system. If the individual had no role in the formation of the intent, but knew in advance that there was a prospect that the system would indeed generate such an intent, maybe the intent is imputable to the human. These are all issues, however, with which courts will need to grapple and the approaches that courts will adopt cannot currently be stated with certainty.
5. Do the existing recognised international crimes make sense if brain technologies have been used? In principle, they do. The requirement for a *mens rea* as an element in such crimes continues to make sense. The following sections of this chapter are designed to give a more specific answer to this question.[4]
6. Does it make a difference if the brain technology malfunctions? The answer to this question will inevitably be linked with the degree to which the brain technology in question affects the individual's ability to form intent or substitutes its own intent in the sense discussed above. If a brain technology such as a BCI misinterprets a thought process or intent that is being sent to it by an operator and if, as a result of that misinterpretation, the weapon is fired at a target other than the one contemplated by the operator, it will be difficult to hold the operator accountable. Of course, if the relevant brain technology has repeatedly malfunctioned beforehand, different considerations will arise, including the wisdom of using it on the occasion in question.

13.004 In the following discussion of specific crimes, the brain technologies that we will be considering are BCIs, ABs, brain-to-brain interfaces (BBIs), brain enhancement and brain degradation. The chapter will base itself on a selection of the international crimes specified in the Rome Statute of the International Criminal Court, that is genocide, crimes against humanity, war crimes and the crime of aggression. The Rome Statute is a treaty that was the subject of careful negotiation and drafting by experts drawn from numerous states. The intention of those experts was that its provisions should reflect customary law, that is law that is binding on all states.[5] It is therefore suggested that the Rome

4 See the discussion of the *actus reus* and *mens rea* issues raised by BCIs in White, ibid, 192–205.

5 As explained to the author by his good friend, Charles Garraway, who was a member of the UK Delegation to the Diplomatic Conference in Rome that adopted the Statute. As to whether the Rome Statute does in fact reflect customary law, see Y Tan, *The Rome Statute as Evidence of Customary International Law* (Leiden University, 9 April 2019), available at https://scholarlypublications.universiteitleiden.nl/access/

Statute is a sensible basis from which to address all five of the brain technologies and thus to produce as comprehensive a set of answers as possible to the key questions posed in the previous paragraph. Self-evidently, this chapter is not a comprehensive treatment of all aspects of international criminal law. It is, nevertheless, hoped that the discussion of the limited number of selected crimes will illustrate the key issues and will assist readers to form their own conclusions.

Taking the selected international crimes in turn, the discussion will start with a brief statement of the crime as set forth in the Rome Statute. Article 9 of the Statute refers to the *Elements of Crimes* and describes the function of these elements as being to assist the Court (that is, the International Criminal Court (ICC)) in the interpretation and application of the crime provisions of the Statute. Article 21(1)(a) of the Statute then requires the Court to apply in the first place the Statute, the *Elements of Crimes* and the Rules of Procedure and Evidence. These *Elements of Crimes* were also negotiated by eminent national experts and were adopted by the Rome Statute Review Conference in 2010.[6] The list of elements of each of the chosen crimes will be stated. Thereafter, each crime and its elements will be assessed by reference to such of the five brain technologies as are of relevance, and hypothetical examples will be used to illustrate key points to the extent that this is thought to be useful. **13.005**

The modes of criminal participation, defences and the mental elements in crimes that are stipulated in the Statute will then be discussed. It will be appreciated that available evidence and the facts as found by the Court will be among the factors that determine whether a particular charge is indeed proved. **13.006**

13.2 A BRIEF HISTORICAL PERSPECTIVE

Under the Charter of the Nuremberg International Military Tribunal,[7] the power was given to that Tribunal to deal with crimes against peace, war crimes **13.007**

item%3A2978427/view and A S Galand, 'The Nature of the Rome Statute of the International Criminal Court (and its Amended Jurisdictional Scheme)' (2019) 17(5) *Journal of International Criminal Justice* 933–56. The end conclusion, where genocide, crimes against humanity and war crimes are concerned, is that the reflection is close but not completely perfect.

6 Review Conference of the Rome Statute of the International Criminal Court, Kampala, 31 May to 11 June 2010, International Criminal Court publication RC/11: the *Elements of Crimes* is available at https://www.icc-cpi.int/sites/default/files/Publications/Elements-of-Crimes.pdf.

7 The Charter of the Nuremberg International Military Tribunal is annexed to the Agreement by the Government of the United Kingdom of Great Britain and Northern Ireland, the Government of the

and crimes against humanity alleged against the major Nazi war criminals. Crimes against peace were stated in the Charter to consist of 'planning, preparation, initiation or waging of a war of aggression, or a war in violation of international treaties, agreements or assurances, or participation in a common plan or conspiracy for the accomplishment of any of the foregoing'.[8] This is mentioned at this stage in the chapter to show that notions of a crime of aggression date back some 80 years. War crimes are described in the Charter, so far as relevant, as 'violations of the laws or customs of war. Such violations shall include, but not be limited to, murder, … wanton destruction of cities, towns or villages, or devastation not justified by military necessity.'[9] Crimes against humanity were expressed in the charter as including 'murder … committed against any civilian population, before or during the war' or persecution on political, racial or religious grounds in exercise of or in connection with another crime within the Tribunal's jurisdiction.[10]

13.008 Article 6 of the Charter stated that '[l]eaders, organisers, instigators and accomplices participating in the formulation or execution of a common plan or conspiracy to commit any of the foregoing crimes are responsible for all acts performed by any persons in execution of such plan'. Article 7 asserted that '[t]he official position of defendants, whether as Heads of State or responsible officials in Government Departments, shall not be considered as freeing them from responsibility or mitigating punishment', while '[t]he fact that the Defendant acted pursuant to order of his Government or of a superior shall not free him from responsibility, but may be considered in mitigation of punishment if the Tribunal determines that justice so requires'.[11]

13.009 The trial of war criminals in the Far East was provided for in the Charter of the International Military Tribunal for the Far East (sometimes also referred to as the Tokyo Military Tribunal).[12] The Charter provided, inter alia, for the trial of crimes against peace and what were described as conventional war crimes, a notion that was stated to comprise violations of the laws or customs of war. Article 6 of that Charter stipulated that the official position an accused had

---

United States of America, the Provisional Government of the French Republic and the Government of the Union of Soviet Socialist Republics for the prosecution and punishment of the major war criminals of the European Axis, signed at London, on 8 August 1945 (IMT Charter).

8 IMT Charter, ibid, Art.6(a).

9 IMT Charter, ibid, Art.6(b).

10 IMT Charter, ibid, Art.6(c).

11 IMT Charter, ibid, Art.8.

12 See General Orders Number 20 issued by the Supreme Commander of the Allied Powers on 26 April 1946.

had or the superior orders he had received would not be sufficient to free him from criminal responsibility but might, if justice so required, be considered in mitigation. It therefore follows that the potential responsibility of those in positions of authority, the absence of a defence simply based on compliance with orders of a superior and the important concept of individual criminal responsibility all date back to 1945.

Finally, it should be noted that the jurisprudence of the International Criminal Tribunals for the Former Yugoslavia[13] and for Rwanda[14] has advanced international criminal law substantially. It is, however, not thought to be necessary to consider the statutes and casework of those tribunals at this stage. Brief mention should also be made of the agreement dated 14 August 2000 between the United Nations and the Government of Sierra Leone pursuant to UN Security Council Resolution 1315 (2000), which established the Special Court for Sierra Leone. This shows that, in situations where the ICC is unable to act for whatever reason, ad hoc arrangements for the exercise of international criminal justice might be made, subject to the willingness of states to make the necessary arrangements. **13.010**

13.3 A DISCUSSION OF SELECTED ROME STATUTE CRIMES

While the negotiators may have intended that the Rome Statute should reflect customary law and thus reflect rules and crimes that, respectively, bind and apply to all states, it is worthy of note that, at the time of writing, only two of the five permanent member States of the UN Security Council are parties to the Statute – namely, France and the UK – while the remaining P5 states – namely, China, the Russian Federation and the US – are not. **13.011**

The offences over which the ICC has jurisdiction are listed in the Rome Statute as follows: Genocide under Article 6, Crimes against humanity under Article 7, War Crimes under Article 8 and the Crime of Aggression under Article 8bis. In the following sections, a selection of the crimes that seem to be of potential relevance to the subject of this book will be considered.[15] It should **13.012**

13 The UN Security Council adopted Resolution 827 on 25 May 1993 and adopted the Statute of the International Criminal Tribunal for the Former Yugoslavia (ICTY), which was annexed to a report of the UN Secretary-General: UNSC, *Report of the Secretary-General Pursuant to Paragraph 2 of Security Council Resolution 808* (1993), UN Doc. S/27504 (3 May 1993).

14 Acting under Chapter VII of the UN Charter, on 8 November 1994 the UN Security Council adopted Resolution 955 (1994) establishing the International Criminal Tribunal for Rwanda (ICTR), the Statute of which was annexed to the Resolution.

15 Not all crimes of such potential relevance are considered, only a limited selection.

be noted that, in becoming party to the Rome Statute, a number of states have expressed certain national positions. It should also be noted that certain states of military importance are not parties to the Treaty.

13.013 Article 1 of the Statute specifies that the ICC's exercise of jurisdiction 'shall be complementary to national criminal jurisdictions'. Article 17 provides that a case will be inadmissible before the ICC if: it is being investigated or prosecuted by a state which has jurisdiction over it, unless the state is unable or unwilling genuinely to carry out the investigation or prosecution; the case has been investigated by a state that has jurisdiction and a decision has been made not to prosecute, unless the decision resulted from the unwillingness or inability of the state genuinely to prosecute; the person has already been tried and the Court would not be permitted to try the case; or the case is not of sufficient gravity to justify further action by the Court.[16]

13.014 The United Nations (UN) Security Council also has the power to refer a situation to the ICC, including in cases where the state having the usual jurisdiction over an accused person is not a party to the Rome Statute.[17] If no permanent Security Council member exercises a veto, a referral to the ICC may appear to be a more likely event than the creation of an entirely new tribunal, but neither option can be excluded.

13.015 In the following discussion of specific crimes, reference is made to the acts of the 'perpetrator', which causes one to wonder who exactly the perpetrator is when brain technologies are being used. If a BCI is being used, for example to enable the operator to control a weapon system by thought or intent, it would seem to the author that the perpetrator must be that operator, probably jointly with the commander or other person(s) on whose instructions the operator is acting. If an AB system is enabling the autonomous operation of a weapon system, the author suggests that the perpetrator of the action taken by that weapon system is the operator who initiated the autonomous mission together with the person(s) on whose instructions the operator is acting. If a BBI system was being used to decide on military action such as an attack, the roles taken by the various persons involved in that BBI-enabled decision-making process will determine which of those individuals can properly be regarded as giving the instructions on which the operator is acting. If the military activity consists

---

16 Rome Statute of the International Criminal Court, Rome, 17 July 1998, 2187 UNTS 3, Art.17(1). Factors to consider when determining unwillingness or inability are given respectively in Art.17(2) and (3). Note also Art.53.

17 Rome Statute, ibid, Arts 12(2) and 13(b).

of a human degradation operation in which a BCI is being used to degrade the performance of personnel belonging to the adverse party, the perpetrator of that operation will, as with other operations involving BCI use, be the operator of the BCI along with the commander or other person(s) (involved in the BBI) on whose instructions the operator is acting.

The previous paragraph provides some provisional suggestions. It will, however, be for the ICC to interpret how the Statute's provisions apply where new and emerging technologies are being used. **13.016**

13.3.1 Genocide by killing

To the extent that is relevant to this intended discussion, the Rome Statute defines genocide as: **13.017**

> For the purpose of this Statute, "genocide" means any of the following acts committed with intent to destroy, in whole or in part, a national, ethnical, racial or religious group, as such:
>
> (a) Killing members of the group;
> (b) Causing serious bodily or mental harm to members of the group; ...[18]

These are the two potential methods of committing the crime that will be considered. Where genocide by killing is concerned, the elements of the crime are: **13.018**

> 1. The perpetrator killed one or more persons.
> 2. Such person or persons belonged to a particular national, ethnical, racial or religious group.
> 3. The perpetrator intended to destroy, in whole or in part, that national, ethnical, racial or religious group, as such.
> 4. The conduct took place in the context of a manifest pattern of similar conduct directed against that group or was conduct that could itself effect such destruction.[19]

It follows from this that genocide by killing involves the killing of members of a specific national, racial, ethnical or religious group based on the fact that they are members of that group and the attacker must intend to destroy either the whole of that group, or part of it, as such. The relevant part must be a substantial part, that is a part which is significant enough to have an impact on the group as a whole: in the case law this has been described by reference to a numerical percentage of the group, a geographic area, or the part's functions **13.019**

18 Rome Statute, ibid, Art.6.
19 Elements of Crimes, n.6, Art.6(a) (footnote omitted).

with respect to the group.[20] Moreover, such an attack must be associated with a clear pattern of similar behaviour against the same group, or the singular attack must have been capable of producing the specified result, that is, destroying the whole or a significant part of the group. So, either a singular attack destroys the whole group or a sufficient part of it, or there is a pattern or sequence of behaviour of a similar nature that generates a similar effect.

13.020 Imagine that State A's senior leadership gives instructions for an attack against minority Group Z, which resides in State B territory but which has been associated with some troublesome activities in the border area between the two states. State A's tactical planners, intelligence assessors, operational and senior commanders confer using BBI technology. Having reviewed the input from multiple sensors that are located on board drones controlled by operators using BCI technology, the intelligence analysts are able to pinpoint where a substantial proportion of the group are collocated. Missiles are launched and these then employ AB technology to guide them to the location where Group Z population members are. The warheads aboard the missiles explode, and large numbers of civilians representing a substantial part of Group Z as a whole are killed. If the required facts and intent can be proved, the action may well be genocide. The State A senior leadership's intent will be critical. Specifically, the ways in which the BCI, AB and BBI technology are used do not relieve the leadership of State A of responsibility. The clear evidence of a genocidal intent will be demonstrated by the instructions that State A's leadership gives. The fact that they use BBI to confer is not relevant; the relevant point is the intent to commit genocide that has been formed by human beings using available technology. This is also not affected by the use of BCI to control the drones – it is the human operators' intent that is merely translated into action by the BCI. Where the AB aspect is concerned, if the AB is merely guiding the weapon to co-ordinates that reflect targeting instructions formulated by

20 International Tribunal for the Prosecution of Persons Responsible for Serious Violations of International Humanitarian Law Committed in the Territory of the Former Yugoslavia Since 1991, *Prosecutor v Radislav Krstić*, Case IT-98-33-A (Appeals Chamber Judgement of 19 April 2004), para.15; International Criminal Tribunal for Rwanda, *The Prosecutor v Clément Kayishema and Obed Ruzindana,* Case ICTR-95-1-T (Trial Chamber II Judgment of 21 May 1999), para.97; International Tribunal for the Prosecution of Persons Responsible for Serious Violations of International Humanitarian Law Committed in the Territory of the Former Yugoslavia Since 1991, *Prosecutor v Radoslav Brđanin*, Case IT-99-36-T (Trial Chamber II Judgment of 1 September 2004), para.702; Extraordinary Chambers in the Courts of Cambodia, *Case 002/02*, Case File No. 002/19-09-2007/ECCC/TC (Judgment of 16 November 2018), para.802; International Criminal Court, *The Prosecutor v Omar Hassan Ahmad Al Bashir*, Case ICC-02/05-01/09 (Separate and Partly Dissenting Opinion of Judge Anita Ušacka, Pre-trial Chamber I Decision on the Prosecution's Application for a Warrant of Arrest against Omar Hassan Ahmad Al Bashir of 4 March 2009), para.67; ICJ Genocide Judgement, paras 198–200.

human commanders, then the use of the AB also does not affect the point that the intent is formed by and in humans. If, however, it is the AB that decides to attack the specific target, and if the AB is so designed that it is capable of forming a genocidal intent, matters become more complex, particularly where the human commander or decision-maker has no such intent. There is the danger that the intent truly lies with an AB system that, on current legal interpretations, cannot be the subject of criminal law process or sanctions.

If the killing or, as the case may be, the causing of bodily or mental harm, is committed with the human-formed intent to destroy a protected group as such in whole or in part, the actual realisation of that outcome is not necessary for guilt to be established and there is no threshold of the number of victims necessary to establish genocide.[21] Element 4 stipulates that the conduct must take place in the context of a manifest pattern of similar conduct directed against that group or must be conduct that could itself effect such destruction. The correct interpretation of this element is yet to be settled.[22] **13.021**

If evidence of genocidal intent is absent, the available evidence may support other charges under the Statute. **13.022**

13.3.2 Genocide by causing serious bodily or mental harm

The second method of committing genocide that we shall consider consists of causing serious bodily or mental harm to members of the group and comprises the following elements: **13.023**

1. The perpetrator caused serious bodily or mental harm to one or more persons.[23]
2. Such person or persons belonged to a particular national, ethnical, racial or religious group.
3. The perpetrator intended to destroy, in whole or in part, that national, ethnical, racial or religious group, as such.

---

21 International Criminal Tribunal for Rwanda, *The Prosecutor v Jean-Paul Akayesu*, Case ICTR-96-4-T (Trial Chamber I Judgment of 2 September 1998), paras 497–498; International Criminal Tribunal for Rwanda, *The Prosecutor v Laurent Semanza*, Case ICTR-97-20-T (Trial Chamber III Judgment and Sentence of 15 May 2003), para.316; International Tribunal for the Prosecution of Persons Responsible for Serious Violations of International Humanitarian Law Committed in the Territory of the Former Yugoslavia since 1991, *The Prosecutor v Goran Jelsić*, Case IT-95-10-T (Trial Chamber Judgment of 14 December 1999), para.100.

22 In issuing an arrest warrant against then President Al Bashir of Sudan, the majority of the ICC's Pre-Trial Chamber suggested that the element means that the crime of genocide is only completed when the relevant conduct presents a concrete threat to the targeted group, or part thereof: ICC, *Prosecutor v Omar Hassan Ahmad Al Bashir*, Case ICC-02/05-01/09 (Decision on the Prosecutor's Application for a Warrant of Arrest against Omar Hassan Al Bashir, 4 March 2009), para.124.

23 A footnote indicates that '[t]his conduct may include, but is not necessarily restricted to, acts of torture, rape, sexual violence, or inhuman or degrading treatment'.

4. The conduct took place in the context of a manifest pattern of similar conduct directed against that group or was conduct that could itself effect such destruction.[24]

13.024 As elements 2, 3 and 4 match the corresponding elements of genocide by killing, the discussion of them above will not be repeated.

13.025 One can imagine the use of a BCI-controlled system to deliver, for example, a chemical substance that is designed to cause serious illness to large numbers of the members of a group. Equally, one can consider as an example the possible use by a state of a virus which is designed to target members of a particular ethnic group and which affects the genetic profile of the persons it infects so as to cause serious illness and/or nasty medical effects. Activities of those kinds would potentially amount to genocide if all of the elements of the crime, as discussed in subsection 13.3.1, are present. Equally, if activities of the kind discussed above affect certain members of the group but are accompanied by other activities that adversely affect other members of the targeted group to the required degree, then genocide may also be established, again provided all elements of the crime can be shown.

13.026 Alternatively, imagine that the chemical substance that is referred to in the previous paragraph is located in warheads mounted on mobile artillery pieces that are controlled by autonomous systems based on AB technology. The AB system repeatedly fires these weapons at locations which are inhabited by members of a particular racial group. The mere fact that the weapons are repeatedly fired at the same racial group would not, per se, prove that genocide is being committed. Moreover, the autonomous nature of the targeting decision-making might make it hard to demonstrate the genocidal intent that is a key part of the crime.

13.027 The word manifest, used in element 4, indicates that it is sufficient if, viewed objectively, there was a clear pattern of genocidal action. An introductory element under Article 6 of *Elements of Crimes* states:

> Notwithstanding the normal requirement for a mental element provided for in article 30, and recognizing that knowledge of the circumstances will usually be addressed in proving genocidal intent, the appropriate requirement, if any, for a mental element regarding this circumstance will need to be decided by the Court on a case-by-case basis.

24 Elements of Crimes, n.6, Art.6(b).

The facts of a case, as established from the evidence, will be vitally important. **13.028**

13.3.3 The crime against humanity of murder

Crimes against humanity under the Rome Statute consist of specified acts 'when committed as part of a widespread or systematic attack directed against any civilian population, with knowledge of the attack'.[25] In this subsection the crime against humanity of murder is considered. The phrase 'attack directed against any civilian population' is stated by Article 7(2) of the Statute to involve 'a course of conduct involving the multiple commission of [one of the specified acts] against any civilian population, pursuant to or in furtherance of a State or organizational policy to commit such attack'.[26] **13.029**

The elements of the crime against humanity of murder are: **13.030**

1. The perpetrator killed one or more persons.
2. The conduct was committed as part of a widespread or systematic attack directed against a civilian population.
3. The perpetrator knew that the conduct was part of or intended the conduct to be part of a widespread or systematic attack against a civilian population.[27]

In introducing the section of the *Elements of Crimes* dealing with crimes against humanity, the document notes that such crimes are 'among the most serious crimes of concern to the international community', that they 'entail individual criminal responsibility' and that they 'require conduct which is impermissible under generally applicable international law'. A nexus is required between the perpetrator's murderous act and the widespread or systematic attack against a civilian population referred to in Article 7(1). The perpetrator must also have had knowledge that their conduct was part of, or they must have intended that conduct to be part of, the widespread or systematic attack. Section 13.1 explains that this element 'should not be interpreted as requiring proof that the perpetrator had knowledge of all characteristics of the attack or the precise details of the plan or policy of the State or organization'. An attack is widespread if it is 'massive, frequent, carried out collectively with considerable seriousness and directed against a multiplicity of victims'.[28] This may be a cumulative effect of a series of inhumane acts or the singular effect of an **13.031**

25 Rome Statute, n.16, Art.7(1).
26 Rome Statute, n.16, Art.7(2)(a).
27 Elements of Crimes, n.6, Art.7(1)(a) (footnote omitted).
28 ICC, *The Prosecutor v Jean-Pierre Bemba Gombo*, Case ICC-01/05-01/08 (Pre-Trial Chamber II Decision Pursuant to Article 61(7)(a) and (b) of the Rome Statute on the Charges of the Prosecutor against Jean-Pierre Bemba Gombo of 15 June 2009), para.83.

inhumane act of extraordinary magnitude.[29] A systematic attack 'refers to the organised nature of the acts of violence and the improbability of their random occurrence'.[30] 'Attack directed against a civilian population' means a course of conduct involving the commission of multiple acts specified in Article 7(1) of the Statute, such as murder, against a civilian population in furtherance of a state or organisational policy.[31] The policy aspect presupposes active state or organisation encouragement or promotion of an attack against a civilian population.[32]

13.032 So it is clear that an isolated attack using a BCI-controlled drone against civilians which is not linked to widespread or systematic attacks cannot be a crime against humanity. Equally, the use of an autonomous AB-enabled weapon to introduce electrodes via the bloodstream into the brain of a leading civilian of the adverse party would also only constitute a crime against humanity if it were to be linked to a widespread or systematic attack and if the other crime against humanity elements were to be present, for example knowledge or intent. As an alternative, imagine a sequence of autonomous AB-enabled attacks, perhaps in association with other forms of attack, all directed against a particular civilian populated area. Subject to the specific facts and to fulfilment of all of the elements of the crime, such activity is capable of being a crime against humanity.

13.3.4 War crimes

13.033 Article 8 of the Rome Statute classes as war crimes susceptible to the jurisdiction of the Court, respectively, grave breaches of the Geneva Conventions 1949,[33] and other serious violations of the laws and customs applicable in international armed conflicts;[34] in the case of a non-international armed conflict, serious violations of common Article 3 of the Geneva Conventions 1949,[35] and other serious violations of the laws and customs applicable in non-international

29 See, for example, International Tribunal for the Prosecution of Persons Responsible for Serious Violations of International Humanitarian Law Committed in the Territory of the Former Yugoslavia since 1991, *The Prosecutor v Vidoje Blagojević and Dragan Jokić*, Case IT-02-60-T (Trial Chamber I, Section A Judgment of 17 January 2005), para.545.

30 ICC, *The Prosecutor v Germain Katanga*, Case ICC-01/04-01/07 (Pre-Trial Chamber I Decision on the evidence and information provided by the Prosecution for the issuance of a warrant of arrest against Germain Katanga of 6 July 2007), para.33.

31 Elements of Crimes, n.6, Crimes Against Humanity, Art.7, Introduction, para.3.

32 Ibid.

33 Rome Statute, n.16, Art.8(2)(a).

34 Rome Statute, n.16, Art.8(2)(b).

35 Rome Statute, n.16, Art.8(2)(c).

armed conflicts.[36] The discussion in this chapter, insofar as it addresses war crimes, will limit itself to a number of such crimes specified in Article 8(2)(b) that seem particularly relevant to the matters discussed in this book. The crimes listed in Article 8(2)(b) are identified as 'serious violations of the laws and customs applicable in international armed conflict, within the established framework of international law'.[37]

The introduction to Article 8 of *Elements of Crimes* explains that war crimes must be interpreted within the established framework of the law of armed conflict. In relation to the last two elements of each crime, it is also noted, inter alia, that there is no requirement for a legal evaluation as to the existence or nature of the armed conflict. However, the factual existence of a situation of armed conflict is, of course, an essential requirement for the commission of a war crime. **13.034**

13.3.5 War crime of attacking civilians

The Statute describes this war crime as '[i]ntentionally directing attacks against the civilian population as such or against individual civilians not taking direct part in hostilities'.[38] The elements of the crime are: **13.035**

1. The perpetrator directed an attack.
2. The object of the attack was a civilian population as such or individual civilians not taking direct part in hostilities.
3. The perpetrator intended the civilian population as such or individual civilians not taking direct part in hostilities to be the object of the attack.
4. The conduct took place in the context of and was associated with an international armed conflict.
5. The perpetrator was aware of factual circumstances that established the existence of an armed conflict.[39]

It is a clear breach of the distinction principle to make peaceable civilians the object of an attack, irrespective of the nature of the weapon or technology that is used. The Court will determine, by reference to the evidence in the particular case, who in fact directed the attack. If AB technology is used to enable autonomous attacks and if it is the AB system that decides upon the target that is to be chosen, the linked questions for the Court to decide are who **13.036**

36 Rome Statute, n.16, Art.8(2)(e).
37 Rome Statute, n.16, chapeau to Art.8(2)(b).
38 Rome Statute, n.16, Art.8(2)(b)(i).
39 Elements of Crimes, n.6, Art.8(2)(b)(i).

was the perpetrator and was it the perpetrator or the AB system that directed the attack that is decided upon by the AB system, not by a human being.

13.037 If the president, prime minister or minister of defence of a country were to direct that a specific attack take place, there would seem to be every reason to regard that individual as the perpetrator for the purposes of criminal responsibility. The commander of the military unit that undertook the attack, along with other persons involved in the conduct of the attack, may also be held individually criminally responsible. The facts found by the Court based on the evidence will determine whether the commander and the other persons referred to in the previous sentence are criminally liable, and if so, whether their liability is as perpetrators of the substantive crime, or on the basis of the extended forms of responsibility set out in Articles 25(3) and 28 of the Rome Statute.[40]

13.038 It is important to note that if the object of the attack was civilian persons who were taking a direct part in the hostilities, element 2 of the offence will not have been satisfied and the crime will not therefore have been committed. The object of the attack will consist of the persons whom the attack is intended to kill, injure or disable.

13.039 Element 3 makes it clear that the person who is found by the Court to be the perpetrator of the crime must have intended to make the civilian population, or individual civilians not taking part in the hostilities, the object of the attack. If the pilot of an aircraft that is equipped with BCI-enabled missiles is instructed to fly to a specified location where they must employ the BCI technology to fire a stand-off missile towards a target identified to them in terms of geographical co-ordinates, it will be for the Court to decide whether, before they caused the BCI to release the weapon, the pilot knew (and therefore intended) that the object of the attack was 'the civilian population as such or individual civilians not taking direct part in hostilities'.

13.040 Likewise, it will be for the Court to determine on the basis of the evidence whether the land commander and weapon operators in a military unit that employs autonomous AB-enabled mobile artillery systems intended that the civilian population as such or individual civilians not taking direct part in hostilities would be the object of the attack. That may be a difficult issue where autonomous systems are concerned. A key issue is likely to be what

40 Note, however, that Rome Statute, n.16, Art.28 deals specifically with command responsibility in relation to commanders and other superiors with regard to the international crimes provided for in the Statute.

the commander and/or operators knew about the targets that the autonomous artillery system could be expected to select as its targets. If, for example, it could be shown that the target recognition software was so set up that the system would interpret population centres as targets to be attacked, and if it could be shown that the person(s) found by the Court to be the perpetrator knew this to be the case and intended that attacks against civilian population centres should take place, element 3 will likely be satisfied. If the commander or operator(s) did not and could not know the civilian nature of the targets the AB system was likely to select, they cannot have formed the required intent and, on that basis, element 3 of the crime will not have been established.

13.3.6 War crime of attacking civilian objects

The Statute describes this war crime as '[i]ntentionally directing attacks against civilian objects, that is, objects which are not military objectives'.[41] The elements of the crime are the following: 13.041

1. The perpetrator directed an attack.
2. The object of the attack was civilian objects, that is objects which are not military objectives.
3. The perpetrator intended such civilian objects to be the object of the attack.
4. The conduct took place in the context of and was associated with an international armed conflict.
5. The perpetrator was aware of factual circumstances that established the existence of an armed conflict.[42]

It is a breach of the principle of distinction to make civilian objects the object of attack irrespective of the nature of the weapon or technology that is employed. Element 1 is in similar form to the first element discussed in subsection 13.3.5 and the comments made there in relation to directing an attack apply equally to this crime. Military objectives are defined in Article 52(2) of Additional Protocol I to the Geneva Conventions 1949 (API) (see Chapter 4, section 4.5.1). As to civilian objects, reference should be made to Article 52(1) of API and to Chapter 4, section 4.5.2. It should be noted that dual-use objects are military objectives. 13.042

Where the language used in the elements of this crime is identical to that discussed in subsection 13.3.5 above, the observations made in that subsection will apply similarly to the present crime. If the perpetrator intends to make military objectives the object of the attack, this offence is not committed. If 13.043

41 Rome Statute, n.16, Art.8(2)(b)(ii).
42 Elements of Crimes, n.6, Art.8(2)(b)(ii).

incidental damage was unintentionally caused to civilian objects, this offence will also not have been committed.

13.044 Accordingly, if a person found by the Court to be the perpetrator who directed the attack (see discussion in subsection 13.3.5) caused a BCI-enabled weapon system to target a civilian apartment block which was not a military objective, that person would be guilty of the crime if they intended to make that civilian object the object of the attack. If an AB-enabled weapon system was being used, for example the AB-enabled mobile artillery system mentioned in subsection 13.3.5, and if the Court has found that the accused person was a perpetrator who directed the attack, determining whether the perpetrator intended to make the civilian object the object of the attack will involve considering all of the evidence on that issue. If the AB technology is designed to make autonomous attack decisions, a specific decision made by the AB system may or may not reflect the intentions of the commander and/or operator that initiated the mission. If, however, the evidence shows that the AB system was programmed to interpret civilian objects as military objectives which it is then programmed to attack, the commanders and operators of the mission who knew this to be the case and who intended civilian objects to be targeted may well be guilty of the offence.

13.3.7 War crime of excessive incidental death, injury or damage

13.045 The Statute describes this war crime as '[i]ntentionally launching an attack in the knowledge that such attack will cause incidental loss of life or injury to civilians or damage to civilian objects or widespread, long-term and severe damage to the natural environment which would be clearly excessive in relation to the concrete and direct overall military advantage anticipated'.[43] The elements of this crime are the following:

1. The perpetrator launched an attack.
2. The attack was such that it would cause incidental death or injury to civilians or damage to civilian objects or widespread, long-term and severe damage to the natural environment and that such death, injury or damage would be of such an extent as to be clearly excessive in relation to the concrete and direct overall military advantage anticipated.
3. The perpetrator knew that the attack would cause incidental death or injury to civilians or damage to civilian objects or widespread, long-term and severe damage to the natural environment and that such death, injury or damage would be of such an extent as to be clearly excessive in relation to the concrete and direct overall military advantage anticipated.

43 Rome Statute, n.16, Art.8(2)(b)(iv).

4. The conduct took place in the context of and was associated with an international armed conflict.
5. The perpetrator was aware of factual circumstances that established the existence of an armed conflict.[44]

This war crime reflects the proportionality rule as set forth in Articles 51(5)(b) and 57 of API (discussed in Chapter 4, section 4.7). The meaning of the word 'perpetrator' was discussed above in section 13.3. Element 1 requires that the perpetrator actually launched the attack. It will be for the Court to apply the idea of launching to the facts that it finds in a specific case. It would seem clear that the operator of a BCI-enabled weapon launches an attack if their thought or intent is translated by the BCI system into the firing of the weapon in accordance with their thought or intent. It will be for the Court to decide whether the commander and/or other individuals can, in addition to the BCI operator, be regarded as having launched a BCI-enabled attack. If AB technology is used to enable autonomous attacks and if it is the AB system that decides upon the target that is to be chosen, the linked questions for the Court to decide are who was the perpetrator and was it the perpetrator or the AB system that launched an attack if the attack was decided upon by the AB system, not by a human being. 13.046

While the war crime is clearly based on the Article 51(5)(b) API proportionality rule, the wording of the war crime differs in the three following respects. 13.047

1. The offence refers to causing excessive damage to the natural environment. If the part of the natural environment that is targeted is, however, a military objective, damage to that part would not be 'incidental' for the purposes of this offence. Moreover, if the damage to the natural environment is not widespread, long-term and severe, that damage would not, it seems, fall to be considered under the collateral damage aspect of the offence; that is however an interpretation point on which the Court will need to decide.
2. The incidental damage to civilians, civilian objects or the environment must be 'clearly' excessive which implies that there is a margin of appreciation. Marginal excessiveness would not appear to be sufficient for these purposes. The Court may takt the view that the excessiveness of the collateral damage that was expected must have been such that no reasonable decision-maker would have decided to proceed with the attack.
3. By referring to 'overall' military advantage, the Statute would seem to be noting the views of a number of states, as reflected in statements made on ratification

44 Elements of Crimes, n.6, Art.8(2)(b)(iv) (footnotes omitted).

of API, to the effect that it is the military advantage anticipated from the attack considered as a whole that must be considered.[45]

13.048 It follows from this that the operator, relevant commander and other participants in the use of a BCI-enabled weapon system to undertake an attack will only be criminally responsible for this offence if:

1. the evidence shows that the particular individual launched that attack;
2. the collateral damage as a whole that was, or that should have been, expected was clearly excessive in relation to the anticipated military advantage; and
3. the element of the collateral damage consisting of damage to the natural environment (if any) consisted of widespread, long-term and severe damage to a part of the natural environment that was not at the time a military objective.

13.049 Likewise, the operator or commander of an operation using AB-enabled weapon systems to undertake autonomous attacks will only be criminally responsible for this offence if the available evidence shows that the three features listed in the previous paragraph are present and if all of the elements of the crime are established.

13.050 Element 2's wording '[is] such that it would' appears to indicate that the nature and circumstances of the attack, taking into account the information that was reasonably available[46] to the perpetrator at the time when deciding to undertake the attack, rendered it evident then that the attack would cause incidental death, injury and damage that would be clearly excessive in comparison to the anticipated military advantage. This particular aspect may not pose problems in relation to BCI-enabled operations, because the human operator of the BCI system and the associated commander will be the persons whose actual or constructive knowledge will be the focus. With an AB-enabled autonomous attack system, the issue will be whether the autonomous nature of the attack decision-making means that there is no relevant human being who can be shown to have had either actual or constructive knowledge. The Court will no doubt consider the available evidence and will decide whether the

45 Consider, for example, the statement made by the UK on ratification of Protocol Additional to the Geneva Conventions of 12 August 1949, and Relating to the Protection of Victims of International Armed Conflicts, Geneva, 8 June 1977, 1125 UNTS 3 on 28 January 1998, para (i). See similar statements by Australia, Germany, Italy and the Netherlands and the statement made by France on ratification of the Rome Statute, n.16, on 9 June 2000, para.5.

46 See AMW Manual, Commentary to Rule 14, para.6 citing UK Manual, para.5.20.4; AMW Manual Commentary to Rule 32(a), para.3; Newport Manual para.8.8; *Prosecutor v Stanislav Galić*, Case Number IT-98-29-T, Trial Chamber Judgment (Int'l Crim Trib for the Former Yugoslavia 5 December 2003, para.58).

circumstances indeed rendered it evident that the proportionality rule would be breached to the required degree, that is that the collateral damage would be clearly excessive.

Element 3 stipulates that the perpetrator must know that the attack will breach the proportionality rule. Any state of mind less than knowledge is not sufficient, and it will be for the Court to decide, based on the available evidence, whether the required knowledge of the accused can be inferred from the facts as found. **13.051**

13.3.8 War crime of employing poison or poisoned weapons

The Statute describes this crime as '[e]mploying poison or poisoned weapons'.[47] The elements of this crime are: **13.052**

1. The perpetrator employed a substance or a weapon that releases a substance as a result of its employment.
2. The substance was such that it causes death or serious damage to health in the ordinary course of events, through its toxic properties.
3. The conduct took place in the context of and was associated with an international armed conflict.
4. The perpetrator was aware of factual circumstances that established the existence of an armed conflict.[48]

The prohibition of the use of poison or poisoned weapons is discussed in Chapter 6, subsection 6.6.2. As noted there, this prohibition reflects long-standing customary law. The crime will therefore apply irrespective of the way in which the poison is used in warfare. If, therefore, an operator employs a BCI system in conjunction with a weapon that uses a poison as the means of causing injury, illness or death to an adverse party during an international armed conflict, this war crime will have been committed. Equally, if an operator equips an AB-enabled weapon system with a substance or a warhead that uses a poison to cause injury, illness or death to an adverse party during an international armed conflict, the war crime will have been committed. **13.053**

The discussion of the notion of perpetrator given in section 13.3 above will apply equally in relation to this war crime. It should be remembered, however, that other bases for criminal liability in respect of this and other international crimes are provided for in Articles 25(3) and 28 of the Rome Statute. **13.054**

---

47 Rome Statute, n.16, Art.8(2)(b)(xvii).

48 Elements of Crimes, n.6, Art.8(2)(b)(xvii).

13.3.9 War crime of employing weapons, projectiles or materials or methods of warfare listed in the annex to the Statute

13.055 The Rome Statute war crime consists of '[e]mploying weapons, projectiles and materials and methods of warfare which are of a nature to cause superfluous injury or unnecessary suffering or which are inherently indiscriminate in violation of the international law of armed conflict, provided that such weapons, projectiles and materials and methods of warfare are the subject of a comprehensive prohibition and are included in an annex to this Statute ....'[49] At the time of writing, no weapons, projectiles or materials or methods of warfare have been included in an annex to the Statute. This is therefore an offence which is not yet complete and cannot therefore yet be made the subject of a charge.

13.3.10 The crime of aggression

13.056 The crime of aggression is defined in Article 8bis of the Rome Statute as follows:

> 1. For the purpose of this Statute, "crime of aggression" means the planning, preparation, initiation or execution, by a person in a position effectively to exercise control over or to direct the political or military action of a State, of an act of aggression which, by its character, gravity and scale, constitutes a manifest violation of the Charter of the United Nations.
> 2. For the purpose of paragraph 1, "act of aggression" means the use of armed force by a State against the sovereignty, territorial integrity or political independence of another State, or in any other manner inconsistent with the Charter of the United Nations. Any of the following acts, regardless of a declaration of war, shall, in accordance with United Nations General Assembly resolution 3314 (XXIX) of 14 December 1974, qualify as an act of aggression:
>
>   (a) The invasion or attack by the armed forces of a State of the territory of another State, or any military occupation, however temporary, resulting from such invasion or attack, or any annexation by the use of force of the territory of another State or part thereof;
>   (b) Bombardment by the armed forces of a State against the territory of another State or the use of any weapons by a State against the territory of another State;
>   (c) The blockade of the ports or coasts of a State by the armed forces of another State;
>   (d) An attack by the armed forces of a State on the land, sea or air forces, or marine and air fleets of another State;
>   (e) The use of armed forces of one State which are within the territory of another State with the agreement of the receiving State, in contravention of the conditions provided for in the agreement or any extension of their presence in such territory beyond the termination of the agreement;

49 Rome Statute, n.16, Art.8(2)(b)(xx).

(f) The action of a State in allowing its territory, which it has placed at the disposal of another State, to be used by that other State for perpetrating an act of aggression against a third State;
(g) The sending by or on behalf of a State of armed bands, groups, irregulars or mercenaries, which carry out acts of armed force against another State of such gravity as to amount to the acts listed above, or its substantial involvement therein.

The elements of the crime are as follows: **13.057**

1. The perpetrator planned, prepared, initiated or executed an act of aggression.
2. The perpetrator was a person in a position effectively to exercise control over or to direct the political or military action of the State which committed the act of aggression.
3. The act of aggression – the use of armed force by a State against the sovereignty, territorial integrity or political independence of another State, or in any other manner inconsistent with the Charter of the United Nations – was committed.
4. The perpetrator was aware of the factual circumstances that established that such a use of armed force was inconsistent with the Charter of the United Nations.
5. The act of aggression, by its character, gravity and scale, constituted a manifest violation of the Charter of the United Nations.
6. The perpetrator was aware of the factual circumstances that established such a manifest violation of the Charter of the United Nations.[50]

It is immediately apparent from Article 8bis(1) that only persons who are in **13.058** very senior political or military positions in a state are capable of committing the offence. Those who exercise control over or direct the state's military action will be restricted to prime ministers, members of the war cabinet, such as ministers of defence, chiefs of the defence staffs, commanders in chief of the respective armed forces and relatively few others. It is the involvement of those senior persons in the planning, preparation, initiation or execution of the relevant act that will constitute the crime. More junior planners will not be covered by this offence. Paragraphs 1 and 2 of Article 8 make it clear that, to be an act of aggression, the activity must breach the UN Charter and must come within paragraph 2. It will be recalled from Chapter 9, section 9.2 that the threat or use of force breaches Article 2(4) of the UN Charter, subject to Articles 42 and 51.

Article 8bis(2) makes it clear that declaring war before the commission of **13.059** the relevant act does not disqualify that act from characterisation as an act of aggression. While this will be a matter for the Court to rule upon if necessary, the phrase in para.2, 'any of the following acts', might be interpreted as limiting acts of aggression to acts of the listed kinds or, alternatively, might be

50 Elements of Crimes, n.6, Art.8bis.

seen as characterising the listed activities as illustrative of acts that are acts of aggression.

13.060 It is, however, evident that the technologies discussed in this book would be capable of involvement in acts that come within this crime. Weapons that are controlled or triggered using BCI technologies, such as missiles, are capable of being used by the armed forces to bombard or attack the territory of another state contrary to Article 8bis(2)(b) and (d). A decision to undertake such an attack could be reached during discussions facilitated by BBI technologies. Autonomous weapons that employ AB technologies could be programmed by the armed forces to search for particular targets within the territory of the victim state and attack them, again in breach of Article 8(bis)(2)(b) and (d). BCI-controlled and autonomous AB-enabled systems might be used to enforce a blockade and might even be involved in its declaration and notification. However, while brain technologies in general might well in future be involved in the actual execution of an act of aggression, it may, but will not necessarily be, by means of BBI technology that the planning, preparation or initiation or execution of the act might be undertaken, and it is the taking of those steps by the specified senior individuals that constitutes the crime, as elements 1 and 2 of the elements of the crime specify.

13.061 Element 2 makes another point of importance to this discussion, namely that the perpetrator must be a person. This effectively excludes any suggestion that an AB system that autonomously performs a hostile act in another state's territory might be liable under this crime. Element 3 tells us that for the crime to take place, the forceful event must actually happen. Awareness by the perpetrator of the factual circumstances mentioned in element 4 does not, it is believed, require that the perpetrator have any specific understanding of the UN Charter. The perpetrator must be aware of the factual circumstances and those circumstances must be such that the Charter is breached.

13.062 The word 'manifest' in elements 5 and 6 should be given its normal, dictionary meaning, namely, when used adjectivally, 'clear and obvious'.[51]

13.063 If the use of a BBI for decision-making at senior levels is capable of giving rise to criminal liability under this offence, it is evident that great care will be required to ensure that the thoughts and intents that are transmitted and exchanged through the system are formulated with suitable care. It is clear

51 Vienna Convention on the Law of Treaties, 23 May 1969, 1155 UNTS 331, Art.31 and *Compact Oxford English Dictionary*, 3rd edn (Oxford University Press, 2005), 619.

that the most stringent controls will be required, that thoughts and intents must be accurately transmitted and received, and that safeguards are in place to ensure that ill-advised action is, as far as possible, prevented.

14

THE LAW ON BRAIN TECHNOLOGIES IN WARFARE: CONCLUSION

14.1 ANSWERING SOME QUESTIONS

14.001 It would be pointless in this closing chapter to try to provide a summary of all that has been discussed in Chapters 1 to 13. On the other hand, it is only right that some answers be offered to the list of pertinent questions that were posed in Chapter 1, section 1.4. So we will start by doing just that. For ease of reference, each question is set forth below and is accompanied by the author's suggested responses. Readers will of course have their own views and what are offered are merely some personal reflections that are intended to facilitate thought on these difficult issues. The questions and associated thoughts are as follows:

14.002 1. Isn't brain technology really the same thing as artificial intelligence?

14.003 Absolutely not. Artificial intelligence (AI) consists of the application of computer-based technology to simulate the human ability to gain knowledge and skills by means of experience, training and/or education. Taking the brain technologies that we have been considering in turn, a brain-computer interface (BCI) can be used either to monitor and perhaps interpret the activity of a brain or to adjust or manipulate the performance of a brain. Computers are involved, but their role is as a channel of communication between the human operator and the brain via the electrodes. Artificial brains (ABs), particularly those exclusively employing computer technology, get closest to AI, particularly where they take the form of artificial general intelligence (AGI).

However, the distinction remains between intelligence as a product of the operation of the brain and the brain itself, and AB technology is aimed at replicating the brain as distinct from mimicking one of its products, namely intelligence. Brain-to-brain interfaces (BBIs) also use computers, but again merely to facilitate direct communication between the human brains engaged in the BBI-enabled activity. Brain enhancement, as we saw in Chapter 10, is all about the use of the three previously discussed technologies, among other things, to enhance cognitive performance, while brain degradation would employ some of the same techniques to have the opposite effect. Key, therefore, to the distinction is the fundamental difference between the brain and intelligence, the former being the device and the latter being its product. So no, brain technologies are not just AI in different clothing.

2. What are the brain technologies that seem likely to be of most relevance to military operations? **14.004**

The five technologies that have been addressed, BCIs, ABs, BBIs, brain enhancement and brain degradation, on current understanding, would seem to be the technologies of greatest potential military relevance. It must be emphasised, however, that the science in this field seems to be advancing rapidly, and the possibility that other brain technologies of military relevance will emerge in the future can by no means be excluded. Equally, it is entirely possible that at least some of the potential applications of each technology mentioned in this book do not prove to be militarily useful and are not, therefore, taken forward. **14.005**

3. Which of these brain technologies have been demonstrated in some form and which are entirely theoretical? **14.006**

As noted in the opening paragraph of this chapter, BCIs have been demonstrated in various contexts in the medical sphere. The technology that enables both monitoring of brain activity and interference in or manipulation of that activity therefore exists. The only area of uncertainty is the extent and nature of its military application, but that will become clear in due course. That there will be military applications seems to be certain. Scientific work in a variety of settings is seeking to produce AGI. In many ways, that can be regarded as the main goal of AI research, and it seems clear that it is merely a matter of time before that goal will become a reality.[1] At the time of writing, however, we must classify AB technology as largely theoretical. However, the organoids and assembloids discussed in Chapter 2 are likely to prove to be an **14.007**

---

1 See Chapter 2, subsection 2.5.1.

important stepping stone towards the accomplishment of AGI. Likewise, AB technologies involving natural or synthetic brain material must also at present be regarded as theoretical possibilities, but again the extent of international research in this sphere makes it likely that, in time, this variety of brain technology will be realised. Whether what will be simulated is a full human brain capability or something less remains to be seen. The author rather suspects that the latter will be the case.

14.008 The science that underpins the BBI concept has been successfully demonstrated. The next stage will be the expansion of the science to involve larger groups of individuals and the conversion of that science into a technology capable of employment in real-world scenarios. Brain enhancement is not a new idea. As we have seen, drugs have been used for that purpose in the past. The use of BCIs to stimulate brain activity for medical purposes shows that the employment of such technology to enhance military performance is a realistic prospect. In Chapter 11, various methods that are or seem likely to enable the degradation of human brain performance were described, it being noted that sometimes the degradation of human performance is achieved by prompting a reaction that indicates the proper functioning of the brain.

14.009 Accordingly, most of the techniques referred to in the book reflect either technologies that exist and are employed for other purposes in medical treatments or are the subject of science that has been demonstrated in experimentation reported in peer-reviewed publications.

14.010 4. What are brain-computer interfaces, artificial brain technologies and brain-to-brain interfaces?

14.011 These three notions have been appropriately described in Chapters 2 and 3, and it is not necessary to repeat those explanations here.

14.012 5. How do *jus in bello,* as it applies to targeting, special protection, weapons, methods of warfare and neutrality, and the law on the resort to the use of force, apply to the use of the five brain technologies?

14.013 Chapters 4, 5, 6 and 7 deal with the application of the principles and rules of the *jus in bello.* Chapter 8 deals with the implications of neutrality law for the employment of brain technologies while Chapter 9 addresses the requirements of the *jus ad bellum* where brain technology use is concerned. In all of these chapters, the relevant provisions of existing law have been examined to determine the qualities that brain technologies must exhibit in order to be compliant. That approach is not intended to imply that existing international law is going to prove adequate to address the perceived challenges posed by these new and emerging technologies. Concerns, for example those mentioned in Chapter 3, may well, in time, precipitate the generation, adoption and implementation of new legal rules, or at least of new best practice, to address these concerns. However, experience with the practical employment of these technologies is likely to be required in order to specify the exact contours of ethical concern and to tease out the precise legal provisions and other practical arrangements that are required to address those concerns. Any attempt to work out what new law is needed should start with an assessment of the applicability of the law that we currently have. This book in no way seeks to pretend that existing law has all of the required answers to the issues posed by emerging brain technologies. The book does, however, seek to state what that law is as clearly as possible in order to provide a basis on which future legal requirements can be assessed. Moreover, pending the adoption of such new legal rules, it is the law discussed in this book that will determine the confines of what is permitted.

6. What are the legal rules dealing with the enhancement and degradation of the human brain? **14.014**

The existing applicable law has been set forth respectively in Chapters 10 and 11. In planning the book, the view was taken that human enhancement and degradation are topics that are distinct from those discussed earlier in the book and that they therefore require ad hoc treatment separately from discussions centred on the law of targeting, weapons, neutrality and *ad bellum*. **14.015**

7. Are there other issues that are relevant? **14.016**

Most certainly there are other important issues that need to be considered. While the focus of the present book is justifiably on international law, a vitally important issue is the ethical acceptability or otherwise of each of the five brain technologies. Is it ethically acceptable to interfere with the human brain, for example to promote greater efficiency and timeliness in military decision-making? Should certain kinds of brain technology be prohibited in warfare? Is it sensible to talk of prohibiting particular brain-related military capabilities, or prospective capabilities, without at the same time considering a prohibition of the threats that inspire their possible adoption. Put another way, if it is rapid threats enabled by digital warfare and hypervelocity missiles that motivate the adoption of brain technologies of significant concern, shouldn't those rapid threats also be banned, particularly if no alternative technologies are available to counter such threats? Certainly, seeking to prohibit measures that may be **14.017** perceived as essential for national security or even survival seems unlikely to attract state support. However, the author is convinced that the ethical disquiet that brain technologies are likely to generate will be the chief driver of legal developments in this field.

14.018 The serious data protection issues arising particularly from BCI use are also discussed in the book, and related points are made in section 14.4 below.

14.2 TIMING OF THE BOOK

14.019 As the research for the book progressed, it became increasingly clear that now is indeed the right time to be writing and publishing this book. BCIs have been used in the medical sphere extensively and there is considerable resulting empirical information on which to base the assessments that have been offered in the previous chapters. Where BBIs are concerned, the concept has been proved, the scientific paper has been published in a peer review environment, so that which might once have appeared to be science fiction now has the character of science fact. Considerable research effort is being devoted to the development of AGI and ABs based exclusively on computer systems. Science has grown brain material with the evident intention of producing ABs that incorporate natural or synthetic brain matter. For many decades, armed forces personnel have taken a variety of substances in an effort to enhance their own performance and numerous scientific reports show that BCIs can be applied to achieve similar medical improvements, a development that suggests the adaptation of that same science to perform military tasks. Likewise, attempts to degrade enemy performance are nothing new. If BCI and, in due course, AB technology can be employed to achieve that outcome, this option is likely to attract the interest, and no doubt the investment, of states and military leaderships.

14.020 So, while significant gaps persist in our understanding of the functioning of the human brain, attempts to replicate the object itself and the kinds of performance that a brain exhibits, to influence it, to observe what it is doing and to enhance its activity surge forth.

14.021 There can be no doubt that these developments must have attracted the attention of the arms industry around the world and of military researchers in diverse states. While brain technology research is the exclusive subject of specialist journals and many publications, including those referenced in this volume, sources discussing military research in this field, while by no means absent (note for example the Defense Advanced Research Projects Agency (DARPA) announcements on the topic), are certainly less plentiful. It would be naive to assume from this that there is little military brain research taking place. A more realistic interpretation would bear in mind the secretiveness that normally surrounds cutting-edge military research and would assume that 'under the bedclothes', as it were, activity is at least as frenetic as that seen in the medical context. Perhaps the current heightened sensitivities among the major powers of the world will increase those sensitivities and the consequent reluctance to disclose what is taking place.

The 175 states that are party to Additional Protocol I to the Geneva Conventions 1949 (API) are, as Chapter 6 explained, legally obliged to determine whether new weapons and weapon systems that they are studying, developing or acquiring comply with their international law obligations. The same legal review duty applies to new methods of warfare that they are planning to adopt. A flick through the chapters of this book will reveal to the casual observer that brain technologies raise many and varied legal and ethical issues. The author does not claim to be a specialist in the field of ethics but does believe he has a thing or two to offer where international law is concerned. So, another key purpose of this book is to offer a helping hand to anyone whose unenviable task it is to provide authoritative legal advice in connection with any of the five technologies listed in the opening paragraph of this chapter. **14.022**

14.3 *LEX LATA VS LEX FERENDA*

The discussion in this book has centred on the law that currently exists, the *lex lata*. Whether and how that law applies in novel circumstances inevitably has an element of *lex ferenda*, law that is thought to be desirable for the future. The International Court of Justice (ICJ) has expressed its view on the applicability of existing core principles of distinction and superfluous injury/unnecessary suffering to weapons and methods of warfare of the past, present and future,[2] but whether they do so apply will depend on: 1. whether binding treaties can be adopted to which sufficient states are willing to become party, or 2. whether a general practice of states accepted as law in that respect emerges.[3] For the latter to happen, we need to wait for the relevant technologies to emerge, for **14.023**

2 ICJ, Nuclear Weapons Advisory Opinion on the Legality of the Threat or Use of Nuclear Weapons [1996] ICJ Reports 226, 35 ILM 809, para.86.

3 Charter of the United Nations and Statute of the International Court of Justice (UN Charter), 1 UNTS XVI, Art.38(1)(b).

the legal positions of states to be clearly expressed either in their actions or in authoritative expressions of state practice that reflect *opinio juris*, and for those legal positions to achieve the level of generality required to convincingly support the existence of binding customary rules.

14.024 Of the brain technologies that we have discussed, that which is arguably the most mature is BCIs. The intrusive access that BCIs afford to the thoughts and emotions of individuals raises the most profound, indeed disturbing, concerns. Somewhat ironically, it is understood that the more precise the intrusion, the greater the prospect for specific medical treatments to address some of the most troublesome challenges to brain health. The irony lies in the fact that the more intrusive interventions are liable, with advances in science, to give the intervenor the greatest potential access to private, innermost ideas, beliefs, feelings, worries, and so on. Access of that kind poses the most acute challenges in the field of human rights, data protection and, most particularly, privacy rights. Somehow, simply to label such data as 'personal data' does not seem to do justice to the extent of the associated intrusion. The idea of access that lays bare the very soul of an individual must cause readers to pause and ask themselves whether this really is a direction in which we wish to go.

14.025 Perhaps the way to look at these matters lies in recognising that there are trade-offs to be made, and those trade-offs vary depending on the circumstances in which the technology is to be used. In the medical sphere, the 'unlocking' of patients suffering from locked-in syndrome, the development of treatments to alleviate some of the worst symptoms of Parkinson's disease, the provision of effective help to paraplegics, all give the most valuable hope to the affected patients, and the development of these technologies for those purposes is, we would all agree, undoubtedly a good thing. If cost-benefit analysis of such technologies is to be conducted, the potential benefits for those individuals must weigh most heavily in that balance, while the drawbacks for others must be considered and minimised.

14.026 To apply that cost-benefit approach to the military employment of BCIs, and for that matter of other brain technologies, due account must be taken of the likely characteristics of the battlefield of the future. The increasing role of digital capabilities in warfare, the advent of hypervelocity missiles and the use of saturation threats (currently in the form of drones) are but three examples of evolving trends that can, the author suggests, be summarised as 'more and more and faster and faster'. Confronted with ever more rapid threats, speed of decision and speed of response become critical to effective defence. The traditional approach to military operations has involved careful consideration of alternatives, the development of options by planning staffs, the adoption of a plan by the commander, the communication of that plan to the deployed units and its subsequent execution. In a future environment where the opportunity for effective response shortens considerably, BCIs and BBIs may prove to be of increasing importance.

Von Clausewitz was right about warfare being 'a mere continuation of policy by other means'.[4] The author senses, however, growing distaste among many for the slaughter of combatants and civilians alike that is such a frequent feature of modern warfare. The potential development of an ability directly to influence the minds of pivotal members of the opposing government or regime may well be seen[5] as a more attractive option for bringing wars to a rapid conclusion, and the employment of some of the technologies we have been discussing may help to achieve that more clinically precise engagement of adverse party leaders. **14.027**

14.4 SO WHAT ARE THE KEY LEGAL AND POLICY ISSUES?

The answer, of course, is that there are many such issues with which we have grappled in the preceding chapters. In the next few paragraphs, the author merely highlights a few points that seem to him to deserve particular emphasis. **14.028**

In the BCI, BBI and brain enhancement contexts, there can be no doubt that the requirement for freely given and informed consent will be an issue in the military context. The personal motivations of the individual that underlie the provision of that consent may include loyalty to the team, wishing to be seen by colleagues in a good light, the belief that giving consent may help to achieve career advancement, or merely the recognition that allowing the conduct of a particular intrusive procedure may enable the successful conduct of a perhaps important military operation. None of those private motives, per se, would cause the consent, for example, to the intrusive insertion of electrodes, to be other than freely given. However, consent cannot be free if the individual has been ordered by a superior authority to submit to the procedure. Moreover, if action falling short of the giving of direct orders is taken by superior authority and has the effect of eroding the freedom with which the individual decides whether to consent, this may also have the effect that the resulting consent is **14.029**

4 C von Clausewitz, *On War* (A Rapaport (ed), 1832), Book 1, para.24.
5 The principle of distinction, and the rules that give effect to it, must nevertheless be complied with.

not freely given. These are among the factors that may sometimes cause difficulty in establishing the freedom of expressed consent.

14.030 Issues also arise from the need for the consent to be not only free but also informed. The information that the individual must receive for the consent to be informed will include the short-, medium- and long-term known side-effects, areas of medical and scientific uncertainty in this regard, and the likelihood of each of the known side-effects applying in the individual's case. Each of these aspects would need to be clearly communicated to, and understood by, the consenting individual. Orders and instructions will need clearly to set forth how the individual should be informed, by whom, where and when, and those orders and instructions would need to be adhered to. It is difficult to understand why a soldier undertaking such a procedure as part of military preparation during military operations should be any less informed than a civilian in advance of a medical operation. Perhaps what is needed here is the establishment of standard procedures to apply in both military and non-military contexts.

14.031 Data protection issues are, as noted in section 14.3, a major concern. The ultra-personal nature of private thoughts and emotions, the access thereto that BCIs seem likely to give, the damaging mental and emotional consequences for individuals of the inappropriate accessing or subsequent handling of such materials all lead to the conclusion that dedicated regulation is needed in which the interests of the data subject are most carefully safeguarded. There are competing interests at work here, and national legislation will need to balance them most carefully.

14.032 The continuing discoveries arising from brain science and the application of those advances to develop new technologies will, the author believes, in time affect very many aspects of our daily lives. New law, and the adaptation of existing law to the circumstances brought about by the new technologies, will be required. If brain technologies are to be employed first in the peacetime, medical and commercial contexts, the likelihood is that regulations and best practice guidance will also first be developed in those spheres. The uses of these technologies include enhancing feelings of well-being, promoting efficiency in the workplace, accelerating education, improving cognitive and sporting performance, and assisting with concentration, relaxation or sleep.[6]

---

6 HRC, Impact, opportunities and challenges of neurotechnology with regard to the promotion and protection of all human rights, A/HRC/57/61, 8 August 2024, available at https://digitallibrary.un.org/record/4060417?ln=en&v=pdf (HRC Report), para.10.

Current doubts as to the effectiveness of these devices and their long-term effects will be addressed in the coming years.[7] So common sense suggests that the arrangements that are developed for commercial applications of such technologies will at least inform how they will be used by the armed forces and in connection with hostilities. It will only, however, be when specific applications of a particular brain technology in the military environment are considered that clear rules can be devised. While at this stage in the evolution of the science matters must inevitably be expressed in somewhat general terms, it is now that those responsible for the conduct of military affairs should start to consider whether the law that we have is adequate to deal with the conduct of military affairs in this new era, or whether we need new law. Whether by reinterpreting the law we have or developing new provisions, human rights of individuals, privacy rights and the data rights of citizens must be carefully safeguarded,[8] and the brain systems and processes that are developed must be appropriately transparent.[9]

14.5 THE ROLE OF THINKING AND THE STATUS OF THOUGHTS

It is self-evident that a great deal of thought will be required in order to work out how to adjust our ways of living, and fighting, to cope with what brain technologies will bring. Indeed, one of the more intractable issues that the discussion in this book raises is the very status of thought itself. **14.033**

In a world in which the formulation of a specific thought can alone trigger events which have consequences, what are the responsibilities of the human being for those thoughts? Is a human being liable for the injurious or damaging consequences if a mere thought of theirs, when received and interpreted by a BCI, initiated the damaging or injurious action? Does it make a difference if the BCI misinterpreted the thought of the BCI operator, and consequently initiated action which the human operator never intended? How can one prove the disparity between the operator's thought and the BCI's interpretation of that thought? In a legal tradition where it is either an observable act or a distinct failure to act where action is required that must have occurred for legal liability to arise, how do we deal with something as nebulous, as transient, as **14.034**

---

7 A Wexler and P Reiner, 'Oversight of Direct-to-Consumer Neurotechnologies' (2019) 363 Science 6424.

8 Consider M Ienca and others, 'Brain Leaks and Consumer Neurotechnology (2018) 36(1) *Nature Biotechnology* 805–10.

9 Note, for example, D Berrick, 'BCI Technical and Policy Recommendations to Mitigate Privacy Risks', *Future of Privacy Forum*, 15 February 2022, available at https://fpf.org/blog/bci-technical-and-policy-recommendations-to-mitigate-privacy-risks/.

insubstantial as a thought becoming the initiator of what might prove to be the most disastrous chain of ensuing events? These are all vitally important questions that will need to be tackled, perhaps in part at least by the development of new law.

14.035 Or, is there indeed an act involved here? Does the act consist of the operator putting on their electrode-bearing headset in the first place? Is that the act which signifies that the operator is acknowledging their responsibility for the thoughts that they develop while the headset is in place? If that is the case, how does this work when the individual has had electrodes inserted into their brain? Is the act of giving the free and informed consent to the insertion of the electrodes the event that signifies the acknowledgment by the subject individual of responsibility for every thought that they have while the electrodes are in place? If that were to be so, it would place huge significance on the giving of the consent and would require that this legal implication of the giving of that consent be explained in most thorough detail to the relevant person.

14.036 This causes the author to wonder whether future law will need to distinguish between thoughts. At the risk of misquoting *Animal Farm* again, we would potentially be in a situation in which 'all thoughts are equal, but some thoughts are more equal than others'.[10] Perhaps, in time, science will distinguish between the thoughts that a BCI will translate into action of the kind specified in the thought and the thoughts which do not have that effect. If that were to be so, and if individuals equipped with the relevant electrodes could be trained to limit action-initiating thoughts to relate only to lawful action, that might be a way ahead. For the time being, however, it suffices to point out that linking legal responsibility to thought alone poses numerous complex problems which may be difficult to solve.

14.037 A closely linked question is at what point do the characteristics of machines and humans start to merge? In the discussion in the earlier chapters, we wondered at what point devices become part of the human who operates them and when human beings become a component in a machine system. The author offers the view that the distinction between human and machine continues to make sense so long as the machine constitutes a tool that the human is employing for the performance of a task. The distinction between 'man and machine' starts to break down the more integrated the implementation and the human become the one with the other. When that integration is such that

10 G Orwell, *Animal Farm: A Fairy Story* (17 August 1945): 'All animals are equal but some animals are more equal than others.'

the two become indistinguishable, arguably the machine has become part of the human and vice versa. That, in a sense, is another way of representing the issues that arise, for example, when the BCI electrodes are physically inserted into the brain of the BCI-enhanced individual. Arguably, when that happens the individual and the BCI system have become integrated with one another to such a degree that what the machine does can properly be treated as the action of the individual and vice versa. This suggests that, when conducting weapon reviews of the sort discussed in Chapter 6, the technology should be considered in its application to the particular individual. This would make sense, because the ability of the specified individual to formulate and limit thoughts as required by the discussion in the preceding paragraphs of this section will determine whether and how the composite weapon system can be used lawfully. This all raises profound and complex legal issues which can only really be resolved when the exact contours of the emerging technology, in its relevant applications in warfare, are known and understood.

14.6 PERSONALITY EFFECTS

A linked issue associated with the use of BCI technology is the potential effect on the personality, and even the mental well-being, of the BCI-equipped individual. It is, for example, imaginable that by gaining access to that individual's innermost thoughts, by influencing them and by linking them directly to action, including violent action involving death, injury and damage to third-party persons and objects, aspects of the personality of that individual may be changed. Logic suggests that the individual may become more cautious about what to think. They may perhaps seek to avoid thought as a personal policy aimed at preserving, as far as possible, their individual privacy. One can certainly imagine a person with an outgoing personality becoming more hesitant, introspective, cautious and uncertain. This, if it is right, suggests that the very individuality of a person may be affected. If so, one rather wonders whether this is really a technology that we want? That leads the author back to the discussion in section 14.3 about cost-benefit analyses. The cost-benefit analysis for a person with locked-in syndrome would perhaps run along the lines of 'this technology can to a degree loosen some of the constraints that your condition imposes on you but means that your private thoughts can, to an extent, be deduced from the read-out from the BCI'. That same cost-benefit approach when applied to the use of such BCIs in other contexts, such as in connection with military operations, might lead to the conclusion that the privacy, personality, infection, internal injury and other costs and potential costs outweigh 14.038

the anticipated benefits. It will therefore, perhaps, be only when assessing the benefits, disadvantages and potential disadvantages in the context of a specific use of the technology that a balanced judgement can properly be made.

14.039 Another linked question that was posed in Chapter 3, section 3.10 is at what point does a person cease to be responsible for their own actions? A number of key questions were identified there. Perhaps the more general conclusion to draw is that this and other issues associated with brain technologies probably require new law and evolving guidance. Different states are likely to adopt different approaches, but it occurs to the author that states might find it useful to confer with one another on these matters with a view to adopting common understandings as to the issues and preferred approaches to dealing with them.

14.7 SOME FINAL REMARKS

14.040 This has not been an easy book to write. The subject is complex. The science is still emerging. The ways in which the technologies will be used cannot yet be precisely stated. The legal issues that are involved are serious and tricky, and how these issues will be resolved will only really be determined when we know more about the technologies. And yet, states will need to develop policy on these topics sooner rather than later, and there is a relative absence of guidance in the military context to assist them.

14.041 So the author reminds the reader of the Martens Clause, the 1907 iteration of which states:

> Until a more complete code of the laws of war has been issued, the High Contracting Parties deem it expedient to declare that, in cases not included in the Regulations adopted by them, the inhabitants and the belligerents remain under the protection and the rule of the principles of the law of nations, as they result from the usages established among civilized peoples, from the laws of humanity, and the dictates of the public conscience.[11]

14.042 If we can, therefore, agree that the customary principles and, arguably, the customary rules of the LOAC apply to the use of brain technologies during hostilities, this at least gives us a basic foundation on which to build new law. If the current fractured geo-strategic relationship between states persists, the adoption of new law is likely to be problematic. In that circumstance, the author suggests that states should still consult with one another with the aim

11 Hague Convention (IV) Respecting the Laws and Customs of War on Land, The Hague, 18 October 1907, Preamble, para.8.

of achieving collective understandings as to how to deal with the many problem areas that we have addressed. Informal understandings between states, while they certainly do not impose legal obligations on the participants, can nevertheless be useful ways of achieving common approaches to difficult issues like these.

Finally, if this book can be of some assistance to those involved in the development of national policy and in the conduct of international engagement in this area, the author's not inconsiderable efforts in putting this book together will have been worthwhile. **14.043**

INDEX